Evidence-based LSP

Linguistic Insights

Studies in Language and Communication

Edited by Maurizio Gotti,
University of Bergamo

Volume 47

PETER LANG
Bern · Berlin · Bruxelles · Frankfurt am Main · New York · Oxford · Wien

Khurshid Ahmad & Margaret Rogers (eds)

Evidence-based LSP

Translation, Text and Terminology

PETER LANG
Bern · Berlin · Bruxelles · Frankfurt am Main · New York · Oxford · Wien

Bibliographic information published by Die Deutsche Bibliothek
Die Deutsche Bibliothek lists this publication in the Deutsche Nationalbibliografie; detailed bibliographic data is available on the Internet at ‹http://dnb.ddb.de›.

British Library Cataloguing-in-Publication Data: A catalogue record for this book is available from *The British Library,* Great Britain

European Symposium on Language for Special Purposes (14th : 2003 : University of Surrey)
Evidence-based LSP : translation, text and terminology. –
(Linguistic insights : studies in language and communication ; v. 47)
1. Sublanguage – Congresses
I. Title II. Ahmad, Khurshid, 1948– III. Rogers, Margaret, 1949 May 27–418

ISBN-13: 9783039111879

ISSN 1424-8689
ISBN 978-3-03911-187-9

Hochfeldstrasse 32, Postfach 746, CH-3000 Bern 9, Switzerland
info@peterlang.com, www.peterlang.com, www.peterlang.net

This volume is dedicated to the memory
of John McHardy Sinclair (1933–2007),
a true scholar whose originality, open-mindedness
and energising spirit of enquiry inspired
many corpus linguists following in his wake.

Table of Contents

Part Two

Part Three

Part Four

Part Five

Previous Publications: European Symposia on LSP

Articles based on papers given at the European symposia on LSP have been published in the following volumes:

Fachsprache 1979. Sonderheft 1: Zweites Europäisches Fachsprachensymposium, Bielefeld 1979. Wien: Braumüller

Høedt, J. / Lundquist, L. / Picht, H. / Qvistgaard, J. (eds) 1982. *Pragmatics and LSP.* Proceedings of the 3rd European Symposium on LSP. Copenhagen. August 1981. Copenhagen: Copenhagen Business School.

Perrin, Michel P. (ed.) 1985. *Pratiques d'aujourd'hui et besoins de demain. Actes du 4ème symposium Européen sur les langues de spécialité.* Bordeaux: Université de Bordeaux II.

Cornu, A-M. / Vanparijs, J. / Delahaye, M. / Baten, L. (eds) 1986. *Beads or Bracelet? How do we approach LSP. Selected papers from the Fifth European Symposium on LSP.* Leuven: Instituut voor Levende Talen.

Laurén, Christer / Nordman, Marianne (eds) 1988. *Special language. From humans thinking to thinking machines.* A selection of papers from the 6th European Symposium on LSP. Vaasa/Vasa 1987. Clevedon: Multilingual Matters.

Laurén, Christer / Nordman, Marianne (eds) 1988. *From office to school. Special language and internationalization.* A selection of papers from the 6th European Symposium on LSP. Vaasa/Vasa 1987. Clevedon: Multilingual Matters.

Brekke, M. / Andersen, Ø. / Dahl, T. / Myking, J. (eds) 1994. *Applications and implications of current LSP research.* Proceedings from the 9th European Symposium on LSP, Bergen 1993. Vols. I-II. Bergen: Fagbokforlaget.

Budin, G. (ed.) 1996. *Multilingualism in specialist communication – Multilinguisme dans la communication spécialisée – Mehrsprachigkeit in der Fachkommunikation.* Proceedings from the

10th European Symposium on LSP, 1995. Vienna: Infoterm. Vols. I-II.

Lundquist, L. / Picht, H. / Qvistgaard, J. (eds) 1998. *LSP. Identity and interface. Research, knowledge and society.* Proceedings from the 11th European Symposium on LSP, 1997. Vols. I-II. Copenhagen: Copenhagen Business School.

Mayer, Felix. (ed.) 2001. *Language for Special Purposes: Perspectives for the New Millennium.* Proceedings from the 12th European Symposium on LSP, 1999. Vols. I-II. Tübingen: Gunter Narr Verlag.

Koskela, M. / Laurén, Ch. / Nordman, M. / Pilke, N. (eds) 2002. *Porta Scientiae. Lingua specialis I-II.* Proceedings from the 13th European Symposium on LSP. Vaasa/Vasa: University of Vasa.

Acknowledgements

The organisation of an international conference always requires a number of committed and dedicated people: LSP 2003 was no different. Our thanks go in particular to the AILA Scientific Commission on Language for Special Purposes under the leadership of Professor Christer Laurén, University of Vaasa (Finland). Colleagues at the University of Surrey, especially Sarah Priston and Sophie Gautier O'Shea, deserve special thanks: Sarah and her team for handling the finances and organisational matters and Sophie for her help in the preparation of the manuscript. We are indebted to Dr Bassey Antia, University of Maiduguri (Nigeria) for his help in planning the Conference Programme and looking after the delivery of the lectures and workshops. Dr Antia and Dr Maria Teresa Musacchio provided substantial editorial advice on an earlier version of the Conference Proceedings. Finally, we would like to acknowledge David Cheng's expert help in managing the conference database and website.

This volume comprises a selection of papers from the Conference Proceedings (available at < http://www.surrey.ac.uk/translation/events/LSP2003_proceedings.pdf >). We are grateful to the authors for revising their articles and for their patience. Professor Maurizio Gotti provided much needed moral support as the Series Editor of *Linguistic Insights*. We gratefully acknowledge his support and encouragement.

Khurshid Ahmad
Margaret Rogers

Dublin/Guildford May 2006

Foreword

In post-modernist circles *evidence* is perhaps regarded as a commitment to a positivist approach to scholarship and research. Discussions surrounding the subject of terminology, one of the earliest aspects of Language for Special Purposes (LSP) to be studied systematically, certainly reveal different philosophical stances. In practice, however, the interpretation of evidence can be contrasted with intuitive speculation, which can be regarded as a comparatively weak basis for many activities in which LSP studies are applied, including language planning, LSP pedagogy, technical authoring, specialist translation and terminography / lexicography. In this respect, parallels can be drawn with areas of specialist activity such as medicine and foreign-language teaching where recent developments focus on an evidence base of therapies and classroom behaviour respectively rather than on systems of belief. In this vein, the current volume addresses a number of aspects of what can be broadly called evidence-based LSP studies. The contributions are drawn from papers presented at the 14th European Symposium on Language for Special Purposes held in Guildford at the University of Surrey, in co-operation with the AILA Scientific Commission on Language for Special Purposes.

This volume is divided into five Parts, each Part being further sub-divided into chapters. The first two Parts deal with two principal sources of evidence: LSP text corpora and citation patterns in specialist communication. The third Part deals with dichotomies in LSP research and highlights the role of evidence, touching on some ideological questions. The final two Parts deal with the potential applications of an evidence-based approach: first, in the area of terminology and knowledge management, and secondly, in the challenges of LSP translation, on which an evidence-based approach may shed particular light.

Overall, the volume aims to give a sense of the different kinds of evidence which LSP studies embrace, while at the same time indicating the importance of how that evidence is interpreted in different applications, languages and cultural environments.

Khurshid Ahmad
Margaret Rogers

Part One
Corpora as Evidence of Language Use

Linguistic investigations have over the last 50 years moved between introspective and observational methods with experimental methods much less in evidence. It is clear from the contributions in the first Part of this volume that the observation of language-in-use through the use of text corpora, including electronic corpora, is buoyant in current studies in Language for Special Purposes (LSP). The advent of computers on the research scene focused attention on the old debate of theory-driven versus data-driven approaches to the study of 'grammars'. It is the legacy of some of that early work in corpus linguistics that we see here now.

Part 1 is introduced by chapters contributed by John Sinclair, one of the pioneers of corpus linguistics since the 1960s, and by Joanna Channell, one of the few truly applied linguists with extensive consultancy experience. Starting with a review of the use of computers in the analysis of natural languages, Sinclair describes and evaluates developments from formal models through early 'natural' language processing (NLP) to the current situation. He points out the difficulties which the processing of 'open text' poses for explaining the way that words make meaning, at the same time indicating a way forward through the construction of what he calls 'local grammars' based on observed patterns in textual data. Illustrating the local-grammar approach in relation to the word *trouble* based on the evidence of the 500m.-word Bank of English, he demonstrates that neither NLP techniques nor conventional grammatical and semantic constructs are necessary to the analysis. The reader may also begin to imagine the possibilities of local grammars for the analysis of LSP texts such as definitions, as suggested by Sinclair. The sources of evidence on which Joanna Channell draws in her consultancy research include written texts classified by genre, interviews, electronic corpora, observations of meetings, and so on. Using 15 case studies ranging from cross-cultural problems experienced by employees of a multinational company to assessment criteria for UK National Vocational Qualifications, she illustrates how a range of approaches from applied linguistics can be employed with LSP data in order to identify the source or sources of communication problems and to propose – in non-technical terms – concrete solutions in a non face-threatening way. The role of the evidential base in validating the recommended solutions is argued by Channell to be crucial from the perspective of the client who has commissioned the research.

In order to investigate whether English has, as often claimed, influenced Italian scientific writing, in the third chapter Federica Scarpa undertakes a diachronic study of extracts from textbooks on dermatology over 60 years, focusing on one particular dermatological process. Within a Hallidayan framework, her analysis suggests a qualified 'yes', but it is also argued that such developments should be seen as a 'positive step towards a true internationalization of the paradigms of science'. Starting from a different perspective, namely that of translation, the influence of English on Italian scientific writing is also the topic of Maria Teresa Musacchio's chapter on information structure. This is explored using a parallel/comparable corpus of English source texts, their Italian translations and Italian original texts in the domain/genre of popular physics articles. Musacchio concludes that the translators in her sample do to some extent reproduce the information structure of the original English texts, resulting in a degree of 'unnaturalness'.

The fifth chapter introduces an area of research of safety-critical importance. Peter Ragan's contribution on the role of cross-cultural factors in pilot-controller communication is based on three case studies. While controlled languages are typically considered culture-neutral, Ragan demonstrates that cultural factors can in fact influence interactions and decisions, meaning that 'Airspeak' as a controlled language needs to be studied on the evidential basis of available corpora in order to better understand its use and how this relates to prescribed forms and meanings.

The intersemiotic relationship between text and image and its automation is of growing importance in modern communications. The research project reported in the sixth chapter by Chris Handy and Khurshid Ahmad investigates how the consistency of the 'manual' indexing of images through linguistic means may be subject to less variability when carried out by domain experts rather than by lay viewers, in so far as experts more consistently select and name the physical characteristics of the image for indexing purposes. Handy and Ahmad's domain of investigation is the 'collateral text' accompanying images of a crime scene investigation conducted by the police.

They conclude that the linguistic performance of the experts studied can be characterised by a local grammar which is not applicable to the text produced by novices. They suggest, however, that the production of such collateral texts is responsive to training.

Within the broad genre of technical writing, the final chapter in this first Part is an investigation of the hybrid phenomenon of deverbal nouns – which exhibit characteristics of both verbs and nouns – in a Norwegian manual used on oil platforms and concerned with steam generation and distribution. Following a morphological analysis of the 154 types (not tokens) of deverbal nouns identified, Øivin Andersen discusses some ways in which these are not typical nouns as a word class. It is also pointed out that such 'nouns' frequently exhibit 'logical polysemy' i.e. have a dynamic and a static sense; some can also be shown to have an argument structure. Extending the analysis to a pragmatic level (information structure), Andersen concludes that this under-researched area (in relation to LSP) is promising for future research, particularly in terminology.

The seven chapters in this first Part demonstrate a wide range of approaches to the use and interpretation of evidence in the study of special languages from the automatic processing of extensive electronic text corpora to case studies, from dermatology to air safety, and from nominal grammar to information structure. In keeping with the current growing academic interest in multimodality, the construction of an LSP evidence base for image and speech/language is also discussed. The implications of this plethora of approaches and subjects are equally wide, moving from the highly specific, for example, implications for training in particular domains or areas of activity, to general principles such as Sinclair's highly productive notion of local grammar, one that has particular resonance for the analysis of LSP texts, which are generally more highly constrained at all levels than general-purpose texts.

JOHN SINCLAIR

Language and computing, past and present

The use of computers in the study of language is almost as old as computers. The first computer applications were, as the very name suggests, concerned with numbers, though Turing's original designs would apply equally well to character strings. However, despite the handling difficulties and the defensive ring of mathematicians, computational linguistics was under way by around 1960.

It was originally powered by early Chomskyan theory and the simple generative-transformational grammars of the era. Unlike traditional linguistics, which was not very rigorous in notation, Chomsky adopted the conventions of mathematical logic, and his grammars looked – and were – eminently computable.

Soon the profession was listening to messages which have become all too familiar – the trumpeting of success which turns out, on closer inspection, to be failure. For example, Thorne/Bratley/Dewar (1967):

> In this paper we describe a program which will assign deep and surface structure analysis to an infinite number of English sentences [and] which also, to some extent, simulates the way in which [the native speaker] perceives this structure.

Chomsky is rightly respected for insisting that grammars must be finite since they fit into people's heads, and that there is no limit to the number of well-formed sentences that the grammars can recognise as well-formed. A grammar containing a single "recursive" rule (where the same symbol appears in both halves of a statement and therefore the rule can be re-applied any number of times) is enough to comply with this requirement, but a grammar of that specification will not necessarily generate all and only the well-formed sentences of any natural language. Nor does Thorne, Bratley and Dewar's program. Nor do any subsequent software systems, as we shall see.

With this as my starting-point, I would like to review the development of the computer analysis of natural language, starting just after the middle of last century.

1. Early theory

Although Chomsky's perspective on language, his formalism, his notation, his style of argument and his descriptive priorities were all novel and refreshing, he made little innovation at the level of the description of English, and defended his rather conservative position stoutly, for example opposing the motion in a debate in 1968 entitled "That traditional grammar should be ended, not mended" (Chomsky 1969). His concentration was always on the formal properties of grammars rather than the nuts and bolts of text samples, and this is clear from his identification of three types of adequacy (Chomsky 1964). Although he abandoned these after a few years, probably because he could not define them with his normal standard of explicitness, they reveal a lot about his priorities. The first level is *observational* adequacy, which means just making sure that the grammar fits the facts, and all the facts. The second level is *descriptive* adequacy, which is making sure that the description is a comprehensive account of the way in which the language operates. The third level is *explanatory* adequacy, where the design of the grammar explains how this language, and all other languages, are organised.

Forty years later, no-one has reached even the level of observational adequacy for any natural language, and there are no signs of anyone getting near. Since there is no limit to the number of well-formed sentences of a language, it would actually be difficult to judge when observational adequacy had been achieved. We can look at splendid efforts to attain this state, like LGSWE[1] and see immediately how far they fall short. Chomsky, however, is only concerned with the top level, explanatory adequacy, and takes the other two for granted, which puts him well beyond the reach of scientific assessment. The evaluation of grammars to choose the best one will take place once there are lots of grammars of lots of languages, all of which have explanatory adequacy (and therefore also descriptive and observational adequacy). This will be some time in the very distant future, and only optimists in good health should wait for it.

These issues were either not clear to, or were ignored by, the early computational linguists such as Thorne, Bratley and Dewar, who treated Chomsky's fragments of English grammar as the basis of an entirely practical, coal-face parser, and proceeded to implement it. But the two intellectual arenas of Chomskyan abstraction and computational applications parted company in the early seventies, particularly when it became clear that the control over the types of rules and their ordering became hopelessly over-complicated in practice. One indication of the change in the wind came with Terry Winograd, who used a non-formal grammatical model, Halliday's Systemic Grammar, on which to base his outstanding work of moving objects around a three-dimensional space using English sentences (Winograd 1972).

2. Natural Language Processing

Computational linguistics no longer had a theory. This is a serious matter for a technologically oriented discipline, because the theory is the basis of the interpretation of results. Theories relate through descriptions to the data of the discipline, which in the case of linguistics is languages. But in this case, because of the hostile stance of Chomsky in relation to data, there was no externally validated data, and the potential of the computer to process large text files was ignored.

1 The Longman Grammar of Spoken and Written English. See Biber et al. (1999) and my review, Sinclair (2001a)

It is difficult to imagine the predicament of a discipline without either a theory or data – both headless and legless at the same time. It was a desperate situation. However, around this time Artificial Intelligence was very fashionable and had clear affinities with the study of languages, so for some years most of the computational linguistic effort was confined to the illustration of specimen cases of ambiguity, "garden-path" structures, and the like[2]. Although the discipline was now called "Natural Language Processing" (NLP) this did not signify any surge of interest in naturally occurring language. The unfortunate use of the term "natural" was not a pre-emptive strike against data-oriented linguists, because the computational linguists of the time had no reason to suppose that such people existed[3]. It was – perhaps insensitively – used to distinguish research into what was deemed likely to occur in ordinary language from work in the structure of artificial languages for computer operations.

What happened was that the discipline turned in on itself; researchers became absorbed in the technology for its own sake, the mechanisms whereby things were achieved, regardless of whether it was worthwhile to achieve them. Goals were specified in terms of interim results, without reference to wider horizons; so making a part-of-speech tagger that "worked", that was "XX% accurate" and so on, became freestanding aims, and the rationale for wanting a part-of-speech analysis was not argued through.

About this time – the middle eighties – the new age of applications dawned. Information Science came of age, and needed all sorts of repositories of information and all sorts of methods of retrieving it. "Fuzzy matching" became the pride of the packages, but unfortunately fuzzy matching was too fuzzy to be of much use. Language text ap-

2 See Appendix item 5, which is only a year or two old.
Another research line was and still is the statistical manipulation of texts – usually very large collections of texts. While overlapping in some respects with corpus study, and able to impact on the world with, in particular, the beginnings of speech recognition, the data need of this group is just masses of text, with no notion of corpus structure or the origins of the texts.

3 If an anecdote will help here, some twenty years ago I was at a conference in Brighton when Fred Jelinek, the father of speech recognition, tracked me down in my hotel, amazed, as he said, to find that I was still alive.

peared to be intransigent and much too volatile and unpredictable to be an acceptable medium for storing and handling information. The massive web search engines of today are still seriously hampered because most of the information that is in electronic form is in the form of texts, and always will be – and texts cannot be understood by existing search engine software.

After an early acquaintance with corpora, the NLP community judged that the most urgent need was for lexicons – word lists which specified for each word some constraints upon its occurrence. Very considerable resources were expended on this kind of work in the nineties, and continue today. To begin with, they followed the usual NLP procedure of concentrating on any technique that seemed to be effective, like type-feature-structure, without consideration of the theoretical model it projected, and more recently the work has developed into various ontologies which are often attractive abstract structures, but which, since they do not accurately reflect the way in which people use words, have no obvious applications[4].

3. Present-day NLP

The following is illustrative of the concerns of the community of computational linguists; it was sent to the Corpora list on 9.10.2003:

> I am trying to develop a tagger for a highly agglutinating language known as Manipuri, falls under Tibeto Burman class of language. I want to develop a POS tagger for this language. There is no previously developed tagger for this language. I also think that for a language like Manipuri, morphological analysis will be an important task for assigning POS category to each word in a corpus. which one of the two approach – rule based or stochastic based will be appropriate for my task.
> Please let me know your comments. If stochastic approach is appropriate please advice me how to proceed.

4 See the Appendix, items 7, 9 and 10

The reason why the correspondent wishes to develop a tagger is completely taken for granted. I know of no member of the NLP community who would question the need, the value, the priority of this considerable expenditure of resource. There is no tagger for Manipuri, and so there should be one. Also, a tagger without any delimiter means a POS (part of speech) tagger. All languages should have one, it is implied. Whether there is any consensus about the parts of speech appropriate for Manipuri is obviously not an issue.

The notion of parts of speech is clearly a theoretical postulate – it rests on the assumption that all the words of a language can be classified into a reasonably small number of classes, based on the relationships they contract with the surrounding words. But there are problems, even for English, the most studied language in the computer era. For one thing, current POS taggers for English waver between a dozen and four hundred parts of speech. Some of this can be accounted for by subcategorisation, but by no means all of it. Secondly, an EC-sponsored project some ten years ago demonstrated vividly that there is no correspondence at all among the POS tagsets of even the closely related languages of western Europe (and the Finnish representative was always on hand to sabotage any prospect of common ground). In a recent paper (Sinclair 1999) I suggest that the hypothesis of part-of-speech classification should be limited to exclude certain words and types of word. In any case, the labelling of parts of speech is of no value in itself, and is only justified either theoretically, as part of a fully articulated descriptive apparatus, or practically, if it is an essential step either in a satisfactory description or in a successful application.

The writer of the Manipuri query lives in an ordered world where there are two, and only two, approaches to POS tagging – the rule-based and the stochastic. A mixture of the two is not envisaged. The researcher either devises a set of rules which correctly assigns tags to each word, or trains a stochastic tagger with a sample of hand-analysed data from which it works out the likelihood of certain words matching certain tags.

Neither of these procedures is able to deliver a satisfactory result; while margins of error are claimed to be miniscule, they are in fact substantial. The high frequency of small and simple words means that claims of 97% accuracy and more are routine, but "accuracy" means simply assigning the tag that the researcher thinks is correct. There is a circularity here, but everyone seems to be so happy with it that one can hardly call it a vicious circularity.

The attitude of not looking outside the toolkit continues in NLP. There is no appeal to theory, nor any to practical utility. No justification is offered for strategies, categories and concepts other than the solving of technical problems, the assumption being that these solutions will lead to breakthroughs in performance in the real world. But despite the practical aims, everything is still measured within the discipline. Typically there are perpetual signs of progress and encouraging developments; the technological barriers are said to be falling all the time, and vast areas of potential applications are forever opening up. Sometimes the linguistic naivety is breathtaking. The Appendix to this chapter contains a few typical assessments of work in progress, culled from the announcements of events in the last year or two. They speak for themselves.

4. Current problems

Some commentators will disagree with this sketch of half a century of development of a discipline, and indeed it is an oversimplification. The theory, while long decoupled from the practice, still has a strong influence on the thinking. It cannot play the support role that is normally expected of theories, nor bring clarity to difficult interpretations, but for many it still guides the style of research, and it still dominates the attitudes to data. In particular, there is no expectation of insights from the data – only problems that have to be solved at a sub-theoretical level. The general attitude, which clouds the judgement of many in the profession, is that we know all we need to know about the major languages, and all that is required is to overcome a few low-level problems and apply this knowledge to the betterment of mankind.

The problems, however, are proving to be intractable. Techniques of analysis, honed over decades and tested on extremely tricky invented sentences, have a poor success rate with corpora. While individual programs for a certain kind of tagging or analysis may claim high accuracy and coverage, no grammar claims to be able to provide a satisfactory analysis of "open text" – that is, text which is just copied from current usage, without pre-processing. No lexicon is near explaining the way words make meaning in open text, no automatic translation routine is anywhere near satisfactory with open text.

At present, when an application requires a good standard of performance, the difference is made up by human intervention, and this is recognised as costly and restrictive. Where the scale of an operation makes it impossible to make use of human skills, for example the search engines on the world-wide-web, the performance of the software is so bad it is a standing joke. As usual, however, we are offered wonderful new resources just around the corner, where the "semantic web", powered by ontologies that are not in contact with open text, will at last deliver intelligent answers to search questions[5].

When a problem is viewed from an inappropriate perspective it may look excessively complicated, more complicated than it actually is; so when problems turn out to be more tricky than expected, the reason for the difficulty could either be in the problem itself or in the viewpoint of the observer, who will be guided by a model of explication. So when we encounter increased complexity, as well as marshalling the resources to tackle it we should also investigate the role played by the theory. Computational resources are nowadays so powerful that they may divert attention from the best way of viewing a problem in favour of massing computer power to solve it. We are now in the era of deploying terascale resources, but even those will not solve problems if they are (a) poorly-understood and (b) to do with the creation of meaning.

5 See the Appendix, for example items 4 and 9.

5. Pinning down the text

Throughout the development of computational approaches to linguistics there has been a series of tactics to avoid the horrors of open text: constraints, limitations, sublanguages, controlled languages, domain-specific varieties, and so on. Here the apparent needs of those working in applications chimed in with those who had a broader perspective. Most of the early applications of computers to texts concerned technical manuals and highly specialised forms of the language, and so – apparently – reduced the scope of the problem even though some extra complications might be added because of the specialised nature of the material.

There was a hidden agenda here also. The language of scientific statement was thought to be particularly clear, simple, economical, objective, unbiased and important; amid the clamour of the media, what is now called "spin", the irresolvable arguments of the soft sciences and the vague and contorted transcripts of conversations, the quiet statements of eternal truth found in the sciences stood out as attractive models for communication, especially in the context of machines both needing crisp information and showing great potential for storing and retrieving it. From a practical point of view also, such simple and direct sentences would probably be easier to incorporate into a Chomskyan grammar, sharing as they do many features of the "kernel sentences", the central constructs of early generative grammars.

Unfortunately, the sort of Platonic discourse that was envisaged as the ideal sublanguage was not found; nor were any other sublanguages of any extent. The writer of scientific statement has at his or her command all the normal resources of the language, plus often some extra features that have developed for the special communication needs. True, some applications requiring only small changes in revising or "relocalising" a document can benefit from memories that use previous states of the documents as support for human editors, and speed up routine jobs. These can be beneficial to the users, but their lack of generalisability means that they have no impact whatever on the description or understanding of languages.

6. The role of ordinary language in computers

We are left in a difficult stand-off position. We cannot make descriptions of languages which are adequate for the uncompromising needs of current computers, their architecture, their assumptions, their conventions. So we cannot use our ordinary languages in computers, either for communication with the computers or for the efficient storage of information in text files. The simulations that we are familiar with in operating systems and programming languages are very superficial disguises for machine instructions, and of course do not mean what they would mean in a human language[6]. Information scientists regard texts as virtually unstructured containers of vague and partial information, and think that they require an external scaffolding to be built to give the information some recognisable shape and retrievable organisation.

We do not at present know if such an expensive and inefficient strategy is necessary. Human beings work with texts, spoken and written, and find them adequately organised, in fact often very helpfully structured, flexible too. The needs of computers appear to be quite alien to the human world, and we do not know if in other circumstances computers might not have been designed to be more amenable to the human way of communicating. Digitisation, for example, the key weapon of information science, puts information well beyond the reach of humans, but readily manipulable in machines.

6 There is some discussion of these points in Sinclair (1999b, 2001b, 2003)

7. An alternative position

It is at least arguable, given the background of computational approaches to language, that part of the problem lies in the lack of theoretical underpinning to the tools of description, and that the received attitudes to data hamper the search for a means of understanding how meaning is created in texts. Perhaps ultimately the human language faculty will turn out to be just too human to be replicated (*not* simulated) in a machine, and we will return to external organisations and aids to get as close as possible to the structure of texts, in order to retrieve information from ordinary language. But the difficulty of a task is not an excuse for avoiding it, and it is now a priority to model language structure as revealed by insights directly derived from data, without external analytical schema being imposed on the data[7].

Starting with large amounts of language data, such as are now readily acquired and routinely processed in computers, recurrent patterns can be identified, initially without reference to any particular language. This is a pivotal point, because it offers a starting point which contrasts sharply with the rich awareness of the language that characterises NLP searches.

This approach is called nowadays *corpus linguistics*. It is almost as old as any other kind of computational linguistics, beginning in the early sixties in USA (Francis/Kučera 1979) and UK (Sinclair et. al. 1970) at around the same time. It was slow to develop, for several reasons. One was that the figure of one million words – the size of the Brown corpus – mesmerised a generation of researchers, and there was no impetus to build larger corpora. A second reason was that the technology required for corpus research contrasted in several respects with that required for fast numerical processing, and the latter had priority until the 1980s. It is important to stress that text processing was regarded as a strange occupation until the popularity of computer typesetting made large collections easy to acquire. The digitisation of libraries came later.

7 An extended discussion of this point can be found in Sinclair (2004).

Another reason for the slow rate of development was that for many years the study of corpora was unacceptable to linguists who adhered to Chomskyan doctrine for the reason that the dogma held that no "interesting" information could be acquired from the study of language in use. Even now corpus linguistics is still derided by Chomsky himself and many of the faithful (Aarts 2000).

In the first stages of corpus building, the perspective is that of the computer scientist managing a data stream. The fact that the data stream is language text has no meaning in the beginning – it is a linear string of characters, and as such it can be exhaustively described. The alphabet of characters can be compiled, and recurrent sequences of various lengths can be identified. Constraints on the occurrence of characters or strings can be worked out.

8. Tokenisation

The first step in modifying the character string into a language text is called *tokenisation*. Certain characters are designated as boundary markers of tokens – principally the space character in alphabetic scripts, but also some punctuation marks, for example in English the apostrophe and the hyphen. The token is held to be a rough guide to the units of meaning, but not a definitive one.

Note that the linguistic information supplied is the minimum to enable the job to be done. Note also that the correspondence between tokens and viable units of meaning in a language is assumed to be faulty from the start. Nevertheless such a tokenisation will result in a string of tokens most of which are at least contenders for components of meaningful units. And, of course, the tactical decisions made at this stage have a profound effect on the view of the language that is achieved later on. The handling of other punctuation marks, capital letters, numerals and other non-alphabetic characters during the tokenisation process will have an influence on the final appearance of the text, and the results will be non-negotiable. Corpora tokenised by different methods are only very roughly comparable; the same corpus tokenised by different methods will yield different statistics.

A moment's consideration of the role of the period character ".", will suffice to illustrate the job of tokenisation. Its function at the end of sentences has a knock-on effect on the initial capitalisation of the next word; its function in various kinds of abbreviation and its optionality in different styles ("r.p.m." or "rpm." or "rpm" ?) gives it an uncertain status. One period in a row of periods has another set of functions entirely.

So tokenisation is at best a low-level practical task that allows study to commence, yet once tokenised in one way a corpus is rarely tokenised a second time. There are no principles of tokenisation, and judgement is by results only, a typical NLP task – if it seems to work, give thanks and leave it alone. It is not surprising, then, that all sorts of problems loom for the researcher who thinks that the tokens are actually linguistic units.

The cautious approach to corpus research assumes that several more steps in analysis will be necessary before the linear units into which the corpus is divided correspond accurately enough with meaning-bearing entities. It was easily demonstrable that combinations of tokens are often closer to meaning-bearing units than individual tokens, which are often undifferentiated with respect to meaning because of being incomplete. I use the term *lexical item* for one or more words which together realise a single unit of meaning.

9. Idiomaticity and lexical items

The idiomaticity of language now takes centre stage; formerly it had two loosely related meanings: *idiom* referred to one of a small number of unusual combinations that were fairly stable multi-word lexical items, and *idiomatic* referred to well-written text that flowed freely and used the characteristic phraseology of the language. These two ideas are now seen in the context of a continuum of *coselection*; at one end, where coselection is relatively fixed, are the idioms[8], and next to them are lexical items with internal variation, then collocations which are not regular enough to form part of the items. At the other end of the continuum are single-word lexical items which attract little or no collocational patterns – like technical terms, perhaps.

From a computational point of view the lack of a reliable unit of meaning complicates the issue; if each successive string of up to seven or so words can realise one lexical item in its entirety, or seven separate lexical items, or any number in between, perhaps with some discontinuity thrown in, the job of identifying the units is a major one. Also the frequency information that arises initially from counting the tokens must gradually be replaced by figures derived from counting the lexical items. So each time a multi-word lexical item is identified, the whole corpus should be retokenised and all the frequencies recalculated, all the collocations revalidated.

In addition to the computational problem of gathering and evaluating the evidence for multi-word units, we must also concede that it is unlikely that the lexical items will be reliably identified by automatic process. In the first attempts at compiling a corpus-driven lexicon, many of the decisions will have to be made by lexicographers on a provisional basis, gradually refined by the cyclical process of retokenisation.

10. Local grammars

We return to the question of language variety, sublanguages and the difficulty of providing a theory and descriptive framework for the

8 Some newer writers in the field are using *formulaic* for heavily coselected passages. I am not happy with this term, because it draws attention to the aspect of fixity in coselection. This focus on fixity also characterised early attempts to bring coselection into language teaching. The other aspect – variation – is at least as important. Terms like *coselection* and *idiomaticity* are neutral, and I prefer them.

range of variation that is observed in texts. Attempts up to date have mainly added complications to an ever-growing general grammar on the assumption that all sentences must be fully explained in a single-pass grammar. This could be too restrictive an assumption.

Ever since it became possible to store documents in electronic form it has been clear that many of the patterns and combinations that appear in the texts are not capable of being described by any grammar of the language. Some are small-scale tokens like sums of money, dates and measurements; others are more substantial multi-token strings like place names, titles and addresses[9]; still larger are semi-codes like descriptions of chess matches or knitting patterns, stock movements and currency fluctuations. As well as these obvious ones, there are many where superficially the sentences are mainly familiar but where there are some special features or strange phraseology. Of the former, the language of full-sentence dictionary definitions is a clear and well-described exemplar (Barnbrook 2002). In these the only unusual feature is that one or more words is in bold face, but there are two other points to note, first that all the sentences are declarative, and the other that regardless of their "normal" grammar they each divide into a *definiens* and a *definiendum*, as definitions traditionally do. Faced with alternative analyses, by normal grammar or by the special grammar of definitions, the second seems altogether more appropriate (Barnbrook/Sinclair 2001).

We have thus proceeded by stages to describe a form of English, full sentence definition, which is almost identical to the rest of the language, and which is readily understood by any competent reader; we are suggesting that, while it can be accounted for in a general grammar in the usual way, there is an alternative grammar, written just for this variety, which interprets the sentences in a way that "knows" from the beginning that they are definitions. Sentences which have a similar form to a definition, like "A mortgage is a stone round your neck." must not of course be sent to this special grammar, or

9 There are already a number of projects which research into these areas; what is called *named entity recognition* in NLP is a process of finding named entities, classifying them and parsing them; as in most of NLP there is no theoretical place for this important work, and only limited practical value.

nonsense will result – a mortgage will be classed as a hypernym of "stone", like granite or basalt, and the phrase "round your neck" will be understood as a discriminator – how you distinguish this kind of stone from the others.

We must recognise the need for a large number of these *local* grammars, as they are called. Small and large, petty or profound, they are necessary because a general grammar cannot in principle do what they do – it cannot provide totally different interpretations of the same sentence, and it cannot handle all the details and byways of the full spread of a language. If a general grammar was extended to cover the second point it would essentially incorporate the local grammars inside itself.

A wide portfolio of local grammars is the simplest design option at present. They would have first chance at an incoming sentence, and they would consist of two components: an input filter to admit only appropriate sentences, and a parser to show the way the sentence makes its meaning. Where there is no real difference between the local grammar and a general one, like the discriminators in a definition, the segments concerned can just be referred to the general grammar (after any local significance has been recognised, like matching sequences in a definition grammar). So after contact with any relevant local grammars, the residue of the sentence would be handled by a simple general grammar – which if local grammars handle most of the meaning of a sentence might be a very basic one.

A portfolio of local grammars might overlap with each other, criss-cross and offer interpretations at all levels of language description. There is no limit to the number and type of them, and there is no requirement for them to be comprehensive; they only offer to do things that are impossible, inconvenient or weakly-handled in a general grammar.

Such a model is messy and could be complex in operation compared with a single general grammar, but it seems to be closer to the way language is used. The utopian scene is of a large computer into which texts are introduced, and which outputs descriptions of them which are regarded as satisfactory accounts of how the patterns in the language of the texts gives rise to reasonably stable meanings. There is little hope of that happening in the foreseeable future. However, very basic grammars can be replicated on machines, and the distributed model of local grammars offers some chance of improving the present state of the machine "understanding" of text.

11. Word and lexical item

I usually finish a general discussion with an example taken directly from a corpus, because there is still very little replicable research that has been published. These examples have frequently been misunderstood as instances of practical lexicography, but – while they often are relevant to lexicography – they are principally intended to demonstrate a relationship between meaning and form which is established before any division into grammar and lexis is imposed on the data. A multi-word lexical item such as those below usually conforms superficially to grammatical norms, but the tokens that appear in it do not deliver grammatical information. They are there as physical components of the item. This argument is supported by the fact that some sequences do not conform to the expected grammatical norms (for example after *borders on the* an adjective can appear without a noun head, such as *surreal, excessive, eccentric*). In the same way some lexical items include unique tokens of a lexical nature, for example *loggerheads* in *at loggerheads, kith, plight* and *troth.* Some accounts of idioms use such deviations as criteria for the identification of an idiom, and they certainly point to the likelihood that within a lexical item the conventions of both grammar and lexis are suspended.

The word-form *trouble* in English is quite common; at the time of writing, February 2004, there are 43,405 instances of it in the Bank of English which stands at a little over 500 million words.

The principal collocates by t-score are *in* and *was.* Other forms of the verb BE are also prominent, giving a summary picture as follows[10]:

10 For an account of t-score see Stubbs (1996). In this section a word-form is printed in italics and a lemma is in small caps; so *trouble* refers to that string

(1)	*in*	11210
(2)	BE	5214

Since many of the co-occurrences of *in* and *trouble* are not in the sequence *in...trouble*, the prominence of the verb BE is much greater than it looks. The next set of collocates are the personal pronouns, especially *he* and *I*, but they are not very strong numerically.

By far the commonest positioning of *in* and *trouble* is adjacent, i.e. *in trouble*, but sometimes another word intervenes. The main words are the adjectives *deep, serious, big, real, dire* and *financial.*

This evidence suggests a lexical item in English whose most characteristic realisation is: BE *in trouble*

The adjectives that are attracted to this item suggest that to be in trouble is an unfortunate situation, and that it often is to do with money.

At this point I would like to remove this item from the concordance, and see what is revealed in the remainder of the data. Unfortunately there is no precise way of doing this with the software at my disposal, and the best I can do is to remove all the instances of *in trouble*, leaving over a thousand discontinuous forms among the remaining 38,428 instances.

The second layer of collocation is *into* and verb forms *get, got, ran, run,* which can be summarised as follows:

(3)	*into*	2967
(4)	GET	1678
(5)	RUN	721

A form of *get* or run appears in 81% (2,399 occurrences) of the occurrences of *in trouble,* so we can postulate a lexical item realised by GET\|RUN *into trouble.*

There is a question whether this is the same lexical item as the first one, especially since there are a number of instances of GET *in trouble*, mainly in American English. The collocating adjectives, *serious, deep* and so on, and *financial,* are the same, so we could see *in*

of seven characters between spaces, while BE refers to *am, are, is, was, were, be, being, been.*

trouble as mainly indicating a state, and *into trouble* a direction. A composite lexical item would consist of:

Lexical item 1

(6) BE *in trouble*
(7) GET *in trouble*
(8) GET *into trouble*
(9) RUN *into trouble*

At this point we now remove *into trouble*, in the same crude way as before. This leaves 36,306 instances of *trouble*, though we know that quite a number of them should really have been taken out.

The picture changes, and we now have collocations as follows:

(10)	1. *is*	6455
(11)	2. *the*	4886
(12)	3. *that*	1589

This tells us that within five words of *trouble*, these three words are prominent. An English speaker's intuition will probably suggest straightaway the phrase:

(13) *the trouble is that*

and that is indeed the almost invariable pattern. It is a lexical item used to introduce a complication or a counterattack on a position in a discussion.

We can explore this item through another perspective to reach another item:

Phraseological item 2

(14) *the X is that…*

where X is one of: *problem, fact, truth, trouble, result, reality, point, idea, reason, irony*

Here is another kind of multi-word item – the *phraseological* item, or *phrase* item for short[11]. Instead of having a constant core of one or more "vocabulary" words, these items have as their core one or more of the common words, often called "grammatical words", though that would be a misnomer on this occasion. These words provide a quasi-grammatical frame within which selections are made from lists of vocabulary words, often quite long lists, and with the possibility of various subsidiary choice sets; so *trouble* and *problem* go together, and perhaps *fact* and *truth, point* and *idea.* There is as yet no established method of classifying these *semantic preferences.*

At this point we now make the best attempt at removing instances of this item, in this case by deleting the sequence *trouble is* wherever it occurs, leaving 33,521 instances. Looking at the collocation profile of these, the result is that another two words come to the top:

(15)	*had*	3207 (HAVE 7977)
(16)	*with*	4578

There is also a strong tendency to *colligate*[12] with an *ing*-word, a present participle. This is a new lexical item; the typical phrasings are:

Lexical item 3

(17) *had trouble X-ing* and *had trouble with X*;

We now remove as many instances of this item as we can, by deleting all cases of forms of HAVE *trouble.*

This has not accounted for all the instances of *trouble with*, and when we explore these more closely, another pattern emerges:

(18) *the trouble with… is*

11 See Renouf and Sinclair (1991) for the introduction of this category.

12 *Colligation* is Firth's (1951) term for the co-occurrence of words realising grammatical categories.

This pattern recalls the previous phraseological item 2, and could be regarded as a variant of it:

(19) the trouble (with X) is that

It is difficult to find the collocates because of the possible overall length of the pattern; the best probe I can do suggests that only one other word, *problem* alternates with *trouble*, so it is probably a minor variant.

We now remove all instances of *trouble with*, leaving 27,704 instances. The word that comes to the top is *no*, with 1,711 occurrences, and HAVE again, making a basic pattern HAVE *no trouble* followed frequently by an *-ing* form. The chances are that this is a variant of the previous lexical item 3, HAVE *trouble X-ing* and the cotexts should be examined for overlap. Before that we should note that *at all* is a frequent internal collocate, and that *in* often comes before the *-ing* form. So some realisations of this item can be quite long:

HAVE *no trouble at all in X-ing*

Seven choices are taken simultaneously in this variant of the item.

We now remove all instances of *no trouble*, leaving 26,581 lines. Now the top collocate is *out*, and the familiar phrase *out of trouble.* This, while much less frequent, is related in meaning to *in trouble*, lexical item 1, and a careful analysis of the two cotexts would be needed to make a case for merging the two as variants of the one item.

We now remove *out of trouble*, and see what comes to the top in the remaining 25,713 instances. It is *any*, and on inspection this seems not to be a new item in itself, but part of the consequence of making one of the other items negative. So we do not delete it, but pick the next most prominent collocate, which is *cause*. There are 1,371 occurrences of the lemma CAUSE, indicating the strong presence of a lexical item that is quite familiar:

Lexical item 4

CAUSE *trouble.*

We now remove CAUSE *trouble* from the concordance, leaving 25,092 lines, and look at the collocational profile of this remainder. The pattern is beginning to break up, partly because of the inefficient tools for removing instances of an established lexical item. Several of the collocates realise small optional variations of frequent items, like the adjectives *serious, financial*, and *much* and *a lot of.*

The most prominent new word is *there*, signalling an item which has the form:

Lexical item 5

there BE *trouble <location>*[13]

Here there are some interesting extras like *afoot, ahead, looming* and *brewing.*

For the last few details we just move down the list of significant collocates, without attempting to remove new items. The new items to emerge are compounds, *trouble-free* (LI 5) and *trouble spots* (LI 6), small items like the two with *worth, worth the trouble* (LI 7) and *more trouble than X* BE *worth* (LI 8).

The two verbs *started* and *began* lead to another pattern, *the trouble began/started*, usually followed by *when* (LI 9). We have found several kinds of prefatory phrase including *the trouble.*

To assess what proportion of the overall occurrence of *trouble* has been accounted for in these multi-word lexical items, we will now attempt to delete all the instances of words that seem to be mainly leftover variations of lexical items we have already accounted for. Again this is rough justice, and we delete all instances of the following tokens:

there, serious, lot, free, spots, deep, big, little, worth, financial, started, began

13 I use a sans-serif typeface within angle brackets to indicate – informally – general semantic preferences.

At this point we can note that well over half the instances have been assigned to one or other of the items. Of the original 43,405 there are only 18,945 left.

New collocates include a few more compounds like *heart trouble* (LI 10), *crowd trouble* (LI 11), *trouble-makers* (LI 12), and *asking for trouble* (LI 13), *trouble flared <timing>* (L I4), TAKE *the trouble to* (LI 15), *sign of trouble* (LI 16) and *spell trouble* (LI 17). These have only a hundred or two occurrences, and so they do not appear until the large patterns have been removed.

The patterns, even this far inside the patterns for *trouble*, are strong and complex, as we can see from *sign of trouble*, LI 17 above. The most common usage of this core phrase is in *at the first sign of trouble*, and there are cases without *at* and without *the*; likewise there are alternatives to *first*, for example superlatives like *least,* or *a* or *no*.

What emerges from this brief probe, using tools that were not designed for the job, is a picture not unlike a dictionary entry. The main formal difference is that each lexical item has its own unique componence, and is in no way "a meaning of 'trouble'". Indeed the semantic subtlety of the notion of "trouble" is exposed in this analysis, and no dictionary would be likely to analyse the word in this way.

This sketch of *trouble* has not been comprehensive nor very precise. But how successful has it been in describing the characteristic usage of the word? There are still around 20,000 instances that we may not have accounted for. One way to check – another rough and ready device – is to take an unbiased sample of the whole concordance and see how much of it is adequately covered. I have taken, for the sake of time and space, only 25 instances, evenly spaced arithmetically from the whole concordance. There is no guarantee that this list, or any other, is representative of the concordance as a whole, but equally there is no reason to believe that it is not a fair reflection.

1	Sabaru's wheels were worth £2,000.	Trouble	flared after thousands of race
2	that knowledge in that time.	Trouble	is you couldn't you could you
3	them alone. They don't cause any #	trouble.	But Heather doesn't want to go
4	and digital TV channels such as	Trouble,	Bravo, Challenge TV and Living
5	Soviet Union or in any way causing	trouble	to Mr Gorbachov, who, at least
6	hopes today and storing up economic	trouble	that will disappoint them
7	in his cabin to sort out some engine	trouble.	After the engineer had gone off
8	his own business was in financial	trouble	and it was for this reason that
9	much space out wide was asking for	trouble.	Coming out of what Redknapp
10	a heavy West Indian accent who had	trouble	with Sawyerville. He finally got
11	care to know that the writer had	trouble	with the topic--it wants to know
12	I'm pitching poorly, if I'm having	trouble	making the pitches I want to make
13	a week off work because he is having	trouble	riding light since an illness
14	you get there, will lead you into	trouble.	This month, I'll be offering
15	Another forgotten horse, Looks Like	Trouble,	still faces a long road back, but
16	Puck (Stanley Tucci) to make	trouble:	misapplying love potions,
17	she would surely have started making	trouble	about it sooner. But Henrietta
18	before the car developed mechanical	trouble	again. But he still timed 1min 24.
19	on Walsall fighting their way out of	trouble	with a battering Rammell. A fifth
20	was the very knowledge of possible	trouble	with adults that led to vandalism.
21	At worst, they are storing up real	trouble	for the months to come.
22	I think that invariably stops the	trouble	right away. My overriding
23	any bad news. I asked him what the	trouble	was and he replied, `Your company
24	the RSA Inquiry see this page). The	trouble	is that the RSA echoes many other
25	it was true. And this was the	trouble:	the script's many departures from

Table 1. Concordance of the word *trouble.*

Two of these instances show *Trouble* as part of a proper name, and so can be ignored henceforth. Most of these are familiar enough from the analysis above. The ones that we have missed and that occur more than once are:

6. *storing up economic trouble*, also 21, *storing up real trouble for*
This is a smallish pattern, but should be recorded, especially in the form with *for*. There are indications that it is quite complex, with *up* obligatory, *for* normal, and very often a modifier of *trouble.* What follows *for* is interesting – a reflexive like *herself, later* or *the future.*

16. *make trouble*, also 17 *making trouble*
This is a more substantial omission. A rough search suggests that there may be over 400 instances of such a pattern, very often with *for.*

Single occurrences that are familiar phrasings:

9. *asking for trouble*
There are more then 200 instances that follow this pattern, almost all with *asking* as the realisation of ASK, and many showing that this phrase is almost nominalised, in examples like *This is asking for trouble.*

14. *will lead you into trouble.*
This is a minor and quite elaborate item, requiring a pronoun (usually) or a noun phrase, and with a small variant *LEAD X out of trouble.*

18. *the car developed mechanical trouble*
With 7. *some engine trouble* this instance points to a small cluster of patterns. You can develop engine trouble or something related to it, or develop a health problem like heart trouble or kidney trouble. There is still not much evidence on which to propose lexical items, because most of the patterns occur with a frequency of less than 50.

22. *stops the trouble*
There is a small item here, *STOP the trouble.*

For instances nos. 19 and 20 there is very little repeated pattern. There are a few instances of *FIGHT X's way out of trouble*, and some of *possible trouble*, but on present evidence we are now scraping the bottom of the barrel.

12. Conclusion

The practical exercise indicates that some twenty-plus multi-word items account for most of the patterning of the word *trouble.* Most of these were found in the collocational searches, and the only one that seems to have slipped through the net is MAKE *trouble.* That it to say, it is a reasonably prominent phrasing and we are left wondering why it did not make the top of the significance list.

Only two of the 23 instances picked to check on the coverage were not fairly clear instances of one of the lexical or phrasal items. It would be sensible to repeat this checking operation because we might have picked an odd selection; after two or three selections it is very unlikely that we will encounter anything else that the procedure has missed.

This is a single, "thin" exploratory probe into a large and complex lexical organisation, and it only shows some of the distinctions that have to be made. Work on other items will no doubt gather and consolidate as well as atomise – there are signs even here, in the phrasal item 2, that some of the uses of *trouble* will be dispersed into other items altogether.

Note that each item is associated with a unique componence of words, even though the variations, which are plentiful, may occasionally overlap with each other. So instead of a multiplicity of "meanings" of *trouble* we have a number of meaningful items each of which contains *trouble* as one of its components.

Note also that this analysis has been carried out without recourse to the normal descriptive arsenals. There has been hardly any need for grammatical or semantic terminology. Also there are no tags, no annotations, nothing but plain text; the only statistics are a simple significance test, that is used as a matter of convenience until a more appropriate measure is devised. In other words, we have arrived at a fairly comprehensive and accurate description of the role of *trouble* in English without requiring the resources of NLP nor of conventional grammar and semantics.

There was no attempt to avoid using these resources; they are available on my computer whenever I need them. For this exercise I would argue that I achieved better results without using them – and without making the semantic assumptions of lexicographers either.

This claim takes us back to the underlying contention of the study. The axioms and apparatus and traditions of linguistic theories that were devised before corpus evidence became available need to be revised in the light of that evidence, because it shows that a language in use does not behave in the ways predicted by the theories. Where the theory has slipped away long ago, as in the case of NLP, new links with corpus-informed theoretical positions need to be formed so that the power and sophistication of the software tools of NLP can be applied both to the development of the theories and to applications that work in the world.

References

Aarts, B. 2000. Corpus linguistics, Chomsky and Fuzzy Tree Fragments. In Mair and Hundt, 5-13.

Barnbrook, G. 2002. *Defining Language.* Amsterdam/Philadelphia: John Benjamins. Studies in Corpus Linguistics 11.

Barnbrook, G. / Sinclair, J. 2001. Specialised corpus, local and functional grammars. In Ghadessy, M., A. Henry and R. Roseberry (eds) *Small Corpus Studies and ELT.* Studies in Corpus Linguistics 5, Amsterdam/Philadelphia: John Benjamins, 237-276.

Biber, D. / Johansson, S. / Leech, G. / Conrad, S. / Finegan, E. 1999. *The Longman Grammar of Spoken and Written English.* London: Pearson Education.

Chomsky, N. 1964. Current Issues in Linguistic Theory. In Fodor J and Katz J. (eds) *The Structure of Language.* Englewood Cliffs, Prentice-Hall, 62-79.

Chomsky, N. 1969. Should Traditional Grammar be ended or mended? *Educational Review 22/1,* 5-17.

Firth, J. 1951. Modes of meaning. In Firth 1957.

Firth, J. 1957. *Papers in Linguistics 1934-1951,* London: Oxford University Press.

Francis, W. / Kučera, H. 1979. *Manual of Information to accompany a standard Sample of Present-day Edited American English, for use with digital computers.* Providence, R.I.: Department of Linguistics, Brown University.

Mair, C. / Hundt, M. (eds) 2000. *Corpus Linguistics and Linguistic Theory.* Amsterdam/Atlanta: Rodopi.

Renouf, A. / Sinclair, J. 1991. Collocational Frameworks in English. In Aijmer, K. / Altenberg, B. (eds) *English Corpus Linguistics: Studies in Honour of Jan Svartvik.,* London: Longman, 128-143.

Sinclair, J. / Jones, S. / Daley, R. 1970. *English Lexical Studies*. Birmingham University, for the Office for Scientific and Technical Information

Sinclair, J. 1999a. A way with common words. In Hasselgård, H. and S. Oksefjell (eds) *Out of Corpus: Studies in Honour of Stig Johansson* Series Language and Computers: Studies in Practical Linguistics 26: Amsterdam/Atlanta: Rodopi, 157-175.

Sinclair, J. 1999b. New roles for Language Centres: the mayonnaise problem. In D. Bickerton / Gotti, M. (eds) *Language Centres: Integration through Innovation,* CercleS (Conféderation Européenne des Centres de Langues de l'Enseignement Superieur) Secretariat, Department of Modern Languages, University of Plymouth, 31-50.

Sinclair, J. 2001a The Deification of Information. In Thompson, G. and Scott, M. (eds) *Patterns of Text: in honour of Michael Hoey*. Amsterdam/Philadelphia: John Benjamins, 287-314.

Sinclair, J. 2001b. Review of Biber et al. *International Journal of Computer Linguistics* 6/2, 339-359.

Sinclair J. 2003. Can we have a conversation with a computer? In Bondi, N. and Stati, S. (eds) *Dialogue Analysis 2000 Selected papers from the 10th IADA Anniversary Conference, Bologna 2000* Beiträge zur Dialogforschung Band 25. Tübingen: Max Niemeyer Verlag, 79-92.

Sinclair, J. 2004. Intuition and annotation; the discussion continues in *Advances in Corpus Linguistics: Papers from the Twenty-second International Conference on English Language Research on Computerized Corpora*. Göteborg 22-26 May 2002 edited by Karin Aijmer and Bengt Altenberg.

Stubbs, M. 1995. Collocations and semantic profiles. *Functions of Language* 2/1, 23-55.

Winograd, T. 1972. *Understanding Natural Language*. Academic Press.

Appendix

Note: These are quotations that have appeared on the Corpora List in the last few years that are indicative of NLP attitudes to research and applications. I have left them anonymous, but I expect that their authors would in the main stand by them.

1. Automatic summarization and question answering (QA) are now enjoying a period of revival and they are advancing at a much quicker pace than before.

2. The increasing importance of Corpus Linguistics is mainly due to its contribution to practical applications in Computational Linguistics.

3. As natural language products play an increasingly more prominent role in the market for knowledge management, information extraction, search and navigation…

4. The ultimate goal of the Semantic Web is to allow machines to share and use knowledge worldwide in a scalable, adaptable and extensible manner, without any central authority and just a few basic rules.

5. Linguistic engineering and language processing is confronted with new issues. Indeed, it is now necessary to work not only on isolated sentences or utterances, but on entire structured or unstructured texts too

6. Moreover, texts are rarely tagged or digitised. However, text processing requires pre-processing in order to conduct syntactical, semantic and pragmatic analysis.

7. During last years, some generic ontologies become available and a lot of research projects tried to take into account semantic aspects to obtain more precise results for IE systems. Meanwhile, important efforts concentrate on developing tools for semi-automatic building of domain-specific ontologies, based on IE and text-mining techniques.

8. MWUs [multi-word units] are used frequently in everyday language, usually to express precisely ideas and concepts that cannot be compressed into a single word. A considerable amount of research has been devoted to this subject, both in terms of theory and practice, but despite increasing interest in idiomaticity within linguistic research, many questions still remain unanswered.

9. Attention is being drawn to new aspects of ontology research such as ontology coordination and mapping – aspects that are particularly relevant for distributed environments such as Knowledge Grid and Semantic web.

10. From this perspective, lexicographers, lexical semanticists and ontologists are joining forces to build innovative systems for integrating ontological knowledge with lexical and semantic resources.

11. Although XML is a useful representation language, its use alone does not solve all the problems and choices with respect to the representation style

12. Recent years have seen the development of techniques and resources to support robust, deep grammatical analysis of language in real-world domains, for instance in flexible human-computer dialog systems […] and speech-to-speech translation […]. The demands of these types of tasks have driven significant advances in areas such as parser efficiency, hybrid statistical/symbolic approaches to disambiguation, and the acquisition of large-scale lexicons. In response to these successes deep language processing is starting to be deployed in commercial applications such as automated email response.

13. Corpus-based methods both in linguistics and NLP need breakthroughs for further development. [...] Combining corpus-based methods with linguistic formalisms may give rise to a new type of linguistics.

14. Due to recent advances in statistical methods and machine learning approaches for NLP and in efficient processing algorithms for high-level grammar formalisms, there are now highly promising attempts to combine shallow and deep processing techniques.

JOANNA CHANNELL

The other side of the LSP fence: Commercial language consultancy and research

1. Introduction

LSP research, in common with applied linguistics generally, has a low profile as a problem-solving approach in the public arena. When leaders in an organisation, be it business, governmental or public, identify a communication issue, their first instinct is to phone for a management consultant or an occupational psychologist. Even if they are aware of LSP research they are unlikely to know anything of the kind of problems it can tackle and the ways that linguistic analysis can add value to their business. This means that many opportunities for the application of the theories and methodologies of LSP research are being lost, and as a consequence that LSP is not fulfilling its potential.

When conducting consultancy research, there are two challenges for the consultant linguist: first, to understand how non-linguists understand and try to tackle language issues; and second, to find ways to communicate the insights of research in usable and understandable forms. This chapter therefore focuses on how LSP issues are understood by non-linguists in businesses and organisations; with the aim of helping practitioners to promote the practical application of LSP research worldwide[1]. Specific questions include:

1 I am grateful to the following groups and individuals who helped to shape the arguments and ideas in this paper: the audience at LSP 2003, Margaret Rogers, Vijay Bhatia, Anthony Johnson, Michael Stubbs, Martin Cutts, the participants at Birmingham English Language Postgraduate conference 2003, and all the people involved in the consultancy, training and research projects mentioned.

- What types of LSP issues do non-linguist business and organisational language users focus on or problematise?
- How do they conceptualise and articulate "language" as an "issue"?
- What outcomes do business and organisational users seek from specialist consultancy?
- Which theoretical and methodological approaches are relevant?
- How can we promote LSP research in organisations and businesses?

Before looking at these questions, I will first clarify the distinction between consultancy and academic research and give an overview of the projects which I will use to provide illustrations and data.

2. Definition of the distinction between consultancy research and academic research

Academic research is inspired by the wishes and interests of the researcher; in contrast, consultancy research is inspired by the needs, wants and beliefs of the client who commissions it: the client defines the research agenda. Unlike the case of academic research, it is the client who has the idea and then seeks a researcher or consultant to carry out the work. Many types of consultancy research require an open competitive tender to win the contract. Once the contract exists, the client pays for the research and usually insists on complete control of the data and results.

3. Overview of projects used as case studies

For the purpose of this chapter, I have selected, from my last 15 years of consultancy and research, 15 pieces of work which fulfil certain criteria:

- First, that they were consultancy as defined in (2);
- Second, that they are pieces of consultancy that included language and communication research and advice.
- Third, that they were commissioned by an organisation or by individuals who do not have specialised knowledge about the nature of language.

This set of examples is therefore not a controlled sample, but rather a set of case studies. The list below is intended to give a sense of the scope of the types of organisations, issues raised and approaches used. Some client organisations have published, or given permission for publication of, accounts of the research carried out for them, others have wished to preserve anonymity. Further reading about some of these projects can be found in Campanelli, Channell et al. (1994), Campanelli/Channell (1996), Channell/St John (1996), Channell (1997), Channell (2000), St John/Channell (1996).

Client company or organistion	Questions and issues	Data
Multinational manufacturer of cleaning products	cross-cultural communication between employees from different countries	company memos, videos of meetings, recordings of phone calls
UK Government (Employment Dept)	How can Jobcentres prepare for the Single European Market?	Interviews
UK Government (Employment Dept)	How can we collect accurate data about training? What do people understand by the term *training*?	CoBUILD corpora, focus groups, survey questionnaire
UK Government (Employment Dept)	How can we collect accurate data about qualifications?	CoBUILD corpora, focus groups, interviews
UK Government (Employment and learning)	Why does everybody tell us that National Vocational Qualifications are hard to understand?	Corpus of NVQ texts, CoBUILD corpora, focus groups, interviews
Burton on Trent Community Partnership	Evaluation of TESOL provision	Classroom observation, analysis of policy documents, interviews
Local authority (City Council)	What are the most effective ways for our receptionists to direct phone calls and visitors to the right place?	Participant observation; audio recordings, development session
Local authorities (different ones)	We want to have a plain language policy – so we need to agree what that is and train people to do it	Policy documents; samples of letters, information sheets, memos.
City Council (large British city)	Our auditors needs to communicate their technical findings to people in all the Council's departments	current audit reports.
City Council, Transport Department (large British city)	How can we best communicate and consult with the public about road schemes?	letters, circulars
	What are the best ways of responding to enquiries from the public?	sample of letters, emails, revisions to letters
Social Services Inspectorate	Can you help an inspector whose reports do not match our usual format and style?	examples of reports, drafts of the individual's reports
National consumer body	The standard of letters going out from the complaints staff is not high enough.	samples of letters, existing templates, existing 'boilerplate' text.
EPSRC Engineering Doctorate programme at Univ. of Surrey	We want our engineers to be better prepared for writing up the portfolio for the Eng.D	'best example' portfolios, published articles.
South Yorkshire Widening Participation Partnership	Evaluate the structures and management board of the partnership	interviews, transcript of management meeting

Table 1. Overview of 15 example research and consultancy projects.

This list consists mainly of projects where the resources for them came from public funds, some via departments of the UK government, some via local authorities or other agencies. There is also, of course, language-issue research being commissioned by private sector organisations. However my specialisation and my network of contacts has mainly been in the public sector.

Written texts	7 projects
Spoken interaction	2 (job c2 (job centres, receptionists)
Both spoken and written	6 projects

Table 2. Types of data.

4. What types of LSP issues or themes were raised in these projects?

The first overarching theme is that of written texts which do not fulfil their communicative purposes. In some cases, this would be from the originators' point of view in the sense that text writers produce a text or texts which do not lead to the desired result.

One example given by staff in a large British City Council's Transport Department is where they need to inform people that the road outside their house is going to be resurfaced. So they would produce a circular letter and deliver it to each house, conveying the information that the road was to be resurfaced, and the request to park cars elsewhere while this was being carried out. When the engineers arrive to carry out the work, the majority of residents have apparently not read this letter, and have not moved their cars, and it causes difficulties for all concerned. Events like this led the Transport Department to approach language specialists at the Plain Language Commission (see website reference, and Cutts 1996). The PLC team, of which I was a member, organised workshops and training sessions looking at how the local government officers could produce letters which would have a better chance of being read and thus produce the action from recipients that the writers wanted.

The second way in which texts do not fulfil their communicative purposes is from the readers' point of view. This is where the people who are the intended readers or users of particular documents complain of difficulties of understanding. An example of this would be the British Government's vocational qualifications initiative of the early part of the 1990s, where a new policy set in train a comprehensive review and standardisation of all vocational qualifications, including the development of new VQs for areas of work which had not previously had qualifications, and in all cases, the development of a competency framework for assessment (for more on VQs and competency-based assessment, see Mansfield/Mitchell 1996).

Almost immediately, the Confederation of British Industry produced a report from a survey of members which showed that employers welcomed the whole VQs initiative but found the documentation difficult. Trade unions, colleges and learners groups reported difficulties in understanding and working with the texts. As a result, the relevant government department, then called the Employment Department, commissioned a large-scale piece of research which aimed to find out why people found the VQ documentation difficult to understand (see Channell/St John 1996).

A second theme in several pieces of work is cross-cultural communication issues. These could be intercountry or interlingual, one example being the multinational chemical company which moves their people around from country to country, so people with a number of different language backgrounds work together, to some extent using English as a lingua franca. Some people in the company had begun to feel that while everyone's English was at an appropriate level, there were still some issues of misunderstanding and ineffective communication and they wondered if LSP analysis could help them to understand the nature of the miscommunication they observed.

More often, though, the cross-cultural communication issues that I have encountered have been about an institutional or group culture which is effective within the organisation but is not understood outside. So, for example, taking again the example of the City Council, there was a need for highways engineers to communicate cross-culturally by sending out letters to the public which avoided technical terminology about road design or traffic management.

The third overarching issue would be that we often found ourselves looking at individuals' repertoire of communicative skills. Using the transport engineers again as an example, they would need to discuss a road design and to present this technically at the relevant council committee. They might also need to explain the same material in a non-technical way to a resident living in a particular street. So I would analyse this as two different aspects of their repertoire of communicative skills.

The fourth theme is that very often the issues of text are about genre. Sometimes what we have looked at has been texts which are poor and communicatively ineffective examples of a particular genre, so for example, looking at letters to customers which respond to complaints, that is a recognisable sub-genre of letters and there are effective and ineffective ways of writing those kinds of letters. Another category of research would be the case where a whole genre fails to be effective for its communicative purpose. An example of this is the work on National Vocational Qualifications (mentioned previously). The teams who developed the new NVQs created a novel genre which had not existed before. However, it initially developed as a genre which instead of communicating a clear idea of what the qualification was about, and what a learner needed to do to gain it, was judged as difficult to read and use.

The final and critical issue that comes up in all of this type of consultancy is the issue of prescription versus description. While an applied linguist always must approach data using a descriptive approach and set of techniques, it is necessary in consultancy research that eventually the researchers would move on to saying "you need to do this". That is to say, that they would move to being prescriptive (see Shuy 1998 and Channell 2001 for the importance of giving clear advice).

5. Which theoretical and methodological approaches are relevant?

Applied linguistics (AL) provides an underlying ethical and philosophical approach to language research (exemplified by, for example the

British Association for Applied Linguistics 1994 *Recommendations on Good Practice in Applied Linguistics*; see also Stubbs, 1996 section 1). AL and LSP also provide a set of tools and approaches which can be used to analyse any aspect of language and language behaviour. Among all of the possible approaches, my work has repeatedly drawn on a small number which have proved their worth as durable, effective in producing results and understandable by the non-linguist clients they were used with. Table 3 shows these.

Needs analysis	10 projects
Genre analysis	8 projects
Pragmatics	7 projects
Conversation Analysis/DA	6 projects
Thematic analysis	4 projects
Error analysis	4 projects
Corpus linguistics	3 projects

Table 3. Approaches from AL and LSP.

Needs Analysis here is used in the broadest sense of analysing what is needed in order to provide recommendations, or training and coaching. However, it has its roots in the LSP-style needs analysis for language teaching, associated with the rise of communicative language teaching in the 1970s.

While this is not the place to attempt a definition of genre analysis, I can say that the reason that genre approaches are so relevant to consultancy research is that they approach texts in context and ask "why" questions. Thus Bhatia (personal communication) identifies 3 levels or perspectives on discourse:

- Discourse as text
- Discourse as genre
- Discourse as social practice

and poses the question, relevant to any consultancy project on language: "why do people write the way they do and what makes this possible?"

Closely related to genre-based approaches are approaches from pragmatics, which have been relevant in seven projects. The three main areas drawn from pragmatic theory are the maxims of conversation originating in the work of Paul Grice (1967, 1968, 1981). The second is Brown/Levinson's (1987) framework looking at politeness and analysis of power relationships in spoken interactions, and also between writers and readers of documents. The third area is that of cross-cultural pragmatic failure, a term first used by Jenny Thomas in her 1983 article of that name which was about foreign language speakers. However the concept is equally useful and applicable to institutional cross-cultural communication such as that between a large organisation and people outside it: its customers, or service users, or clients.

Research methods drawn from other disciplines have been used alongside approaches from AL. The main approaches are listed in Table 4.

Focus groups	3
Survey questionnaires + statistical analysis	2
Job analysis	6
Evaluation metrics	1
Structured or semi-structured interviews	7

Table 4. Research methods and approaches drawn from other disciplines.

Sections 3, 4 and 5 have attempted to provide an overview of the case studies, viewed from the LSP practitioner's perspective. I now turn to the other perspective, that of the clients who seek help with language issues.

6. Why do organisations seek consultancy or research and what outcomes do they seek?

The reasons for seeking specialist support from an LSP analyst are often one or more of the following:

- People in the organisation feel that it needs to improve communication or they want to influence another organisation or individuals to improve their communication.
- They have received complaints, or negative media coverage, or an external body is putting pressure on them to evaluate or improve.
- They are stuck and they wonder if applied linguistics can help, even though they do not really know what it is.
- LSP analysis has been helpful to them before (or they have heard that it was helpful to another organisation).

Having sought specialist research and consultancy, generally the organisations reviewed here would be looking for a report with four main areas of content:

a) Explain why the present situation is as it is. Do not give us technical language.
b) Justify your analysis but do not overwhelm us with academic detail.
c) Tell us what is working and what is not working.
d) Give us something we can use to improve (although we might easily ignore your recommendations, see Shuy 1998).

At this point, two developments may occur. On the one hand, the organisation may welcome the report and recommendations and set about making changes. Shuy (1998) sets out a paradigm case of a positive response:

> "[...] [the organisation] admitted its weakness, co-opted the linguist who had been working against them in a lawsuit, asked for help, created a well-

> protected administrative entity that nurtured the project, took the advice of the trainers, and implemented a new language policy that had at the least the strong potential for continuation."
> (Shuy 1998: 45)

On the other hand, the organisation may react negatively. People may misunderstand what LSP consultants have done, fail to value the insights of their approaches, or specifically work against implementtation of their suggestions (again, see Shuy 1998 for some examples). It is useful to recognise two sources for potential resistance: some will be the general resistance to change, to outside evaluation, to self-examination which has been well identified in the management literature on organisational change (for a review of the literature on this in a higher education context, see Blackwell/Preece 2001); and some will be specifically around the different beliefs about language which specialists and non-specialists hold, to which I now turn.

7. Conceptualisation of "language" by non-linguists

To ensure the success of consultancy research, it is important for LSP practitioners to remember that their specialist knowledge and experience of language lead them to have a conception of the nature of language which is very different from that held by non-linguists (see Shuy 1998: 120ff for similar points). Roberts (2003: 145) says that at this point in the research relationship, "the unremarkable and naturalised ways of doing and being an Applied Linguist are confronted by the 'other'" To draw on a current popular metaphor, it sometimes feels as if "LSP consultants are from Mars and clients are from Venus". The main differences of perception would include:

LSP practitioners (from Mars)	Clients/non-linguists (from Venus)
▪ everything about language is negotiable and changeable ▪ every use of language is situated ▪ we separate form from function as a matter of course.	▪ we all know a language, so we are our own experts ▪ there are correct and incorrect ways of writing and speaking ▪ language is the way it is and it can't be done differently or better.

The different perspectives on and conceptions about language held by linguists and non-linguists pose specific issues in the establishment of a productive working relationship and that topic alone could fill the rest of this chapter (see Shuy 1998, Channell 2001, Roberts 2003 for ideas about how to establish such a relationship). However, here I continue with the theme of "the other side of the fence" by looking in more detail at the conceptualisation of language by non-linguists as exemplified in the 15 research projects under review. Experience suggests that non-linguists:

- see language as "a bunch of discrete units" which can be put together in any way the writer likes (Shuy 1998)
- can recognise a successful text but cannot explain why it is successful
- confuse brevity with simplicity and clarity
- demonstrate a low awareness of the relationship between language use and its context
- are unaware of the value of distinguishing form from function (medium from message).

I will now use a particular project as a source of examples of some of these points, as well as a case study which demonstrates effective communication between the research team and the client.

8. The language of occupational standards and vocational qualifications

This project is an example of good practice in that the client (the UK Government) recognised the existence of a specific language issue and sought specialist research and consultancy in order to learn more about the problem and to move towards a solution. "National Vocational Qualifications" (usually known as NVQs and in Scotland, Scottish Vocational Qualifications) is the unified system of vocational qualifications developed in the United Kingdom during the first part of the 1990s. The National Vocational Qualification "Statement of competence" details the outcomes that an individual has to be able to achieve in order to be considered competent in the occupation covered by the NVQ. Documentation was designed which was (and is) used by learners, tutors and assessors. The introduction of NVQs/SVQs was a revolutionary and important step forward in the delivery of vocational education in the UK (see Mansfield/Mitchell 1996 for more on the development of vocational qualifications).

As mentioned earlier, Government research had shown that users/readers reacted negatively to the language of NVQ texts. A research team based at the University of Birmingham[2], and also including expert occupational standards developer Bob Mansfield, was commissioned to identify the features of the texts which caused users' negative reactions. Part of the research involved analysis of a corpus of NVQ texts (2 million words), looking for frequent patterns and comparing them with patterns in the CoBUILD Bank of English. The research identified 16 different language features which made the texts difficult for their readers and then suggested ways to avoid these features and create more accessible texts. Example 1 shows an extract from the level 1 qualification for hairdressing (as it was before revision).

2 Members of the research team were: Joanna Channell, Malcolm Coulthard, Alice Deignan, Neil Drave, John Sinclair, Maggie Jo St John

Example 1: Text: NVQ level 1 in hairdressing, 1996. UK Government, National Vocational Qualifications and Scottish Vocational Qualifications. (text has since been revised) (see Channell/St. John 1996).

Element: Cutting hair into a layered form so that the inner hair is shorter than the outline hair length
Range: On straight and curly hair, wet and dry hair. With and without partings and fringes.
Performance criteria:

a) Established natural hair fall and movement by examination
b) Determined natural hair growth characteristics by checking hairline
c) Combed or brushed hair into position for cutting
d) Positioned client's head at the appropriate angle for efficient operation
e) Made small neat sections
f) Combed sections to control the hair
g) Followed guidelines throughout the cut
h) Achieved style blending short layers into longer edges
i) Club (blunt) cut to achieve maximum weight
j) Tapered hair using scissors or razor to reduce bulk and length
k) Thinned hair using scissors or razor to reduce bulk
l) Used mirrors to check balance throughout
m) Showed client the effect of the cut using a back mirror
n) Followed safety and hygiene procedures
o) Completed cut within 30 minutes

This text would be used by an assessor who is assessing (in this case) a trainee hairdresser, to check that this trainee can do the things that they need to be able to do to be a competent hairdresser. Each qualification is divided into elements which cover different aspects of doing the job. Then for each element there is a listing of exactly what someone needs to demonstrate to show their competency. So this is a competency based system of assessment. The research questions here were first "why is it that people found this text difficult to use?" and then "why did the authors of this text write it the way they did?".

This extract exemplifies a number of linguistic features which the researchers identified as the cause of the general negative comment about NVQ/SVQ texts. These included:

- Presence of unknown collocations (for example "performance criteria")

The VQ texts contained many combinations of words which did not appear in the CoBUILD Bank of English and which we therefore concluded were likely to be combinations which readers would never have previously seen. If there are a few of these in a text, there is not a problem because readers use their knowledge of constituent lexical items to work out what the collocation means but if a text contains hundreds of never-before-seen collocations we believed it leads to difficulties with understanding.

- Missing words/note form

The performance criteria in this example are not full sentences. Material has been omitted to make them shorter. The absence of reference to agents, patients or context makes it difficult to understand who is doing what and to whom. Partly this came from a drive for brevity, in the mistaken belief that if a text was shorter, then it was also easier to understand. Now, a text with elements missing is fine if the reader knows what the text is about, but if the reader is trying to learn about something new from the text, then they cannot reconstruct the missing elements.

- Non-standard use of lexis (for example "range")

There were many instances in NVQs of lexis being used with a special, often technical, meaning. In this text, an example would be the word *range*.

9. Confusing brevity with clarity and simplicity

A competency-based description of a particular job-task produces a detailed and complex text. The amount of text needed to specify precisely all the aspects of a particular task is lengthy, as we see with the hair-cutting example. There was therefore a drive, as NVQs developed, to keep the texts as concise as possible. Attempts to make texts shorter often had the effect of making them much more difficult to understand.

The following examples from the text of the (then) qualification in retailing/store management show difficulties with texts which have been abbreviated into a type of note form.

> Example 2: Performance criterion from retailing
> Stock quality not meeting specification identified and reported

Here the passive voice verbs disguise who is to do what and to whom. Agentless passive voice verbs were pervasive in the VQ texts (the frequency was even higher than in scientific writing), and our focus group participants picked this feature out as something which they found off-putting.

The amount of material omitted to produce the note form make recovering meaning challenging, even with cotext. The recovered meaning would be something along the lines of:

> *Stock of a quality which does not meet its specification is identified and reported to an appropriate person.*

The drive for brevity in these texts also led writers to omit logical stages in an argument. While this can be a perfectly legitimate device for making a text more concise, it may cause difficulties for readers who are not familiar with the topic material. They are expected to infer logical stages, rather than having them made explicit. For example:

> Example 3: Performance criterion from retailing
> (g) displays are constructed safely by staff and are completed within the required time limits

is more difficult to understand than the longer version with more of the relevant text present:

> *While displays must be constructed safely by staff, they must also be completed within the required time limit*

In the original text the contrast between the two requirements, and the difficulty of complying with both at the same time, is left implicit.

To make matters worse, the logical connections are obvious to someone who already has expertise in an area. So the designers seemed to fail to appreciate that someone learning about this as a new topic might miss the absent logical connections.

Another method for packing information which occurred in the NVQ texts at that time was to put information into large nominal groups. So a large nominal group would be used to describe entities or refer to processes, rather than using a full sentence to do this:

> assembled displays are constructed...

(above) is more difficult than:

> *When you assemble displays you must construct...*

because in the original text the agent, the person who assembles the displays, is left implicit.

> Example 4: Performance criterion from retailing
> Details of stock received and held accurately recorded

has a six-word noun phrase which is the patient of the verb *recorded.* It is harder to process than the longer version:

> *Details of the stock which has been received and which is already held must be accurately recorded.*

So again we have a complex set of concepts packed down by writers who believed that if they could make the text shorter then it would be easier to understand and what they actually achieved was the opposite.

10. Vague language

Given the requirement to describe as precisely as possible the various job tasks for occupations, the researchers hypothesised that the presence of vague language might be another source of difficulties in understanding (for a general description of vague language, see Channell 1994 and on writing, Channell 1999). One example was the presence of the number approximator *at least* + a number.

Example 5: Element from Office Administration Level 1 (1996 version, since revised)

element: Communicate effectively

Performance criteria:
1 Collect full data to compose **at least 3** messages to specified individuals
2 Receive **at least 3** telephone calls for self and others, passing on the message immediately
3 Pass on **3** messages by telephone to specified individuals
4 In a simulation call to the emergency services impart all the necessary information including-correct emergency service; name and job title; location of accident problem; nature of accident problem
5 Receive **at least 3** simple job instructions (either oral, written or diagrammatic) and carry out the job
6 Complete **at least one** relevant form, writing accurately and legibly
7 Receive & direct **at least 1** visitor ensuring: visitor greeted promptly & courteously; needs identified; only disclosable information given; **all** visitors directed/escorted appropriately; reasons for delay/non- availability explained politely; security & safety procedures followed
8 Produce **at least 1** simple sketch to satisfy an identified need

In example 5, the developers of this Standard mostly fixed on three as the number of occurrences required to demonstrate competence, though in two cases, they decided that one is enough. It is notable that performance criterion 3 does not say "at least". The potential problems of understanding which can be seen here are:

at least can be interpreted vaguely
the assessor can ask for a larger number
in some cases it appears to be redundant

Arguably, *at least* is redundant in most of these occurrences. Furthermore, it will lead to different individual assessors interpreting the element in different ways. Some might decide that the specified number is what they require; while others might think that if the text says *at least* then that means that they should require more than the number specified.

In this piece of consultancy research the team was able to do three things which were helpful to the Government department which commissioned the work. We:

- showed that NVQ texts are a distinctive genre
- identified 16 different linguistic features which were causing problems to readers
- recommended strategies for rewriting and redevelopment of the texts.

Our results and recommendations were persuasive to the client because we backed our findings with the presentation of quantitative data from our comparative analysis of different corpora. So they could see that these were not our subjective opinions about the texts. Apart from making the results convincing, this had the positive outcome that we avoided alienating the writers and developers of NVQs by criticising their work (our suggestions for clearer writing are in St. John/Channell 1996; for the specific response of one of the training organisations (the Construction Industry Training Board), see the Plain Language Commission website, and for general material on clearer writing see Cutts 1996). We showed that we understood the constraints of the writing task which they had been set and the strategies they had used to accomplish it.

11. Conclusions

I would like to see a world in which, if someone is heading an organisation which identifies an issue with language, the first strategy they think of is to call on an applied linguist; and that they do this as readily as they would reach for any other type of management or financial or human resources consultant. The 15 case studies on which this chapter is based all demonstrate the practical value of LSP consultancy to organisations, businesses, consumers, writers and readers. My conclusion is therefore that it is essential that AL and LSP get better known (as well known as occupational psychology or management sciences).

I believe there is a need for a major international effort to raise the profile of applied linguistics and within this, the LSP perspective. Currently much organisational consultancy is carried out either by people applying psychology or applying management sciences. I am clear that applied linguistics has a legitimate and needed place alongside these two.

Roberts described her 2003 paper as a "call to arms" (2003: 133) to the applied linguistics community to 'bring practical relevance and problem solving to the centre of our work." I would go further, in suggesting that the relevant professional associations might do more than they currently do to promote AL.

I therefore conclude with some suggestions for how LSP practitioners might, individually and collectively, promote their work to a wider audience. These are to:

- raise the profile of applied linguistics in commercial and public sector arenas, nationally and internationally (individually, by publication and presentation, collectively by organising events and conferences designed to communicate LSP to potential users and beneficiaries)
- follow the model of other professional areas (for example applied psychology) – psychology has been immensely successful in selling itself outside academic psychology to organisations, to

governments, to businesses as having a range of expertise that they can make use of. So psychology has a high profile in public perception and I think, particularly in a British context, that it is a good model to follow, in terms of how the psychology profession has achieved that.

- network with other types of "expert" consultants
- use concrete examples of useful analysis
- use communication failures as a way to "pitch" for consultancy business
- be available and easy to find
- adopt and maintain a neutral rather than a "critical" stance.

Much has been achieved in the arena of linguistics applied to education and language learning; there remains much more to do in other areas of language in working life.

References

Bhatia, Vijay (personal communication) Genres in written discourse. Presentation at a workshop at the Association for Business Communication European conference. Lugano, May 2003.

Blackwell R. / Preece D. 2001. Changing Higher Education *International Journal of Management Education* 1/3.

British Association for Applied Linguistics 1994. *Recommendations on Good Practice in Applied Linguistics.*

Brown, P. / Levinson, S. C. 1987. *Politeness: some universals in language use*. Cambridge: Cambridge University Press.

Campanelli, P. / Channell, J. 1994. *Training: the word and the concept.* London: Employment Department Research Series.

Campanelli, P / Channell, J. 1996. *The conceptualisation of qualifications by individuals*. London: HMSO.

Channell, J 1994. *Vague Language.* Oxford: Oxford University Press.

Channell, J. / St John, M. 1996. The Language of Standards. *Competence and Assessment* 31, 2-6.
Channell, J. 1997. How to implement plain language in standards of competence. *Competency* 5/1, 26-32.
Channell, J. 1999. Vagueness in written English. *Modern English Teacher* 8/4, 26-30.
Channell, J. 2000. Working on the telephone – how telephone receptionists work with language. In Coulthard, M., J. Cotterill / F. Rock (eds) *Dialogue Analysis VII: working with dialogue*. Tübingen: Max Niemeyer Verlag.
Channell, J. 2001. Review of Shuy 1998. *Language in Society* 30/1, 107-110.
Cutts, Martin 1996. *The Plain English Guide*. Oxford: Oxford University Press.
Grice, H. P. 1967. Logic and Conversation. In Cole, P. / Morgan, J. L. (eds) *Syntax and Semantics*. New York: Academic Press.
Grice, H. P. 1968 Utterer's meaning, sentence meaning and word meaning. *Foundations of Language* 4, 1-18.
Grice, H. P. 1981. Presupposition and conversational implicature in Cole, P. (ed.) *Radical Pragmatics*. New York: Academic Press.
Mansfield B. / Mitchell, L. 1996. *Towards a competent workforce*. London: Gower Publishing Limited.
Roberts, C. 2003. Applied Linguistics Applied. In Sarangi, S. / van Leeuwen T. (eds) *Applied Linguistics and Communities of Practice*. British Association for Applied Linguistics and Continuum.
Shuy, R. W. 1998. *Bureaucratic Language in Government and Business*. Washington: Georgetown University Press.
St John, M. / Channell, J. 1996. *Language Issues in NVQs and SVQs*. Department for Education and Employment: Competence and Assessment Briefing Series 12.
Stubbs, M. 1996. *Text and Corpus Analysis*. London: Blackwell.
The Plain Language Commission, recent projects. <http://www.clearest.co.uk/recentproj.htm> [accessed 18 January 2004].
Thomas, J. 1983. Cross-cultural pragmatic failure. *Applied Linguistics* 4/2, 91-110.

FEDERICA SCARPA

Using an Italian diachronic corpus for investigating the "core" patterns of the language of science*

1. Introduction

The influence of English on Italian LSPs – especially at the lexical level – is a well-documented phenomenon (among others, see Dardano 1994 and Cartago 1994). Such an influence has been postulated also on the patterns of text production in terms of a higher level of linearity and comprehensibility, at least for the special language of economics (Cozzi 1996: 327). To a certain extent, this would also entail that, in the last 30 years or so, under the influence of the English language of science, a variation has occurred in the meaning-making practices of the Italian scientific community (Lemke 1991). In this chapter I tentatively aim to test the true extent of the influence of scientific English on its Italian counterpart at linguistic levels other than terminology. In so doing, I also hope to provide a small contribution to the hypothesis of "core" patterns in scientific discourse across different languages, which is implied in Halliday's "prototypical syndrome of features that characterizes scientific English" (1993: 54). To this end, I have monitored over a 60-year time span the evolution of the Italian language of the specialized subject field of dermatology by investigating a small corpus (60,411 words) of texts, mainly on the topic of acne, written by a variety of authors and belonging to the

* My heartfelt thanks to my father for his invaluable help in suggesting most of the textbooks included in the corpus, for finding them – in a few cases in his personal library but more often in public libraries in Rome – and, in many cases, photocopying the relevant parts for my use. A dermatologist himself, as his father was before him, he was only too glad to give me his advice and support, and I benefit from both.

genre 'textbook on dermatology'. The specific patterns of scientific language which have been monitored for development over time are mainly by-products of 'grammatical metaphor', the process whereby meanings are multiply-coded at the level of grammar, which Halliday/ Martin (1993) see as the most characteristic feature of the written "discourse for doing experimental science". These patterns are: simple structure of clauses and sentences, choices realizing the Theme, nominalization and cohesive devices of conjunction.

The basic assumption underlying my study is that, under the influence of English, the Italian language of science has varied its patterns of text production in terms of a higher level of technicality and abstraction (Martin 1991). To monitor this hypothesized evolution, I investigated the lexicogrammatical patterns used for organizing information in portions of the different texts 'doing the same things', i.e. describing the age of onset of acne, and defining and classifying the terms *comedone* and *acne*.

2. My corpus

According to the typology of corpora proposed by Laviosa (2002: 33-38), the material used in the present study is a written corpus which is a sample (portions of texts selected according to the topic of interest, i.e. acne), diachronic (texts produced over a relatively long time span, i.e. 1939-2000), terminological (texts originating within a specialized subject field, i.e. dermatology), and single monolingual (one set of texts all in Italian).

Looking in more detail at the 'sample' category, the sample texts contained in the corpus can really be considered to be full texts because of the very nature of the textbooks they were taken from, which are divided into various chapters/sections, each centred on a different topic.

The corpus is also predominantly (18 out of 20 texts) non-translational, consisting of Italian texts by authors – highly reputed university professors whose textbooks were very influential in their own time – writing in their native language. The only texts which are translational (Andrews/Manganotti 1964; Fitzpatrick/Johnson/Polano/Surmond/Wolff 1992), i.e. not originally produced in Italian but translated from English, make up between the two of them only 2,489 words out of the total 60,411 (4.1%) and have been included to provide a benchmark for the comparison between the predominantly non-translational element of the corpus and two original English textbooks (Rook/Wilkinson/Ebling 1979; Caputo/Ackerman/Sison-Torre 1990).

However, there are at least two discrepancies in the design of the corpus, which are both due to the objective difficulty of finding in both private and public libraries medical textbooks dating before 1980, because of the obvious problems linked to the relatively quick 'ageing' of their contents:

1) the texts published in 1939 have a much lower level of similarity concerning the topic, because they do not deal specifically with acne but much more generally describe diseases manifesting themselves via dermatological signs (e.g. chicken-pox, rubella);
2) the word counts of the sub-corpus for the 1960s/1970s and the sub-corpus for the 1990s are considerably smaller than those of the other two sub-corpora:

Time span	**1930s/1940s**	**1960s/1970s**	**1980s**	**1990s/2000**
Total word count	24,988	6,526	19,102	9,795

Table 1. Word count of each sub-corpus.

Moreover, of the three texts published in the 1960s/1970s, one is a translation (Andrews/Manganotti 1964) and one more strictly belongs to the genre 'compendio' (Tagliavini 1973), i.e. a small guide on the morphology of dermatological diseases, where the text is only ancillary to the illustrations.

The corpus has been investigated both automatically, by using the suite WordSmith Tools by Oxford University Press when looking for lower-level features in individual words and word-clusters (e.g.

cohesive devices and nominal groups), and manually when searching for higher level patterns in and between clauses and sentences.

3. Sentence and clause structure

Different languages present information in a different order and therefore vary quite considerably in the way their syntax encourages different types of sentence structure and thematization, even though some genres are more different than others (see Maia 1997). Given that Italian syntax, just like other Romance languages, allows for a greater complexity of structure than English, I started my analysis by considering the average sentence and paragraph lengths in the texts of the corpus, expecting to find a progressive shortening of both over time:

Time span	**1930s/1940s**	**1960s/1970s**	**1980s**	**1990s/2000**
Mean sentence length	53.76	25.64	37.85	32.16
Mean paragraph length	545.70	130.21	212.42	140.11

Table 2. Word count of mean sentence and paragraph length.

As shown from the table above, sentence and paragraph lengths have indeed reduced over time, though not in the gradual way I expected. The sharp drop in the figures for the 1960s/1970s, however, can be at least partially explained by the imbalance in the corpus design mentioned earlier. Interestingly, without the translational text (Andrews/ Manganotti 1964) the values for the 1960s/1970s sub-corpus have a slight increase in both parameters (sentence length = 26.62 and paragraph length = 136.56), which somehow corroborates my prediction of a progressive shortening of sentence and paragraph length over time, given the well-known tendency of translators to maintain the sentence structure of the source text. However, in this word count a sentence has been typically considered as ending with a full stop, question mark or exclamation mark (and followed by a capital letter), a constraint which does not take into account the possibility that some functional changes may have occurred in Italian punctuation rules over the 60 years spanned by the corpus, possibly also under the influence of English discourse. For example, let us consider the following four instances, all dealing with the age of onset of acne, where such a functional evolution of punctuation seems in fact to emerge:

(1) La malattia compare frequentemente all'epoca della pubertà (di qui il nome di acne giovanile); ha decorso molto cronico con alternative di miglioramenti e di esacerbazioni: scompare qualche volta spontaneamente coll'avanzare dell'età, oppure sotto cure opportune generali e locali, ma si ripresenta con facilità. In alcuni casi si vede la malattia presentarsi per la prima volta nella età adulta: spesso sono in giuoco in questi casi moventi interni speciali (vedi eziologia). (Radaeli 1948)

(2) L'acne è una condizione molto comune nell'adolescenza: nella sua forma conclamata interessa il 40-50% dei giovani; questa incidenza aumenta notevolmente se si tiene conto della occasionale presenza di comedoni e pustole soprattutto nei maschi della stessa fascia anagrafica. Compare alla pubertà tra gli 11 e i 13 anni e raggiunge la più alta incidenza tra i 15-17 anni. Le forme più gravi si osservano in circa il 3% dei maschi, meno frequentemente nelle donne. (Angelini and Vena 1985)

(3) L'acne volgare colpisce in genere soggetti con un range di età variabile da 13 a 24 anni con ampie oscillazioni individuali. L'acne può persistere o anche comparire oltre questa età e ad essere colpita, in questi casi, più di frequente è la donna. (Vena and Cassano 1998)

(4) Esordisce alla pubertà con un picco di incidenza e gravità fra i 14 e i 17 anni nelle femmine e fra i 16 e i 19 anni nei maschi. E' rara l'insorgenza in età più precoce e la durata oltre i 30 anni. (Rebora and Marchesi 2000)

Whilst all four excerpts consist of paratactically related clauses (both below and above the clause complex level), there is a progressive reduction in the use of colons and semi-colons, which in the two most recent excerpts have been substituted by full-stops. In this respect, Angelini and Vena's excerpt provides an intermediate link in this gradual shift between Radaeli's use of colons and semi-colons – where commas could have in fact been more congruently used (all first three clauses have the same grammatical Subject *malattia*) – and the two most recent excerpts.

Closely linked to the greater length of sentences is the issue of their grammatical intricacy, with clause complexes in earlier texts tending indeed to contain more clauses than later texts but with no comparable shift from a hypotactic to a paratactic type of relation between clauses. Though the earlier Italian texts contain undoubtedly more hypotactical links than the later ones[1], their level of grammatical intricacy is still relatively low compared to contemporary non-specialised texts.

A more fundamental shift is exemplified in Text 1 (see Appendix) and is the transition to a progressively more technical and abstract scientific discourse, as reflected in the gradual building up of that "taxonomizing focus" which Martin (1991) sees as distinguishing scientific discourse from other types of texts. Though Martin's observation is of course valid for other scientific discourses than English, as far as the Italian corpus on acne is concerned in the earlier texts such taxonomies do indeed exist[2] but tend to be implicit in Trimble's sense, i.e. where "all of the classifying information is included but is not stated as such" (Trimble 1985: 90). As such they are not 'complete' classifications, which are explicit in that they provide three kinds of information: the item being classified, the class to which the item belongs and the basis (or bases) for classification (Trimble 1985: 86). Whilst the first excerpt (Radaeli 1948) in Text 1 is merely a physical description of the comedone, in the second (Monacelli/Nazzaro 1967) the relational process (*costituiscono*) introducing *comedones* in the very first clause establishes some level of abstraction by identifying comedones as the *lesioni elementari primitive* of acne and then roughly distinguishing them into two subclasses on the basis of the differences between them (*incassati in un orifizio follicolare* and *disposti alla sommità di una piccola rilevatezza biancastra rotondeggiante*). The classification of comedones becomes progressively more explicit and elaborate in the later texts until, in the most recent one (Rebora/Marchesi 2000), the taxonomy is built first by establishing a superordinate (*Il comedone è una dilatazione dell'infundibolo del pelo...*) which is then broken down into two subclasses (*comedoni aperti* and *comedoni chiusi*), both elaborated by the appositions *punti neri* and *punti sottopell"* and defined in terms of the differences be-

1 See for example in Radaeli (1948) the hypotactical clause (*se il follicolo viene [...]*) in the second line of the definition of "comedone" in Text 1 (Appendix).

2 See for example the extended classification of different types of jaundice taking up to three-quarters of the whole text in Ferrari (1939).

tween them (*con orifizio dilatato di colore scuro* vs. *con orifizio molto piccolo (...), vere microcisti follicolari*).

Such an evolution makes it not unreasonable to hypothesize that, under the influence of the English pedagogic discourse of medicine, its Italian counterpart may have acquired a standardized pattern for constructing explicit (complete) taxonomies. The tendency to taxonomize and, more generally, to heavily organize and classify information in checklists, seems in fact to be a feature of the English discourse of science and, in the case of acne, in both the English textbooks taken as reference (Rook/Wilkinson/Ebling 1979 and Caputo/Ackerman/Sison-Torre 1990) comedones are classified very explicitly indeed.

Turning now to definitions, the rhetorical organization of the texts of the corpus does not show an equally clear evolution as in the pattern of classification. Text 2 (see Appendix) consists of the definitions of *acne* in all the texts of the corpus but two (Radaeli 1948 and Ribuffo 1987), where the pathology is never formally defined. In all cases, the definition of acne is also the first sentence of the text[3] and consists of a Token (the technical term to be defined)[4], an identifying relational process (*è, si intende, si definisce*) and a Value (the information needed to define the term) (Martin 1991: 311-313). The ten definitions vary in terms of the amount and precision of the information they provide: in Trimble's sense (1985: 75-79) most are simple, i.e. made up of one sentence (Andrews/Manganotti 1964; Monacelli/ Nazzaro 1967; Panconesi 1982; Binazzi 1985; Sapuppo 1986; Fitzpatrick et al. 1992; Rebora/Marchesi 2000), as opposed to complex (or

3 In both the texts where acne is not formally defined, the first sentence focuses instead on the symptoms and signs of acne: "Nella sintomatologia dell'acne volgare bisogna portare l'attenzione sopra due ordini di fatti; le alterazioni della secrezione e della eliminazione del sebo cutaneo ed i fatti infiammatori follicolari e perifollicolari" (Radaeli 1948); "Il quadro inizia con seborrea e comedoni (acne comedonica), i quali si presentano come punti neri localizzati a livello dell'orifizio follicolare. Compaiono successivamente, sempre in sede follicolare, lesioni a carattere infiammatorio sotto forma di rilievi papulosi e di pustole (acne papulo-pustolosa)" (Ribuffo 1987).

4 In Binazzi (1985), where the Token is referred to anaphorically as *così*, the technical term "acne" is the title of the section, only one line above the definition.

expanded), i.e. definitions incorporating a description and/or classification (Angelini/Vena 1985; Cerimele/Saccabusi 1988; Vena/Cassano 1998). The simple definitions are either (overwhelmingly) formal, i.e. containing all three basic defining elements – the term being defined, the class of which it is a member and the sum of the differences distinguishing this term from all other members of the class – or, in only one case (Sapuppo 1986), non-formal (there is no clear statement of the differences).

Definitions, however, provide a very good example of the evolution of some of the choices which realize the Theme in the texts of the corpus. From a comparison between the two earliest definitions of acne in the corpus (Andrews/Manganotti 1964; Monacelli/Nazzaro 1967), in the translational text (1964) the term to be defined is Subject-Theme in an unmarked topical position (*L'acne volgare è...*), whilst in the non-translational text (1967) the term *acne giovanile* is encapsulated in a prepositional phrase (Adjunct) (*Con il nome di acne giovanile ... si intende...*) in a marked pre-topical position. Assuming that the translation (1964) has maintained the same word order as the original[5], such a difference is consistent with Evangelisti's (1994) findings in her contrastive analysis of Italian and English textbooks on psychology: in English definitions, the term to be defined was introduced straight away and functioned as Subject-Theme (*X is...*), whilst in Italian definitions there was a preference for the less linear and compact structure *Con X ci si riferisce a....*, where the term to be defined was encapsulated in a prepositional phrase in a marked pre-topical position followed by an impersonal verb functioning as topical Theme (see *si intende* in Monacelli and Nazzaro 1967 and *Si definisce* in Binazzi 1985). As all the later texts in the corpus except Binazzi (1985) and Rebora/Marchesi (2000) use the pattern *X is...*, it is not unreasonable to speculate that there has been some influence from English on Italian definitions in the choice of the Token as realizing the Theme.

5 "Acne is a chronic inflammatory disorder [...]" (Rook/Wilkinson/Ebling. 1979) and "Acne is an extremely common disorder [...]" (Caputo/Ackerman/Sison-To 1990).

Turning now to the choice of the characteristic elements which realize the Theme outside definitions, rather expectedly in later texts the most recurrent Themes are nominalizations, whilst in earlier texts there was a wider variation of thematization in relation to a higher flexibility of word order of Italian compared to English. In partial accordance with Nwogu/Bloor's (1991: 380) findings relating to medical research articles, I found a progressive increase of the following two syntactical items functioning as Theme: "simple/complex nominal group" (functioning as non-agent Subject of passive clauses) and "prepositional phrase (Adjunct) plus nominal group". As for the third typical realization found by the two researchers, i.e. "adverbial group (Adjunct) plus nominal group", an analysis of the adverbs ending in the suffix *-mente* has yielded the following results:

	Sentence-initial adverbial groups[6]	**Total hits**	**%**
1939-1948	16	260	6.15
1964-1973	4	105	3.80
1982-1988	25[7]	219	11.41
1992-2000	12	131	9.16

Table 3. Word count of adverbs ending in *–mente.*

Looking at the percentage column of the Table above, an increase of adverbs in thematic position seems indeed to emerge, though not as progressively as expected, whilst the low percentage for the 1964-1975 set could once again be partially explained by the discrepancy in the corpus design relating to the 1960s/1970s texts. The high percentage of sentence-initial adverbs in the 1982-1988 set could be ascribed to a particularly marked influence of English word-order rules on Cerimele/Saccabusi's (1988) language, whose text, in fact, also happens to be the longest for this time span (7,745 words). Interestingly,

6 Sentence- initial adverbials are those occurring after a full-stop, a semi-colon, a colon and an open parenthesis sign and can also be pre-modified by grammatical items like *più* (e.g. *Più frequentemente*) and *solo* (*Solo raramente*).

7 Mostly, though not exclusively, in Cerimele and Saccabusi (1988). An interesting observation about the influence of English on Italian punctuation is that in the 1982-1988 texts the sentence-initial adverbial is only occasionally followed by a comma, whilst in the 1992-2000 set it usually is.

however, at the level of individual texts, the one having the lowest percentage of hits per 1,000 tokens (3.58%) in the whole corpus is the translational text by Fitzpatrick et al. (1992), with the possible exception of the even lower percentage (1.89%) relating to the very brief compendium (530 words) by Tagliavini (1973).

I also found a very slight but rather consistent increase in the thematization and, more generally, in the use of selected conjunction groups functioning as logical connectors between clauses and sentences:

	1939-1948		**1964-1973**		**1982-1988**		**1992-2000**	
	s.i.	**other**	**s.i.**	**other**	**s.i.**	**other**	**s.i.**	**other**
In effetti	-	-	-	-	1	1	1	-
In realtà	-	-	-	-	1	1	2	-
D'altronde	-	-	-	-	5	-	1	-
In primo luogo	-	1	-	-	-	-	1	-
In tal modo	-	2	-	-	3	-	1	1
Nonostante	1	-	-	-	-	-	2	1
D'altra parte	1	1	-	-	-	-	4	-

Table 4. Word count of specific conjunctive expressions (s.i. = sentence initial).

The only conjunctive which seems to have clearly shifted its position at the beginning of the message is *d'altra parte*, whilst *in effetti*, *in realtà* and *d'altronde* seem to have suddenly appeared in the Italian language of dermatology – both as sentence openers and not – in the 1980s. Both the shift in the position of *d'altra parte* and the rather recent appearance of *in effetti, in realtà* and *d'altronde* might once again be not unreasonably explained by the influence of a literal translation of the English adversative conjunctive expressions *on the other hand* (mostly sentence opening) and *in fact*.

4. Nominal style

Nominalization is the linguistic resource par excellence of technicality and abstraction (Martin 1991: 315). This feature is also to be found in Radaeli's (1948) text, where the use of grammatical metaphors is more frequent than expected, given the traditional importance allocated by Italian authors to the verbal process: e.g. in Text 1 [...] *dovuta ad un aumento di secrezione con secondaria* (instead of "al quale ha fatto seguito una") *ipercheratosi dello sbocco follicolare;* [...] *è ammissibile che alla determinazione dei* (instead of "a determinare I") *fatti infiammatori acneici concorra l'azione di microrganismi*. Still, in the corpus there is a progressive increase of nominalizations. This shift of emphasis towards objects rather than processes – with the resulting grammatical foregrounding of identifying relational processes – can be found especially in the explanatory portions of the texts, which are organized through actions ordered in time (Martin 1991: 323). For example, the material process *se il follicolo viene compresso fra due unghie si vede che il punto nero si solleva seguito da una specie di vermiciattolo bianco-gialliccio untuoso al tatto* (Text 1) is realized verbally as a clause in Radaeli (1948) and, a few lines after the definition of *comedone* provided in Text 1, in Panconesi (1982) [8] but – if referred to at all – in later texts is realized nominally (*la spremitura*)[9]:

(5) La spremitura del follicolo pilosebaceo corrispondente lascia uscire un filamento biancastro, untuoso e molliccio, di 2-3 mm di lunghezza [...] (Monacelli/Nazzaro 1967);

8 *[...] dà origine alla formazione del cosiddetto filamento seborroico (che può essere osservato macroscopicamente spremendolo ad esempio dalle ali del naso di un soggetto 'seborroico') considerato il pre-comedone* (Panconesi 1982).

9 As further evidence of the progressive nominalization of the Italian medical language, in the first two excerpts of Text 1 the material verbal process *lascia / fa uscire* (plus Object) becomes an abstract relational process realized by the structure Empty verb (*dà adito / si ottiene*) plus nominal group in the last two excerpts.

> La spremitura del follicolo fa uscire [...] il comedone, formazione biancastra cilindrica, costituita da sebo, cellule cornee [...] (Binazzi 1985);
> La sua spremitura dà adito alla fuoriuscita di un corpicciolo vermiforme biancastro (Sapuppo 1986);
> Con la spremitura dei comedoni aperti si ottiene l'uscita di materiale grasso vermicolare (Cerimele/Saccabusi 1988).

This shift towards the nominal style is closely connected to a corresponding depersonalization and objectification of discourse, entailing the gradual disappearance of the researcher as participant. In particular, concerning the use of personal reference, this is one of the aspects of cohesion distinguishing earlier from later textbooks. For example, the first person personal pronoun *noi* has been found only in De Filippi (1939) (2 hits) and Radaeli (1948) (1 hit); the clitic *ci* has been found in Ferroni (1939) (3 hits), De Filippi (1939) (5 hits) and Radaeli (1948) (2 hits), and only once in Vena/Cassano (1998); the possessive pronoun *nostr** occurs once in Ferrari (1939), twice in Radaeli (1948) and once in Andrews/Manganotti (1964). The fact that personal structures are so scarce in later textbooks[10] points to a progressively lower focus on the researcher as a participant and, more generally, on individuals[11], which I think is a rather unfortunate evolution in the discourse of this field. After all, if what Sacks (1985, quoted by Francis/Kramer-Dahl 1991: 340) wrote about neuro-psychology can be applied to medicine in general, medicine is a discipline on the borderline between the natural 'hard' sciences and the human 'soft' sciences, and therefore its scientific rigour should be tempered by the fact that it has the human subject at its centre.

10 Of course a more thorough search could be conducted, e.g. for items in the first-person plural ending in *-amo* and *-emo*.

11 A further example of such a progressive depersonalization is provided by the count of the occurrences of the inanimate item *studi* as Theme-Subject of a predicate usually referring to an animate agent (e.g. *evidenziare, indicare, presentare and so on*). The influence of English can once more be hypothesized on the basis of the increase over time of such pattern: out of a total of 11 hits in the corpus for the item *studi* (1 in Ferrari 1939, 1 in Angelini/Vena 1985, 1 in Ribuffo 1987, and 8 in Vena/Cassano 1998), the specific pattern under consideration occurred 5 times, 4 of which in the 1998 text (and the remaining one in the 1987 text).

5. Conclusions

There are three speculative conclusions that can be drawn from this study. The first is related to the question: To what extent has English influenced Italian text production patterns in this particular genre? Based on my findings, I believe that the increase over time of any of the patterns taken into account can indeed be correlated to the influence of the norms and conventions of scientific English on its Italian counterpart. Of course, these results should be further substantiated in the same corpus by similar findings in different patterns, such as the investigation of generic organization, aspects of modality and the use of the passive voice. Another possible field of enquiry could be opened up by the cross-checking of these results against findings from searches conducted on a bilingual comparable corpus made up of the Italian texts considered in this study and a number of English textbooks on the same topic, possibly published over the same time span. However, one important fact that has emerged from this study and should not be overlooked is that the discursive patterns of different authors writing in the same years (especially in the 1982-1987 texts) can be more or less anglicized, a lack of consistency that could be investigated not only in relation to the authors' personal style and mastery of the Italian language, but also in terms of more objective factors such as the age of the author and the pedagogic function of the text he is writing.

The second conclusion relates to the question: To what extent does such an influence entail a shift toward higher comprehensibility? Going back to Cozzi's (1996: 337) observation for the Italian LSP of economics that the influence of English has resulted in a higher level of linearity and comprehensibility, it could be argued that the rise in the level of cohesion (higher degree of cohesion), syntactic simplification (higher frequency of parataxis and nominal style) and explicitness (of classifications and definitions) found in the diachronic corpus could result in a discourse which is more easily accessible by learners. However, it must also be said that, as for its English counterpart, the massive – and occasionally excessive and inappropriate – use of grammatical metaphor in the resulting Italian discourse makes it so lexically dense and "incongruent" that at times – as Halliday (1993: 70, 84) himself remarks – one cannot help feeling that discourse is unnecessarily made more difficult to understand than it need be. In this sense, 'learning science' is not strictly the same thing as learning the language of science and the authors of textbooks should be motivated not only by the functional constraint of purpose (higher objectivity) but also by the contextual constraint of the assumption that the level of knowledge of their readers is relatively low (Nwogu/Bloor 1991: 382-383).

The third and last conclusion relates to the question: To what extent do the results of the study confirm Halliday's postulation of "core" patterns in the discourse of science across different languages? The specific patterns of scientific discourse which I have monitored for development over time (simple structure of clauses and sentences, choices realizing the Theme, nominalization and conjunctives) are all by-products of grammatical metaphor and therefore have all – to a greater or lesser extent – characterized the Italian texts of the corpus well before the 1960s-1970s[12], the decades when English supposedly started to exercise its influence. This is true also for other features such as a "taxonomizing focus" and the preference of both languages for building definitions through relational processes of the identifying type. A clear pattern that seems to emerge from the study, however, is that through its influence English has greatly amplified some features of the Italian discourse of science, such as the nominal style and the related progressive depersonalization of prose. Following Lemke's dynamic perspective of text production[13], such changes should be mostly viewed in the light of the mind-boggling progress made by medical research in the last 60 years and the consequent evolution in the practices and the discourse of the Italian scientific community. The influence of scientific English on other scientific languages like

12 See Halliday and Martin (1993: 15) seeing in Galileo's Italian an example of instantiation of grammatical metaphor, ie. the union of nominalization with recursive modification of the nominal group that is the semiotic realization of the birth of science.

13 "the text is a product and a record of meaning-making processes which are essentially dynamic. These processes are social semiotic practices, the signifying practices of a community" (Lemke 1991: 36).

Italian can therefore be considered as the construction of an increasingly technical and abstract scientific discourse across different languages, functioning as a common "semiotic technology" (Martin 1991: 307), because it enacts today's broad consensus about what constitutes scientific practice (Halliday 1993: 67). The evolution of the Italian language of dermatology under the influence of English, therefore, should not be seen in negative terms as a loss of individuality and distinctiveness but rather as a positive step towards a true internationalization of the paradigms of science.

References

Caputo, R. / Ackerman, A.B. / Sison-Torre, E.Q. 1990. *Pediatric Dermatology and Dermatopathology*. Philadelphia/London: Lea and Fabiger.

Cartago, G. 1994. L'apporto inglese. In Serianni, L. / Trifone, P. (a cura di) *Storia della lingua italiana*, vol. III. Torino: Einaudi, 721-750.

Cozzi, T. 1996. Tradurre testi di economia. In Cortese, G. (a cura di) *Tradurre i linguaggi settoriali*. Torino: Cortina, 325-327.

Dardano, M. 1994. L'influsso dell'inglese sull'italiano di oggi". *Terminologie et Traduction* 1, 145-161.

Evangelisti, P. 1994. Strategie dell'informazione scientifica nel discorso psicologico italiano e inglese: la definizione nei testi introduttivi. In De Mauro, T. (a cura di) *Studi sul trattamento linguistico dell'informazione scientifica*. Roma: Bulzoni, 195-227.

Francis, G. / Kramer-Dahl, A. 1991. From clinical report to clinical story: Two ways of writing about a medical case. In Ventola, E. (ed.) *Functional and Systemic Linguistics*. Berlin/New York: Mouton de Gruyter, 339-368.

Halliday, M.A.K. 1993. On the language of physical science. In Halliday, M.A.K. / Martin, J.R. (eds) *Writing Science: Literacy and*

Discursive Power. London/Washington D.C.: Falmer Press, 54-68.

Halliday, M.A.K. / Martin, J.R. 1993. General orientation. In Halliday, M.A.K. / Martin, J.R. (eds) *Writing Science: Literacy and Discursive Power*. London/Washington D.C.: Falmer Press, 2-21.

Laviosa, S. 2002. *Corpus-based Translation Studies. Theory, Findings, Applications*. Amsterdam/New York: Rodopi.

Lemke, J. 1991. Text production and dynamic text semantics. In Ventola, E. (ed.) *Functional and Systemic Text Semantics*. Berlin/New York: Mouton de Gruyter, 23-38.

Maia, B. 1997. Sentence structure and thematization in comparable and parallel texts. In Klaudy, K. / Kohn, J. (eds) *Transferre Necesse Est*. Scholastica, 541-547.

Martin J.R. 1991. Nominalization in science and humanities. Distilling knowledge and scaffolding ext In Ventola, E. (ed.) *Functional and Systemic Text Semantics*. Berlin/New York: Mouton de Gruyter, 307-337.

Nwogu, K. / Bloor, T. Thematic progression in professional and popular medical texts. In Ventola, E. (ed.) *Functional and Systemic Text Semantics*. Berlin/New York: Mouton de Gruyter, 369-384.

Rook, A., / Wilkinson, D.S. / Ebling, F.J.G. [3]1979. *Textbook of Dermatology*. Oxford: Blackwell, 2 vols ("Seborrhoea", "Comedones", "Acne", 1712-1731).

Sacks, O. 1985. *The Man Who Mistook His Wife for His Hat*. London: Picador.

Trimble, L. 1985. *English for Science and Technology*. Cambridge: CUP.

i) The corpus 1939-1948

Cappelli, J. 1943. *Le infezioni sessuali*. Milano: Vallardi ("Sifilide congenita", 246-249).

De Filippi, P. 1939. Malattie infettive. In Ferrata, A. (a cura di) *Diagnostica medica differenziale*, I. Milano: A. Wassermann & C., 1094-1117.

Ferrari, G. 1939. Itteri. In Ferrata, A. (a cura di) *Diagnostica medica differenziale*, vol. I. Milano: A. Wassermann & C., 225-254.

Ferroni, F. 1939. La cianosi. In Ferrata, A. (a cura di) *Diagnostica medica differenziale*, vol. I. Milano: A. Wassermann & C., 455-465.

Radaeli, F. 1948. *Malattie cutanee*. Milano: Vallardi ("Acne volgare o giovanile", 309-31).

Zavattari, E. 1939. Malattie parassitarie da parassiti animali. In Ferrata, A. (a cura di) *Diagnostica medica differenziale*, I. Milano: A. Wassermann & C., 1160-1168.

ii) The corpus 1964-1973

Andrews, G.C. / Manganotti, G. 1964. *Malattie della pelle*. Torino: Minerva Medica ("Acne polimorfa – rosacea", 403-409).

Monacelli, M. / Nazzaro, P. 1967. *Manuale di dermatologia e venereologia*. Milano: Vallardi ("Malattie delle ghiandole sebacee", 780-791).

Tagliavini, R. (a cura di) 1973. *Dermatologia nella pratica medica. Compendio di dermovenereologia*. Milano: CIBA-GEIGY Farmaceutici ("Acne volgare, Rosacea", 27, 178).

iii) The corpus 1982-1987

Angelini, G. / Vena, G.A. 1985. *Manuale di dermatologia*, II edizione. Roma: Universo ("Acne volgare", 268-273).

Binazzi, M. 1985. *Manuale di dermatologia e venereologia*. Bologna: Esculapio ("Acne", 397-401).

Cerimele, D. / Saccabusi, S. 1988. Acne polimorfa giovanile. In Serri, F. (diretto da) *Trattato di Dermatologia*, III, Padova: Piccin, 1-28

Panconesi, E. 1982. *Manuale di dermatologia*. Firenze: USES ("Acne", 179-182).

Ribuffo, A. 1987. *Manuale di dermatologia e venereologia*, III edizione. Roma: Lombardo ("Patologia del follicolo pilo-sebaceo", 55-65).

Sapuppo, A. 1986. *Clinica dermosifilopatica*, II edizione. Padova: Piccin ("Dermatosi con pustole follicolari", 140-146).

iv) The corpus 1992-2000

Caputo, G. 1998. Isotretinoina sistemica nell'acne. In *L'acne incontra l'esperto*. Roma: Performance, 69-76.

Cavicchini, S. 1998. Le cicatrici dell'acne: opzioni terapeutiche. In *L'acne incontra l'esperto*. Roma: Performance, 61-67.

Fitzpatrick, T.B. / Johnson, R.A. / Polano, M.K. / Surmond, D. / Wolff, K. 1992. *Atlante di dermatologia*, tradotto dal dott. Stefano Veraldi, II edizione. Milano: McGraw-Hill Italia ("Malattie delle ghiandole sebacee e apocrine").

Rebora, A. / Marchesi, L. 2000. Acne e rosacea. In Cainelli, T. / Giannetti, A. e / Rebora, A. (eds) *Manuale di dermatologia medica e chirurgica*. Milano: McGraw-Hill Italia, 267-276.

Vena, G.A. / Cassano, N. 1998. Patogenesi dell'acne. In *L'acne incontra l'esperto*. Roma: Performance, 7-24.

Appendix

i) Text 1

Definitions of *comedone*

Il comedone si presenta come un punto nero della grossezza di un capo di spillo o di un grano di miglio che occupa lo sbocco dilatato di un follicolo: se il follicolo viene compresso fra due unghie si vede che il punto nero si solleva seguito da una specie di vermiciattolo biancogialliccio untuoso al tatto. Il comedone è costituito da cellule cornee e da sebo. (Radaeli 1948)

I comedoni costituiscono le lesioni elementari primitive; appaiono come piccoli punti neri più o meno evidenti, incassati in un orifizio follicolare o disposti alla sommità di una piccola rilevatezza biancastra rotondeggiante. La spremitura del follicolo pilosebaceo corrispondente lascia uscire un filamento biancastro, untuoso e molliccio, di 2-3 mm di lunghezza, con l'estremità biancastra o nerastra in rapporto all'ossidazione dei lipidi della cheratina e all'accumulo di polvere sulla parte scoperta. (Monacelli/Nazzaro 1967)

Il comedone così formato (miscela di strato corneo, di germi, di lieviti, di lipidi e di pelo) può essere aperto verso l'esterno con il quale parzialmente comunica attraverso il tappo ipercheratosico-pigmentario (punto nero) o chiuso perché il poro residuo del follicolo è divenuto solo virtuale. (Panconesi 1982)
La più semplice è l'acne comedonica, caratterizzata dalla presenza di un rilievo papulo-nodulare biancastro miliare, del diametro di 1-2 mm, sulla cui superficie, con l'aiuto di una lente, si può riconoscere lo stoma accollato (comedone chiuso) oppure dilatato ed ostruito da materiale nerastro (comedone aperto). La spremitura del follicolo fa uscire, in entrambi i casi, il comedone, formazione biancastra cilindrica, costituita da sebo, cellule cornee, detriti e germi: la zona nera nella parte distale del comedone aperto è costituita da polvere e da melanina. (Binazzi 1985)
La massa cheratinica e lipidica piuttosto compatta che in questo modo viene a formarsi, riempiendo il lume dell'unità pilosebacea, forma un tappo a livello della apertura dilatata, dando così origine ad un comedone chiuso ("punto bianco"). Se invece questa massa comedonica protrude dal follicolo, si ha un comedone aperto ("punto nero": il colore è legato all'ossidazione dei lipidi). Con l'ulteriore distensione del follicolo le pareti si fissurano e si rompono: ciò porta al passaggio nel derma di sebo, cheratina e batteri ed alla conseguente formazione delle lesioni infiammatorie (papule, pustole, noduli, cisti). (Angelini/Vena 1985)
L'epitelio in tale sede mostra infatti un'esaltata attività proliferativa ed un turnover cellulare accelerato; la conseguente ipercheratosi provoca l'ostruzione del dotto pilosebaceo. In tal modo insorge il comedone chiuso, che, attraverso processi infiammatori, può evolvere nelle altre lesioni tipiche dell'acne; il comedone aperto, invece, si forma quando le alterazioni della cheratinizzazione interessano anche l'acroinfundibolo; in quest'ultimo caso però il suo contenuto può essere agevolmente eliminato. (Vena/Cassano 1998)
Il comedone è una dilatazione dell'infundibolo del pelo contenente soprattutto cheratina, ma anche lipidi, pigmenti melanici, batteri microaerobi (specialmente Propionibacterium acnes) e peli. Si distinguono comedoni aperti con orifizio dilatato di colore scuro ("punti

neri") e comedoni chiusi con orifizio molto piccolo ("punti sottopelle"), vere microcisti follicolari. (Rebora/Marchesi 2000)

ii) Text 2

Definitions of *acne*

L'acne volgare è una malattia infiammatoria cronica dei follicoli pilosebacei, caratterizzata da comedoni, papule, pustole, cisti e noduli; l'affezione è sempre preceduta da una seborrea. (Andrews/Manganotti 1964)

Con il nome di acne giovanile (da ακνη= punta) si intende una dermatosi molto comune caratterizzata da manifestazioni cutanee polimorfe, costituite prevalentemente da comedoni, papule e pustole, che si manifesta nel periodo puberale in soggetti con terreno seborroico. (Monacelli/Nazzaro 1967)

L'acne, detta anche acne volgare o acne polimorfa o acne giovanile, è una dermatosi cronica infiammatoria del follicolo pilosebaceo e del tessuto peri-follicolare caratterizzata dalla presenza di comedoni, pustole, papule, papulo-pustole, eventualmente di noduli e cisti, localizzata al volto e al torace di giovani di entrambi i sessi, dal decorso prolungato e, nei casi più gravi, dal trattamento assai difficile. (Panconesi 1982)

L'acne è una dermatosi cronica infiammatoria del follicolo pilosebaceo a patogenesi multifattoriale. Essa è clinicamente caratterizzata dalla formazione di comedoni aperti e chiusi, papule, pustole, papulopustole, noduli e cisti ed interessa le aree ricche di ghiandole sebacee, quali il viso, le spalle e le regioni mediotoraciche. L'affezione risolve spontaneamente nei primi anni della seconda decade di vita. (Angelini / Vena 1985)

Si definisce così (ακμη in greco significa fioritura) una dermopatia caratterizzata da lesioni del follicolo pilo-sebaceo nelle sedi della seborrea. (Binazzi 1985)

L'acne volgare o giovanile è una forma morbosa estremamente frequente che senza predilezione di sesso insorge in genere alla pubertà e tende a risolvere verso il 20o-25o anno di età; non raramente si evidenzia familiarità. (Sapuppo 1986)

Definizione. L'acne volgare è una malattia del follicolo pilo-sebaceo che inizia con cheratinizzazione anomala della porzione più bassa dell'infundibolo (infrainfundibolo), con accumulo di materiale sebaceo e cheratinico e conseguente dilatazione del follicolo stesso (comedone), che secondariamente va incontro a flogosi. È caratterizzata dalle seguenti lesioni che possono essere tra loro variamente associate: comedoni , papule, pustole, noduli, cisti. Tale molteplicità giustifica la denominazione di acne polimorfa; in genere primo a comparire è il comedone che è lesione non infiammatoria. Esito non obbligatorio è la cicatrice che può essere atrofica o cheloidea. (Cerimele/Saccabusi 1988)

L'acne è un'infiammazione cronica dell'unità pilo-sebacea di alcune aree (volto e tronco); compare nell'adolescenza e si presenta sotto forma di comedoni, papule, noduli, cisti o papulo-pustole; spesso, ma non sempre, esita in cicatrici atrofiche o ipertrofiche. (Fitzpatrick et al. 1992)

L'acne è una patologia che interessa l'unità pilosebacea. A dimostrazione di ciò depone anche il fatto che i follicoli pilosebacei rappresentano l'unica struttura follicolare reperibile nella cute acneica e che il loro numero risulta molto più elevato nei soggetti affetti da acne. (Vena/Cassano 1992)

Per acne si intende un processo infiammatorio delle unità follicolo-sebacee caratterizzato da papule, pustole e talvolta noduli ed esiti cicatriziali, la cui lesione elementare è il comedone. [...] Le acni si distinguono in acni endogene e acni esogene. (Rebora/Marchesi 2000)

Maria Teresa Musacchio

The distribution of information in LSP translation. A corpus study of Italian

1. Introduction

Research in LSP translating has shown that in science and technology target texts are expected to sound natural and idiomatic – that is, to leave readers under the impression that they are originals. On closer inspection, the assessment of how natural an LSP translation sounds often rests on an evaluation of quality and consistency of terminology – in particular 'extended' or compound terms, subtechnical vocabulary and specialised phraseology. Yet terminology only makes up a small part of a technical or scientific text: corpus analysis has shown that in these areas too the most frequent words are mainly closed-class, general-language words. It is clear, then, that the naturalness of LSP translations derives from a blend of different elements, lexical as well as syntactic – not to mention stylistic conventions as to text types. Moreover, if special language texts are considered that are not drafted in English – the international *lingua franca* of science and technology – they are supposed to reproduce the information structure that is typical of their language. Based on the extent of adherence to target-language specific norms and conventions, researchers have variously concluded that translation gives rise to a "third code" (Frawley 1984), that has to be studied as a genre of its own (Baker 1993) and that translating as a process is subject to source language interference (Toury 1995). Pursuing the idea of linguistic features that are typical results of translating, Baker (1993: 243-245) has classified them in six categories – 'explicitation', simplification, normalisation of grammar, avoidance of ST repetitions, naturalisation (exaggerating features of the target language), and distinctive distribution of lexical items. Subsequent research has identified other possible categories such as natural linear order and structural weight of sentences, (possible) ambiguity, limits to sentence reordering, separating and linking of clauses (Doherty 1997a and 1997b). It can be argued that these classifications are overlapping to a greater or lesser extent. For example, simplification is a way to reduce structural weight, while separating or linking clauses can be regarded as a process of naturalisation, and normalisation of grammar reflects attempts to re-create the natural linear order of TL sentences. In this chapter, Doherty's terminology will be preferred because it focuses more on the syntactic and textual aspects of the influence of a source language on a target language.

Considering the nature of the corpus analysed in this chapter – popular science articles – another relevant perspective to this kind of investigation is the one offered by Myers (1992: 142) who points out that in scientific journal articles the material is organised hierarchically according to the scientist's argument and to an arrangement of time in parallel series of events. This creates a *narrative of science*, whereas popular science articles construct a chronological narrative of scientific facts, focus on the observation of nature following the natural history tradition and therefore provide a *narrative of nature*. On a textual level, then, popular science articles – compared to scientific journal articles – show a distinctive organisation, syntax and vocabulary. In *Scientific American*, for example, editorial changes in syntax to fit the conventions of the genre take three forms "(1) rephrasing of introductory statements as questions and answers; (2) rephrasing of compound and complex sentences into several more simple sentences; and (3) rephrasing passive and impersonal constructions in active voice" (Myers 1990: 175).

2. The distribution of information

Linguistic research in the distribution of the elements making up a message in different languages shows that the representation of the information is language-specific and that there are language-specific focus-attributing positions within the syntactic structure of sentences. With reference to the language pair that will be compared and contrasted in this chapter – English and Italian – it should be pointed out that in English, right-branching clauses are easiest to comprehend. Extensive clause embedding renders sentences awkward and indeed incomprehensible if the clauses are positioned initially in the sentence, where the length and complexity of the clauses contravenes the principle of end-weight (Quirk/Greenbaum/Leech/Svartvik 1985: 49-52). In Italian the principle of end-focus also applies as the most important information is usually placed at the end of the sentence (Benincà/Salvi/Frison 1991: 121). However, Italian exhibits several structures where constituents are extracted and moved to the initial position of the sentence in a sort of "free zone" (Benincà 1993: 255) in order to reduce structural weight. Further, according to Halliday/Martin (1993: 16) languages have a distinctive way of constructing reality in science; English follows empiricist lines, French rationalist ones. If French is taken to be a typical example of a Romance language, it is even clearer that there is a language-specific distribution of information. In translating, then, awareness of the different distribution of information in SL and TL is important for successful communication as it is "a function of optimal processing conditions, varying according to language specific parameters" (Doherty 1997b: 72). In LSP translating this is even more important as adequate transfer of contents is essential.

3. Method

This corpus-based investigation is carried out in two stages. In the first stage, features of information structure and focus-attributing positions are studied in a corpus of English-Italian translations of popular physics articles to identify examples where wording does not appear to reflect the natural Italian word order. In the second stage these features are compared with those of a corpus of original Italian articles on the same topic to see if the Italian information structure is used in translation or whether target texts reproduce the original English information structure. Corpus analysis is partly computer-assisted using dedicated software – WordSmith Tools (Scott/OUP 1998). The corpus is also compared with the contemporary Italian component of a larger corpus of nuclear physics jointly developed by the University of Surrey and the University of Trieste (Ahmad/Musacchio 2003). The aim of analysis is to trace strategies that can be implemented in LSP translating and translation revision (1) to balance information structure or (2) reduce structural weight of sentences, (3) to improve cohesion and (4) re-instate the typical Italian construction of reality along logical lines in popular science. Given the relevance of content in science these aspects will also be studied with a view to detecting possible ambiguities.

4. A corpus of popular science texts on particle physics

The corpus developed for investigation consists of popular science articles on particle physics published over a 10-year period.

The articles were taken from the American monthly *Scientific American* and from the Italian monthly *Le Scienze*. *Scientific American* has a general readership, though many of its readers have some kind of scientific or technical training (Myers 1990: 144). Articles are written by research scientists by invitation or by the magazine staff and are close in form to scientific articles. *Le Scienze* started off as the Italian translation of *Scientific American*, but in the last decades it has published both translations from *Scientific American* – which still make up most of the articles in the magazine – and articles written by Italian research scientists and scientific reporters. Its readership is very similar to that of *Scientific American*. There are two components to the corpus: (1) a parallel component made up of 9 English articles published by *Scientific American* from 1993 to 2003 and their Italian translations published by *Le Scienze* over the same period and (2) a comparable component consisting of 9 articles originally written in Italian and published by *Le Scienze* in the same 10-year period. The number of articles selected for inclusion in the corpus was dictated by the translations published by *Le Science* on the topic and thus determines corpus size. Corpus size and composition are summarised in Table 1 below. A list of the articles in the corpus is given in the Appendix.

	English parallel component, 1993-2003	Italian parallel component, 1993-2003	Italian comparable component, 1993-2003
	Scientific American	Le Scienze	Le Scienze
Tokens	40,633	41,414	41,417
Sentences	1,765	1,802	1,516
Sentence length	21.57	22.52	26.21
Paragraphs	172	166	188
Paragraph length	236.24	251.89	220.54

Table 1. A parallel/comparable corpus of popular science articles.

5. Analysis

The corpus was first analysed using WordSmith Tools. Statistical information about the three components of the corpus given in Table 1 above reveals what follows:

- Though the number of articles is the same, Italian translations and original Italian articles tend to be longer than the original English texts. In particular, translations are longer even if in some cases they are abridged versions of the source texts.
- Sentence length is roughly comparable in the English and Italian parallel sections of the corpus; sentences are slightly longer in the Italian comparable sections of the corpus. This may point

to an influence of English on Italian translations, especially considering that sentence length is as high as 31.51 and 35.82 in the popular science and secondary-school textbook component of the Italian corpus of nuclear physics developed by the Universities of Surrey and Trieste (Ahmad/Musacchio 2003).[1]

- Translated Italian articles tend to reproduce the paragraphing of the English source texts. The shorter number of paragraphs in the parallel Italian component is a consequence of text abridging during the process of translating, revising or editing. On the contrary, original Italian articles alternate short and long paragraphs so that overall number of words per paragraph is lower – 220.54 compared to 236.24 of original English articles.

Myers' remarks (1990: 175) about editorial changes in textual organisation in popular science are also worth investigating in a preliminary stage. As to rephrasing of introductory statements, questions and answers appear in three of the nine English articles, in two of their translations and in two of the comparable Italian articles. Most articles, though, start with some kind of historical background or background information on the topic. This confirms Myers' view (1990: 188) that research in particle physics is not so amenable to being turned into a narrative of nature as – say – biology. Rephrasing of passive and impersonal constructions in the active voice can be gleaned by running concordances of words designating people involved in research and mentioned in the articles to emphasise the activity of the scientists. In the parallel Italian component there are 104 occurrences of words such as fisico (physicist = 5), fisici (physicists = 52), teorico (theorist = 1), teorici (theorists = 29), sperimentatore (experimenter = 1) and sperimentatori (experimenters = 16). In the comparable Italian component there are 35 occurrences of these words (fisico, 3; fisici, 29; sperimentatore, 2; sperimentatori, 1). Clearly, in this case Italian translations are influenced by the source text.

These preliminary data warrant further investigation into popular article organisation and structure in English and Italian.

1 The total size of these components of the corpus is 185,985 tokens.

5.1 Information structure

The typical, subject-verb-object (SVO) word order in English starts with given information and then moves on to new information. This order of given-new information or theme-rheme makes it easier for receivers to understand the message. New information is normally to be found at the end of the clause. When an initial element is the focus, it is prominent – this creates emphasis. As in English, the unmarked word order in Italian is SVO and the information structure is based on the information-flow principle of given and new and the principle of end-focus.

To promote an unmarked theme to marked theme, however, Italian has the same options as English – fronting, left and right hand dislocation, clefting, and inversion, but may resort to them more or less frequently. A simple way to promote the verb to marked theme is subject-verb inversion. In English inversion is a relatively rare phenomenon, especially in academic prose – approximately 500-600 occurrences per million words (Biber/Johansson/Leech/Conrad/Finegan 1999: 926). As a consequence of greater morphological inflection, Italian has a freer sentence structure and inversion is more common. For example, verbs of happening such as *accadere*, *succedere*, *avvenire* usually cause the subject-verb order to be inverted. As can be seen in the following example, the natural Italian word order one expects when *accadere* is used was not re-created in the translation:[2]

(1) Before the advent of the Standard Model, physicists had become used to experiments producing unexpected new particles or other signposts to a new theory almost before the chalk dust had settled on the old one. They have been waiting 30 years for that to happen with the Standard Model. (Kane 2003)[3]
Prima dell'avvento del modello standard i fisici si erano abituati al fatto che gli esperimenti producessero particelle inattese o altri indizi che puntavano verso una nuova teoria, quasi prima che la precedente fosse stata completata. Da 30 anni si aspetta che una cosa del genere accada con il modello standard. (Kane 2003)

2 Underlining indicates parts that are relevant to current discussion.
3 For references of corpus articles see the list in the Appendix.

In other cases the reasons why information flow is impaired in Italian translations are more complex. In the example below the two sentences are joined by the coordinating conjunction *e* ('and'), but *very well tested* is translated using explicitation in the form of a very long relative clause which sits clumsily in the middle of the sentence and makes information focus more difficult to identify. This form of explicitation is reinforced by the adjunct *correttamente*:

(2) The Standard Model is very well tested. It predicted the existence of the W and Z bosons, the gluon and two of the heavier quarks (the charm and the top quark). (Kane 2003: 73)
Il modello è stato sottoposto a innumerevoli verifiche, che ne hanno immancabilmente confermato la validità, e ha correttamente previsto l'esistenza dei bosoni W e Z, dei gluoni e di due dei quark più pesanti ("charm" e "top"). (Kane 2003: 42)

Considering that Italian tends to move peripheral information to the left, an implicit relative clause at the beginning of the sentence could balance information structure in Italian. Further, the information provided in the relative clause is redundant and can be more concisely expressed by the adjunct *correttamente*:

(3) Sottoposto a innumerevoli verifiche, il modello ha correttamente previsto l'esistenza dei bosoni W e Z, dei gluoni e di due dei quark più pesanti ("charm" e "top").

Similarly, in the following example, the long noun group followed by two relative clauses and used as theme in the original English text forces the translator to resort to parataxis in Italian to simplify the sentence, but information focus – progress made in the construction of the accelerator – is lost as indeed is part of the information (which will take the major responsibility for constructing the accelerator itself), probably because it is thought to be redundant in Italian.

(4) This vast and technologically challenging project, coordinated by CERN (the European laboratory for particle physics), which will take the major responsibility for constructing the accelerator itself, is already well under way. (Smith 2000: 71)

> Questo progetto, di eccezionale livello tecnologico, è già in fase avanzata di realizzazione ed è coordinato dal CERN, il Laboratorio europeo per la fisica delle particelle. (Smith 2000: 63)

Again, fronting the relative clause would help restore information balance:

(5) Coordinato dal CERN (il Laboratorio europeo per la fisica delle particelle), questo progetto di eccezionale livello tecnologico è già in avanzata fase di realizzazione.

5.2 Structural weight

In English, the preferred distribution of elements follows the principle of end-weight: long and complex elements are placed towards the end of the clause so that receivers can decode the message more easily. In Italian, new information comes at the end of the sentence while more peripheral information is moved to the "free zone" on the left. Somewhat conflicting strategies are used in English and Italian and should be handled carefully in translating from one language to the other.

In the following English sentence, the specification *so far to no avail* is added at the end of the sentence according to the principle of end-weight. In Italian the English word order is preserved contravening the idea of end-focus. The problem is compounded by keeping the long adjunct *at their highest-energy colliders* in mid- rather than left-peripheral position and what the comparable corpus confirms to be two unusual collocations in popular physics, *massime energie* and *cercare la presenza di qc*. The comparable corpus further indicates that active forms with subjects such as *experimenters* are not common in Italian popular science articles, where an impersonal form introduced by *si* or a passive is preferred.

(6) Experimenters, however, have searched at their highest-energy colliders for particles predicted by supersymmetry, so far to no avail. (Jolie 2002: 71)
I fisici sperimentali, però, hanno cercato alle massime energie raggiungibili negli acceleratori la presenza di particelle previste dalla supersimmetria, finora senza successo. (Jolie 2002: 47)

Senza successo is a literal translation of *to no avail* which is used here instead of the standard equivalent adverb *invano* as in the proposed revision of the translation below:

(7) Pur sfruttando le più elevate energie raggiungibili dagli acceleratori, finora si sono purtroppo cercate invano tracce delle particelle previste dalla supersimmetria.

Another problem is created by clauses between brackets or dashes, which do not take the same position in Italian as they do in English. Preservation of the English structure violates the natural word order of Italian:

(8) Third, CP symmetry – essentially, the symmetry between matter and antimatter – must be violated. (Quinn/Witherell 1998: 79)
Infine, la simmetria *CP* – essenzialmente la simmetria tra materia e antimateria – deve essere violata. (Quinn/Witherell 1999: 69)

Explicitation of the link between the main clause and the clause between dashes and subject-verb inversion would help to keep structural weight under control:

(9) Infine deve essere violata la simmetria *CP*, cioè – in sostanza – la simmetria tra materia e antimateria.

In the following example structural weight in the Italian translation is increased by positioning peripheral information – introduced in English by although – in mid-sentence and by the implicit concessive clause where the gerund rappresentando, which refers cataphorically to the subject of the mentre-clause, coppie di quark. After a concessive clause introduced by pur one expects to find the subject – either explicit or implied. In this case, however, the subject is further removed by subject-verb inversion.

(10) Whereas quarks do not exist freely in nature, mesons do – although they are often unstable. (Cline 1994: 45)

(11) Va ricordato che i singoli quark non esistono liberi in natura mentre – pur rappresentando stati spesso instabili – esistono coppie di quark, i mesoni appunto. (Cline 1994: 51)

In Italian the position of the clause between dashes makes the contrast *quarks do not exist – mesons do* less sharp. To reduce structural weight and keep information focus on the contrast, subject-verb inversion can be used:

(12) In natura non esistono quark liberi, mentre sono presenti coppie di quark, cioè i mesoni, anche se spesso rappresentano stati instabili.

Similar problems originate from the position of adverbs or adverbials. In the following Italian translation the adjunct individualmente is placed after the operator and before the main verb as individually is in English. The Italian equivalent of the adverb, individualmente, is ambiguous and così followed by a sebbene-clause makes for heavy reading of the sentence:

(13) So although charge and parity symmetry are individually broken by neutrinos, in combination their dictates would seem to be obeyed. (Quinn/Witherell 1998: 77-78)

(14) Così, sebbene le simmetrie di parità e di carica siano individualmente violate dai neutrini, sembra che vengano rispettate quando sono applicate in combinazione. (Quinn/Witherell 1999: 68)

In the proposed revision of the translation below così at the beginning of the sentence is replaced by dunque, a more frequent cohesive device in the comparable Italian component of the corpus (see 5.3 below); individualmente is substituted by the unambiguous adjunct in singoli casi and se takes the place of quando as the more frequent subordinating conjunction used in the comparable Italian articles to introduce what are actually hypothetical and not temporal clauses:

(15) Per quanto in singoli casi siano violate dai neutrini, le simmetrie di parità e carica paiono dunque rispettate se si applicano in combinazione.

5.3 Cohesion

Compared to English, Italian is known to prefer longer, more complex sentences where complexity is often the result of hypotaxis. As can be seen from Table 1 above, corpus analysis of sentence length confirms that sentences are longer in the comparable, original Italian component.

As to sentence complexity, a comparison of subordinate clauses in the parallel and comparable components of the corpus by looking at occurrences of subordinating conjunctions – such as *perché, poiché, affinché, sebbene, anche se, se, quando, mentre, senza*, and so on – shows that frequencies are broadly similar. There is, however, a difference in the distribution of some coordinating conjunctions as shown in Table 2.

	Parallel Italian component	*Comparable Italian component*
Dunque	8	27
Quindi	27	49
Ma	140	97
Cioè	10	35
Infatti	6	25

Table 2. Occurrences of some coordinating conjunctives.

The higher frequencies of *dunque, quindi, cioè* and *infatti* in the comparable component suggest that in popular physics translations the number of conclusive and explicative cohesive links should be increased. On the contrary, the higher frequency of but in the parallel component may point to a preference for a different text organisation based on contrast as highlighted by adversative conjunctions and reflected in Italian translations.

According to Halliday/Hasan (1976) cohesion is created by reference, substitution, ellipsis, conjunction and lexical cohesion by collocation or reiteration – repetition, synonymy or near-synonymy, superordination or use of general words. In English science cohesion is often created by reiteration. In Italian reiteration by means of repetition is avoided for stylistic reasons unless it causes ambiguity. In technical and scientific texts it is particularly important to avoid involuntary ambiguities as this impairs adequate text decoding. In the following example, cohesion is achieved in English by noun repetition. In this case repetition is not necessary in Italian and can be replaced by ellipsis:

(16) Little ripples in these fields carry energy and momentum from place to place, and quantum mechanics tells us that these ripples come in bundles, or quanta, that are recognized in the laboratory as elementary particles. For instance, the quantum of the electromagnetic field is a particle know as the photon. (Weinberg 1999)

(17) Piccole increspature in questi campi trasportano energia e impulso da un luogo a un altro, e la meccanica quantistica ci dice che queste increspature arrivano a pacchetti, o quanti, identificati in laboratorio come particelle elementari. Per esempio, il quanto del campo elettromagnetico è una particella ormai ben nota: il fotone. (Weinberg 1999: 50)

In other cases English repetition at the end of a sentence and at the beginning of the following sentence is reproduced in Italian. This does not improve cohesion in Italian while it increases structural weight.

(18) Up and down, strange and charm, and bottom and top are closely related to each other and are paired into "families". Up and down, for instance, are the two lightest quarks and belong to the first family. In each family one quark has an electric charge of 2/3 (up, charm and top), and the other has an electric charge of –1/3 (down, strange and bottom). (Cline 1994: 41)

(19) Le coppie su e giù, strano e incantato, basso e alto, che sono costituite da quark strettamente correlati, rappresentano tra "famiglie". Su e giù, per esempio, sono i quark più leggeri e appartengono alla prima famiglia. In ogni famiglia uno dei due quark ha carica elettrica pari a 2/3 (su, incantato e alto), mentre l'altro ha carica –1/3 (giù, stano e basso). (Cline 1994: 47)

At least one repetition could be avoided in Italian by text re-organisation and ellipsis:

(20) Le coppie su e giù, strano e incantato, basso e alto, che sono costituite da quark strettamente correlati, rappresentano tra "famiglie": alla prima appartengono per esempio su e giù, i quark più leggeri. In ogni famiglia uno dei due quark ha carica elettrica pari a 2/3 (su, incantato e alto), mentre l'altro ha carica –1/3.

As can be seen, fronting of the anaphoric *alla prima* [...] makes the paratactic *sono* [...] *e appartengono* unnecessary. As a result the sentence is more concise.

Another frequent type of cohesion is given by substitution. In the following example, *such a decay* in the English original refers back to a previously mentioned *decay*. Cohesion is further created by conjunction as sentences 2 and 3 of the original text are connected by the conjunction *e* in Italian. However, in these sentences the English SVO structure is closely rendered in Italian:

(21) In late 1993 such a decay was seen at the Cornell electron-positron storage ring. Only a few such events have been detected so far. Calculating the likelihood of this process is quite difficult. (Cline 1994: 46)

(22) Alla fine del 1993 un simile decadimento è stato osservato nell'anello di accumulazione elettroni-positroni di Cornell. Pochi di questi eventi sono stati finora rivelati e calcolare la probabilità di un simile processo è molto difficile. (Cline 1994: 52)

In the example, a slight ambiguity is created by *simile* as a translation of *such*. When *simile* is used as a premodifier it is a synonym of *tale*, another equivalent of *such* in Italian. In the comparable component of the corpus, however, it is always used as a postmodifier meaning *similar to*. Further, in this component of the corpus *simile* has 9 occurrences and *tale* 46, whereas in the parallel component occurrences are 26 and 7 respectively. A concordance of *simile* from the comparable component of the corpus shows how it is used in popular physics:

e adottando un dispositivo sperimentale concettualmente	**simile**	a quello sopra menzionato, furono in grado di	Realis~1.txt 89
miliardi di kelvin. Si ipotizza che una transizione di fase	**Simile,**	in senso inverso, sia possibile all'interno di alcune	Ilplas~1.txt 80
in alto nella pagina a fronte, la QCD (o qualunque teoria	**Simile)**	permette di scrivere la massa di ciascuno come	Modell~1.txt 48
ad esempio, le proprietà del protone si calcolano in modo	**simile**	a quelle di un nucleo di 3He fatto di quark (due u e	Modell~1.txt 45
ha sfidato i fisici nella sua comprensione, ha una intensità	**simile**	a quella elettromagnetica ed è oggi unificata con	Laviol~1.txt 32

Table 3. A concordance of *simile* from the comparable component of the corpus.

Taking all these aspects into consideration leads to formulate the following alternative translation where cohesion is increased by making the link between sentence 2 and 3 more explicit using *quindi* rather than *e* and placing *finora* in its standard position according to the comparable component of the corpus, i.e. in clause-initial position. Finally, demonstrative reference in the English original (*this process*) is rendered by the periphrasis *un processo del genere* to avoid repetition of *tale* (*tale decadimento/tale processo*):

(23) Alla fine del 1993 si è osservato un tale decadimento nell'anello di accumulazione elettroni-positroni di Cornell. Finora sono stati rivelati pochi di questi eventi, quindi è molto difficile calcolare la probabilità di un processo del genere.

5.4 Construction of reality in Italian popular science

Halliday/Martin (1993: 16) propose that different languages construct reality in science in distinctive ways. Further investigation in this area will be needed to test the validity of the idea. If we consider the following sentence taken from the parallel Italian component of the corpus:

(24) Uno dei principali scopi della fisica, forse il primo in assoluto, è quello di comprendere l'affascinante varietà della natura in modo unificato. (Weinberg 1999: 376)

It is clear that the problem is not so much the close rendering of the English SVO word order:

(25) One of the primary goals of physics is to understand the wonderful variety of nature in a unified way. (Weinberg 1999)

The sentence does not sound quite natural in Italian, though it is not an example of a "third code" in Frawley's sense. The following sentence from the comparable Italian component of the corpus shows how reality is constructed in Italian popular physics and may help to identify what went "wrong" in the translating process:

(26) Uno degli sforzi della fisica moderna è quello di cercare di descrivere queste forze in modo unificato, come aspetti diversi di un'unica interazione. Ma una teoria unificata non c'è ancora [...]. (Gruppo Athena 2002: 58)

In Italian then, one cannot *comprendere* ('understand'), but can *descrivere* ('describe') in a unified way. Another important clue is provided by the second sentence in the comparable Italian text where *una teoria unificata* ('a unified theory') sums up the concept expressed in the preceding sentence: by the time Italian readers get to the verbal group (*è quello di comprendere*) they have formed expectations as to how the sentence will unfold and an adjunct such as *in modo unificato* is not very likely to take clause-ending position. A more readily understandable Italian version would be as follows:

(27) Uno dei principali scopi della fisica, forse il primo in assoluto, è quello di ricondurre a una teoria unificata/descrivere tramite un'unica teoria l'affascinante varietà della natura.

As can be seen, the problem does not only lie in the choice of words and collocations, but also in the position of the adjunct *in modo unificato*. To sum up, English presents the process as the discovery of unity behind the variety of nature. Italian prefers to look at it as the formulation of a theory that can account for different phenomena in nature.

Another example of the interplay between syntax and semantics in the construction of reality in Italian popular science is the following:

(28) In the 1980s nuclear theorists proposed that superviolent collisions were not necessarily the only way to see supersymmetry; they predicted that a different form of supersymmetry could exist in certain atomic nuclei. (Jolie 2002: 71)

(29) Negli anni ottanta alcuni teorici ipotizzarono che le collisioni ad altissime energie non fossero necessariamente l'unico modo per rivelare la supersimmetria; secondo le loro previsioni, una forma di supersimmetria differente poteva esistere in certi nuclei atomici. (Jolie 2002: 48)

The comparable component of the corpus shows that Italian prefers an impersonal form or a passive to active sentence such as *alcuni teorici ipotizzarono* unless the difference between the work of theoretical and experimental physicists is foregrounded. In other words, in this case Italian takes for granted that in physics a theory can only be put forward by a physicist and the explicitation is considered redundant. Moreover, the anaphoric *secondo le loro previsioni* is ambiguous because in the preceding sentence theorists did not *predict* but *ipotizzarono* ('proposed' or 'hypothesised'). Finally, the rather clumsy, close rendering of the English SVO suggests that fronting of the adjunct *in certi nuclei atomici* improves information balance and reduces structural weight:

(30) Negli anni ottanta fu avanzata l'ipotesi che le collisioni ad altissime energie non fossero necessariamente l'unico modo per rivelare la supersimmetria; secondo tale ipotesi, in certi nuclei atomici poteva esistere una diversa forma di supersimmetria.

6. Conclusions

Analysis of the parallel and comparable components of the corpus suggests that in translation, reproducing the natural linear order of the target language implies an awareness of information structures and focus-attributing positions of elements in the sentence, a feeling for structural weight and knowledge of cohesive strategies and typical ways to construct reality in Italian in the field and genre.

The illustration of translation problems by contrasting sentences from translated articles with similar sentences in the original Italian articles shows how a comparable corpus can help in the process of translating and revising. In short, results indicate that translating and revising popular physics articles are not just a question of care in the selection of terminology, subtechnical vocabulary and specialised phraseology, but also require consideration of the interplay between syntax and lexis and make it necessary to take into account factors affecting the ways in which clauses are adapted to context or varied for adequate focus and emphasis in the target language.

References

Ahmad K. / Musacchio M.T. (2003) Enrico Fermi and the making of the language of nuclear physics. *Fachsprache – The international Journal of LSP, research, didactics, terminology* 25/3-4, 120-140.

Baker, M. 1993. Corpus linguistics and translation studies – implications and applications. In Baker M. / Francis G. / Tognini-Bonelli E. (eds) *Text and Technology. In Honour of John Sinclair*. Amsterdam/Philadelphia: John Benjamins, 233-250.

Benincà, P. / Salvi, G.P. / Frison, L. 1989. L'ordine degli elementi della frase e le costruzioni marcate. In Renzi, L. & Salvi, G.P. (a cura di) *Grande grammatica italiana di consultazione, I.*. II ed. Bologna: Il Mulino, 115-225.

Benincà, P. 1993. Sintassi. In Sobrero, A.A. (a cura di) *Introduzione all'italiano contemporaneo. Le strutture*. Roma/Bari, Laterza, 247-290.

Biber, D. /, Johansson, S. / Leech G. / Conrad, S., / Finegan, E. 1999. *Longman Grammar of Spoken and Written English*. Harlow: Pearson.

Doherty, M. 1997a. 'Acceptability' and language-specific preference in the distribution of information, *Target* 9/1, 1-24.

Doherty, M. 1997b. Textual garden paths – parameterized obstacles to target language adequate translations. In Hauenschild, C. / Heizmann, S. (eds) *Machine Translation and Translation Theory*. Berlin/New York, Mouton de Gruyter, 69-89.

Frawley, W. 1984. Prolegomena to a theory of translation. In Frawley W. (ed.) *Translation: Literary, Linguistic, and Philosophical Perspectives*, London and Toronto: Associated University Presses, 159-175.

Halliday, M.A.K. / Hasan R. 1976. *Cohesion in English*. Harlow: Longman.

Halliday, M.A.K. / Martin, J.R. 1993. *Writing Science: Literacy and Power*. London/Washington, D.C.: The Falmer Press.

Myers, G. 1990. The social construction of popular science: The narrative of science and the narrative of nature. In *Writing Biology. Texts in the Social Construction of Scientific Knowledge*. Madison, WI./London: The University of Wisconsin Press, 141-192.

Quirk, R. / Greenbaum, S. / Leech, G. / Svartvik, J. 1985. *A Comprehensive Grammar of the English Language*. Harlow: Longman.

Scott, M. / Oxford University Press 1998. *WordSmith Tools Manual*. Available: <http://www.liv.a.c.uk/~ms2928/wordsmit.htm> [accessed: 2001-2003].

Toury, G. 1995. Beyond descriptive studies. Towards laws of translational behaviour. In *Descriptive Studies and Beyond*. Amsterdam/Philadelphia: John Benjamins, 259-279.

Appendix

i) Scientific American *articles*

Cline, D.B. 1994. Low-Energy Ways to Observe High-Energy Phenomena. *Scientific American*, September, 40-47.

Close, F.E. / Page, P.R. 1998. Glueballs, *Scientific American*. November, 80-85.

Duff, M.J. 1998. The Theory Formerly Known as Strings. *Scientific American*, February, 64-69.

Jolie, J. 2002. Uncovering Supersymmetry. *Scientific American,* July, 70-77.

Kane, G. 2003. Physics Beyond the Standard Model. *Scientific American*, June, 68-75.

Llewellyn Smith, C. 2000. The Large Hadron Collider. *Scientific American*, July, 71-77.

Nauenberg, M. / Stroud, C. / Yeazell, J. 1994. The Classical Limit of an Atom, *Scientific American*. June, 44-49.

Quinn, H.R. / Witherell, M.S. 1998. The Asymmetry between Matter and Antimatter, *Scientific American*. October, 76-81.

Weinberg, S. 1999. A Unified Physics by 2050? *Scientific American*, December. Available: <http://www.sciam.org> [accessed: July-August 2003].

ii) Italian translations published by Le Scienze

Cline, D.B. 1994. Nuove tecniche per la fisica delle alte energie. novembre, 46-54.

Close, F.E. / Page, P.R. 1999. Le glueball. *Le Scienze*, febbraio, 48-53.

Duff, M.J. 1998. La teoria un tempo chiamata 'delle corde'. *Le Scienze*, giugno, 90-95.

Jolie, J. 2002. Rivelare la supersimmetria. *Le Scienze*, settembre, 46-53.

Kane, G. 2003. La fisica, oltre il modello standard. *Le Scienze*, luglio, 38-45.

Llewellyn Smith, C. 2000. Il Large Hadron Collider. *Le Scienze*, settembre, 62-71.

Nauenberg M. / Stroud, C. / Yeazell, J. 1994. Il limite classico di un atomo. *Le Scienze*, agosto, 74-79.

Quinn, H.R. / Witherell, M.S. 1999. L'asimmetria tra materia e antimateria. *Le Scienze*, febbraio, 66-71.

Weinberg, S. 1999. Una fisica unificata entro il 2050? *Le Scienze*, dicembre, 48-56.

iii) Italian comparable articles published by Le Scienze

Antinori, F. / Quercigh, E. 199x. Il plasma di quark e gluoni, *Le Scienze Quaderni*, n. 125, 90-94.

Bellettini, G. 1997. La scoperta del quark *top*, *Le Scienze,* settembre, 32-39.

Beltrametti, E. 1997. Realismo classico e realtà quantistica. *Le Scienze*, settembre, 4-11.

Franzini, P. 1997. La violazione della simmetria *CP*. *Le Scienze Quaderni* 103, 68-70.

Franzini, P. / Franzini, P. / Lee-Franzini, J. 1999. La fisica di Dafne. *Le Scienze*, giugno, 60-66.

Gruppo ATHENA 2002. La fabbrica degli atomi. *Le Scienze*, novembre, 56-63.

Lodi Rizzini, E. / Venturelli, L. / Zenoni, A. 1998. Atomi esotici e antiatomi. *Le Scienze*, luglio, 40-46.

Morpurgo, G. 1996. Modelli a quark e QCD, *Le Scienze*, settembre, 74-80.

Peruzzi, G. 2000. La costante di Planck compie cento anni. *Le Scienze*, novembre, 4-9.

PETER H. RAGAN

Cross-cultural communication in aviation

1. Introduction

The combination of communication, culture, and knowledge is usefully studied with close attention to the context in which the communication takes place. In international civil aviation, flight crews communicate with one another and with air traffic controllers using a specialized and highly contextualized language known as radiotelephony phraseology, pilot-tower or controller communication, among LSP instructors and researchers.

Widespread concern over the significant role of language in aircraft accidents and incidents has led to scrutiny of problematic use of this restricted register of English. However, it has received little attention in accident investigations beyond the evaluation of its function in conveying information. Although aircraft accident reports may contain information that points to the relevance of cultural factors, culture is rarely officially identified as an important variable for a variety of reasons and has not been connected with language use.

Sapir has observed that "we may think of language as the symbolic guide to culture" (1964: 63). Language use on the flight deck of international commercial aircraft presents an opportunity to study how national culture affects flight crew-air traffic controller communications. This study of cross-cultural communication in aviation argues that it is necessary to promote awareness of intrinsic functions of language in use, namely how language functions to communicate meaning as content, interpersonal relationship, and technical organization at clause level, and of the impact of national culture on language use by pilots and air traffic controllers in order to improve flight safety. It presents different perspectives on Airspeak, characterizes the significance of culture in its use, and presents three case studies of the contribution of culture to the breakdown of pilot-controller communication.

2. Perspectives on Airspeak

The International Civil Aviation Organization (ICAO) monitors aviation internationally, including use of this language, as does the Federal Aviation Admission (FAA) in the U.S.A. and other government agencies in various countries. It specified English as the "international language of the air" and is responsible for (1) establishing and reviewing international standards for the licensing of personnel and aircraft operation, (2) developing principles and techniques of international air navigation, including meteorology, radio communications, and rules of the air, and (3) currently requiring that applicants for airline transport pilot rating must "be able to read, write, and understand the English language and speak it without accent or impediment of speech that would interfere with two-way radio conversation." And the flight instructor is the judge of language proficiency!

This state of affairs is changing, however. The contributions of language to aviation accidents and incidents has led ICAO to recently establish "minimum skill level requirements for language proficiency for flight crews and air traffic controllers, develop an ICAO language proficiency rating scale applicable to both native and non-native speakers language; and recommend a testing schedule to demonstrate language proficiency" (Mathews 2003: 7) to go into effect within a few years time.

Airspeak is a singularly context bound special language with its emphasis on the human-machine interface (HMI) and the safe conduct of air transport. A restricted register like this is associated with distinctive probabilities of language use both of discourse functions and the weighing of choice in lexis and grammar. Figure 1 highlights this situational context:

1. PARTICIPANTS (Who's involved?) – Pilots and air traffic controllers
2. TEXT (What type of language?) – Airspeak (restricted register of English)
3. MODE (What use?) – Air-ground communication
    a. PURPOSE (Why?) – Direct, inform, question, request, respond
    b. CHANNEL (How?) – Spoken
4. FIELD (What is the focus of the activity?) – Aircraft take-off, flight, landing, etc.
5. TENOR (What is the relation between participants?) – ATC directs/controls pilots

Figure 1. Description of situational context for Airspeak.

There is a constant and very pressing concern that the aviation industry has in dealing with the HMI and the need for safety. For a flight crew communicating on the flight deck of a BOEING 747-400, this translates into the immediate presence of an aircraft weighing in at 396,900 kg (875,000 lb). The presence of this technology causes informational exchange to take priority over social and organizing functions of language and the wording that expresses them. Two studies illustrate the effect that prioritizing the use of language for information exchange has on communication.

John Sinclair (2001) has explored the "deification of information" which he associates with the increasing use of networked computers. He suggests this deification is a consequence of a human-machine interface incorrectly presented as being inter-active, and essentially operating as a one-way type of communication. The result is an increasing inability to handle the vast amounts of information made available by computers. While described as interactive, computer operation in fact transforms users to mere "clickers" who use their *mouses* (plural of the pointing device *mouse*) to respond to the machine's agenda. While interacting with the machine, there is virtually no need for social discourse and the linguistic skills it requires.

Similarly, in the aviation context, the increasing computerization of the cockpit of commercial aircraft and demands of technology aboard a commercial jetliner lead to one-way communication. In a study entitled "A Comparison of Cockpit Communication B737 – B757," Costley, Johnson, and Lawson compared communication on the flight decks of Boeing 37-200, 737-300, and the 757 aircraft, airplanes that display a progressive dependency on the computer. Data (involving 16 captains and 11 copilots) gathered from climb, cruise and descent sequences indicated a significant decrease in interpilot communication as the cockpit automation increases, although pilot activity rates on aircraft with fully automated flight decks are equal to that of conventional cockpits. Computer reliance negatively impacted flight crew interaction in general, and interpersonal language use in particular.

The perception of Airspeak that emerges from the demands of the Human-Machine Interface suggests that for flight crew and air traffic controllers, there are:

- a preoccupation in the cockpit with the communication of information and the discourse functions associated with it; and
- a tendency toward isolation of the individual members of the flight crew at work in the cockpit, with little opportunity to use discoursal and lexicogrammatical functions associated with interpersonal and organizing language behavior (or to learn them in the case of non-native speakers with poor English proficiency.

The situational dependence of Airspeak is readily seen through both the personal experience reported by pilots and qualitative and quantitative analyses of the use of Airspeak. Qualitative, content-oriented studies of actual language use, such as those found in NTSB Air Accident Reports substantiate the nature of this language use. So do the quantitative studies derived from compilations such as the Air Traffic Control Corpus of the Linguistic Data Consortium (2002) with its 70 hours of controller and pilot transmissions from three international airports of the U.S.A. All of these data illustrate correct and incorrect, appropriate and inappropriate use of Airspeak. They all bear witness that Airspeak is idiosyncratic, predictable, and problematic. Figure 2 summarizes evidence and gives examples of these specific features of Airspeak.

FEATURE	EVIDENCE
1. IDIOSYNCRATIC	DEPENDENT ON THE SITUATION
(primarily refers to content outside any written text but known to communicators)	
	DISJUNCTIVE & ABBREVIATED WORDING
	(discontinuous and leaves out words)
	SIMPLIFIED & FORMULAIC
	(relies on prepared phraseology rather than spontaneous speech)
Examples:	"CLIMB AND MAINTAIN 3000"
	"I NEED YOU TO FLY TEN"
	("I need you to fly ten mile legs in the holding pattern")
	"YOU'RE CLEAR TO LAND ONE TWO ZERO: FIFTEEN"
	("degrees/ wind knots")
2. PREDICTABLE SITUATION-DEPENDENT	OPENING AND ANSWERING SEQUENCES
	(controller/pilot calls, informs, requests, directs, checks, and so on, in response to a "mini-situation," for example, take-off, approach)
Example: Edinb:	"CALEDONIAN NINE FOUR FOUR YOUR CLEARANCE"
	BR944: "NINE FORTY FOUR GO AHEAD"
3. PROBLEMATIC (potential)	MIX OF NON-STANDARD UTTERANCES, EXCHANGES, AND CULTURAL IMPRINT
Example:	"NEGATIVE SIR WE JUST RUNNING OUT OF FUEL WE OKAY THREE THOUSAND NOW OKAY"

Figure 2. Specific features of Airspeak.

3. The significance of culture

Investigators of the causes of air disasters in the late 1970s came to the disturbing conclusion that the majority, that is, over 70% of air crashes were caused not by failures of equipment or weather but rather human error (Helmreich/Ashleigh 1998).

Problematic language use contributes to such data. In commercial aviation, the cockpit is an environment, a situational context in which a skilled group of individuals perform work that requires high levels of technical skills, and because they work together as crew, high levels of interpersonal skills as well. A crew forms a culture, most simply defined as that which distinguishes one group of people from another (Hofstede/Pedersen/Hofstede 2002). This culture can be supportive or problematic for the interactions that it affects.

The aviation community responded to the problem of human error in the cockpit by initiating psychological training for flight crews in the early 1970s and 1980s. The evolution of this training since then is relevant to any look at culture manifested in language use. Discussions of group and individual behavior in the cockpit promptly led to the notion of "cockpit culture" and gave rise to the associated "cockpit resource management training", or CRM, now a large-scale industry within the aviation profession. From this focus on the cockpit crew, CRM expanded to become Crew Resource Management, and now offers a variety of training modules including cabin crew and other system elements. As it developed, it also had to acknowledge the different types of significant cultures involved, notably occupational, organizational, and national.

Initially CRM was only practiced in the U.S. and other westernized countries. Within these relatively homogeneous national cultures, the effect of culture was generally uniform and therefore masked. However, as Helmreich/Merritt assert, "the potential for misunderstandings in cross-cultural encounters is enormous (1998: 56)"and "language is probably the most fundamental source of problems in cross-national cultural groups" (1998: 202-203). Since so much of CRM is based on communication and command styles, it is not surprising in retrospect that CRM was not very successful when it was exported to some Asian and S. American countries.

An important question, then, is the extent to which national culture affects pilot training and skills, important because by 2000, CRM was promoted all over the world and was even required of all 185 member states of the ICAO (Merritt 1998: 283). Merritt (1988: 284) describes the prevailing view then, which has persisted for many, claiming that:

> within the aviation community [it] has been one of denial or minimization of any national differences – the assumption has been that pilots operate the same types of aircraft and therefore they should be trained to the same standards using the same technique.

This question was fully researched and answered in the work of Ashleigh Merritt (2000). She turned to cross-cultural psychology for guidance in the seminal work of Geert Hofstede (1980, 1991), who studied and derived four dimensions of national culture. Merritt collected data from some 9,400 male commercial airline pilots in 26 airlines in 19 countries in a replication study of Hofstede's indexes of national culture. The successful replication correlations for the dimensions of individualism-collectivism (IDV: 0.96), power distance (PDI: 0.87), masculinity-femininity (MAS: 0.75), and uncertainty avoidance (UAI: .68) (along with additional measures/adjustments relevant to aviation) confirmed that national culture exerts an influence on cockpit behavior over and above the professional culture of pilots, and corroborates that 'one size fits all' training is inappropriate. In other words, CRM practices that were held to be universally applicable are indeed culturally influenced.

Given the problematic nature of communication in cross-cultural encounters and language use in cross-national cultural groups, a view of language solely as a conveyor of information is insufficient to capture the manifestations of culture in text: interpersonal and organizational functions of language also need to be analyzed to account for the interplay of Airspeak and culture.

4. Enlarging the perspective

A functional perspective of language acknowledges that texts are responsive to situational contexts and gives rise to the concept of text types (Halliday 1973). Similarly, Biber (1995: 33) uses the term *register* as a term for a socially perceived text category and *text-type*, a "grouping of texts defined in strictly linguistic terms" which are finally interpreted in terms of purpose and other characteristics of situational contexts (1995: 10). With a systemic-functional model of language, one can move from an extrinsic level, the discourse level of language as purposive behavior, to an intrinsic level, the level of wording, i.e., lexis and grammar. The systemic perspective applied is that the functions of language are reflected in the internal structure: the intrinsic level derives from the extrinsic. This is a parallel interpretation of the concept of functions, which co-occur at the structural level of wording. Biber's multi-dimensional methodology (1995: 136) is based on the premise "that most formal differences reflect functional differences". He also acknowledges and notes the co-occurrence of functions.

Figure 3 below offers a description of how meaning is communicated in the wording of language from a systemic-functional perspective through these three major functions. It also offers a sample of Airspeak to exemplify the analysis of text using these three functions (see also Ragan 1997). The three functions apply to both spoken and written modes of expression, and concurrently convey meaning. The content function communicates information for our understanding of our environment. It is reflective and experiential. Language expresses who/what is involved, what is going on, and under what circumstances.

Airspeak, like all language uses, also has an exchange function. This refers to a two-way interaction that is interactive and interpersonal, and has to do with the social use of language – it is a rich function in the expression of cultural values. We can see this interaction at a simple level in the lexis and grammar of asking questions or making of statements about information, and when we make offers or command action of others in terms of behavior involving 'goods and services'. This function refers to social language use, such as acknowledging relationships, moderating directness, and expressing degrees of politeness.

The third major function is that of organization. Language functions to communicate our sense of the ordering and logic of content and language interaction. Shared meaning is cohesive, coherent and structured. It has a logical structure depending on the type of text it is. A useful way into this function is to think of the features that make language use identifiable according to its text type. For example, a good set of instructions proceeds and is organized in such a manner that we can readily recognize. This is a fascinating area for cultural studies.

1. **Understanding our environment (CONTENT)**
   - It is reflective and experiential
   - Wording refers to who/what is involved, what is going on, and under what circumstances
2. **Acting on others (EXCHANGE)**
   - It is interactive and interpersonal
   - Wording expresses a question, statement, offer, or command, and social indicators, for example, of relationship and politeness.
3. **Ordering spoken and written text (ORGANIZATION)**
   - It is coherent and structured
   - Wording has theme, focus, and logical structure appropriate to its text type

Example: Edinb: "*Caledonian nine four four your clearance*"
BR944: "*Nine forty four go ahead*"

Figure 3. Three major functions of language

One needs to be careful with language use, especially during times of stress and emergency: The multiple functions that language serves need to careful combined. Airspeak is meant to simplify and focus communication, but lacks the means to do so outside of the content function. Awareness of the co-occurrence of these functions is useful as it clarifies the interplay of language and culture, but in the cockpit environment this does not easily take place without recourse to a less-restricted register of English. The example shown in Figure 3 above is a short dialogue between a controller at Edinburgh Airport and the pilot of a private plane with the call number BR944. It models the concurrent expression of the three functions in ideal conditions – there is no emergency taking place.

As for content, the controller identifies the plane being called, "Caledonian 944." He then refers to his purpose for calling, to get "your clearance." He also expresses and initiates an exchange by offering these two partial statements: the "Caledonian nine four four" and "your clearance" identify the pilot's airplane.

An exchange takes place as the controller requests that the pilot acknowledge his call by responding to him. The controller initiates the interaction. The pilot responds with content: he identifies by repeating the call sign of his aircraft, "Nine forty four" as part of the exchange. He then makes a request with the content "go ahead". This refers to the action going on and is also an exchange in that he directly requests the controller to "go ahead" and give him his clearance. It is vintage Airspeak except for the "forty".

With regard to organization, these words exhibit a logical order common to Airspeak, in this case with an opening and answering sequence between the two participants which includes calling, informing, directing, and checking information (by repeating it). This transaction takes place in a manner fully predictable in this particular mini-situational context, the preparation for take-off.

Other forms of analysis at discourse and wording levels in other applications are also fruitful. Linde's quantitative analysis of the role that linguistic mitigation plays in aircraft accidents is an excellent introduction to the exchange function of language, in which language is viewed in its interactive, interpersonal role in communication (Linde 1988). Mitigation refers to the degree of politeness or directness involved in a spoken communication. Linde builds her investigation on the theory of Brown/Levison (1978) who describe politeness as the attempt to avoid face-threatening action.

Chapter 6 of Biber's *Dimensions of Register Variation* (1995) presents an analysis of the relations in Korean among twenty-two registers (10 spoken and 12 written) with respect to six significant dimensions of variation. This is noteworthy because one of these, the "Overt Expression of Personal Stance" "comprises several features reflecting the personal attitudes and feelings of speakers and authors" (1995: 193). Another "Honorification" "shows the importance of social relations and setting [...] and confirms the importance of this system as a separate dimension of register variation in Korean" (1995: 193). In Biber's Appendix 1 there is also a grammatical description of linguistic features in Korean which includes the categories of "sociolinguistic indicators" and "stance markers."

Similar to the systemic-functional perspective, the features described by Linde and Biber are capable of showing nuances of culture in the analysis of intercultural communication. A significant example of this is the use of English in cultures where saving face is highly valued. In the two examples of pilot-controller communication presented below, this is one of many cultural values which potentially affect language use, and ultimately, flight safety.

5. Examples of culture and Airspeak

With the lexicogrammatical functions of content, exchange, and organization as wording in mind, two examples are offered here to model the interplay of culture and Airspeak. These are by no means typical events; they are, in fact, worst-case scenarios. The contribution of cultural factors to aircraft incidents and accidents is a sensitive, complicated, and controversial topic (Phillips 1998), one that is rarely explored in official accident document. Although the overwhelming majority of incidents and accidents have multiple causes, those with cultural components are routinely identified and investigated without reference to culture. Here three examples, one of Avianca, the principal Colombian carrier, and two of Korean Air Lines, offer different insights into the interplay between culture and language.

Figure 4 below offers insight into the interplay between culture and language by looking at the final portion of the transcript of tape recordings made by the cockpit voice recorder of Avianca flight 052 on July 19, 1989. This captures all of the communications among the flight crew and between them and air traffic controllers for the final 11 minutes of that flight (National Transportation Safety Board 1991). The numbers on the left refer to the time of transmission. All Spanish wording has been translated into English as noted. This flight was enroute from Bogota, Colombia via Medilin on the way to JFK Airport in New York. The transmission at 2133.12 hours was the end of communications between crew and air traffic controllers. At approximately 2134 hours, this flight, which had been in a holding pattern over JFK airport, ran out of fuel and crashed in a wooded residential area in Cove Neck, Long Island, New York. Of the 158 persons aboard, 73 died, including the flight crew. .

KEY:	CAM: cockpit area microphone RDO: air-ground communications Initial numbers: points on the flight reconstruction diagram Numbers in parentheses: time in hours, minutes, and seconds

39 (2123:28) CAM: The Avianca captain declares a missed approach by telling his crew, "Give me landing gear up." (Spanish)
45 (2123:43) CAM: The captain says, "We don't have fue..." (Spanish)
46 (2124:06) CAM: The Avianca captain speaks to the first officer, "Tell them we are in emergency."
(Spanish)
47 (2124:08) RDO: The first officer acknowledges an ATC altitude and heading to the JFK controller, adding "...and ah we'll try once again we're running out of fuel."
48 (2124:15) RDO: A controller says, "Okay."
51 (2124:22) CAM: Again the captain tells the first officer to "Advise him we are emergency." (Spanish)
52 (2124:26) CAM: The captain asks the first officer "Did you tell him?" (Spanish)
53 (2124:28) CAM: to which the first officer responds, "Yes, sir, I already advised him." (Spanish)
57 (2125:08) CAM: Again the captain says "Advise him we don't have fuel." (Spanish)
61 (2125:2S) CAM: He repeats "Did you already advise that we don't have fuel?" (Spanish)
62 (2125:29) CAM: The first officer answers, "Yes, sir, I already advise him hundred and eighty on the heading we are going to maintain 3000 feet and he's going to get us back." (Spanish)
64 (2126:35) RDO: A controller says, "I'm going to bring you about fifteen miles NE and then turn you back for the approach. Is that fine with you and your fuel?"
65 (2126:43) RDO: The Avianca first officer answers, "I guess so, thank you very much."
66 (2126:46) CAM: The captain asks the first officer, "What did he say?" (Spanish)
67 (2126:46) CAM: The first officer answers him, "Fifteen miles to get back to the localizer." (Spanish)
70 (2130:32) ·RDO: The controller instructs them, "Avianca 052 climb and maintain 3000."
71 (2130:36) RDO: The first officer responds, "Negative sir, we just running out of fuel we okay three thousand now okay."
76 (2132:49) RDO: Then the first officer calls the JFK controller, "Avianca 052 we just lost two-engines and we need priority please."
78 (2132:54) RDO: The controller responds, "Avianca 052 turn left heading two five zero..." and "Avianca 052 heavy you're one five miles from outer marker maintain two thousand until established on the localizer cleared for ILS two two left."
79 (2133:12) RDO: The first officer in turn responds, "Roger Avianca."

Figure 4. Selected dialogue between AVA 052 Flight Crew and Ground Control.

We can note the role of multiple functions of language in an excerpt from this dialogue taken at 2130:32-36. This excerpt, between an air traffic controller and the first officer of the aircraft, is shown in Figure 5 and is presented with the wording categorized as features of content, exchange, and organization in Figure 6.

(2130:32) "Avianca 052 climb and maintain 3000"
(2130:36) "Negative sir we just running out of fuel we okay three thousand now okay"

Figure 5. Dialogue excerpt between controller and first officer.

CONTENT:

	Participants	Avianca 052
		sir
		we
		fuel
	Actions	climb
		maintain
		running out of
	Circumstance	3000
		Negative
		Just
		Okay

EXCHANGE:
Information (to inform)
Asking:
Stating: Negative, sir we just running out of fuel
we okay three thousand now okay
Goods & services (to get action)
Requesting:
Commanding: Climb and maintain 3000
Relationship markers: sir, just (additional features of exchange)

ORGANIZATION:
Text type: (aviation radio communication features of identifying, commanding, responding)

Figure 6. Wording categorized according to whether content, exchange, or organization is being communicated.

The selected dialogue in Figure 5 is worthy of close scrutiny for it typifies what can be seen throughout the entire recorded dialogue within the cockpit and between cockpit and tower. Here we will only consider some of the highlights of this dialogue. In all of the recorded communications of this flight, the first officer speaks to the tower on behalf of his captain, for he was the better speaker of English. The language he uses gives evidence of his apparent deferential role, both to the captain and to the controller. In his dialogue with the captain, he does not indicate that he has any problem in communicating to the tower about their emergency as ordered by the captain. The captain repeatedly asks him about this; he responds twice with "Yes, sir, I already advised him (2124:28, 2125:29)."

The NTSB Aircraft Accident Report indicates without specific reference that it was likely that the Captain's limited English proficiency "prevented him from effectively monitoring the content of the transmission" made to the controllers by his first officer (1991: 58). The report also notes the failure of the flight crew to communicate effectively among themselves. The NTSB also concludes that "the first officer incorrectly assumed that his request for priority handling had been understood as a request for emergency handling" although the NTSB considered him to be sufficiently proficient in English to be understood by air traffic control personnel (1991: 74-75). The question of whether cultural factors were involved on board AVA 052 should have been, but was never asked.

Clearly cultural factors affected the first officer's communications with air traffic control and with the cockpit crew. The wording evidences what appears to be a deliberate and effective avoidance in his speech of any disagreement or demanding, willful expression of need with the air traffic controllers. He shows an inclination to make polite, submissive responses to the controllers with illogical combinations of concession and emergency, such as in his utterance, "and ah we'll try once again we're running out of fuel" (2124:08).

In a question and answer dialogue noteworthy for its limited and problematic use of Airspeak, a controller who is reacting to his fuel problem asks the first officer, "Is that fine with you and your fuel?" (2126:35), and gets the response, "I guess so, thank you very much" (2126:43). The first officer does repeatedly fail to say the Airspeak word "emergency" to get the landing priority that the flight so desperately needed to touch down before running out of fuel. The controllers did not pick up any indication of a problem until it was too late; they heard only civility. And throughout the dialogue, there is a pervasive, irregular use of Airspeak by both air traffic controllers and the first officer. Yet as part of this inappropriate use of Airspeak, the first officer shows a certain facility in speaking indirectly, non-aggressively, and politely despite the desperate urgency of the situation. This is culture at work. There are indications as well that the first officer may have been speaking in a similar manner to the captain in Spanish.

Other problems contributed to this disaster, such as the failure of the ground relay station to adequately record and report the flight's fuel levels, and inadequate traffic management by the FAA.

Language deficiency was cited by the NTSB accident investigation report as an important contributing factor to the accident. The role of culture figured prominently but was not discussed generally nor with regard to language deficiency. Latino cultures are considered to be collectivist and usually high-context in nature (Rogers/Steadfast 1999). A collectivist culture is one in which the collectivity's goals are valued over those of the individual. High-context cultures are those "in which the meanings of a communication message are found in the situation and in the relationships of the communicators." Nonverbal communication and subtleness in communication are emphasized. One avoids threatening the face of one's conversation partner. The investigation noted that the steward came to the cabin to ask about the status of the flight. The flight engineer, sitting behind the captain, pointed to the empty fuel gauge and made the gesture of cutting the throat to indicate the perilous situation.

Heimlich/Ashleigh (1998: 98-99) suggest both uncertainty avoidance (UA) and power distance (PD) were relevant in this disaster: "Those high in UA are likely to be more committed to a course of action once chosen and less flexible in considering other alternatives. The captain appears to have been committed to reaching New York (1998: 99)." Neither the fuel issue, nor the possibility of diverting to another airport was considered. Heimlich/Ashleigh (1998: 99) note the consequences of culture on the language use:

> The effects of PD are more striking. The flight engineer, although clearly aware of the crisis situation, only communicated the urgency of the situation non-verbally to the steward. Although the Ground Proximity Warning System (GPWS) sounded 15 times during the approach (indicating that the flight was below the glide path for the approach), none of the junior crewmembers expressed concerns. More striking was the behavior of the flight engineer when the captain executed the missed approach. Instead of communicating directly the criticality of the situation, he attempted to show the gravity of the situation

> indirectly by reading from the aircraft operating manual the instructions for executing a missed approach with minimal fuel aboard.

The interplay between culture and language emerges somewhat differently from two accidents of Korean Airlines. There is less cross-cultural sharing between cockpit and tower, but an amazing and startling degree of culture maintenance in the cockpit. Phillips describes the events of the accident in Guam in newspaper style (1998):

> The crew of Korean Air Flight 801 grew nervous as the Boeing 747 approached Agana, Guam, on a rainy night in August. Something didn't feel right. The plane, flown by autopilot, was descending steeply. The crew talked about the attitude, and someone said several times that the airport "is not in sight." But investigative sources said that neither the copilot nor the flight engineer spoke out boldly, as trained, to alert the captain or even to urge breaking off the landing. Alarms suddenly sounded in the cockpit. After an excruciating pause of several seconds, the captain finally cut off the autopilot and prepared to pull up. At almost that moment, the crew of another plane perhaps 50 miles away saw the clouds ahead glow bright red. The airplane struck Nimitz Hill, crashed and killed 228 passengers and crew.

The NTSB determined the probable cause of this accident to be (Aviation Safety Network 2000):

> the captain's failure to adequately brief and execute the non-precision approach and the first officer's and flight engineer's failure to effectively monitor and cross-check the captain's execution of the approach. Contributing to these failures were the captain's fatigue and Korean Air's inadequate flight crew training.

This is summarized in Figure 7:

1. What happened? - Captain conducting a non-precision approach at night time - Airplane struck Nimitz Hill, crashed - 228 (out of 254) fatalities 2. What was the probable cause? - Failure of captain to brief crew adequately and execute the approach - Failure of first officer and flight engineer to effectively monitor and cross-check the captain's execution of the approach - Failure of Minimum Safe Altitude Warning (MSAW) caused KAL 801 to descend below the safe altitude (captain unaware until alarms went off) - Fatigue of captain - Inadequate flight crew training (reliance on automated landing)

Figure 7. Crash of KAL 801 – Boeing 747 (Guam, August 6, 1997) (NTSB, 1997).

A similar disaster occurred in London, England two years later with KAL 8509, a cargo aircraft. It is briefly described in Figure 8.

1. What happened? - Airplane banked and crashed shortly after takeoff - 4 (out of 4) fatalities 2. What was the probable cause? - Failure of captain's Altitude Director Indicator (ADI) - Captain's excessive concern over Distance Measure Equipment (DME) - Captain's ignoring of alarm signaling banking until 12th signal - Failure of flight crew to inform or question captain

Figure 8. Crash of KAL 8509 – Boeing 747 (London, 12/22/99) (Dept. of Transport).

The implications of Korean cultural maintenance in the aviation context are daunting. Rhodes (1998) cites a study by members of the University of Texas psychology department pointing to national culture as a major factor in determining whether pilots trust and prefer automation. In their survey of 5,879 pilots from 12 countries, 100 percent of Korean pilots said they preferred the autopilot, and they noted that Korean aviators report greater shame than pilots of other nationalities when making a mistake in front of their crewmembers. Pedersen, a pioneer researcher in multicultural studies, refers to Duryea's contention that "conflict management in the Asian context has been described as face maintenance, face saving, face restoration, or face loss. Pedersen notes that "face can become more important than life itself as the evaluation of the self by the community is essential to identity (2000: 149).

This brings into focus the import of Phillips' report on KAL 801 above that "the crew talked about the altitude, and someone said several times that the airport 'is not in sight'" (A1). It is not that surprising that "investigative sources said that neither the copilot nor the flight engineer spoke out boldly, as trained, to alert the captain or even to urge breaking off the landing." Is it naïve to suggest that crew resource management training can overcome the cultural experiences of a lifetime? It may be argued that this is a case of cultural values and responses overcoming the need for explicit, aggressive communication. Saying that the airport was not in sight may well have been a mitigated, indirect suggestion or request from the crew to the captain of the kind described in Linde's study. This sort of communication was found in her investigation to be more likely to fail even in cultures without a strong face-saving orientation and even during non-emergency interactions. Such occurrences of cultural domination argue for evaluating cockpit voice recorder evidence in a more sophisticated manner to include the personal, interactive exchange function of language use.

What specific aspects of Korean culture affect air safety? The poor record amassed by Korean Airlines flying operations over the last thirty years and the leak of a KAL Safety Audit (Patterson 1998) give greater insight into the systemic problems that have plagued KAL. It is beyond the scope of this chapter to detail these findings but we may note that we are talking about a subculture within the Korean culture. These factors are listed in Figure 9. Much of the subculture of KAL grows out of a traditional Korean deference to command authority and the authoritarian behavior of many KAL pilots who are air force retirees. there was a rejection of managerial and 'good buddies" concepts of crew resource management (CRM) in favor of a "good boss" model (Last 1988).

1. How does culture generally affect air safety? - Cockpit culture as product of combination of man-machine interface and interpersonal relationships among crew members in flight situation - Mixed response of NTSB investigators to significance of culturally determined behavior - Minor role of cultural factors noted in reports - Cultural issues felt to smack of racism - Cultural factors controversial 2. What specific aspects of Korean culture affect air safety? - Authoritarian behavior of many KAL pilots who are air force retirees - Traditional Korean deference to command authority - Pilot surveys suggestion of problem areas - Koreans ranked highest for trust in automation - Koreans reported greater shame on making mistakes publicly - Rejection of managerial and 'good buddies" concepts of crew resource management (CRM) in favor of "good boss" model

Figure 9. Cultural factors in KAL airplane crashes.

But change has come. The bad publicity that had been generated led to the decision by KAL management to initiate a $200 million Safety Plan, beginning with engaging Boeing Flight Safety to retrain KAL pilots in basic cockpit/crew resource management (CRM) techniques. According to the KAL Annual Report (1999), this includes an "Error management Course" (EMC), an enhanced version of the previous CRM that was designed "to better accommodate Korean cultural idiosyncrasies." To remove the KAL cockpit culture generating conflicts between younger copilots and older, ex-military pilots, KAL has been hiring foreign pilots. These new pilots are also expected to impact the poor English standard language of current pilots, and Berlitz Language Center has been hired to train the Korean pilots. Finally, a profit motive appears to have been replaced by a safety-first attitude. Much of this turn-around continues, although a pilot's strike program in 2001 has led to setbacks: reduction of foreign hires, equalization of salaries, and equal union representation on the flight regulation committee.

6. Conclusion

Changing cultural values and the use of language that manifests them is not an easy task. Part of any change of cultural values must deal with language use since language influences thought and thought language. Language inculcates the broader perspective of a person's or society's customs and value systems. Cultural factors will remain controversial and problematic rather than an integral part of the knowledge base of the aviation industry because of the mixed response of NTSB investigators and other aviation professionals to the significance of culturally determined factors, behaviors and language use, and fear that that such issues smack of racism.

Training programs of any kind need to take into account the pervasive nature of this interplay between culture and language. Aviation professionals need to know how change can take place. Four recommendations are offered to acknowledge the significance of culture and language in international aviation:

1. Airspeak should be researched and studied as a special case of English for special purposes, documenting and contextually studying the ways in which it is not only idiosyncratic and predictable, but also problematic.
2. Non-native speakers of English ideally should be helped to build a foundation of general English proficiency before undertaking their prescribed specialist training in Airspeak.
3. Aviation English training programs for non-native speakers need to contextualize their language teaching and create awareness of and proficiency with the major functions of language expressed in the lexicogrammar, i.e., content, interpersonal exchange, and organization in aviation text types. Crew resource training for native and non-native speakers should include contextualized emergency scenarios that demand the use of social and organizing features of language use in addition to the informative.
4. Language teachers, flight instructors, and aviation administrators should develop a practical and applicable awareness of the disparity

between the prescribed and actual use of Airspeak. Language corpora are available for principled research toward this end. Such knowledge will inform efforts to standardize language use, develop national and international English proficiency testing schemes, and facilitate a creative, effective role for interactive language use in response to plans for modernization such as the FAA's Free Flight program.

References

Aviation Safety Network 2000. *Aircraft accident report. Korean Air Flight 801*. Available: <http://www.ntsb.gov/Publictn/2000/AAR0001.htm> [accessed: August 13, 2003].

Biber, Douglas 1995. *Dimensions of Register Variation.* Cambridge: Cambridge University Press.

Brown, P. / Levinson, S. 1978. Universals in language: politeness phenomena. In Goody, E.N. (ed.), *Questions and Politeness: Strategies in Social Interaction*. Cambridge: Cambridge University Press, 56-289.

Costley, John / Johnson, David / David Lawson 1989. A comparison of cockpit Communication B 737-B757". *5th International Symposium on Aviation Psychology*, Columbus, Ohio, U.S.A. April 17-20. Proceedings 1 [990-26176 10-53]. Columbus, Ohio: Ohio State University, 413-418.

Department of Transport 1999. *Korean Airlines Boeing 747-2B5F, HL-7451*. Available: <Air Accidents Investigation Branch (AAIB)> [accessed: August 13, 2003]

Halliday, M.A.K. 1994. A*n Introduction to Functional Grammar*. London: Arnold.

Helmreich, Robert L. / Merritt, Ashleigh 1998. *Culture at Work in Aviation and Medicine*. Aldershot: Ashgate.

Hofstede, G. 1980. *Culture's Consequences: International Differences in Work-Related Values*. Beverly Hills, CA: Sage.

Hofstede, G. 1991. *Cultures and Organizations: Software of the Mind.* Maidenhead, U.K.

Hofstede, Gert Jan / Pedersen, Paul / Geert Hofstede 2002. *Exploring Culture.* Yarmouth, Maine: Intercultural Press.

Korean Air Annual Report 1999. Available: <http://www.koreanair.com/img/pdf/annual99.pdf>, [accessed: August 15, 2003].

Last, Steve 2000. Eliminating 'cockpit-caused' accidents, error-tolerant crew procedures for the year 2000. Available: users2. ev1.net/~neilkrey/crmdevel/resources/paper/last/last.htm and <http://uers2.ev1.net/~neilkrey/crmdevel/resources/paper/last/last.htm> [accessed: July 25, 2003].

Linde, C. 1988. The quantitative study of communicative success. Politeness and accidents in aviation discourse. *Language in Society* 17/3, 375-399.

Mathews, Elizabeth 2003. Language proficiency requirements for flight crew and air traffic Controllers underscores need for language training programs. *ICAO Journal* 58/4, 7-9, 30-31.

Merritt, Ashleigh 2000. Culture in the cockpit: Do Hofstede's dimensions replicate? *Journal of Cross-Cultural Psychology* 31/3, 283-301.

National Transportation Safety Board 1991. *Aircraft accident report. Avianca, the airline of Colombia*, Boeing 707-321B, HK 2016, Fuel exhaustion, Coveneck, New York, January 25, 1990. NTSB/AAR-91/04.

National Transportation Safety Board 1997. *Aircraft accident report. Korean Air Flight 801.* Agana, Guam August 6, 1997 DCA97MA058. Available: <http://www.ntsb.gov/events/KAL801/default.htm> [accessed: August 10, 2003].

Patterson, Alex 1998, Sept. Korean Airlines audit findings. *Delta Airlines*, Available: <http://www.vision.net.au> [accessed July 24, 2003].

Pedersen, P. 2000. *A Handbook for Developing Multicultural Awareness* (3rd ed.). Alexandria, VA: American Counseling Association.

Phillips, Don 1998, March 18. Is culture a factor in air crash? Guam probe may raise touchy issue. *Washington Post*, A1.

Ragan, Peter 1997. Aviation English: An Introduction. *Journal of Aviation/Aerospace Education & Research* 7/2, Winter (E-RAU), 25-36.
Rhodes, T. 1998, March 19. Asian culture link in jet crashes. London: *The Times*, 19.
Rogers, E. M. / Steinfatt, T.M. *Intercultural Communication*. Prospect Heights: Waveland Press.
Sapir, E. 1964. *Culture, Language, and Personality: Selected Essays*. Edited by David G. Mandelbaum. Berkeley and Los Angeles, Calif.: University of California Press.
Sinclair, J. 2001. The deification of information. In Scott, Mike and Thompson, Geoff (eds), *Patterns of Text: In Honour of Michael Hoey*. Amsterdam/Philadelphia: John Benjamins.

CHRIS HANDY AND KHURSHID AHMAD

Indexer variability in specialist domains

1. Introduction

The problem of indexing images has existed for many years, but has been exacerbated as the number of digital images held in computer databases and on the worldwide web has risen. Experts in domains such as medicine, architecture, engineering, art criticism and crime scene investigation need to be able to locate appropriate images quickly, efficiently and consistently to perform their duties. This is also true of commercial picture libraries. Computers are generally considered an efficient means of generating, maintaining and searching indexes. However, while this is true for textual or numerical data, it is less true for image data and research continues to address the problems of storing and retrieving image data from collections of digital images. There have been two approaches proposed for indexing digital image collections: *Content Based Image Retrieval* (CBIR) and *Text Based Image Retrieval* (TBIR). Both approaches have benefits and drawbacks.

Despite the name, CBIR researchers are focussed on the perceptible features of an image, colour, shape, texture and brightness. There are two original assumptions here: First there is enough information in the perceptible features to extract 'content' details; and, second, given the features are perceptible, and by implication universal, one can find a mathematical description of the features and their distribution. CBIR uses mathematical algorithms to analyse the data stored in the image file itself. Digital images are composed of a series of pixels (picture elements), each having numerical information related to the location of the pixel within the image, the colour and the luminance. The algorithms operate on this information, extracting vector representations of *low-level* features (colour, shape and texture) within the image. These vectors then form the index. There are two methods of specifying a search query: *query by example* and *query by sketch,* (Del Bimbo 1999: 20). With query by example an image similar to the desired image(s) is used as an exemplar image. The system extracts vectors for this image in the same way as for the indexed images and then the extracted vector is compared with those in the database using a distance function for a similarity matching and results are returned to the user. Query by sketch uses a similar procedure, but instead of using a similar image to those desired, the user uses graphics tools embedded within the system to 'draw' the desired image and specify colour distributions and textures (Flickner/Sawhney/Niblack/Ashley/Huang/Dom/Gorkani/Hafner/Lee/Petkovic/Steele/Yanker 1995, Eakins/ Graham 1999). The advantages of such a system are that it is a completely automated, and as such relatively quick (in human terms), though it is computationally expensive. The disadvantage is that users wish to search for objects and concepts, not colours textures and shapes. This is the so-called "semantic gap" (Zhao/Grosky 2002), which impedes the formulation of meaningful queries by users. Formation of meaningful queries is also hampered because of the methods used for specifying the query (queries by example and sketch). Query by example relies on the user having an example query to hand and query by sketch is not intuitive to most users.

Whereas CBIR systems rely on algorithms allowing computers to index (and retrieve) images, TBIR systems rely entirely on human indexers for indices for images. Trained indexers, often specialising in one subject area, allocating pre-defined categories to images (in a similar way to librarians allocating a classification to library books, for example Dewey Decimal). This has the advantage that it allows users to specify a query using keyterms, a way familiar to them, as the terms are part of the user's natural language; it therefore allows searches at a more semantically meaningful level for objects and concepts. The two disadvantages of TBIR is that it is very time consuming for indexers to review a series of images and allocate categories to each image. Estimates range from 7 minutes per image (Getty Images, a commercial image bank) to more than 40 minutes per image (Rensselaer Polytechnic slide collection). Secondly there is little correlation between the indexer's allocated terms and the terms used by retrievers. In a study by Furnas/Landauer/Gomez/Dumais (1983), a less than 20% correlation was identified between an indexer and a retriever in the choice of keyterms. In addition indexers may not be consistent in their allocation of keyterms, i.e. there may be *indexer variation,* making retrieval difficult (Eakins/Graham 1999).

Automating text-based indexing would overcome the time overhead whilst retaining the desired semantic search capabilities. It may be possible to automate text-based indexing by processing extant text associated in some way with an image, so called *collateral text* (Srihari (1995). Keyterms can be extracted from these texts and used to form an index. Extant collateral texts may take the form of captions comprising just a few words, or longer explanatory texts. An image caption, where the text closely describes or annotates the image content may be considered to be *closely* collateral, while a more general text illustrated by an image, such as a magazine article or encyclopaedia entry, may be considered to be *broadly collateral* (Ahmad/Tariq/Vrusias/Handy 2003). Extant texts exist in many specialist domains such as Art, Medicine, Finance and Forensic Investigation. The authors of these texts, domain experts in a specialist domain, tend to use specialist language, that is to say a restricted subset of general language (Harris 1991, Halliday/Martin 1993). Specialist languages are constrained lexically, syntactically and semantically. They exhibit a paucity of verbs, adjectives and adverbs and consequently contain a higher proportion of nouns and noun phrases when compared with general language. Deerwester (1990: 392) states that: "There are usually many ways to express a given concept, so the literal terms in a user's query may not match those of a relevant document." However the adoption of standard nomenclature by specialists within their domain would suggest that this might not be the case between domain experts.

The use of a specialist language by domain experts also makes the processing of their texts to extract keyterms more computationally tractable when compared with processing general language texts. However, experts may differ in their opinions as to the relative importance of artefacts depicted in the image and therefore the indexes produced may suffer from the problem of indexer variation, further complicating retrieval .

A recent research project at the Universities of Surrey and Sheffield (SoCIS[1]) sought to assist crime scene examiners by automating the storage, indexing and retrieval of crime scene records. This work gave rise to our current investigation of indexer variation amongst crime scene examiners. For more information see: Ahmad/Vrusias/Tariq (2002), Ahmad et al. (2003), Vrusias/Tariq/Gillam (2003).

2. Human indexers learning to index

Our hypothesis is that: experts in a specialist domain will be more consistent in which subjects they choose to comment on (within the image) and in their choice of vocabulary and use of grammar than lay viewers. Indeed, Deerwester (1990) "assume[s] that there is some underlying latent semantic structure in the data" and it is our contention that training and experience will consolidate any such underlying latent semantic structure.

An experiment was designed to test this hypothesis. Experts become experts through training and experience and so the effect of training and experience on indexer variation is being examined. Trainee Scene of Crime Investigators were asked to provide captions/explanations for mock crime scene images on their first day of training (at a police scientific support training college). They were asked to provide further captions/explanations on completion of their initial eight week training course. The process will be repeated after they have completed their first six months working in the field. Expert Scene of Crime Investigators, with many years of experience, have also provided captions/explanations for the mock crime scene images.

The police have a duty of confidentiality to victims, witnesses, suspects and criminals, and for these reasons are most reluctant to supply actual crime scene data to researchers, even with personally

1 <http://www.computing.surrey.ac.uk/ai/socis/>.

identifying data removed. However, those who train scene of crime officers regularly produce mock crime scenes for training purposes. As the scenes are for training purposes, they are carefully designed to illustrate the most common aspects of scenes found at a variety of crimes and usually contain a range of objects likely to be of interest to crime scene examiners.

On the first day of their training the trainee crime scene investigators provided descriptions of one mock burglary crime scene (CS3) consisting of 21 images. Following their training they first provided descriptions of the 14 images of a different crime scene (CS1), a murder. A different crime scene was chosen to ensure that subjects had no preconceptions arising from their previous descriptions. They then described the images from CS3 again so that a comparison of the descriptions could be made. Expert crime scene investigators provided descriptions of all of the images from CS1 and CS3. There was a mixture of spoken and written descriptions; the spoken descriptions were transcribed into computer text files from tape, omitting repetitions, false starts, and verbal fillers. The written descriptions were copy typed into computer text files.

3. Analysis of results

Earlier work in subject-specific language (Harris 1991) and later work in lexicography, especially defining lemmas, and certain pragmatic uses of language, for example in telling time or dates (Ross 1993), suggests that local grammars (see Sinclair, this volume) are used in LSP, lexicography and pragmatics. A local grammar is described by Hunston/Sinclair (2000) as "[a] small (but not insignificant) sub-language". As it is claimed that a feature of languages is the use of local grammars (Barnbrook 2002: 73), we examined the captions manually to look for evidence of increased use of local grammars following training and by experts. For each subject the first clause of each caption was examined and a graphical representation of the clause structures used by each subject was produced. Thus a relatively simple graph would indicate a high occurrence of local grammars and a complicated graph would indicate little occurrence of local grammars. Figure 1 above is the graph for subject 3 derived from the captions provided on the first day of the training course.

Figure 1 shows the wide variety of clause forms employed by the trainee crime scene examiner. The examiner starts clauses in nine different ways and employs a total of eighteen different words/word forms in the twenty-one clauses examined.

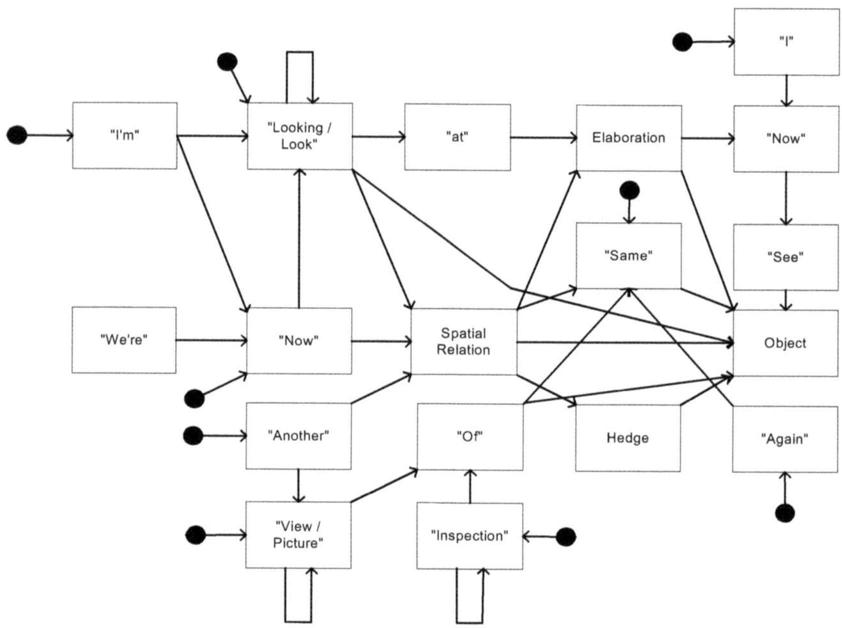

Figure 1. Graph representing the different clause structures used by subject 3 when providing captions to crime scene images at the commencement of training. Note that an arrow returning to the same box from which it originates indicates some modification of the term in the box, for example' close up view' is a modification of 'view'. Black circles represent start points.

Contrast this with Figure 2, which is the graph produced from the same subject's descriptions produced at the end of his training. This shows two ways of starting clauses and six different words/word forms.

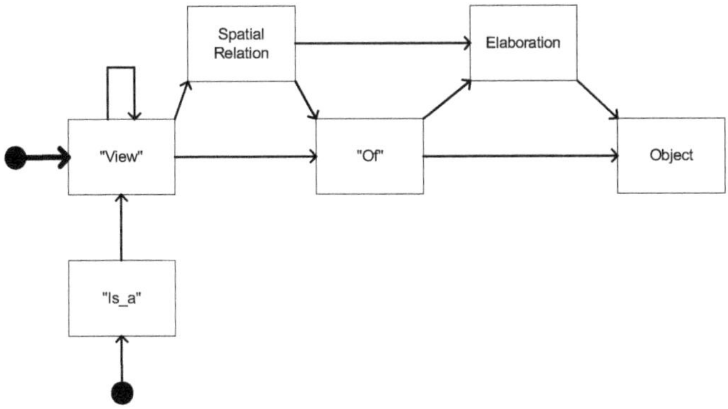

Figure 2. Graph representing the grammatical structures used by subject 3 when providing captions to crime scene images following training. Note that the heavy lines indicate the commonest construct.

When we consider Figure 3, the expert's graph, we see that there is only one way of starting the clause and four word/word formations. This would seem to indicate that, prior to training, the subjects employ little, or no use of patterned clauses governed by a local grammar. Following training there is a greater reliance on local grammars, and the use of local grammars is further refined with experience.

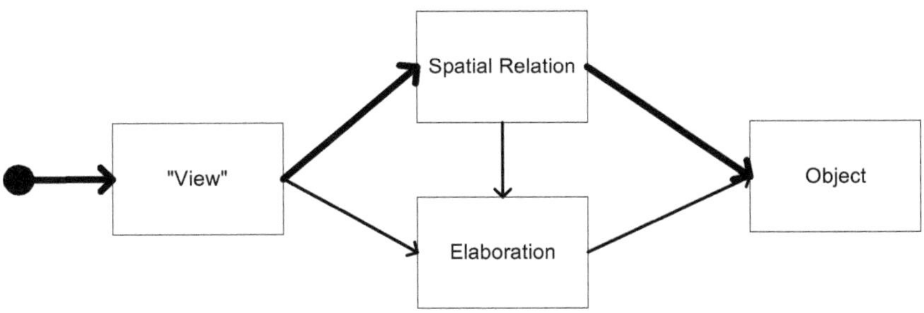

Figure 3: Graph representing the grammatical structures used by an expert. Note simplicity of graph when compared to those of the trainee.

It would appear that experts often include the word *view* as a pivotal word in their local grammar. The word (or its derivatives, *viewed*, *viewing*) appears in 83% of all descriptions provided by the experts. This is compared with 22% for trainees at the start of training and 44% for trainees at the end of training. Examples of the use of the word by experts are:

(1) "View of entrance to main office"
"Entirety view front door of Locard House"
"Further view in living room"
"Close up view of hand bag"

This may reflect the experienced crime scene investigator's desire to provide some locative information in his or her descriptions so that other investigators, lawyers, judges, magistrates or jurors are able to mentally relate the positioning of important pieces of evidence in the crime scene, aiding their interpretation of events. Further evidence supporting this hypothesis comes from the high number of comments from experts regarding the type or positioning of the shot. Examples of these comments include:

"square on"	*"opposite view"*
"scene setting"	*"corner view"*
"side view"	*"close up"*
"interior view"	*"as viewed from"*

Table 1. Examples of comments made by experts regarding the type or positioning of the shot.

It was noted that novices were much more verbose than experts, who were more concise in their descriptions. Calculating the average number of words used by novices at the start of training, novices at the end of training and experts to describe CS3, we can see that the experts use only a quarter of the words that novices use at the start of their training.

Indexer	Average words	Percentage
Novices – Start of Training	1200	100
Novices – End of Training	789	66
Experts	293	24

Table 2. Comparison of the average number of words used by each indexer group to describe all of the images in scene CS3.

Following training the novices showed a 34% decrease in the number of words used to describe the images. Examining the descriptions shows that the novices attempt to provide a complete description of everything in the image whilst the experts are more focussed – they only comment on the items they consider to be of importance or relevant. Table 3 shows an example of this.

Indexer	Description	Words
Novice – Start of Training	I now see the bedroom or one of the bedrooms it looks like a child's bedroom single bed and a cot to the right of the bed there's a bedside cabinet four drawers the bottom two drawers are completely open with some items hanging out the third drawer up is slightly open with an item hanging out and on top of that there's some different toys and ornaments the bed doesn't look like it's been disturbed it's just cuddly toys over the pillow cot the cot is open and the doors the side door is down with a cuddly toy in it and a bike propped up against the wall or a scooter looks like an old scooter propped up against the wall.	124
Novice – End of Training	Now a view of the picture from child's bedroom, single bed, with a cot, to the right of the bed a bedside cabinet with two drawers open a four drawer cabinet a bedside cabinet, the bottom two are open, the third one up is slightly open with some clothing hanging out.	51
Expert	View of ground floor bedroom towards bed and cot (as viewed from door).	13

Table 3. Comparison of the descriptions given for one image (CS3, Image 16) by the different indexer groups.

4. Further work

It appears that the experts consistently use patterned clauses governed by local grammar. The trainees, contrariwise, appear not to use a local grammar as is evidenced by the experts. It is intended to follow up the initial work by conducting similar experiments with the newly trained crime scene examiners after they have been working in the field for around six months to assess the effect of a period of practical experience. Further analysis needs to be undertaken extending the identification of local grammars to more than one clause per description. A detailed comparison of objects described by each subject needs to be completed to ensure that the initial indications provided by the reduction in the number of words employed by experienced subjects is indeed indicative of a more focussed approach. This reduction in word usage may also indicate that experienced subjects use less elaboration and/or conjecture and this should be examined. Lastly an evaluation of the structure of phrases conveying spatial relationships and positional information would, we believe, prove helpful.

5. Afterword

Initial results indicate that there may be some validity to the hypothesis that experts in a specialist domain will be more consistent in their choice of subjects to comment on (within the image) and in their choice of vocabulary and use of grammar than lay viewers. Following training there appears to be a more regular and consistent use of local grammars.

The results also show that the acquisition of experience allows crime scene examiners to refine their use of local grammars. Experienced examiners also seem to place more emphasis on positional information, often using the word *view* as a pivotal word denoting the start of the information. They also are more focussed, only commenting on the essential, or important, items in the image with the result that they are less verbose than novices. The fact that such changes are noticeable after a short training period would indicate that the training is effective and successful.

References

Ahmad, K. / Tariq, M. / Vrusias, B. / Handy, C. 2003. Corpus-Based Thesaurus Construction for Image Retrieval in Specialist Domains. In Sebastiani, Fabrizio (ed.) *Proc. of the 25th European Conference on Information Retrieval Research (ECIR-03), Lecture Notes in Computer Science 2633*, 502-510. Berlin: Springer Verlag.

Ahmad, K. / Vrusias, B. / Tariq M. 2002. Co-operative neural networks and 'integrated' classification. *Proceedings of International Joint Conference on Neural Networks* (IJCNN02). Piscataway, New Jersey: IEEE, 1546-1551.

Barnbrook, G 2002. *Defining Language: A local grammar of definition sentences.* Amsterdam/Philadelphia: John Benjamins.

Deerwester, Scott / Dumais, Susan T. / Furnas, George W. / Landauer, Thomas K. / Harshman, Richard 1990. Indexing by Latent Semantic Analysis. *Journal of the American Society of Information Science* 41/6, 391-407.

Del Bimbo, A. 1999. *Visual Information Retrieval.* San Francisco, USA: Morgan Kaufmann..

Eakins, J.P. 1996. Automatic image content retrieval – are we getting anywhere? *Proceedings of Third International Conference on Electronic Library and Visual Information Research (ELVIRA3)*, De Montfort University, Milton Keynes, 123-135.

Eakins, J.P. 1998. Techniques for Image Retrieval. *Library and Information Briefings 85*, British Library and South Bank University, London, October 1998.

Eakins, J.P. / Graham, M.E. 1999. *Content-based Image Retrieval: A Report to the JISC Technology Applications Programme*. Image Data Research Institute Newcastle, Northumbria, Available: <http://www.unn.ac.uk/iidr/report.html>, [accessed: January 15th, 2003].

Flickner, M. / Sawhney, H. / Niblack, W. / Ashley, J. / Huang, Q. / Dom, B. / Gorkani, M. / Hafner, J. / Lee, D. / Petkovic, D. / Steele, D. / Yanker, P.1995. Query by image content the QBIC system. *IEEE Computer* 28/9, 23-31.

Furnas, G.W. / Landauer, T.K. / Gomez, L.M. / Dumais, S.T., 1983. Statistical semantics: Analysis of the potential performance of key-word information systems. *Bell System Technical Journal,* 62/6, 1753-1806.

Gross, M., 1993. Local Grammars and their Representation by Finite Automata. In Hoey, M. (ed.) *Data, Description, Discourse, Papers on the English Language in honour of John McH Sinclair.* London: Harper Collins, 26-38.

Halliday M.A.K. / Martin J.R. 1993. *Writing Science: Literacy and Discursive Power.* London and Washington D.C.: The Falmer Press.

Harris, Z.S. 1991. *A Theory of Language and Information.* Oxford: Clarendon Press.

Hunston, S. / Sinclair, J.M. 2000. A local Grammar of Evaluation. In Hunston, S. / Thompson, G. (eds) *Evaluation in Text: Authorial Stance and the Construction of Discourse*. Oxford University Press: Oxford, 74-10.

Srihari, R.K. 1995. Use of Collateral Text in Understanding Photos. *Artificial Intelligence Review, Special Issue on Integrating Language and Vision* 8, 409-430. Kluwer Academic Publishers, Netherlands.

Vrusias, B. / Tariq, M. / Gillam, L. 2003. Scene of Crime Information System: Playing at St. Andrews. *Proceedings of the Cross Language Evaluation Forum (CLEF 2003) Workshop*, Amsterdam.

Zhao, Rong / Grosky, William I. 2002. Narrowing the Semantic Gap – Improved Text-Based Web Document Retrieval Using Visual Features. *IEEE Transactions On Multimedia* 4/2, June 2002.

ØIVIN ANDERSEN

Deverbal nouns as hybrids: some textual aspects

1. Introduction

Nominalization has for several decades been a central area of research in general linguistics. The early works of Lees (1960) and Vendler (1967, 1968) had a great influence on later treatments such as Chomsky's analyses in the seventies (Chomsky 1970). The main discussion was whether nominalization was primarily a syntactic or a lexical phenomenon.

Jane Grimshaw's MIT dissertation concentrated on deverbal nominalizations and claimed that certain types of deverbal nouns had argument structure and that the presence of argument structure in nouns correlated with some basic aspectual characteristics of the denotation of these nouns (Grimshaw 1990).

Grimshaw used English data only, but these properties turned out to be relevant for other languages as well, and the semantic and syntactic structure of basic deverbal nouns have been investigated for several languages of the world. However, the pragmatic and text linguistic aspects of the phenomenon have been studied to a much lesser degree.

As far as studies in the field of terminology and LSP are concerned, surprisingly few extensive works on the subject are available. This is rather surprising considering the fact that most introductory text books on terminology and LSP focus on the fact that nominalization is one of the most salient features of LSP texts of all sorts.

Michael Halliday's works constitute an exception to this generalization. His treatment of the role of nominalizations in the development of English scientific writing from Newton and Priestly to the present day is both stimulating and interesting reading (Halliday/Martin 1993).

Against this background I found the need to have a closer look at this type of word formation in Norwegian technical writing. I have gathered my data from one of the system manuals from the Gullfaks A-platform system "Dampsystemet" (Steam Generation and Distribution System), an instruction manual for Norwegian technical personnel at the platform. The dominant text type in the manual is instruction with some passages of pure description. There are no explanatory or expository parts.

2. Deverbal nouns

But first: What is a deverbal noun? A deverbal noun is a noun which is derived from or corresponds to a verb, as in *aktivering,* activation (from *aktivere*, 'to activate'), *sjekk*, 'check' (from *sjekke*, 'to check'). The manual contained 154 deverbal nouns counted as types (the number counted as tokens is considerably higher).

There are several different morphological classes of deverbal nominal suffixes. A number of studies have shown that the different classes tend to behave differently on all levels of description and it is important to distinguish between them.

3. Morphological classes in Norwegian

The most productive of the Norwegian deverbal morphological classes is *-ing*. A list showing the number of occurrences with this suffix and the others in the manual is given in Table 1 where the *-ing* suffix marks more than 50% of the deverbal nouns.

Morphological type	sum
-(n)ing	88
[root]	31
-sjon	16
-asjc	5
Infinitive	4
-anse	2
-sel	2
-skap	1
-t	1
-else	4
Total	154

Table 1. Occurrences of morphological types.

All the nominal types have different types of compound structure. Some forms are simple nouns, like *styring* ('control'), *drenering* ('drain') and *arbeid* ('work'). Others are compound nouns where the first element in the compound may correspond to a sentence constituent function of the corresponding verb, like the direct object in *slangetilkopling* ('hose connection') (*kople slange til noe* ('connect a hose to something'), an adverbial in *kraftforsyning* ('power supply') (*forsyne med kraft,* 'supply with power') or a predicative element as in *rengjøring* ('back washing') (*gjøre noe rent*, literally 'to make something clean'). These compound words may also occur as phrases where the first element occurs in postnominal position as a prepositional modifier. It is generally known that sentence functions like the subject and the direct object are marked in a different manner than adverbial functions (called adjuncts) in the nominalization process. The grammatical subject is usually marked by a possessive construction and the direct object is marked by the preposition *av* ('of'), as in:

(1) Arbeiderens overvåking av dampforsyningen
('The workers' surveillance of the steam production').

However, the possessive subject is hardly ever realised in these kinds of technical texts.

3.1 -ing *nominals*

The *-ing* nominals are the most productive morphological type in Norwegian. A list of some of the *-ing* words are given in List 1.

List 1. *-ing* nominals
Innledning ('introduction'), distribuering ('distribution'), rengjøring ('back wash'), plassering ('location'), fordeling ('distribution'), avblåsing ('blow down'), vannbehandling ('water treatment'), forutsetning ('precondition'), rutinesjekking ('routine checking'), styring ('control', 'stabbing'), overvåking ('monitoring'), aktivering, ('activation'), avstenging ('shut down'), levering ('delivery', 'supply'), produksjonsboring ('production drilling'), regulering ('regulation'), gjennomføring ('completion'), utløsning ('activation'), tilsetting ('addition'), kraftforsyning ('power supply'), isolering ('isolation'), slangetilkopling ('hose connection'), utblåsingssikring ('blow out prevention', 'blow out preventor'), sikring ('securing', 'fuse'), nødavstenging ('emergency shut down'), utprøving ('commissioning'), tilbakemelding ('feed back'), feilsøking ('trouble shooting'), feilretting ('fault removal'), alarmregistrering ('alarm registration'), handling ('action'), opplæring ('training'), erfaring ('experience'), oppbygging ('construction'), skadevirkning ('harmful effect'), langtidsvirkning ('long term effect'), påvirkning ('impact'), drenering ('drain'), trykkavlastning ('pressure release'), åpning ('opening', 'port').

The distribution of morphological types on phrase level for the direct object and word level are given in Table 2. As we can see, transitive derivation with phrase marked derived direct object (the type *tilkopling av slange*, 'connection of hose') is very common with *-ing* nominals.

Morphological type	Phrase with derived direct object	Word		sum
		Compound	single	
-(n)ing	39	20	29	88
[root]	6	16	9	31
-sjon	1	4	11	16
-asje	0	3	2	5
infinitive	1	2	1	4
-anse	0	2	0	2
-sel	0	0	2	2
-skap	0	0	1	1
-t	0	1	0	1
-else	3	1	0	4

Table 2. Distribution of morphological types on the phrase level (with derived direct object) and word level.

Phrase with derived object: *behandling av vann* ('treatment of water')
Compound: *vannbehandling* ('water treatment')
Single word: *behandling* ('treatment')

3.2 Root nominals

Another common type of derivation is the root nominalization where the corresponding nominal is formed with zero derivation from the stem (also called conversion). A list of these is given in list 2:

List 2 Root nominals
Start ('start'), stopp ('stop'), rengjøringsarbeid ('back wash work'), sjekk ('check'), kaldstart ('cold start'), anleggssjekk ('field check'), feltpanelsjekk ('field panel check'), ventilsjekk ('valve check'), uttak ('outlet'), kraftforbruk ('power consumption'), avvik ('deviation'), leveringstrykk ('discharge pressure'), driftsstans ('shut down'), prosessvedlikehold ('process maintenance'), utdrag ('abstract'), krav ('demand'), vedlikehold ('maintenance')

In addition there were seven other morphological types, but none of these are productive suffixes in Norwegian. A survey is given in list 3.

List 3 Low productive types
-sjon, as in dampproduksjon ('steam production'), aksjon ('action'), operasjon ('operation'), konstruksjon ('construction'), modifikasjon ('modification'), korrosjon ('corrosion'), isolasjon ('isolation').
-asje, as in lekkasje ('leak'), pakningslekkasje ('gasket leak').
-else, as in arbeidstillatelse ('work permit'), utstedelse ('issue'), overholdelse, forståelse ('comprehension', 'understanding')
infinitive form: skade ('damage') (from å skade, 'to damage'), miljøskade ('environmental damage')
-anse, as in vannleveranse ('water supply'), dampleveranse ('steam supply')
-skap, as in kjennskap ('knowledge')
-t, as in pumpedrift ('pump running').

4. Prototypical properties of nouns and verbs

Deverbal nouns are hybrid forms between the categories noun and verb. This means more specifically that they share some characteristics typical of verbs and some characteristics typical of nouns. According to Hopper/Thompson (1985) a set of characteristics for the two major parts of speech can be given. Those relevant for our purposes are listed in List 4.

List 4: Prototypical properties of nouns and verbs:

Nouns	**Verbs**
(Specific/anaphoric) reference,	description/no reference
Entities/objects	events
Countability	non-countability
+Pluralization	- pluralization
+ Determiner	- determiner
Static meaning	dynamic meaning
Given/old information	new information
No argument structure	argument structure
Topic	Comment

Typical nouns have specific reference as opposed to typical verbs which do not refer at all. Typical nouns denote countable entities or objects and are easily pluralized as opposed to verbs. Because nouns have entity reference, they typically occur with determiners, again in contrast to verbs. Nouns typically have a static denotation as opposed to verbs, which have dynamic meaning. On the level of information structure nouns tend to occur as sentence topics (or themes) with given or old information, whereas verbs with their associated participants tend to occur as sentence comments (or rhemes).

5. Deverbal nouns as non-prototypical nouns

Deverbal nouns do have reference, but they tend to have generic reference more often than specific reference. When expressing generic reference they often lack determiners, plural markers and have argument structure, especially a derived direct object marked by the preposition *av* ('of'). With generic reference they tend to express a dynamic meaning of process.

The ability to refer is a typical nominal property. The most typical way of reference for nominals in texts is the anaphoric reference where an antecedent is involved. This characteristic is also shared by deverbal nouns:

(2) Ferskvann tilføres matevannstanken gjennom en tilbakeslagsventil 55-152WP. Vannets innløpstrykk kan avleses på trykkindikator 55-PIO013. Vanntilførselen blir regulert av en flottørventil, [...](Chapter 2.2.1)
(Desalinated water is supplied to the water break tank via a check valve, 55-152 WD. The inlet water pressure is indicated on a pressure indicator, 55-PIO013. The water supply is controlled by a mechanical level control valve [...]).

The deverbal noun *vanntilførselen* ('the water supply') refers anaphorically to the first sentence *Ferskvann tilføres matevannstanken* which is the antecedent expression.

Another type of reference is exophoric reference where the sender goes outside the text to refer to events or entities which are assumed to be familiar to the receiver:

(3) Lav-lavt nivå i tanken blir overvåket via nivåbryteren 55-LSLL017, som er innstilt på 816 mm. [...] Fellesalarm 55-UA001 blir utløst på BT i SKR, og alarm 55-LALL017 blir utløst på feltpanalet i M23. Aktivering av nivåbryter 55-LSLL017 vil også stoppe driftsmatepumpen (chapter 2.2.1).
(Level switch low low, 55-LSLL017, trips on low water levels, [...].*Activation of level switch 55-LSLL017* will ...)

The deverbal noun *aktivering av nivåbryter* ('activation of level switch') has not been introduced into the text earlier and the sender seems to imply that procedures for activation of level switch 55-LSLL017 are either taken for granted or considered to be irrelevant in the current context. Here the first alternative seems to be the most likely one.

A third type of reference is the generic reference. This is a rather special and untypical type of reference for nouns. Generic reference with typical nominals can be used in classificatory use with the definite articles in Norwegian (examples 4 and 7), and with the indefinite article in the singular (example 6) and in the indefinite plural (example 5), but the use of a naked form of the noun with generic reference is not so much used with ordinary nouns in Norwegian, especially in classificatory use, and seems to be ungrammatical in English (example 8):

(4) Hest-**en** er et pattedyr. -definite article singular
The horse is a mammal.

(5) Hest-er er pattedyr.-indefinite article plural
Horses are mammals.

(6) En hest er et pattedyr.-indefinite article singular
A horse is a mammal.

(7) Hest-ene er pattedyr. -definite article plural
The horses are mammals.

(8) ?Hest-() er pattedyr.
*Horse is a mammal

However, generic reference with a naked deverbal noun as head is a very common type of reference with deverbal nouns as in example 9:

(9) Generic reference:
Dampen blir brukt til *rengjøring av prosessbeholdere* og forskjellige andre rengjøringsarbeider på plattformen. (chapter 2.1.)
(The steam is used for *steam cleaning / purging of process vessels* and for general cleaning purposes on the platform.)

Here the reference is to *rengjøring* ('cleaning', 'purging') in general and no specific instance of activity is implied.

Table 3 shows that generic reference is the dominant one in this text.

Morphological type	Generic Non-specific	Anaphoric Specific inside text	Exophoric specific/non-specific outside text
-(n)ing	74	8	44
[root]	24	4	6
-sjon	5	9	6
-asje	2	2	2

Table 3. Distribution according to reference type.

Here the exophoric non-specific type in column 4 is a subtype of the generic type in column 2. This explains why the figures do not add up with the sums in Table 2.

Table 4 shows clearly that this type of generic reference with a naked noun is the dominant type in this text, at least with the two most productive morphological forms.

Morphological type	Naked form	Indefinite article singular	Indefinite form plural	Definite article singular	Definite article plural	Sum
-(n)ing	80	1	2	3	2	88
[root]	30	0	0	1	0	31
-sjon	7	0	3	5	1	16
-anse	0	0	0	2	0	2
-sel	2	0	0	0	0	2
-skap	1	0	0	0	0	1
-t	1	0	0	0	0	1
-else	4	0	1	0	0	4

Table 4. Form of deverbal noun (definite, indefinite article, singular, plural).

6. Logical polysemy

Most deverbal nouns are event referring, but some have a dynamic, process meaning of an event and others refer to the result of the event and have a static, result meaning. Many deverbal nouns can have both these meanings. This is a phenomenon called logical polysemy (Pustejowsky 1998: 31ff). Logical polysemy is a type of polysemy which is not idiosyncratically isolated to specific lexemes or terms in a language but which comprises large classes of lexemes. One of the most central and widespread types of logical polysemy concerns the distinction between process and result meanings of event referring nouns. This polysemy is closely related to deverbal nouns but can also occur with other types of nouns. In example 10 we have process meaning and in 11 we have result meaning:

(10) Process:
Standardprosedyre for *isolering* av reguleringsventiler (Dampsystemet chapter 4.2.4)
(Standard control valve *isolation*.)
isolering ('isolation') refers to an unspecified, generic, complex process event.

(11) Result:
Isoleringen i veggene var brennbart
(*The isolation* in the walls was combustible.)
isoleringen refers to the result of the process of isolation, in this case the material used in the process.

In other cases the logical polysemy takes the form of an aspectual difference where the process meaning has a durative or imperfect meaning, as with the root nominal in 12, in contrast to the perfective instantiating meaning of the result meaning of the same nominal in 13:

(12) Process:
Sjekk av manuelle ventiler må stemme overens med sjekklisten.
(Check of manual valves must agree with the check list.)

(13) Result:
Hvis ventilen ikke åpner seg må *sjekken* tas på nytt.
(If the valve does not open the check must be performed once more.)

This is connected to the instantiating meaning of 13 as opposed to the generic meaning of 12. In 13 an important part of the meaning of the nominal is the instantiation of the general event of checking. A closely connected and important difference between 12 and 13 is that pluralization is possible in 13, but not in 12.

As we can see, there are various subtypes of process and result polysemy, but they seem to be variations of the same type of polysemy.

In the Steam Generation and Distribution System manual this polysemy type was very widespread, especially with the two most productive morphological types *-ing* and root nominals, as Table 5 shows. 69 of 88 *-ing* nominals and 29 of the 31 root nominals had logical polysemy.

Morphological type	Yes	No
-(n)ing	69	19
[root]	29	2
-sjon	11	5
-asje	5	0
Infinitive	0	4
-anse	2	0
-sel	2	0
-skap	0	1
-t	0	1
-else	2	2

Table 5. Presence of logical polysemy.

7. Argument structure

The presence of argument structure can best be detected by looking for the realization of the derived direct object at the phrase level, where it is overtly marked by the preposition av ('of'). The phrase type is that of: tilkopling av slange ('connection of hose'), where slange is the derived direct object of tilkopling.

Table 2 showed that many *-ing* nominalizations occurred on phrase level with unpacked derived direct objects. Some of the other forms also had this phrase structure. As list 4 illustrates this is a typical verbal characteristic. Table 6 further illustrates that this verbal characteristic matches with another verbal characteristic: the dynamic, process meaning. All the *-ing* nominalizations in unpacked phrase form with *av*-marked direct objects had dynamic process meaning and only one of the root-nouns had a result meaning. This is a fairly strong indication that presence of argument structure and dynamic meaning tend to merge in showing the verbal side of deverbal nouns.

Morphological type	Process	Result
-(n)ing	34	0
[root]	4	1
-sjon	1	0
-asje	0	0
Infinitive	0	0
-anse	0	0
-sel	0	0
-skap	0	0
-t	0	0
-else	1	2

Table 6. Distribution of process-result polysemy in deverbal nouns with derived direct objects marked by the preposition *av* ('of').

Table 7 shows, further, that those deverbal nouns without logical polysemy (for example those that are unambiguous) tended to have a process meaning with *-ing* nouns (the most productive type) and result meaning with root nouns. This should indicate that deverbal *-ing* nominals are more verbal than deverbal root-nominals in this technical Norwegian text.

Morphological type	process	result	place
-(n)ing	18	1	0
[root]	0	2	0
-sjon	2	3	0
-asje	0	0	0
Infinitive	0	0	0
-anse	0	0	0
-sel	0	0	0
-skap	0	1	0
-t	1	0	0
-else	0	2	0

Table 7. Sense type with absence of logical polysemy.

8. Information structure

From the point of view of information structure information in text sentences can be divided into topic (theme) and comment (rheme) positions. Topic position is the first constituent of the sentence and normally contains the grammatical subject of the sentence, which is typically the point of departure, i.e. what is talked about. The comment position is regarded as being the rest of the sentence, to put it simply. In my data I have classified the deverbal noun types according to this distribution. As is well known, topic vs comment marking typically corresponds to given vs new information.

But this distribution can sometimes be overridden for various information structure purposes. The terms 'given' and 'old' information are often used synonymously in the text-linguistic literature, but for my purposes I feel a need to make a distinction between the two:

Given information is a type of information which is previously introduced in the co-text, usually in comment form. This information is picked up again later and backgrounded by the sender, usually in topic position. Old information, on the other hand, is a type of information that the sender assumes to be known to the receiver without prior introduction. This information may be classified as what Clark (1994) calls common ground knowledge.

Both given and old information are typically linked to reference types of typical nominal expressions. Given information is associated with anaphoric reference where the earlier introduced information is the antecedent (as in example 2 above). Old information is associated with exophoric reference, where the nominal expression refers to a piece of information which is outside the text in the assumed common ground knowledge space of the sender and the receiver (as in example 3 above).

Table 8 illustrates the distribution of the morphological types according to information structure. As we can see the topic and given/old information go together as expected (see also the final item on list 4, where topic position is the typical position of ordinary nouns).

But deverbal nouns can also occur as comments with new information or even with given or old information. This seems to be typical especially of instruction texts. In the manual the instruction passages had almost exclusively the form of imperative clauses. Imperative clauses do not have the regular topic-comment structure and are normally topicless constructions. So the most likely interpretation of the non-typical occurrence of deverbal nouns in comment position is the result of the instruction text type rather than the result of the non-typical character of the deverbal nouns.

Morphologi-cal type	Topic and given information	Topic and old information	Comment and new information	Comment and given / old information	Topic and new nformation
-(n)ing	15	14	25	9	0
[root]	12	5	7	1	0
-sjon	5	1	8	1	0
-asje	1	0	3	1	0
infinitive	0	0	4	0	0
-anse	0	2	0	0	0
-sel	0	1	0	1	0
-skap	0	1	0	1	0
-t	0	1	0	0	0
-else	1	0	3	0	0

Table 8. Distribution according to information structure.

9. Conclusions

This survey shows that deverbal nouns share characteristics of both nouns and verbs. The proximity to the two major parts of speech can be defined in terms of typical features of the two word classes. This has previously been demonstrated on the syntactic level in a number of morphosyntactically-oriented studies in linguistics, but this investigation shows that this is also the case on the textual, pragmatic level.

The study shows that the most productive morphological types are the ones which are closest to the verb, and the relative distance is also revealed by the logical process-result polysemy of the deverbal nouns. The process nominals are closer to the verb than the result nominals, as their semantics would indicate.

The process *-ing* nominals also exhibit argument structure revealed in the derived direct object construction on the phrase level with the argument transfer preposition *av* ('of'). The lack of determiners and modifiers with the nominals in the text and the frequent use of generic reference are further evidence that these nouns are non-typical nouns. These nouns are also quite common as exophoric reference and are thus important as indicators of the professional character of these texts.

This preliminary pilot investigation also shows, I think, that there is a need to study deverbal nominalizations further in LSP. My study has not touched the difficult question of terminology. As Dressler (1989) has pointed out, there are several questions of terminology to be solved.

References

Chomsky, N. 1970. Remarks on Nominalization. In Jacobs, R. A. / Rosenbaum, P.S. (eds) *Readings in English Transformational Grammar*. Waltham, Mass: Ginn and Co..

Clark, H. H. 1994. Discourse in Production. In Morton A. Gernsbacher (ed.) *Handbook of Psycholinguistics*. San Diego: Academic Press, 985-1021

Dressler, W. 1989. Funktion und Textzusammenhang in der Wissenschaftssprache. In Dressler, W. / R. Wodak (eds) *Fachsprache und Kommunikation: Experten im sprachlichen Umgang mit Laien*. Wien: Bundesverlag.

Grimshaw, J. 1990. *Argument structure*. Linguistic Inquiry Monograph 18. Massachusetts Institute of Technology.

Halliday, M.A.K. / Martin, J.R. 1993. *Writing Science: Literacy and Discursive Power*. London: The Falmer Press..

Lees, R.B. 1960. *The Grammar of English Nominalizations*. The Hague: Mouton.

Pustejovsky, J. 1998. *The Generative Lexicon*. Cambridge, Mass.: The MIT Press.

Vendler, Z. 1967. *Linguistics in Philosophy*. Ithaca: Cornell University Press.

Vendler, Z. 1968. *Adjectives and Nominalizations*. The Hague: Mouton.

Part Two
Constructing LSP Texts: Citation Patterns

One of the key ingredients of an LSP text is the manner in which other LSP texts are cited in the text. The citations normally include name(s) of the cited author(s) in the main text, occasionally the title of the cited article or book, and invariably there is a list of references that contains the bibliographic details of the citations. Learning to cite is a key skill in constructing LSP texts and different specialist domains have different styles of citation, each of the styles reflecting the legacy of the particular specialism. More important perhaps is the social aspect of citation: when we cite somebody, we are either accepting or rejecting their authority in the specialism, we are either finding or rejecting hypotheses and evidence; in short the social edifice, particularly the informal aspects of the edifice, are reflected in the citation patterns. Much of the objectivity of specialist disciplines, the claim that a specialism is a specialism almost independent of the personalities and institutions involved, is reflected in the conventionalised manner in which specialists cite their peers. In science and engineering, it is often surnames, for arts and aesthetics full names, and even first names. It seems that no matter what the degree of formality in citation, the process of citation into which researchers are 'socialised', is part of the discipline required for systematic observation, evaluation, representation and analysis – science (Wissenschaft) itself. As an indication of its crucial role, breaking the rather complex and variable conventions of citation has serious consequences within academic communities, often in the form of formalised sanctions against novice students and expert academics alike.

In the first chapter of Part 2, Robert Wilkinson describes citation behaviour in psychology and argues that in this particular specialism, the knowledge of domain culture is crucial. He describes a method for observing citation behaviour, and by implication culture, and reports on a study he has conducted with postgraduate students in the Netherlands. The citation patterns of the students are studied within the scope of a methodology which goes back to Swales' work on academic genre analysis (Swales 1990) and to the more recent – and perhaps more speculative – extensions to the cognitive functions of citation patterns. One key finding of Wilkinson's research is that the study of citation patterns will help us to develop critical skills that, in turn, will enable students to make efficient use of previous findings. Moving from psychology to philosophy, in the next chapter Merja Koskela discusses the function of references in research articles. Koskela's is a more corpus-based approach, but she also builds on Swales' argument that there is a clear link between citation analysis and discourse analysis. Koskela examines texts published over a period of about 40 years in analytical philosophy, looking at the influence of key figures including Alfred Ayer, Bertrand Russell, W.V. Quine and Charles Peirce. For Koskela it is important where the citation was elaborated, either as a verbatim quote, in end-notes or in a bibliography at the end of the text. She looks at cross-citational patterns, negational references and text structure. Her conclusion, which is echoed throughout this second Part, is that a text is merely a trace of its author's behaviour and cannot be used as the sole evidence for discussing that behaviour. However, in the end, the text is all we have.

The Norwegian KIAP project (*Kulturell Identitet i Akademisk Prosa* – 'cultural identity in academic prose') deals with three specialisms – medicine, economics and linguistics – in a trilingual environment, English, Norwegian and French and provides the context for the third and fourth chapters of Part 2, both of which discuss how authors of LSP texts recognise others, mainly through citation patterns. Both studies are corpus-based: Kjersti Fløttum seeks to find citation clusters and Trine Dahl attempts to investigate how metatextual expressions are incorporated into LSP texts. The fifth and final chapter in Part 2 is a case study by Tiina Männikkö dealing with academic historians writing in Swedish; the author tries to find citations of 'events' as stories embedded in academic and popular history texts. The study is a work-in-progress based on a small corpus of five texts from academic journals and a popular history magazine, providing an interesting analysis of an alternative source to citations as support for arguments and claims, namely stories.

In conclusion, this second Part provides an overview of the citation conventions used in a range of disciplines (many of which are social and human sciences) across several languages and cultures; it can therefore serve as a good introduction to this growing aspect of LSP discourse studies.

References

Swales, John 1990. *Genre Analysis. English in Academic and Research Settings*. Cambridge: Cambridge University Press.

ROBERT WILKINSON

Citation behaviour in psychology: Acquiring the domain culture

1. Introduction

Citation is critical to academic writing. Citation allows writers to situate their own work in the context of prior research. In this respect it serves as a marker of the degree of academic socialization (Kaplan 1965; Nicolaisen 2005; Swales 1990). Recent studies have demonstrated the considerable variation between different disciplines in the ways writers cite the authors of published works. For example, Hyland (1999) showed the differences in the frequency and nature of citations in research articles in eight disciplines, and Paul Thompson's study of PhD theses has shown that the differences also depend on the genre (Thompson/Tribble 2001). While these studies demonstrate what writers do, it remains unclear why they do what they do.

Cronin (1984) argued that attributing reasons to why writers cite does not mean that these attributions make the real reasons explicit. There is an "attribution gap" between why writers cite and why we think they cite. Sometimes the reasons may be unknown or even frivolous. A decade earlier Weinstock (1971) had listed a large number of "serious" reasons, among which writers may give credit to authors for related work, may use citations to substantiate claims, may identify the originators of methodology or equipment, may identify further background reading, or even pay homage to pioneers in the domain. However, in Cronin's view, writers may be unaware of why they cite when they cite, and the way in which they cite.

The present chapter reports a case study into how three psychology students acquire a feeling of how they should report previous research in their own texts. The study is part of a larger study situated in the context of a 4-year *doctorandus* (Masters) programme in the Netherlands. The main study comprises a comparative study of a small corpus of psychology texts, and a qualitative longitudinal analysis of samples of work written by psychology students at two moments (approximately two years apart), and an interview study.

2. Background

In academic fields students are assumed to make progress because their writing approximates increasingly the 'norms' established by the specific domain in which they are writing. In this respect, the measure of whether the students meet these norms is not so much that of academic exams and papers, but rather the acceptance of their work in peer-reviewed journals. The norms that students have to meet to be accepted in the domain are not always explicit, for example they cannot be found in style guides such as those of the American Psychological Association (APA). More often they are implicit: students have to reason out for themselves what the domain accepts and what it does not.

However valuable training courses in academic or professional writing may be, it is unlikely such courses can address the features that characterize the norms specific to a relatively narrow domain, such as psychology. To a large extent, students are assumed to assimilate the norms from their reading of the literature, which thus serves as a model for their own writing. However, within all domains there is wide scope for variation within the acceptable norms. Thus the students have to construct a mental model of what the ranges of these implicit norms are. Hence, one would expect exemplars of these "norms to be more or less evident in the students' writing: as students acquire greater expertise in their domain during their academic studies, one would expect their later writing to resemble more closely the features of expert published writing than their earlier writing would do.

This study focuses on citation practices in psychology as an exemplar of the norms of socialized writing in that domain. Citation behaviour among psychology students may be seen as a kind of proxy measure for the degree of socialization into the domain. How citations are used in psychology is both explicit and implicit. Even though the explicit guidelines (i.e. APA) do help aspiring writers with what and how they should report previous research, these guidelines present choices; they do not tell students why they may report in one particular way rather than another. The form a writer chooses and what that implies seem to be critical knowledge for the aspiring writer. However, it has been suggested that writers may not be consciously aware why they choose a particular form: it is part of their tacit knowledge (Hudson 1975; Ravetz 1971). Such knowledge would help novice writers to understand why they themselves may choose particular forms in particular contexts. Moreover, the knowledge would need to be specific for each domain since it is likely that citation behaviour will vary considerably from domain to domain (Hyland 1999). In the field of psychology in particular, Hartley (2001) has commented on the complexity of learning to write according to the conventions of specific genres, and that it takes much time to become 'socialised' into the appropriate disciplinary methods.

Citations can be classified according to surface form, that is whether they are integral or non-integral citations (Swales 1990). Integral citations are defined as those performing a grammatical function within the text, for example as subject or as object of a preposition. Non-integral citations are defined as those in parentheses (brackets or superscript numbers). Following Swales/Thompson/Tribble (2001) have advanced a sub-classification of non-integral (source, identification, reference, origin, plus 'other') and integral citations (verb-controlling, naming, and 'non-citation'). 'Source' indicates a citation where the writer attributes a proposition to one or more specific sources. 'Identification' describes citations where the writer identifies the agent of the action referred to in the sentence. 'Reference' covers citations which refer the readers to other authors by means of expressions such as *see*, *see.*, and *for example*. 'Origin' identifies the originator of a concept or product: this could be a term or expression, or a method (for example, a questionnaire). Among the integral categories, 'verb-controlling' covers citations where the author or authors cited govern a verb, whether in the active or passive form. 'Naming' relates to citations where authors are mentioned in the sentence as part of a prepositional phrase, for example, but do not govern the verb. 'Non-citations' cover references to authors where no identifying date is given; typically this may occur as second mention in the same paragraph. (For a fuller description of these categories, see Thompson/Tribble 2001.)

Citations can also be analysed in terms of cognitive function (Hyland 1999): summary, generalization, or quote, with a category for 'other' too. A 'summary' can be defined as an instance where a writer rephrases in his or her own words the proposition of the original author. In simple terms in this study, a summary is recorded where the writer cites only one author. A 'generalization' may be defined as an instance where a writer attributes facts, findings, observations, and so on, to more than one author. Thus, in simple terms in this study, a generalization is recorded where a citation references two or more publications by the original authors. A 'quote' is defined as an instance where the writer cites the original words of the author, indicating this by using quotation marks.

In this study, measurement of the occurrence of citations according to form and function in the texts of three student writers is compared to the usage in a target domain, as evidenced in a small corpus of psychology texts. However, this does not identify the reasons why the students choose one form or another. For this purpose, data from a semi-structured interview with each student has been used.

3. Method

The students. The three students (let's call them Lisa, Ellen, and Henny) were recruited from a cohort that started their 4-year doctorandus (Masters) programme in 1998. The programme entailed studying in Dutch and English, with most of the work in the first three semesters being in Dutch. From semester 4 onwards, students had increasingly to work in English, even though much of the literature they had read already was written in English. During the fourth semester they had to write a paper in English for the first time. During the third and fourth years, depending partly on the specializations and electives the students choose, they would increasingly write in English. Moreover, because the nature of the studies encourages students to do practical traineeships abroad (in 3rd or 4th year), not only does English play a ever-more dominant role, but the students' study time increases accordingly. Thus, many students of the 1998 intake did not graduate until 2003 (some even later). At the end of their studies students have to write a graduating thesis (Masters thesis). The students have the option to write this in English or in Dutch.

Data. The students' citation behaviour is compared in two ways: across two moments (T1 and T2 – even though the time between T1 and T2 varies from student to student), and with a 'model' of citation behaviour that students might be assumed to target in their writing. The model of citation behaviour was constructed from a subset of a corpus of psychology texts that students may be assumed to have read during their second-year.

Corpus of psychology texts. The corpus was selected from the texts suggested in the second-year psychology manuals or included in the course readers for the year 1999-2000. The inclusion criteria were that texts had to be from psychology journals or from books (collected papers or where chapters were written by different authors). Textbook chapters were excluded, as were articles from popular psychology magazines, newspaper articles, case reports, Internet articles, among others. The lists of articles were checked with the psychology staff responsible for the courses, and a final selection was made. Finally, some selected articles were excluded when they proved to contain no citations, and some suggested articles proved to be unavailable. The subset of the corpus reported here contains 16 articles (109,000 words), covering three genres: research articles (3), theoretical articles (5), and review or overview articles (8). The whole of the review and theoretical articles was included in the analysis. However, in the research articles only the introduction and discussion / conclusion sections were included; method and results were excluded on the grounds that these typically contain few citations, and thus would not provide much input towards a mental model of citation behaviour for the students. While it is not claimed that this subset represents scientific writing in psychology generally, it is held that this represents the kind of scientific writing from which second-year psychology students could construct their own mental model of the citation practice. Thus, the subset comprises texts that the students can be assumed to have read.

Analysis of the corpus and student texts. The corpus was analysed manually. Only one article was available electronically, and the manual analysis is not assumed to be more time-consuming than an electronic analysis. Data were collected on citation form (integral and non-integral citations; Swales 1990; Thompson/Tribble 2001) and citation function (Hyland 1999). The three students' second-year texts (2000) and their graduating theses (2002-2003) were analysed in a similar way to the corpus. The analysis was performed using SPSS 10.1.

Interview study. To obtain information about the reasons that students choose one particular citation technique rather than another, the students were interviewed, among other things, about their citation behaviour in their own writing. For this purpose, citation examples from the students' own second-year paper and their final thesis were used.

The interview was semi-structured and adapted after piloting with first-year PhD students. The interviews were conducted between September 2002 and May 2003. Each interview lasted about one hour. Only parts of the section of the interview dealing with citation behaviour are reported here.

4. Results

4.1. Students' papers

Figure 1 shows the citation types for the three students according to the number of citations used at T1 and T2. At T1 Lisa and Henny show a tendency to use non-integral 'source' citations, whereas the *opposite tendency is apparent in Ellen's writing. At T2 Lisa and* Henny show the same tendency as before, but reveal an increasing use of integral citations. Ellen too shows an increase in integral citations, especially non-citations: this suggests the repetition of authors previously mentioned. Figure 2 shows thc findings in percentages from the corpus subset: the ratio between integral and non-integral citations is almost balanced, with 'source' and 'verb-controlling' types dominating respectively. Comparing the findings for the students with those of the corpus subset suggests that the students, Lisa especially, do tend to move towards the model as presented by the corpus. In proportional terms, the move towards the model is only apparent in Lisa.

Regarding cognitive function, the three students' writing at T1 reveals a complete absence of generalization (see Figure 3); indeed only Ellen uses citations in any other way than as a summary. At T2, however, all three students show some use of generalization, especially Lisa. However, with the possible exception of Lisa, the patterns shown by the individual students differ from that in the corpus, where generalization accounts for 20% of the citations (Figure 4).

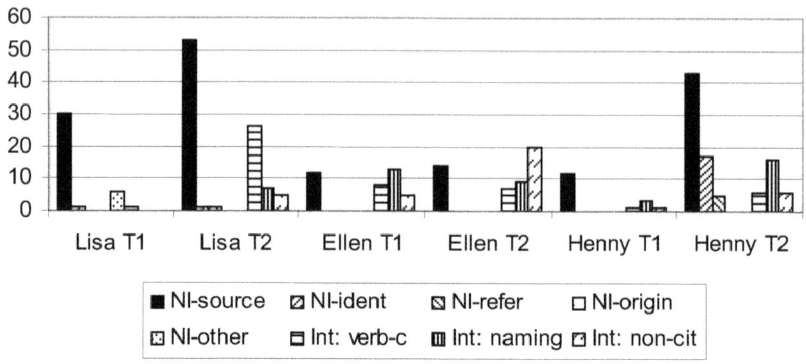

Figure 1. Citation types – Students T1 and T2 (number of citations; NI = non-integral; Int = integral).

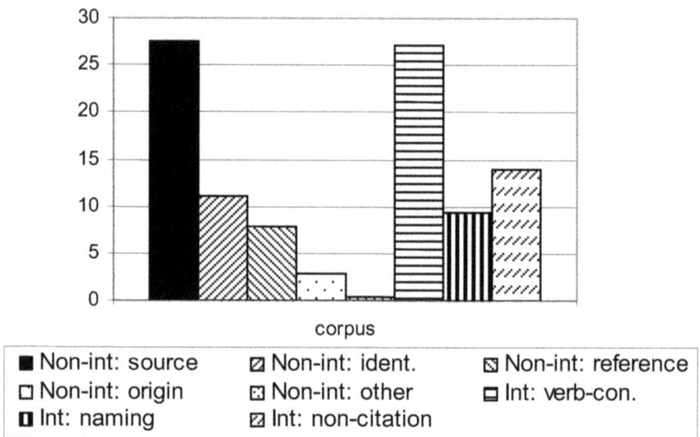

Figure 2. Citation types – corpus (%; NI = non-integral; Int = integral).

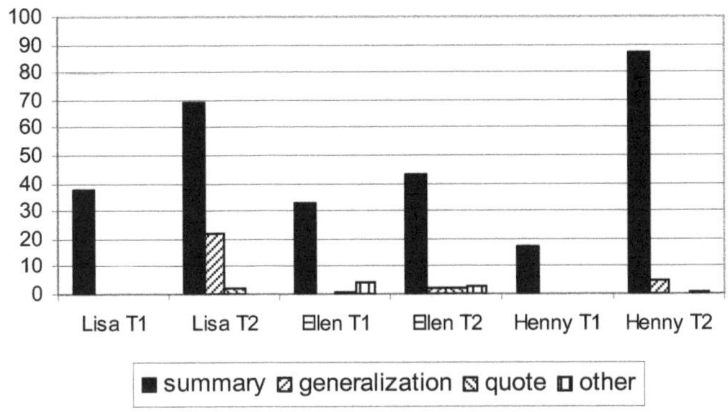

Figure 3. Cognitive function – Students T1 and T2 (numbers of citations).

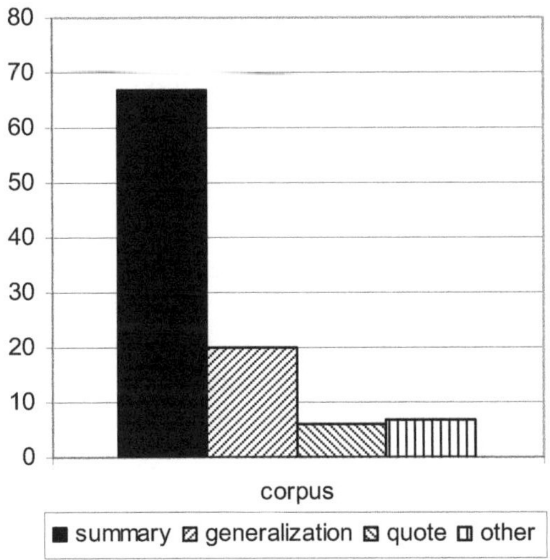

Figure 4. Cognitive function – Corpus (%).

4.2 Interview results: reasons for citation behaviour

The interviews revealed that the students had a wide range of reasons for deciding whether to report previous research by means of a non-integral or integral citation. Because it was not feasible to ask the three interviewees about every citation they used, only a selected number of instances were chosen to represent different ways of reporting previous research. Moreover, as shown in Figure 1, Lisa and Henny showed a marked tendency to use non-integral citations in their second-year paper, although less so in their final paper compared to the corpus. Thus the findings from the three students should be seen as exploratory, and therefore interpreted with a degree of caution.

The reasons for using citations could be classified in three groups: research reasons, discourse reasons, and language and training reasons or writing reasons. Differences between non-integral and integral citations arise chiefly at the sub-divisions of these categories.

4.3 Research reasons

Both Henny and Ellen indicate that they use a non-integral citation to indicate the *source* of information; this may refer to specific findings, definitions, or claims. Example 1 illustrates how Henny describes this (the extract number refers to the sequence in which the extract was discussed during the interview, and the numbers in parentheses refer to the code given to the citation). In this example, Henny emphasizes her reasoning for closely identifying a proposition with its source.

EXAMPLE 1

B Ok, and here [...] you make a comment here "neurochemically this counteradaptation is represented [...]", you give a reference to Di Chiara here, and then a further comment and references to Fromme and D'Amico. What made you do it in that particular way?

Extract 3 (1826, 1827):

Neurochemically this counteradaptation is represented in the decreased levels of dopamine in the nucleus accumbens during withdrawal (Di Chiara, 1997), decreased GABA transmission and increased glutamate transmission (Fromme & D'Amico 1999), while the acute effects of alcohol consumption oppose these reactions.

H For in this article I get to know about the first part, and these other consequences neurochemically I find in this – chapter it was.
B So your reason here would be to put the reference very close to the actual information that you got from that particular source.
H Because if I did it both at the end then some people would say, no Di Chiara didn't say that about glutamate.

Ellen also indicates that she would use a non-integral citation to indicate the importance of the research cited for the student's own study. Yet, the 'importance' reason does not seem to be a consistent choice for using a non-integral citation.

Thus, all three students reported using an integral citation to highlight the *authority or importance* of a study (including the relevance to the student's own research). Example 2 illustrates how Ellen describes her reasoning.

EXAMPLE 2
B Ok, let's move on to the sixth one. Here you begin with a kind of introduction "Once spatial knowledge referring to bla-bla-bla is stored [...]. That can be concluded from a recent research by Schmidt and so on" What made you choose that patterning?
Extract 6 (1967, 1968):
Once spatial knowledge referring to a familiar area is stored, it remains in memory for a very long time. That can be concluded from a recent research by Schmidt, Peeck, Paas and van Breukelen (2000). Schmidt and his colleagues examined the durability of street name knowledge acquired in childhood and the factors that influence this durability.
E Well, I thought it would be clear to start with the conclusion from a research instead of ending with it, so I think that's why I did it like that.
B And is this also because you go on to talk in quite some detail about Schmidt's study?
E Yeah, it was a very important study in relation to my own research.

Somewhat relatedly, all three students used integral citations when they wished to identify the author(s) of research, data, a task, a definition, or an interpretation. Again, Example 3 from Ellen illustrates her reasoning, emphasizing that the integral citation allows her to refer to the authors later with "a shorter reference".

EXAMPLE 3

B Ok, and the fifth one I've selected here. You refer to Joshi, MacLean and Carter here and again you bring it to the fore.
Extract 5 (1962, 1963, 1964):
In a rather recent research Joshi, MacLean and Carter (1999) examined children's routes to school. With our experimental research in mind, results of this study could be very interesting. The research was executed with reference to Hillman's assertion that the spatial development of children who are accompanied to school and to other destinations for a long period is impeded (1993 in Joshi, et al., 1999). Hillman stated this referring to the finding that ever more children (90% in 1990 versus 20% in 1970) are being accompanied to school.

E Yeah, and then people know instantly that Joshi, MacLean and Carter did the research. If I said "In a rather recent research it appeared that children's routes to school were examined" and then I say the name, then I think it's not that clear.

B Ok, does the fact that you refer to Joshi et al. several times later have an influence in why you chose this pattern at the beginning?

E Yes I think so, because in the beginning it's very clear who did it, and afterwards I can make it a shorter reference.

Other reasons given by the students for using integral citations were to highlight the originator of a theory, model, framework, or term (indicated by Lisa and Ellen), and to highlight specificity (a specific study, specific findings, a specific example; for example citing the first author to do something) (indicated by Lisa).

To sum up, research reasons for using non-integral citations were to indicate the source or the importance to one's own study, while research reasons for using integral citations were to highlight the authority or importance of the authors' work, to identify the author (or a definition or interpretation), to highlight the originator of a theory or model, and to highlight the specificity of a particular study.

4.4 Discourse reasons

Only one discourse reason was mentioned for using a non-integral citation. Lisa indicated that it allowed her to *focus on summarizing or combining* results, findings, or statements, as illustrated by Example 4. Because the authors said "the same thing", Lisa indicates that it is easier to read if the sentence is not interrupted by parenthetical citations, but she adds that she would do so if the authors had not said the same thing.

EXAMPLE 4

B OK. The sixth one I chose here. You refer to a number of aspects in primary health care, you list them all and then you give several references afterwards. What made you do that?
Extract 6 (2032):
The most important aspects of PHC are: food and water supply, maternal and child health care, immunisation against major infectious diseases, prevention and control of endemic diseases, basic care of health problems, supply of essential drugs and community mobilisation and awareness (Amanoo-Lartson, Ebrahim, & Lovel, 1985; Boerma, 1989; Starfield, 1992).

L Yes, the list of primary health care is something that many authors wrote about, at least in their introduction. When I read through my articles, I found these different aspects I found them back in different articles, yes, that's why I refer all, since I read them in several references, I'm just going to write that down.

B So would there be a reason why you put them all at the end rather than say indicate against each one?

L I'm starting with?

B Well you might say, for example, "food and water supply" and then give a reference, "maternal and child health care" and then give a reference.

L I see, well this is because they all said the same thing, so this is clearer to read, because if I write brackets after every part, then it disturbs when you're reading, and if they would, for example if the first one would have said different things than the second one, then I would have written that down, for example if food and water supply was only mentioned by the first one. I think I do that somewhere else afterwards. There are a lot of references because everybody said something else.

However, both Henny and Ellen give discourse reasons for using integral citations, in particular because the integral citation allows easy reference forward or backward, as illustrated by Example 5. Here Henny indicates that it is not only the importance of the names of the authors, but particularly the facility it gives her to refer to their names as representing the studies the authors have conducted.

EXAMPLE 5

B Ok, the last one I have here, number 11, in your conclusion part, or discussion part, you refer to several authors here, summing up. "This does not replicate findings by Fowles and Iaboni who demonstrate that" and "following reward in the study of Gomez and McLaren". Are there particular reasons why you use those structures?
Extract 11 (1890, 1892):
Overall, except for a slight increase in HR of abstinent alcoholics in the REW-REW and REW-PUN condition, a decrease in HR was found. This does not replicate earlier findings by Fowles (1988) and Iaboni et al. (1997) who demonstrated an increased HR accompanying reward in normal controls. Additionally, even the failure to find an increased HR following reward in the study of Gomez and McLaren (1997) is incompatible with current findings of a decrease in HR.

H Well, the names are important here. Well, I could have said what they did find and put their names behind it. I explained it earlier. I can now refer to their names.

Lisa also gives a discourse reason for using an integral citation – to focus attention on the topic the writer addresses through particular authors or on a particular study.

In sum, then, the discourse reason for using non-integral citations relates to *focusing on summarizing or combining data* from different authors, whereas the discourse reasons for using integral citations include *facilitating subsequent reference* and *focusing attention on the topic* of the authors cited.

4.5 Language and training reasons

Both Henny and Lisa reported that they used non-integral citations because they had been told that "it had to be this way". In other words, they reported that they were simply *following instructions*. The students did not indicate language or training reasons for using integral citations.

4.6 Variation and no reason

One reason given for switching between integral and non-integral citations was simply for the sake of variety, as shown in Example 6 from Ellen.

EXAMPLE 6

B Ok, and the second extract – we need to look at the two pages here, the one I've selected overruns the page – and you refer to "Research that will be addressed later on in this theoretical introduction showed that" and then the comment and you give the reference here in brackets. Any particular reason that you started that way?
Extract 2 (1942):
Research that will be addressed later on in this theoretical introduction showed that spatial knowledge remained in peoples memory systems for a very long time, and that there were several factors enhancing this durability (Schmidt, Peeck, Paas & van Breukelen 2000).

E Well, that was a very important research, but like the way I referred it that's just one of two or three ways you can do it and well it's not really it wasn't really a conscious choice or anything, it's just that you want some variety in your piece of work.

B Ok, so that's the reason why you would refer to "research that will be addressed later on".

E I could also say like "Schmidt and mm researched this and this and they found that". Sometimes it just looks better or sounds better when you do it like this.

However, occasionally the students did not know why they chose one form rather than another, as to some extent Ellen admits in Example 6 above.

5. Discussion and conclusions

The findings from this case study of three students suggests that they do change their citation behaviour during their time of study, but not all in the same way. They do tend to absorb the domain conventions (culture) as measured by a model of citation behaviour in the corpus of psychology texts the students are assumed to have read. By the time they graduate at Masters level, the students are approaching the norms for the domain, in so far as these are reflected in citation usage.

However, with regard to cognitive function, the three students show only limited change between their first paper in English and their final thesis. The students do not yet seem to have reached a level of expertise in the domain that enables them to generalize easily from previous research. It is difficult to argue that this stems from the students not having read sufficient literature; rather it may have to do with a tendency to report findings separately in a possible desire to highlight slight distinctions between studies. In particular, this may stem from the fact that the students may well be reporting (summarizing) what others have done, rather than reporting their own opinions and deductions, and then using published research to support it. The process that the students are going through at the end of their Masters studies may be a reflection of a similar process observed in other professional domains. Research, especially in medicine, has identified a process of transition in expertise development as students move out from the educational phase of learning and into the world of practice (Schmidt/Boshuizen 1993; Custers/Boshuizen/Schmidt 1998). In this process a person has to reorganize his or her mental structures of knowledge (encapsulation) from individual knowledge bases to a larger, more integrated knowledge bases, which may be stored in the form of scripts (Schank/Abelson 1977). It may be that an increase in the use of generalization (perhaps reflecting a more integrated knowledge base) is a feature that expert psychologists develop during practice, such as during PhD studies.

The students are generally quite able to account for why they chose to use a particular citation form in a specific instance. Previous research has discussed reasons for citing the work of one's predecessors (Cronin 1984; Swales 1990; Thompson/Ye 1991; Jordan 1997). Most information seems to have been gathered from a close analysis of texts. It seems less common for researchers to question the writers why they make specific choices. Both Hyland (1999, 2000) and Paul Thompson (Thompson 1999) have attempted to question informants in the disciplines they analysed. In this study three intermediate writers were interviewed to determine the reasoning underlying the choices they actually made in practice. However, it should be borne in mind that the reasons a student gives in an interview for using a particular citation form may not be the same reasons that the student had in mind at the time of writing. These results nevertheless suggest lines for future research with other groups of writers.

It is valuable to study citation behaviour in a domain like psychology because the ability to make efficient use of the findings from previous research is a critical skill for psychology (and other) students. This is not only because each discipline has its own cultural conventions and norms, but also because the very reporting, acknowledging or accommodating of one's predecessors' research takes up such an enormous part of what one writes in the discipline. Thus, students' writing could benefit from conscious scaffolding based on research in order to socialize the students gradually into the discipline. However, it may be ineffective to require students to generalize from previous research until later in their studies.

6. Acknowledgements

I would like to thank Professor Gert Rijlaarsdam (University of Amsterdam), Professor Arthur van Essen (University of Groningen), and Professor Els Boshuizen (Open University, the Netherlands) for their advice in the construction of this chapter.

References

Cronin, B. 1984. *The citation process: The role and significance of citations in scientific communication*. London: Taylor Graham.

Custers, E.J.F.M. / Boshuizen, H.P.A. / Schmidt, H.G. 1998. The role of illness scripts in the development of medical expertise: results from an interview study. *Cognition and Instruction 16/4,* 367-398.

Hartley, J. 2001. Students, writing and computers. *Psychology Learning and Teaching 1/*1, 10-15.

Hudson, L. 1975. *Human beings: An introduction to the psychology of human experience*. London: Cape.

Hyland, K. 1999. Academic attribution: Citation and the construction of disciplinary knowledge. *Applied Linguistics 20/*3, 341-367.

Hyland, K. 2000. *Disciplinary discourses. Social interactions in academic writing*. Harlow: Pearson Education.

Jordan, R. R. 1997. *English for Academic Purposes. A guide and resource book for teachers*. Cambridge: Cambridge University Press.

Kaplan, N. 1965. The norms of citation behaviour: Prolegomena to the footnote *American Documentation 16/3*, 179-184.

Nicolaisen, J. 2005. The social act of citing: Towards new horizons in citation theory. *Proceedings of the American Society for Information Science and Technology* 40/1, 12-20.

Ravetz, J.R. 1971. *Scientific knowledge and its social problems*. Harmondsworth: Penguin.

Schank, R. C. / Abelson, R. P. 1977. *Scripts, plans, goals and understanding*. Hillsdale NJ: Erlbaum.

Schmidt, H. G. / Boshuizen, H. P. A. 1993. On the origin of intermediate effects in clinical case recall. *Memory and Cognition 21,* 338-351.

Swales, J.M. 1990. *Genre analysis. English in academic and research settings*. Cambridge: Cambridge University Press.

Thompson, G. / Ye, Y. (1991) Evaluation in the reporting verbs used in academic papers. *Applied Linguistics* 12/4, 365-382.

Thompson, P. (1999) Exploring the contexts of writing: interviews with PhD supervisors. In Thompson, P. (ed.) *Issues in EAP Writing Research and Instruction.* Reading: Centre for Applied Language Studies, University of Reading, 37-54.

Thompson, P. / Tribble, C. (2001) Looking at citations: Using corpora in English for academic purposes. *Language Learning and Technology 5/3*, 91-105.

Weinstock, M. (1971) Citation indexes. *Encyclopaedia of Library and Information Science 5,* 16-40.

MERJA KOSKELA

Functions of references in philosophical research articles

1. Introduction

Since Swales' (1986) seminal article on the relationship between citation analysis and discourse analysis, linguistic methods have been used in a wide variety of studies of bibliographical references. Such studies have concerned among other things reporting verbs, their degree of evaluation and their role in the discourse (Thompson/Ye 1991; Thomas/Hawes 1994; Thompson 1996). Most of the studies have concentrated on one field (Koskela 1999; Salager-Meyer 1999), but interestingly, in some studies referential behavior in different fields has been compared (Hyland 2000; Fløttum 2003). My study falls into the first category and concentrates on functions of references within the field of philosophy.

In his study of referential behavior in eight academic disciplines, Hyland (2000) found that philosophy has its own referential profile. Philosophers use a great number of references, often neglect to repeat the explicit reference, and include the name of the cited author in the reporting sentence. In addition, the cited work can be explicitly criticized in philosophy (see also Bloor 1996). My own results (Koskela 2000), based on Swedish philosophical texts support Hyland's results of writing in English, but they also show that there are substantial individual differences within the field of philosophy and differences between different schools of thought, especially between the Analytic tradition and the Continental tradition.

In the present chapter I will study references as discourse features in research articles representing Analytic philosophy from the 1950s and from the 1990s. The starting point of my study is one of the early works on citation analysis, namely Moravcsik/Murugesan's (1975) typology of citations. The typology was originally created as a refining tool for quantitative reference-citation counts aiming at measuring scientific quality. As such it concentrates on single references and their function in the immediate context. In my chapter I will test how the model works in analyzing functions of references in the construction of discourse in whole texts, and therefore I will base my discussion on only five articles, two from the 1950s and three from the 1990s. With the help of the model, I will try to find out if there seem to be functions that vary with time or if there are permanent functions typical of philosophical discourse independent of time.

2. The material of the study

Before turning to the functions of references, I will describe the specimen articles used as material. The two early articles (Weitz 1950; Aldrich 1955) were chosen at random from the first volume of the journal Philosophical Studies (founded in 1950), which describes itself as a journal for philosophy within the Analytic tradition. Even though the opposition between the Analytic tradition and the so-called Continental tradition is today much less focused on than earlier, I chose to look at Analytic philosophy because interviews conducted in connection with a study of philosophical writing (Koskela 2000 and 2003) showed that the Analytic tradition still has a strong position in both Finland and Sweden. For comparison, two articles were chosen from the 1990s volumes of the journal. One article (Creath 1998) was chosen because its topic seemed to be similar to that in Aldrich's (1955), and one other article from the same year (Juhl 1998) was chosen at random. However, Juhl's article turned out to include only one explicit reference to literature. Therefore, the material was later completed by Gampel's (1997) article. In Table 1, I have collected some central features of the material.

Article	Contents	No. of references[1]	No. of endnotes	No. of verbatim quotes	List of references at the end
Weitz (1950)	Relating Ayer to Russell	61	8	5	None
Aldrich (1955)	Quine's idea of meaning and naming	117	1	19	None
Creath (1998)	Quine's view on Peirce	38	0	2	Six entries
Gampel (1997)	Normativity of meaning	34	34	4	None
Juhl (1998)	Conscious experience	1	5	0	Six entries

Table 1. Some characteristics of the example articles.

Compared with Hyland's (2000) findings based on a material of 25 journals from the year 1980 it seems that the number of references in the 1950s papers comes closer to Hyland's material (according to him, there is on average 89 references per paper), whereas the 1990s articles have substantially fewer references. For the 1990s articles, Hyland's result that philosophers use a lot of references does not get much support. Regarding the use of endnotes (footnotes listed at the end of the paper) and a list of references at the end of the paper, there does not seem to be any regularity in the journal: technicalities do not seem to be considered important.

Verbatim quotes are minimal in Hyland's (2000) material, as they are in mine, with the exception of Aldrich's (1955) paper. According to Hyland (2000), summary is a more efficient way of supporting an author's own arguments than verbatim quotes, because others' findings can then be expressed on the author's own terms. However, it is expedient for Aldrich to let Quine talk on his own terms, because Quine's wordings allow for several interpretations, and Aldrich has, no doubt, chosen for quotation the very expressions that support his own views.

1 In counting the references I have followed the guidelines set in Hyland (2000).

Judging by the number of references and the contents of the papers, the material consists of two different types of articles. The articles by Weitz, Aldrich, and Creath take up perennial problems for new discussion, whereas the articles by Gampel and Juhl represent logical reasoning of the kind considered typical of Analytic philosophy. Even here there is variation, however. When Gampel includes names of authors in his text and uses endnotes for details, Juhl hardly mentions any names of other researchers at all.

3. A model for content citation analysis

As already mentioned, Moravcsik/Murugesans's (1975) classification of citations was created to support quantitative citation counts in order to find reliable measures for evaluating research. The model consists of four parameters and is non-dichotomous, which means that all references in the texts are tested with respect to each parameter. The results are then reported in terms of percentages of all references. The model is based on an in-depth study of citations within texts on high-energy physics (namely Physical Review 1968) and is described in Figure 1.

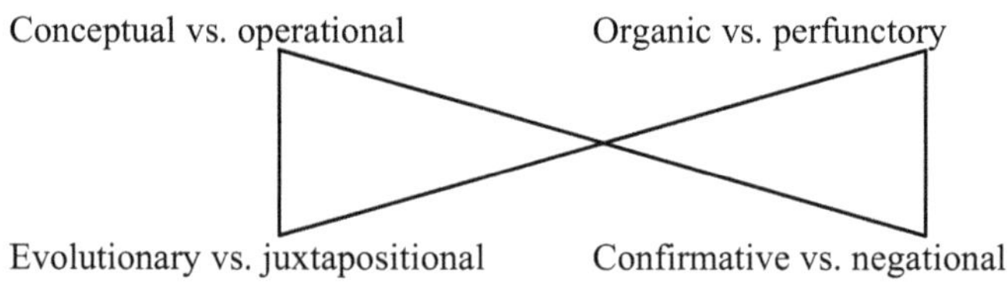

Figure 1. Moravcsik and Murugesan's citation typology (figure from Cronin 1981).

The parameters of the model are the following, i.e. the authors ask if the references are:

a) Conceptual or operational
b) Organic or perfunctory

c) Evolutionary or juxtapositional
d) Confirmative or negational.

Conceptual references refer to a concept or a theory that is used in the referring paper, whereas operational references are made in connection with a tool or physical technique used in the paper. Organic references are important for understanding the referring paper and for the working out of its content. Perfunctory references, on the contrary, are acknowledgements of similar work done earlier. Evolutionary references are such that the whole referring paper is built on them, and juxtapositional references present the referring paper as an alternative to the paper referred to. Finally, confirmative references find the contents referred to correct, and negational find them incorrect or otherwise dispute them (Moravcsik/Murugesan 1975).

In the present chapter I will concentrate on the third category presented above: that is, whether the references are *evolutionary* or *juxtapositional*. This is motivated, in addition to considerations of space, by the fact that all references in my material are conceptual, and that perfunctory references have earlier received a lot of attention (Swales 1986). In the end, however, I will briefly consider *negational* references and their position in the structure of philosophical research articles, because negational references and juxtapositional references share certain common features.

4. Evolutionary and juxtapositional references as text-structuring elements

As mentioned above, evolutionary references form the basis of the referring paper and new thoughts are built on them, whereas juxtapositional references are used in order to provide alternatives to the ideas presented in the paper referred to. However, it must be noted that, at least according to Swales (1986: 50), juxtapositional references only include the offering of "(non-aggressive) alternatives, refinements and extensions", which makes them different from the negational references.

When applying the model to real texts, it soon becomes obvious that it is difficult to categorize single occurrences of references as either evolutionary or juxtapositional. This is the case even if the immediate context of the reference is taken into consideration. Examples 1 and 2 indicate how a single instance of citation can easily be misleading.

(1) For Ayer, philosophy contains no factual assertions, says nothing which is true or false, and in no way competes with science [...] (W50)

(2) Russell sometimes means by *philosophy* analysis as contextual definition [...] but [...] he also at times means by *philosophy* analysis as real definition. (W50)

Judging by the single reference and its immediate context, it would seem that example 1 is neutral and potentially evolutionary, whereas a critical tone can be sensed in example 2, hinting at a possible juxtapositional stance. Therefore, in order to make such a judgment with any degree of accuracy a discourse approach covering the whole text is needed. It is evident that considering single references is a different matter than considering the functions of references within the whole text, and can lead to different interpretations.

In order to be able to consider the whole text, I have drawn a "reference pattern" for whole texts. Table 2 below describes the complete reference pattern of Weitz's (1950) article on philosophy as analysis. The pattern is formed by all instances of references in the different parts of the text. The numbers in parenthesis show how many references to the mentioned author have been used after one another, and the marking of eventual subsections follows the one used in the paper (only Weitz's article is divided into subsections).

I. Ayer	Russell (2)
Russell	Dispute between Russell and Bradley
Hume	Both Russell and Bradley
Ayer (6)	Russell
II. Ayer	Bradley (2)
Russell (13)	**IV.** Hume
Cantor	Ayer (4)
Russell (3)	Hume (7)
III. Russell	Russell (5)
Bradley	**V.** Russell
Russell	Broad
Bradley	Moore (2)

Table 2. The reference pattern in Weitz's (1950) article.

As Table 2 shows, the number of different authors referred to in the article is not high. The main sources are clearly Ayer and Russell, and only after studying the whole pattern can it be concluded that Weitz's citation of Ayer is clearly juxtapositional whereas his citation of Russell and Hume is evolutionary. Actually, this is explicitly expressed in the aims of the paper, but in a pure quantitative analysis this would go unnoticed.

(3) In this paper I shall try to **refute** Ayer's doctrine [...] (W50)

The discourse approach also seems to be needed if we want to categorize Aldrich's (1955) references to Quine as either evolutionary or juxtapositional. The reference pattern in Aldrich's article is presented in Table 3.

Mr. Quine	Lewis (2)
Quine (27)	Quine (6)
Kant	Lewis
Quine	Quine (2)
Eddington	Lewis
Kant	Quine
Lewis (2)	Fichte
Carnap	Quine
Lewis	Hume
Quine	Quine
Vaihiger	White
Quine (28)	Quine (19)

Table 3. The reference pattern in Aldrich's (1955) article. (Names of books not listed.).

In his article Aldrich engages in both evolutionary and juxtapositional accounts of Quine. Interestingly, the evolutionary references often consist of what Hyland (2000: 36) calls "an imagined dialogue". These are cases where the author provides claims on his advisory's behalf, and the references can be characterized as hypothetical rather than actual. See the examples in 4 below:

(4) Quine **may be arguing** a different thesis [...]
He **may be saying** that [...]
His point **might then be** that
Paraphrasing a bit, **one might say** for Quine that [...] (A55)

Clearly, such references would be highly questionable in any other discipline, but they seem to be accepted in philosophy because they help the author to demonstrate which views he supports and which he opposes (Hyland 2000). Most other references to Quine in the article are juxtapositional. In the end, for example, Aldrich (1955) claims that Quine has not been fully aware of the consequences of his position, thus confirming his juxtapositional stance:

(5) I conclude that he (=Quine) **is in effect working** with [...] he **is implicitly laboring** with [...] What I am suggesting is that Quine has **implicitly accepted** this formula – except that he denies A/S [...] **without his realizing it**. (A55)

The question is, of course, whether Aldrich is really citing Quine at all or only creating a convenient opposition for the purposes of his own argument. In that case all Aldrich's comments on Quine would in reality yield a juxtapositional interpretation, and the evolutionary vein could be interpreted as making concessions to proponents of Quine's views.

Interestingly, and possibly illustrating the stable nature of philosophical discussion over the years, Creath in his 1998 paper on Quine's critique of Peirce pursues similar lines as Aldrich did 43 years before him. However, he does not resort to imaginary dialogue. The reference pattern in Creath's paper is presented in Table 4.

Quine	Scheffler
Peirce	Quine (4)
Quine (3)	Weierstrass
Peirce	Quine (2)
Quine (3)	Peirce
Peirce	Quine
Quine (9)	Peirce (4)
Peirce (2)	Quine (2)
Quine	

Table 4. The reference pattern in Creath's (1998) article.

When considering the whole pattern it becomes evident that Creath's citations of Quine are juxtapositional. Example 6 reminds of the argumentation presented by Aldrich in his imagined dialogue. In example 7 Creath is very careful in making the point that his juxtapositional stance on Quine does not automatically lead to taking an evolutionary attitude towards Peirce. Here he differs from Weitz who accepts both Russell and Hume when rejecting Ayer:

(6) […] the very sentence of Word and Object which expresses his (=Quine's) objection to the limit notion also **tacitly concedes** that […] (C98)

(7) Peirce's notion of limit **is at least as adequate** as Quine's notion of conservatism. (C98)

The examples from Creath clearly show that a discourse approach to whether references are evolutionary or juxtapositional reveals new perspectives. As Swales (1986) proposed, it seems that a category of zero, that is a category for references that are neither evolutionary nor juxtapositional is needed here in order to give a correct picture of the functions of references to Peirce.

Now, if we are to judge what philosophers do with references based on this discussion, we can conclude that in the type of philosophical article where they engage in a debate on perennial questions they use references in order to create an authorial self through references (Hyland 2000). Through references they can introduce a claim that they want to take up for discussion (even by means of an imaginary dialogue if needed), and use other references to support their own view against the initial claim. Textually this is achieved by presenting two opposing views, one being evolutionary and one juxtapositional or, alternatively, presenting only one view and taking a juxtapositional stance on it. However, it must be noted that this type of article is not the only type of philosophical research article within the Analytic tradition. In my randomly chosen material of five articles, three articles are of this kind, whereas the other two do not fit into this frame at all since they engage in logical reasoning on its own right without relating it to previous research to a very high degree.

5. Negational references and text structure

Because the juxtapositional stance discussed above tends to be related to negational references, I will briefly discuss the functions of negational references in the five articles I have used as my material. According to Swales (1986) negational references are used typically in the introductions in connection with step 3 in his rhetorical moves model, preparing for present research (especially when creating a research space).

As shown earlier (Crookes 1986; Koskela 2000), the kind of moves structure of article introductions presented by Swales (1990) is best suited for natural science articles. In social sciences as well as in philosophy, such schematic structure is much harder to establish.

Of the five articles in my material, the step of preparing for present research can be found in two articles, and of these two cases negational reference can be found in one, in Gampel's introduction presented in example 8:

(8) (*Step 2:* reporting previous research)
Davidson and Kripke advance quite different arguments, but they share an attempt to undermine certain naturalistic theories.
(*Step 3:* preparing for present research)
Although much discussed, these and other arguments from normativity have been received with **puzzlement and skepticism**. The reason is **that proponents of the arguments** say **surprisingly little** about the precise nature of the claims… (G97)

As we can see in example 8, the negational element is not directly connected with the reference, but is presented afterwards and concerns general reactions as well as nameless proponents of certain arguments. Toning down criticism in this way can at least in part account for the fact that negational references are found to be rare in research articles. As MacRoberts/MacRoberts (1984) have found, there are indeed many clever ways of and different motivations for disguising criticism even though criticism is "the life blood of science". However, as Bloor (1996) and Hyland (2000) show, criticism is more common in philosophy than in other fields. In my material, however, the negational references are found further in the text, in connection with the authors' arguments where they make clear their juxtapositional stance rather than in the moves structures of introductions.

(9) Chalmers' recent arguments (see Chalmers (1996)) that […] is also **shown to be incorrect**. (J98)

(10) Quine's **tortured treatment** of synonymy is partly the result of **his not knowing** what meaning is. (A55)

(11) Kripke's way of expressing the normativity condition […] **is suggestive**…(verbatim quote**). The question is how to make sense of such remarks**. (G97)

(12) Ayer's main point seems to be that Hume's analysis of causation raises no empirical problems. **With this I cannot agree**. (W50)

Example 9 shows that new, previously not mentioned authors can be drawn into the discussion through a negational reference in the middle of the text, if needed. However, most of the negational references concern the authors on whom the citing paper takes a juxtapositional stance (examples 10 and 12). In other words, there are usually some points in the cited works that the author disagrees with, more or less strongly, and these can well be presented through a negational reference. MacRoberts/MacRoberts (1984) suggest that authors do not want to express open criticism of their peers because there is the danger that the criticism can jeopardize their careers or because there is a risk that the paper offered to a journal can be sent for review to the very person criticized. In philosophy, these dangers do not necessarily come to the fore because ancient philosophers are still treated as equal discussion partners. Thus the risk of jeopardizing one's career is less evident. Sometimes, the negational comments are embedded in the referring sentence (as in examples 9 and 10), which makes it possible to single out negational references without considering the whole text. In my material, however, the type where the negational comment follows the reference in a separate sentence, often several sentences away, seems to be more common, which again calls for a discourse approach if the negational references are to be recognized.

6. Conclusion

Textual analysis can never completely explain the motivations behind an author's referential behavior, but it can suggest plausible reasons (Cronin 1981). In this chapter I have tried to establish some functions for references in whole texts that are typical of philosophy as a field of inquiry independent of time. In earlier studies (notably Hyland 2000), it has been shown that philosophy has a distinctive referential profile. This can be explained by the nature of the problems explored, inquiry patterns and knowledge structures as well as by the community conventions of effective argument. According to Hyland (2000) philosophers cite as they do because they tend to construct knowledge through dialogue and discuss old problems all over again in the light of personal engagement. One reflection of this is perhaps also the continuing tradition of not repeating the explicit reference in the text, which is common praxis both in the 1950s papers and in the 1990s papers. In philosophy, references tend to require shared knowledge.

An exploration of the few specimen texts that I have used shows that there is considerable variation in the citing behavior within one single tradition of philosophy, the Analytic one. It can thus be expected that the differences are even more evident if different traditions are accounted for. However, the variation within the Analytic tradition does not seem to be dependent on time: the 1990s papers can remind us very much of the 1950s papers, which tells us that the knowledge structures of the field and its community conventions have not changed substantially in 40 years. Personal preferences undoubtedly affect citation choices, but based on my material it seems that the content and aims of the paper are even more influential. Of course, it can be the case that the type of papers which include logical reasoning with few references was a current trend in Analytic philosophy at the end of the 1990s, but this does not affect the basic knowledge structures essentially, since these papers can again be taken up for scrutiny the way Quine and Ayer have been in other articles in the material.

To conclude, a case in point, quantitative reference-citation counts are still today used to judge the quality of researchers' work and their position in the development of the field. Myfindings once again confirms Swales' (1996: 49) somewhat ironical statement that "a single categorization of citations [...] is a convenient fiction". In addition, there seems to be substantial differences in the results of the categorizations depending on whether the analysis concerns single instances of references or whether it takes into consideration the whole text and its complete reference pattern. Naturally, both approaches could gain in developing their own categorizations. What I hope to have demonstrated, however, is that a discourse approach to references can be very illuminating and useful, especially from an LSP point of view, since it can show us how whole texts and their argumentation structures are constructed through references. A different matter is, of course, that such an approach is far too laborious to be useful in judging scientific quality in large quantities of research articles.

References

Bloor, T. 1996. Three hypothetical strategies in philosophical writing. In Ventola, E. / Mauranen, M. (eds) *Academic Writing: Intercultural and Textual Issues*. Amsterdam/Philadelphia: John Benjamins, 19-43.

Cronin, B. 1981. The need for a theory of citing. *Journal of Documentation* 37/1, 16-24.

Crookes, G. 1986. Towards a Validated Analysis of Scientific Text Structure,. *Applied Linguistics* 7/1, 57-70.

Fløttum, K. 2003. Bibliographical references and polyphony in research articles. In Fløttum, K. / Rastier, F. (eds) *Academic discourse. Multidisciplinary approaches*. Oslo: Novus, 97-119

Hyland, K. 2000. *Disciplinary Discourses: Social Interactions in Academic Writing*. Essex: Longman.

Koskela, M. 1999. Om referenser till vetenskaplig litteratur i svenska filosofiska texter. *Nordica Bergensia* 20, 143-160.

Koskela, M. 2000. *Svenska som filosofins språk*. Vaasan yliopiston julkaisuja. Tutkimuksia 235. Språkvetenskap 38. Vaasa.

Koskela, M. 2003. Svenska och finska filosofers syn på skrivande och språk. In Fløttum, K. (ed.) *Akademisk Prosa,* 1–2003. Skrifter fra KIAP. Bergen: Romansk institutt, Universitetet i Bergen, 37-45.

MacRoberts, M. / MacRoberts, B. 1984. The Negational Reference: or the Art of Dissembling. *Social Studies of Science* 14, 91-94.

Moravcsik, M. J. / Murugesan, P. 1975. Some Results of the Function and Quality of Citations. *Social Studies of Science* 5, 86-92.

Salager-Meyer, F. 1999. Referential Behavior in Scientific Writing: A Diachronic Study (1810-1995). *English for Specific Purposes* 18/3, 279-305.

Swales, J. 1986. Citation Analysis and Discourse Analysis. *Applied Linguistics* 7/1, 39-56.

Swales, J. 1990. *Genre analysis: English in research and academic settings*. Cambridge: Cambridge University Press.

Thomas, S. / Hawes, T. P. 1994. Reporting Verbs in Medical Journal Articles. *English for Specific Purposes* 13/2, 129-148.

Thompson, G. 1996. Voices in the Text: Discourse Perspectives on Language Reports. *Applied Linguistics* 17, 501-530.

Thompson, G. / Ye Y. 1991. Evaluation in the Reporting Verbs Used in Academic Papers. *Applied Linguistics* 12, 365-382.

Appendix 1.

The material of the study

8.1 1950s

Aldrich, V. C 1955. Mr. Quine on Meaning, Naming, and Purporting to Name. *Philosophical Studies* VI/2, 17-26. (Code A55.)

Weitz, M. 1950. Analysis and Real Definition. *Philosophical Studies* 1/1, 1-8. (Code W50.)

8.2 1990s

Creath, R. 1998. Quine and the Limit Assumption in Peirce's Theory of Truth. *Philosophical Studies* 90/2, 109-112. (Code C98.)

Gampel, E. H. 1997. The Normativity of Meaning. *Philosophical Studies* 86/3, 221-242. (Code G97.)

Juhl, C. F. 1998. Conscious Experience and the Non-Triviality Principle. *Philosophical Studies* 91/1, 91-101. (Code J98.)

KJERSTI FLØTTUM

Traces of others in research articles: the citation cluster

1. Introduction

I have argued elsewhere (Fløttum 2003a) that scientific writing can be seen as a tension between progress and continuity – progress in the sense of being original and presenting new findings and continuity in the sense of situating oneself as a researcher in a scientific tradition. In this chapter, I will first give a short presentation of the KIAP project (see also Dahl, this volume) (section 2) and some quantitative results related to the frequency of bibliographical references or citations in research articles (section 3). Second, I will claim that the specific phenomenon of cluster, defined here as the accumulation of three or more bibliographical references, may assume two general functions corresponding to the two dimensions just mentioned: progress and continuity (section 4). I will also argue that even if clustering represents an efficient way of referring to and situating oneself in relation to other relevant research, it may lead to considerable ambiguity and even weaken the academic ideal of clarity. In my summing up and final remarks (section 5), I will point to the importance of taking into account individual differences between articles.

2. The KIAP project

The present study is part of the research related to the multidisciplinary and doubly contrastive KIAP project, short for *Cultural Identity in Academic Prose: national versus discipline-specific* (see <http://www.uib.no/kiap/index-e.htm>, Fløttum/Breivega 2002, Fløttum/Rastier 2003). The KIAP activities are based on the following key issue: Can cultural identities be identified in academic prose, and, if so, are these identities national or discipline-specific in nature? We attempt to answer this question through a *linguistic* and *contrastive* study of English, French and Norwegian research articles within the fields of economics, linguistics and medicine. The central questions we ask are related to authorial presence and stance, to the manifestation of other researchers' voices and to the author's presentation and promotion of their own research. As regards the question whether the cultural identity of academic writers is primarily national or primarily discipline-specific in nature, our findings so far indicate that the discipline dimension seems to be more important (Breivega/Dahl/Fløttum 2002), but the national or language dimension should not be neglected (especially as regards metadiscourse and the use of first person and indefinite pronouns; see Dahl 2003, 2004; Fløttum 2003a, b, c).

The analyses undertaken by the project are based on data generated from an electronic corpus (under construction) comprising research articles representing the three languages and three disciplines (9 subcorpora). At present we are working on 180 articles (20 for each subcorpus), published between 1995 and 2002, which are coded, and constitute *KIAP Corpus 1.* The total number of words is 1,161,488 (English: 493,130, French: 329,049, Norwegian: 339,309). However, many tables, figures and equations have been deleted from the original version of the articles, thus we estimate the original corpus at about 2,000,000 words. It is the body part of the corpus which is investigated here (containing 826,652 words), for example the plain text, corresponding to the article minus (sub)titles, abstract, examples, quotes, figures, tables, equations, notes, bibliography. (For further details on the corpus and the methodological design, see <www.hit.

uib.no/kiap>). For the present study on bibliographical references, one article (frmed18 [French medical text 18] with a count of 3,918 words) was excluded from the search because of the exceptionally high number of references, 468 in all. Thus the total number of articles included here is 179.

3. Bibliographical references (BR) and clusters (CL) in KIAP Corpus 1

We know that the use of citations or bibliographical references is important in scientific texts, and especially so in the genre of the research article. In his study of "interaction through citation", Ken Hyland (2000: 20) claims that "[c]itation is central to the social context of persuasion as it can provide justification for arguments and demonstrate the novelty of one's position." In KIAP, we consider the study of citation or bibliographical references (BR) as an important contribution to the answering of our second research question related to the manifestation of other researchers' work and voices in research articles. We are inspired by previous work undertaken for example by Swales (1986, 1990) and Koskela (1999) on relevant categories for the study of citation, by Hyland (2000) for his results related to differences between various disciplines, by Salager-Meyer (1998) for her studies on reference patterns in medical discourse, and by Valle (1999) for her diachronic analyses of citations in general and clusters in particular.

In KIAP we limited our research to BRs from 1900 to 1999 and ended up with the following four relatively broad categories for investigating the nature and frequency of BRs in our KIAP Corpus 1 material (for explanations, see Fløttum 2003a):

> *R1 – Non-integral reference*, by (superscript) number: *The moon is blue [1].*
> *R2 – Part-integral reference*, by "cited" author's name and/or year of publication in parentheses: *The moon is blue (Smith 1995).*

R3 – *Semi-integral reference*, by the presence of the cited author's name as an integrated element of the citing sentence: *Smith (1995) has observed that the moon is blue.*
R4 – *Fully integral reference*, by quote (defined as 3 or more words) of named author: *Smith (1995) claims: "The moon is blue." / Smith (1995) claims that "the moon is blue."*

Let us now look at some of the quantitative results (for further details, see Fløttum 2003a), according to each subcorpus (English, French, Norwegian) further broken down into economics, linguistics and medicine (Table 1).

ENGLISH subcorpus		FRENCH subcorpus		NORWEGIAN subcorpus	
engecon	24	frecon	26	noecon	29
engling	75	frling	17	noling	38
engmed	41	frmed	36	nomed	39
engall	*46*	*frall*	*26*	*noall*	*35*
ALL: 36					

Table 1. Average number of bibliographical references (BR).

With a total number of 6,413 BRs identified in KIAP Corpus 1, we get an average of 36 per article. This is an interesting result to compare with Hyland's study on BRs in research articles taken from different disciplines in English (Hyland 2000: chapter 2). There are some differences with regard to what is included in our studies, but it is nevertheless worthwhile to note that his figures indicate an average of almost 70 BRs per paper (double our findings, which are based on three languages), but with variations from 24 (in physics) to 104 (in sociology). The only subcorpus which comes close to Hyland's average in our corpus is English linguistics with 75 occurrences per article; this in fact matches exactly the average that Hyland gets for the discipline of applied linguistics (75.3) in his English material. As regards the individual variations between our different subcorpora, English linguistics is clearly the discipline with most occurrences of BRs per article, with an average of 75. There is a considerable gap between this and number two, English medicine, with an average of 41 occurrences. French linguistics displays the lowest number of occurrences, with an average of only 17. We have observed that English linguistics has the highest average in one single article (185 occurrences) and Norwegian economics the lowest (2 occurrences). It should also be noted that there are no clear patterns related to language or discipline in the individual differences between the articles with the highest and the lowest numbers of occurrences.

English	Occurrences	%	FRENCH	Occurrences	%	NORWEGIAN	Occurrences	%
engecon	469	0.42	frecon	511	0.47	noecon	580	0.51
engling	1498	0.88	frling	338	0.49	noling	758	0.84
engmed	810	1.36	frmed	675	1.18	nomed	774	1.79
engall	*2777*	*0.82*	*frall*	*1524*	*0.65*	*noall*	*2112*	*0.85*
TOTAL: 6413 occurrences/frequency: 0.78								

Table 2. Bibliographical references (BR) – occurrences and relative frequency (%).

As shown in Table 2, the average frequency of BRs in our corpus is 0.78. Of the three languages, the Norwegian subcorpus has the highest relative frequency (0.85). But the difference in relation to the English 0.82 is not big. The French subcorpus distinguishes itself by a notably lower frequency than the other two, 0.65. It is difficult to comment on these findings since we do not have similar studies to compare with. According to the traditional view of English explicitness (see Dahl 2003), one would perhaps have expected English to have the highest percentage.

If we now turn to the discipline perspective (not made explicit in Table 2), the medicine subcorpus appears as the clear winner, with a relative frequency of 1.41. This is almost double that for the second-ranked item, the linguistics subcorpus, with a percentage of 0.79. The economics subcorpus has the lowest percentage, 0.47. This result is quite surprising if one considers medicine as a hard discipline. Hyland, in the study mentioned above, presents figures which "broadly support the informal characterisation that softer disciplines tend to employ more citations" (Hyland 2000: 24). In our corpus, and in all the three languages, medicine displays the highest frequency of BRs.

Table 3 represents a ranking list where language and discipline are taken together. From this list we see an interesting division into three groups: The first group is formed by the medicine subcorpora;

the second by English and Norwegian linguistics, and the third group by French linguistics and the three economics subcorpora:

Subcorpus	Relative frequency %
nomed	1.79
engmed	1.36
frmed	1.18
engling	0.88
noling	0.84
noecon	0.51
frling	0.49
frecon	0.47
engecon	0.42

Table 3. "Ranking list" – Bibliographical references (BR) – language and discipline.

As regards the results concerning the distribution of the four BR subtypes R1–R4, the overall results indicate that R1–Non-integral, R2–Part-integral and R3–Semi-integral references are quite evenly distributed (respectively 33%, 26% and 34%; see details in Fløttum 2003a). The R4–Fully integral type–is only represented by 6% of the total BRs. The latter is interesting in relation to KIAP's research question about the way and degree of presence of others in the article. Full integration is rare; an exception was the French linguistics subcorpus in which the R4 references made up 18%, which is notably higher than all the other subcorpora. In general terms, it may be said that the presence of others is submitted to the author's strong control in a way that gives them little possibility to express themselves in their own words.

Finally, I looked at the distribution of BRs over the article sections; there is little variation between languages. Typically about 20% (+/-) of the BRs are found in the Introduction section. The medical articles in all three languages seem to follow the IMRAD norm saying that the majority of the references should be placed in the Discussion section, with some positioning in relation to previous studies in the Introduction section. Except for this particular distribution in the medical articles, BRs are spread all over, but with a low frequency in concluding sections (in the articles which have such sections).

After having carried out this electronic and manual quantitative analysis, yielding the results presented above, we found it necessary to propose some refinements of the existing categories and to undertake more qualitative analyses. Such refinements would make it easier to say something about the function of references in the text, an important aspect which the quantitative results can say little about. In Fløttum 2003a, I have proposed different refinements (for example polyphonic analyses; see Fløttum 2003c, 2005). The one I will focus on here is the cluster (CL), defined as an accumulation of three or more references. CL is a feature which typically occurs in connection with R1 and R2 but also with R3.

There are of course situations where the clustering is practical (for example when referring to a group of publications treating the same subject or belonging to the same tradition), but in many cases it may be relevant to ask why such accumulations occur. Here is an example from engling16 (the article with the highest number of BR occurrences – 185):

(1) However, the relevant dimensions of discourse meaning have proved quite hard to characterize. The tunes have variously been associated with social attitude (O'Connor and Arnold 1961 and in a different sense Merin 1983), illocutionary acts (Liberman and Sag 1974, Sag and Liberman 1975, Liberman 1975), propositional attitudes and maintenance of mutual belief (Ward and Hirschberg 1985, Pierrehumbert and Hirschberg 1990, Bartels 1997), and various notions of information structure or packaging (Halliday 1967a, Jackendoff 1972, Schmerling 1976, Ladd 1980, 1996, Gussenhoven 1983, Selkirk 1984, Terken 1984, Terken and Hirschberg 1994, Morel 1995, Rochemont 1986, Steedman 1991a,b, Zubizarreta 1998). (*engling16*)

The first two clusters are in fact introduced and specified in a quite informative way; but the last one, containing 14 BRs, is introduced rather vaguely by the complex noun phrase "various notions of information structure or packaging". With many clusters like these, it is not surprising that the total number of occurrences attains 185. However, this example must be considered as an extreme one.

Without having studied CLs in detail in KIAP's three languages and three disciplines, we may still establish that they are found in all disciplines and all languages. In the present chapter I will limit my analysis to the French material – the subcorpora with the lowest frequency of BRs.

BRs & CLs / Language & discipline	BR occurrences	BR frequency (%)	CL occurrences	Number of BRs in CLs	Average size of CL	Presence (%) of BRs in CLs
Frecon	511	0.47	33	125	3.8	25%
Frling	338	0.49	15	55	3.7	16%
Frmed	675	1.18	37	142	3.8	21%

Table 4. Frequency of bibliographical references (BR) and presence of clusters (CL) in French research articles.

The results presented in Table 4 allow us to consider clustering as an important phenomenon in research articles. In fact, Valle (1999) in her work on the manifestation of the "collective intelligence" in life sciences over 300 years (1665-1695) observes an increase over time in the clustering practice compared to the use of single, isolated citations (Valle 1999: 396). Without going into the discussion here about the role of the accumulation of research over years, I will just point to the fact that in this material the economics articles contain the lowest frequency of BRs (0.47%; not very different from linguistics with 0.49%) but the highest percentage of BRs embedded in CLs (25%; quite different from linguistics with 16%). The medicine articles are situated between economics and linguistics (21% of BRs in CL). I do not think that these differences are important; what is more interesting is that there are in fact great similarities as regards the quantitative characteristic of the CL. Their average size in all three disciplines is around 3.7-3.8 and 7 is the highest number of BRs in one CL in all three disciplines. However, there is great individual variation within the articles, an observation which I will come back to in my final remarks. First we will look at some examples of the two main functions postulated in the introduction: 1) Clusters indicating continuity and 2) Clusters indicating progress. We will study how they are manifested – what the nature of the CLs is and in what cotext they appear.

4. Nature and function of clusters

I started out this study with the hypothesis that the main function of clusters would be to refer to a scientific tradition and in many cases to situate the author as a researcher in relation to this tradition. Valle (1999) also observes that large clusters tend to appear in for example "historical surveys" of a field. However, I had to revise this hypothesis and formulate a new one according to which clusters not only indicate *continuity* but also *progress*, in the sense that they are used in more or less clearly polemic sequences to signal the author's position within a given subject matter or field. The position often contrasts with and is meant to indicate progress in relation to other researchers' work. The two functions may of course overlap, for example when the author is using different traditions manifested by different clusters to make clear his or her own position. Let us look at some examples:

4.1 Clusters indicating continuity

The clusters assuming this function often refer to a common object of study and/or they contain a verb referring more or less neutrally to the research process in the cited studies – verbs like rapporter ('report') as in (2) and se pencher sur ('look into') as in (3). Explicit credit is quite often given to the cited authors:

(2) La prédominance féminine nette est rapportée dans la plupart des séries [4],[7],[8] comme dans notre série. (frmed06)
(The clear female dominance is reported in most of the series [4],[7],[8] as in ours.)

In (2), the author is claiming that he/she is part of a tradition, while in (3), by means of the cluster, the author is referring to the fact that he/she has an object of study which is common to many researchers.

(3) De nombreux auteurs se sont penchés sur ce problème, tels Higgins J. et Hirsch F. (1970), Rhomberg R.R. (1976), Lanyi A. et Suss E.C. (1982) ou plus récemment Coughlin C.C. et Pollard P.S. (1996). Le Fonds monétaire international (FMI) aborde également la question dans son étude de 1984 [International monetary fund (1984), p. 10-11). Unanimement, l'ensemble de ces articles précise(nt) qu'il n'existe pas de variable de change préférable à une autre. (frecon04)
(Many authors have looked into this problem, for example Higgins J. and Hirsch F. (1970), Rhomberg R.R. (1976), Lanyi A. and Suss E.C. (1982) or

more recently Coughlin C.C. and Pollard P.S. (1996). The International monetary fund (IMF) also looks at the question in its 1984 study (International monetary fund (1984), p. 10-11). All the articles emphasize unanimously that there is no exchange variable which is preferable to another.)

In (4) the author is referring to two traditions; in addition he/she wants to show that the model referred to in the second one (2) is a good one and – when modified (en le particularisant) – fruitful to his/her own research:

(4) On fera donc fond sur deux axes: 1. L'opposition sur laquelle s'est fondé le deuxième regard [...].
2. Le modèle théorique de la Morphologie Distribuée (ou Autonome), cf. Halle et Marantz (1993), Harris (1997), Zribi-Hertz (1998). On montrera, en le particularisant, que ce modèle s'applique sur un mode contrastif à *son* et à *en* [...]. (frling05)
(Thus our basis will follow two axes: 1. The opposition which the second view is based on [...].
2. The theoretical model of the Morphologie Distribuée (or Autonome), cf. Halle et Marantz (1993), Harris (1997), Zribi-Hertz (1998). We will show, by specifying it, that this model can be applied in a contrastive mode to *son* and to *en* [...].)

The function of indicating continuity can have different sub-functions as for example giving historical background, giving credit, assigning priority or gaining support (see Valle 1999: 401). But it is difficult to distinguish them clearly, they often overlap. For that reason it seems fruitful to establish a few but relatively general functions as I have tried to do here.

4.2 Clusters indicating progress

The clusters assuming the *progress* function are often marked by expressions indicating concession, contrast, debate and polemic discussions. In the examples below we find *en revanche* ('on the other hand') in (5) and the polyphonic construction with the adverb *toutefois* ('however', 'nevertheless') in (6) below:

(5) En revanche, Bailey M.J., Tavlas G.S. et Ulan M. (1986), De Grauwe P (1988) et Savvides A. (1992), qui testent eux aussi les deux possibilités, trouvent des résultats plus significatifs quand ils utilisent des taux réels plutôt que nominaux. (frecon04).
(On the other hand, Bailey M.J., Tavlas G.S. and Ulan M. (1986), De Grauwe P (1988) and Savvides A. (1992), who also test the two possibilities, get more significant results when they use real rather than nominal rates.)

A debate is clearly referred to in (5); the cotext also indicates that the author values as positive the findings referred to by the cluster – he/she positions him-/herself as favorable to the research cited by using expressions such as résultats plus significatifs.

In (6), the progress is clearly indicated in that the author proposes a solution to a problem that many have experienced in previous research:

(6) [...] la mesure de la prévalence de ces maladies pose des problèmes [1-4]. On peut toutefois utiliser des estimations. (frmed03)
([...] the measuring of the diseases is problematic [1-4]. One can, however, use estimates.)

In (7) the author makes explicit that there is going to be some debate about the content of the clusters references (cf. seront confrontées) and thus progress:

(7) Dans un premier temps (par. 1), on présentera une liste de caractéristiques, dans l'ensemble bien connues, qui distinguent les deux emplois de *en*, cf. Gaatone (1980), Hulk (1983), Kupferman (1991), Lagae (1994, 1997), Milner (1978), Ruwet (1972). Ces caractéristiques générales seront confrontées ensuite (par. 2, 3) à des exemples tels que [1-4]. (frling06)
(First (par. 1), we will present a list of characteristics, generally well known, which distinguish the two uses of *en*, cf. Gaatone (1980), Hulk (1983), Kupferman (1991), Lagae (1994, 1997), Milner (1978), Ruwet (1972). Then these general characteristics will be tested (par. 2, 3) on examples like [1-4].

4.3 "Play" between different traditions

In some cases, the two functions overlap in the sense that the author may set up a play between different traditions without taking an explicit position him- /herself, as in the following:

(8) Les locutions prépositionnelles *à travers* et *au travers (de)* confrontent la recherche linguistique à un défi qui nous paraît exemplaire à plus d'un titre. Certains synonymistes (par exemple, Bénac 1956: 964; cf. aussi le TLF) soutiennent que [...]. D'autres auteurs, comme Dupré (1972: 2579-2580), Grevisse (1986: § 924), Hanse (1983: 943-944) ou Spang-Hanssen (1963: 231-233), plaident, à l'inverse, pour une "synonymie grammaticale" entre les deux expressions. [...]. Si nous voulons élucider la notion – particulièrement obscure – de "synonymie grammaticale", différentes voies s'offrent à nous. (frling17)
(The prepositional locutions *à travers* and *au travers (de)* give linguistic research a challenge which to us seems exemplary in more than one way. Some synonymists (for example, Bénac 1956: 964; cf. also TLF) claim that [...]. Others, like Dupré (1972: 2579-2580), Grevisse (1986: § 924), Hanse (1983: 943-944) or Spang-Hanssen (1963: 231-233), argue, on the contrary, for "grammatical synonymy" between the two expressions. [...]. If we want to elucidate the particularly obscure notion of "grammatical synonymy", different orientations are available.)

The two functions A and B are very broad and may of course be subject to refinements, along different dimensions, for example along positive and negative axes. The continuity function is perhaps mostly positive in that the researcher often refers to a tradition which has meant much to his/her own research while the progress function may have negative implications in the sense that the researcher often positions him/herself by refuting or showing insufficiencies in other researchers' work.

Another fruitful development of the study of BRs and of clusters is to look at them in a more explicit polyphonic perspective, i.e. in relation to the idea of the presence of several voices in one and the same text, and even in one and the same utterance. This is an interesting perspective which clearly brings in not only the traces of others, but also the traces of self, i.e. the voice of the author. (For an elaboration of this perspective, see Fløttum 2003c, 2005).

4.4 Ambiguity

I would like to come back, briefly, to the problem of ambiguity mentioned in the Introduction. Clustering is an efficient way of referring to the work and the voices of other researchers which are relevant in one's own research. Different norms imposed by the research article may however contribute to rendering the message unclear and even ambiguous. On the one hand the research article is submitted to a standard length which cannot be transgressed; on the other hand there is a norm saying that one should position one's work in relation to existing traditions. These two might come in conflict with each other: referring to a tradition necessitates a certain amount of space. To solve this problem clusters have proved to be an efficient means. However, the clustering may render the information which one wants to convey unclear, as in example (1) above. Here are two other examples:

(9) Trois dimensions se dégagent, qui coexistent pour tout ou partie selon la réalité du réseau considéré (Bakis H. (1993), Lazega E. (1994), (1998), Marrel P (1998)).
Une dimension physique [...]. : Une dimension fonctionnelle [...]. Une dimension relationnelle [...]. (frecon03)
(Three dimensions appear, which coexist wholly or partly acccording to the reality of the considered network [Bakis H. (1993), Lazega E. (1994), (1998), Marrel P (1998)). A physical dimension [...]. : a functional dimension [...]. A relational dimension [...].)

One could imagine that each cited researcher in (9) is responsible for one of the three dimensions mentioned, but this is not made explicit neither in the cluster sentence nor in the presentation of the three dimensions below. One does not get to know why the three researchers are referred to: do they all point to the three dimensions or does each point to one, for example? Let us look at (10):

(10) La sémantique formelle [...] est en train d'annexer d'une part le domaine réservé au discours, et celui du traitement du langage en contexte, à savoir la pragmatique (cf.Kamp & Reyle 1993, Chierchia 1995, Asher 1993). (frling11)
(Formal semantics [...] is annexing on one hand the domain reserved for discourse, and the one of language treatment in context, i.e. pragmatics (see Kamp & Reyle 1993, Chierchia 1995, Asher 1993)).

Do the three cited researchers represent formal semantics or the other fields mentioned, or are they all claiming the view presented?

In the following example, one could ask what kind of *étude spécifique* ('specific study') the references refer to:

(11) Les traitements de substitution (méthadone, buprénorphine,...) prescrits aux Urgences n'ont pas été étudiés ici. Ces prescriptions pourraient faire l'objet d'une étude spécifique [10], [11], [12]. (frmed20)
(The substitution treatments (methadone, buprenorphine,...) prescribed at Emergency have not been studied here. These prescriptions could be subject to a specific study [10], [11], [12].)

5. Summing up and final remarks

The use of bibliographical references represents an explicit way in academic discourse to refer to and to position oneself in relation to a given scientific tradition (the function of *continuity*) as well as to point to divergences in relation to others' work and to point to the progress represented by one's own (the function of *progress)*. The clusters may be considered as a particularly efficient way of fulfilling either of these two functions. We have also seen that clusters are used in all three disciplines studied here, slightly more frequent in economics than in medicine and in linguistics. In KIAP we want to continue these studies in order to look into the frequency of this phenomenon in articles from the same disciplines, but written in English and in Norwegian.

We have also seen that clusters are not always very reader-friendly in the sense that the reader may wonder what is really meant by referring to the studies in question, and what it is that is actually said in them.

I would also like to mention that even if clusters are present in all disciplines there are considerable individual differences within the articles. In economics, for example, ten (half of the subcorpus) of the articles do not use clusters at all; in one article there are 20 clusters, while the other nine have either only 1 or 2 clusters. In linguistics too ten articles do not display clusters. In the other half of this subcorpus, there is variation between 1, 2 and 3 clusters. Finally, in the medicine subcorpus, only 4 articles do not contain clusters. The variation in the other articles is between 1 and 7.

This might of course be due to pure coincidence, but the differences might also point to the fact that the text manifested in the genre of the research article leads a life of its own (for a similar argument, see Breivega 2001). Within the textual norms that exist, there is room for individual variation. But this explanation may not be satisfactory. The activities and the practice behind each article, i.e. the research process in given communities, and the position of the actual research could also be important in this context and contribute to the explanation of individual article differences (see Berge 2003). Object of study, methodology and the phase in which the research presented is placed (start, work in progress or end; new or well-established field) are important factors in this context. I will not go further into these more practice-oriented and even sociological questions here, but they are important if one wants to look at the phenomenon of clustering in a more comprehensive context. Last but not least, they are important from a genre perspective. The genre of the research article is not necessarily something very stable, but rather dynamic and tightly related to its socio-professional context (for further KIAP studies, see Fløttum, Dahl and Kinn (forthcoming)).

References

Berge, K. L. 2003. The scientific text genres as social actions: text theoretical reflections on the relations between context and text in scientific writing. In: K. Fløttum / Rastier, F. (eds) *Academic discourse. Multidisciplinary approaches*. Oslo: Novus, 141-157.

Breivega, K. R. 2001. *Vitskaplege argumentasjonsstrategiar. Ein komparativ analyse av superstrukturelle konfigurasjonar i medisinske, historiske og språkvitskaplege artiklar*. Dr.art. thesis. University of Bergen.

Breivega, K. R. / Dahl, T. / Fløttum, K. 2002. Traces of self and others in research articles. A comparative pilot study of English, French and Norwegian research articles in medicine, economics and linguistics. *International Journal of Applied Linguistics* 12/2, 218-239.

Dahl, T. 2003. Metadiscourse in research articles. In Fløttum, K. / Rastier, F. (eds) *Academic discourse. Multidisciplinary approaches*. Oslo: Novus, 120-138.

Dahl, T. 2004. Textual metadiscourse in research articles: a marker of national culture or academic discipline? *Journal of Pragmatics* 36/10, 1807-1825.

Fløttum, K. 2003a. Polyphony and bibliographical references. In Fløttum, K. / Rastier, F. (eds) *Academic discourse. Multidisciplinary approaches*. Oslo: Novus, 97-119.

Fløttum, K. 2003b. Personal English, indefinite French and plural Norwegian scientific authors? *Norsk Lingvistisk Tidsskrift* 21/1, 21-55.

Fløttum, K. 2003c. Polyphonie dans les textes scientifiques. Etude de deux cas français. In Olsen, M. (ed.) *Polyphonie – linguistique et littéraire*, VII. Roskilde: Samfundslitteratur Roskilde, 111-129.

Fløttum, K. 2003d. The French pronoun "on" in academic discourse – indefinite versus personal. In Hajičová, E., Kotěšovcová, A.,

Mírovský, J. (eds) *Proceedings of CIL17*, CD-ROM. Matfyzpress, MFF UK. Prague.

Fløttum, K. 2005. The self and the others – polyphonic visibility in research articles. *International Journal of Applied Linguistics* 15/1, 29–44.

Fløttum, K. / Breivega, K. 2002. Cultural identity in academic prose: national versus discipline-specific. In Koskela, M. / Laurén, C. / Nordman, M. / Pilke, N. (eds) *Porta Scientiae II. Lingua specialis.* Vaasa: Proceedings of the University of Vaasa. Reports 96, 533-545.

Fløttum, K. / Rastier F. (eds) 2003. *Academic discourse. Multidisciplinary approaches.* Oslo: Novus.

Fløttum, K. / Dahl, T. / Kinn, T. forthcoming. *Academic Voices – across languages and disciplines.* Amsterdam/Philadelphia: John Benjamins.

Hyland, K. 2000. *Disciplinary Discourses: Social Interactions in Academic Writing.* Essex: Longman/Pearson Education Limited.

Koskela, M. 1999. Om referenser till vetenskaplig litteratur i svenska filosofiska texter. *Nordica Bergensia* 20, 143-160.

Salager-Meyer, F. 1998. Reference patterns in medical English discourse. In Lundquist, L. / Picht, H. / Qvistgaard, J. (eds) *LSP. Identity and interface. Research, knowledge and society.* Proceedings from the 11th European Symposium on LSP, 1997. Copenhagen: Copenhagen Business School., 495-504.

Swales, J.M. 1986. Citation Analysis and Discourse Analysis. *Applied Linguistics* 7/1, 39-56.

Swales, J. M. 1990. *Genre analysis: English in academic and research settings*. Cambridge: Cambridge University Press.

Valle, E. 1999. *A collective intelligence: The life sciences in the Royal Society as a scientific discourse community, 1665-1965.* Doctoral thesis. Anglicana Turkuensia 17. Turku: University of Turku.

TRINE DAHL

Accommodating the reader: Metatext in research articles. A report from the KIAP project[1]

1. Introduction

In the academic world it becomes increasingly important to get the message across. In other words, the further development of our professional life depends to a great extent on how our findings are received in the research community we are a part of. This again implies that we need to argue our case well and try to anticipate the reader's reaction to the claims we make in our texts. We must, to use Michael Hoey's words, be aware of the text as "a site for interaction" (Hoey 2001: 10).

One way that we can provide assistance to the reader in the processing of our text is to make use of metatextual devices. These are devices that do not contribute to the propositional content of the text; rather, they help organise it and act as clues to the reader about what the writer is doing at a particular point in the argumentation. This phenomenon is of course not restricted to academic contexts, but previous studies have shown that it plays a prominent role in teaching and research mediation (Crismore/Markkanen/Steffensen 1993; Bunton 1999; Hyland 1999; Mauranen 2002; Thompson 2003). However, it has also been shown that various disciplines exploit metatext differently, even within the same genre (Hyland 1998). The same is true for different languages (Mauranen 1993; Valero-Garcés 1996).

1 This project is financed by the Research Council of Norway. See also Fløttum, this volume.

In this chapter I would like to bring these two variables, that is, discipline and language, together in order to discuss which seems to be more decisive in terms of metatext use. Do linguists have their own style when it comes to offering assistance in the form of metatextual expressions, or is it rather the case that for example Norwegian researchers clearly form a group here, regardless of whether they are linguists, economists or researchers within other disciplines? This is an issue which belongs in the framework of the KIAP project[2]. In this short chapter I will focus primarily on metatext in English and Norwegian, but results and comments concerning French, the third language involved in the project, are given in sections 5 and 6 (Dahl 2004 for a more detailed presentation and discussion of metatext in the KIAP project).

2. What is metatext?

The concept of *metatext* is not easily definable. Other terms in use include "meta-comments" and "metadiscourse". We often distinguish between "metatext" and "metadiscourse", using "metatext" to refer to one category within the broad concept referred to as "metadiscourse". "Metatext", then, is used to refer to elements serving a primarily textual function, while "metadiscourse" covers this in addition to meta-elements which function primarily on the interpersonal level, establishing a rapport with the reader (Vande Kopple 1985; Crismore/Farnsworth 1990). Let me illustrate this difference with a couple of examples (all the examples given are from the KIAP corpus):

Metadiscourse

Textual metadiscourse=metatext:

2 KIAP: Kulturell Identitet i Akademisk Prosa (Cultural Identity in Academic Prose); see section 3.

(1) This paper is organized as follows:...
(2) In this section, we discuss...
(3) We have argued above for the use of...

Interpersonal metadiscourse:

(4) If you are like me and find it implausible that...
(5) Why were these forms retained and those forms lost?

In this chapter I have restricted my investigation to metatextual expressions. These have been grouped into two categories, namely what I call "locational metatext" and "rhetorical metatext". Examples 1, 2 and 3 above contain both types, with *this paper* (1), *this section* (2) and *above* (3) as locational metatext and *organized* (1), *discuss* (2) and *argued* (3) as rhetorical metatext. So, while locational expressions guide the reader through the text by reference to the text and its parts, rhetorical expressions provide overt information to the reader about what discourse act the writer is performing, thereby easing the processing effort needed to interpret the message. I include only verbs in this category.

3. Corpus and methodological issues

My investigation of metatext belongs in the much broader framework of the KIAP project (<www.hit.uib.no/kiap>; Breivega/Dahl/Fløttum 2002; Fløttum 2003a, Fløttum 2003b). This is a linguistically based project aiming at identifying cultural identity in academic texts. It is a doubly contrastive project taking both discipline and language into consideration.

We are interested in writer manifestation as an expression of cultural identity, and we want to see if such identity is linked primarily to the author's native language culture or primarily to the disciplinary culture he or she is socialised into. The languages involved are English, a world language and a popular object for studies within academic discourse; French, also a world language, but one which has not been studied much in the context of writer identity; and Norwegian, definitely not a world language and hardly studied at all in such a context (an important exception is Breivega 2001). We have looked specifically for authors in the three languages who are likely to be native speakers. As for disciplines, we study representatives of the three major scientific fields, namely natural science (represented by medicine), social science (represented by economics) and the humanities (represented by linguistics).

Our final corpus will consist of approximately 450 research articles divided over the three languages and three disciplines. At present we are working with 180 articles, called Corpus 1. This corpus consists of some 800,000 words, a figure which only includes the so-called body part of the article. Abstracts, headings, examples, tables, footnotes, references etc., have been stripped off. The list of search items has been established through a combined process of armchair linguistics, manual work with the texts in a pilot phase, as well as inspiration from previous studies. The automatic search process produces lists of occurrences of each search item in its context. As is often the case in such automated searches, the program turns out hits which are not relevant for the investigation. Let me give a few examples of such noise in the corpus:

(6) his influential 1985 *paper* on…
(7) The definite *article* appears as an epithet…
(8) emergency caesarean *section* was less likely among younger mothers…
(9) countries with per capita income *below* $1500 in 1985…

As a consequence we have to go through the lists manually in order to weed out irrelevant hits.

4. Results and discussion

The findings are presented in tabular form below, with data on the two languages in Table 1 and data on the three disciplines in Table 2 (locational) and Table 3 (rhetorical). The figures given are the relative frequencies expressed as the percentage which the number of occurrences represents in relation to the number of words in the relevant (sub)corpus.

English	*Norwegian*
0.37	0.34

Table 1. Metatextual elements: Overall relative frequency in English and Norwegian.

We see from Table 1 that as regards language, English and Norwegian scientific writers display a very similar pattern of metatext usage. When it comes to discipline, Tables 2 and 3 show that economists use more metatext than linguists, and that these two use a lot more than the medical writers. These two tables also reveal that locational metatext is more frequent than rhetorical, that is in economics and linguistics. In the medical texts the situation is the opposite. I will comment on this point below.

Discipline	*English*	*Norwegian*
economics	0.30	0.30
linguistics	0.21	0.20
medicine	0.02	0.01

Table 2. Locational meta-elements for two languages and three disciplines.

Discipline	*English*	*Norwegian*
economics	0.19	0.18
linguistics	0.18	0.11
medicine	0.05	0.04

Table 3. Rhetorical meta-elements for two languages and three disciplines.

From these results we may conclude that for these two languages the discipline variable seems to be the important one in the study of metatext. English and Norwegian economists, as well as linguists and medical researchers accommodate their readers in a very similar way. The only exception seems to be the linguists' use of rhetorical metatext. A closer look at the meta-elements for this group reveals that this result to a great extent is due to English linguists being frequent users of the verbs *argue* and *discuss*, while Norwegian linguists use the corresponding verbs *argumentere* and *diskutere* only modestly[3].

So, were these results what we had expected or not? As regards the language variable, our hypothesis was that English scientific writers use more metatext than Norwegian (Breivega/Dahl/Fløttum 2002). This was not really confirmed by the results of my investigation. On the basis of these findings, we might claim that both English and Norwegian are representatives of so-called reader-oriented cultures (Hinds 1987). Anna Mauranen's description of the Anglo-American writer as someone who invites the reader "to take a tour of the text together with the author, who acts as a guide" (1993: 16), may also be extended to the Norwegian scientific writer. An example from one of the Norwegian economics texts in our corpus provides support for this claim:

(10) La meg derfor bare gi et lite hint om sammenhengen nå, og invitere leseren til å lese seg videre ned gjennom artikkelen for å få med seg detaljene.
[Let me therefore just hint at the connection now, and invite the reader to read on through the paper to pick up all the details.]

As for the discipline variable it was unexpected that economics texts in fact had a higher frequency of metatext than linguistics texts. One of our hypotheses was that linguists would be more visible as writers in their texts than economists and medical writers (Breivega *et al.* 2002). However, my investigation into the use of metatext has shown that the economist is very much present in the text, particularly in the function of the guide providing signposts which the reader can use when navigating within the text. It is in fact in the locational metatext category that we see the clearest differences between the economists

3 It was suggested by John Swales in the discussion of the present paper that this difference might be due to the more competitive environment of the Anglophone world of linguistics.

and the linguists. If we again take a look behind the figures we find that the difference to a great extent can be pinned down to a difference in frequency of a few meta-elements. The words in question are *article/paper* and *section* and their Norwegian counterparts. It almost seems to be a genre requirement that the research article within economics should refer to itself and its parts throughout the text and in particular in the introduction part of the article, providing the reader with a schematic outline of the paper:

(11) The rest of this paper is organized as follows. *Section 2* briefly describes [...] We present our model of information sharing in *Section 3*, where we show that [...] *Section 4* describes some of the central bank's activities that are [...] *Section 5* concludes and suggests avenues for further investigation.

Linguists, too, often do this, but the feature is less consistently observed in that discipline.

Let us now take a closer look at medicine, the discipline where there were relatively few metatextual elements. The figures in Tables 2 and 3 indicate a dichotomy between economics/linguistics on the one hand and medicine on the other. To use Bazerman's words, there seems to be a difference in how "language accomplishes the work of science" (Bazerman 1988: 291). Research articles in the humanities and social sciences also display similarities in terms of text structure, but they are far from being as homogeneous in this respect as articles within the natural sciences. The medical articles in our corpus all follow the expected IMRD structure (Swales 1990), even articles which are more theoretically oriented than the traditional reporting from a study undertaken. The use of this formalised structure to present one's research data implies that all the information chunks find their given place within the text. This is understood by writer and reader and, as a consequence, there is no need to specify where in the text information is found by means of locational metatextual expressions. When it comes to rhetorical metatext, we saw from Table 3 that there was more of this in the medical texts than of the locational type. Even so, there was much less such metatext, too, in the medical articles compared to economics and linguistics. What turns out to be the case is that in the medical texts the research process has turned textual in a different way than in the other two disciplines. What I mean by this is that the writing tradition within that discipline allows for the presentation of research data as an account of research acts which to a lesser degree must be turned into discourse acts than is the case in economics and linguistics. A high number of verbs in the medical articles are of the research process type, such as

(12) I *carried out* a study…
(13) I *examined* the qualitative data…
(14) We *entered* all data on…
(15) We *excluded* patients with a…

One explanation for this may be that the medical researchers work with physical objects and measurements, while economists and linguists typically work with more abstract notions. They have to create connections and to some extent construct consequences through the interpretation of data to a greater extent than the medical writers, who in many cases may refer to natural laws and report according to standardised procedures. The same thing is reflected in the very low frequency of references to the medical article as a text, and the high frequency of the word *study*, which has not been included as a locational metatext item.

5. What about French?

As can be seen from Tables 4 and 5 below, French authors use far less metatext than their English and Norwegian colleagues. The main difference in the locational category may be spotted in the occurrences of words referring to the text itself (for example in French *article*) and to parts of the text (in French *section*, *paragraphe*, *partie*). Such words are very common in English and Norwegian research articles, at least within economics and linguistics. It is, however, not just in the use of these locational expressions that the difference is observed. We also see it in the use of locational words pointing backwards and forwards (for example *above*, and *below* and their Norwegian and French counterparts) and *now* (Norwegian *nå*; French *maintenant*). This seems to indicate that French writers are less concerned about the function of guiding the reader through the text than English and Norwegian researchers.

Discipline	*English*	*Norwegian*	*French*
economics	0.30	0.30	0.10
linguistics	0.21	0.20	0.10
medicine	0.02	0.01	0.02

Table 4. Locational meta-elements for three languages and three disciplines.

Discipline	*English*	*Norwegian*	*French*
economics	0.19	0.18	0.06
linguistics	0.18	0.11	0.09
medicine	0.05	0.04	0.04

Table 5. Rhetorical metatext for three languages and three disciplines.

6. Concluding remarks

I claimed in section 4 that discipline seemed to be the decisive factor in terms of metatext. However, the inclusion of French articles has changed the picture somewhat. What now seems to be the case is that when comparing English and Norwegian, discipline matters more, in that for both these languages the frequency of metatext was quite similar within the three disciplines irrespective of language.

The French results, on the other hand, revealed lower frequencies of metatext in both economics and linguistics. In fact, the figures for these two disciplines were quite close to what was recorded for the medical texts. From this two conclusions may be drawn, one relating to language and one to discipline.

As regards language, it seems clear that from a metatext perspective English and Norwegian represent reader-oriented cultures. The role of the academic author seems to be that of taking the reader by the hand and guiding him or her through the text. French academic writers, on the other hand, take a different view of their role in the mediation through text. They present their argumentation and leave it up to the readers to find their way through the text. Hence, these results relating to metatext seem to indicate that French represents a writer-oriented culture. Whether French academics are able to switch between the reader-oriented way of writing when producing articles in English – which they must if they want a wider audience – and their native writer-oriented approach, is something that remains to be investigated. A study of Spanish scientists writing in English indicates that this is no easy task (Valero-Garcés 1996).

When it comes to the discipline variable, we have seen that English and Norwegian academic writers are marked by the practices of their discipline. Economists in both these two languages are the most frequent users of signals to their readers about how to handle the text. This is particularly true for locational metatext providing navigation signals. Linguists, too, provide their audience with metatextual clues to ease the text processing. The medical writers, on the other hand, rely on the IMRD format in the structuring of their material. Little extra processing help is offered in the form of metatext. This contributes to the impression of the medical texts as accounts which are closer to the research process than is the case for the economics and linguistics texts. This is probably due to the fact that in the latter two disciplines, research results are to a large extent created through the argumentation built up within the text, in contrast to medical research which typically takes place in the laboratory by means of commonly acknowledged methods and procedures.

References

Bazerman, C. 1988. *Shaping written knowledge: The genre and activity of the experimental article in science*. Madison, WI: The University of Wisconsin Press.

Breivega, K. 2001. Vitskapelege argumentasjonsstrategiar. Ein komparativ analyse av superstrukturelle konfigurasjonar i medisinske, historiske og språkvitskaplege artiklar. Unpublished PhD thesis, University of Bergen.

Breivega, K. / Dahl, T. / Fløttum, K. 2002. Traces of self and others in research articles. A comparative pilot study of English, French and Norwegian research articles in medicine, economics and linguistics. *International Journal of Applied Linguistics* 12/2, 218-239.

Bunton, D. 1999. The use of higher level metatext in PhD theses. *English for Specific Purposes* 18, Supplement 1, S41-S56.

Crismore, A. / Farnsworth, R. 1990. Metadiscourse in popular and professional science discourse. In Nash, W. (ed.) *The writing scholar: Studies in academic discourse*. Newbury Park, CA: Sage, 118-136.

Crismore, A. / Markkanen, R. / Steffensen, M. 1993. Metadiscourse in persuasive writing. A study of texts written by American and Finnish university students. *Written Communication* 10/1, 39-71.

Dahl, T. 2004. Textual metadiscourse in research articles: a marker of national culture or of academic discipline? *Journal of Pragmatics* 36/10, 1807-1825.Fløttum, K. 2003a. Personal English, indefinite French and plural Norwegian scientific authors? Pronominal author manifestation in research articles: A cross-linguistic disciplinary study. *Norsk Lingvistisk Tidsskrift* 21/1, 21-55.

Fløttum, K. 2003b. Bibliographical references and polyphony in research articles. In Fløttum, K. / Rastier, F. (eds) *Academic discourse. Multidisciplinary approaches*. Oslo: Novus, 97-119

Hinds, J. 1987. Reader versus writer responsibility: A new typology. In Connor, U. / Kaplan, R. (eds) *Writing across languages: Analysis of L2 text*. Reading, MA: Addison-Wesley, 141-152.

Hoey, M. 2001. *Textual interaction. An introduction to written discourse*. London: Routledge.

Hyland, K. 1998. Persuasion and context: The pragmatics of academic metadiscourse. *Journal of Pragmatics* 30, 437-455.

Hyland, K. 1999. Talking to students: Metadiscourse in introductory textbooks, *English for Specific Purposes* 18/1, 3-26.

Mauranen, A. 1993. Contrastive ESP rhetoric: Metatext in Finnish-English economics texts. *English for Specific Purposes* 12, 3-22.

Mauranen, A. 2002. "One thing I'd like to clarify…". Observations of academic speaking. Available: <http://www.eng.helsinki.fi/hes/Corpora/one_thing.htm> [accessed: May 9, 2003].

Swales, J. 1990. *Genre analysis. English in academic and research settings*. Cambridge: CUP.

Thompson, S. E. 2003. Text-structuring metadiscourse, intonation and the signalling of organisation in academic lectures. *Journal of English for Academic Purposes* 2, 5-20.

Valero-Garcés, C. 1996. Contrastive ESP rhetoric: Metatext in Spanish-English economics texts. *English for Specific Purposes* 15, 279-294.

Vande Kopple, W. 1985. Some exploratory discourse on metadiscourse. *College Composition and Communication* 36/1, 82-93.

TIINA MÄNNIKKÖ

The presentation of series of events in academic and popularised articles in the field of history

1. Background

History as a discipline originally evolved through spoken stories and pure literature to what it is today (see *Herodotos historia* 2000; Martin 1987; Steinmetz 1995). The task of the historian has been defined as "to ascertain, describe, and interpret particular events, developments and situations of the human past" (Kristeller 1961: 87). Therefore there will always be a connection between narratives and academic history, because some narrative features, for example the chronology of the events and people involved in these events, will always exist in historical research. When academic texts are popularised they can be expected to become even more narrative. According to the instructions for popularised writers, they should aim at writing narrative texts and think of themselves as storytellers instead of researchers (Fjæstad 1993; Laurén/Myking/Picht 1997; see also Melander 1987; Koskela/Pilke 2001).

The aim of my research is to compare academic and popularised articles in the field of history in order to answer the question "why do we popularise history?", comparing narrative aspects in the chosen articles. In this chapter I aim to examine whether the difference between academic and popularised articles can be found in the way they make use of stories, i.e. to what extent academic and popularised articles in the field of history include story-like parts. The term "story" will in this study refer to all series of events that recapitulate past time events with human actors involved. One criterion of a story is that it should include at least two event clauses[1] that are ordered according to the original time line of the events[2].

Myers (1990), who has analysed both scientific and popularised texts in the field of gene technology, claims that historical chronology, human actors and audience are features that are conventionally excluded from research reports. According to Myers (1990), research articles only include a logical sequence of experiments, not any sequence of events, but popularised articles introduce the discovery made as an event and the researchers as actors. They also include time expressions that guide the reader through the chronological sequence of events.

2. Materials and method

The material for this study consists of two parts. Firstly, there are five articles published in the Swedish academic journal *Historisk Tidskrift* ('Historical Journal', *my transl.*) between 1997 and 1999. Secondly there are five popularised articles published in the Swedish popularised magazine, *Populär Historia* ('Popularised History', *my transl.*) between 1997 and 1998. All the articles are written in Swedish by Swedish academic historians who work at a Swedish university in the Department of History or the Department of General History. In the following I will refer to the academic articles with the abbreviations A1-A5 and to the popularised articles with the abbreviations P1-P5.

The study consists of two parts. To be able to study the stories included in the articles from a semantic point of view, I will first examine the event clauses used in the articles. I am interested in cases where the writer recapitulates events in the so-called storyworld with clauses in the simple past or historical present tense. By "storyworld"

1 An event clause is a main clause in simple past or historical present tense and expresses a non-iterative, specific, completive and affirmative event (Polanyi 1982).

2 Compare Labov (1972) and Fleischman (1990).

I understand events that have happened in another time, often another location and are populated by other participants[3] compared with the actual world of the writer and the reader (Polanyi 1989: 15). When these clauses form a series of at least two events, they meet the criteria of a story in this study[4].

To illustrate the method, I will first give two examples from my material of which the first (Ex 1) does not meet the criteria of a story and the other (Ex 2) does. I will also give my own *translations* into English. The numbers in brackets refer to the numbers of the sentences.

(1) (12) Genom 1917 års familjerättsliga reform vidtog den svenska staten långtgående åtgärder för att förbättra de utomäktenskapliga barnens ställning. (13) Under 1800-talet hade samhällets insatser för ogifta mödrar mestadels bestått i att hjälpa dessa att bli av med sina barn, genom utplacering i fosterhem eller barnhem. (14) Tanken bakom det tidiga 1900-talets reformer var istället att möjliggöra för mödrarna att själva ta hand om sina barn. (15) Men det samhälleliga stöd som erbjöds genom barnavårdsmannainstitutionen var samtidigt förbundet med kontroll av barnens omvårdnad och av hur moderskapet, och faderskapet, utövades. (16) Med 1917 års lag fick alla svenska barn för första gången rätt till två föräldrar. (A4)
(12) On the basis of the reform concerned with family rights 1917 the Swedish state made far-reaching changes to improve the position of children born out of wedlock. (13) In the 19th century the efforts of society to help unmarried mothers had mostly consisted in helping them to get rid of their children by placing them in foster homes or children's homes. (14) The intention behind the early 20th century reforms was, on the contrary, to make it possible for the mothers to care for their children themselves. (15) But the social support offered by the child welfare officer's institution was at the same time connected with control of the children's care and of how the moherhood and fatherhood was practised. (16) Thanks to the law of 1917 all Swedish children were for the first time given the right to two parents. (A4)

(2) (60) År 1385 återgick de västskånska städerna och borgarna från hanseaterna till den danska kronan i enlighet med fredsbestämmelserna i Stralsund 1370. (61) Samma år uppnådde Olof kunglig myndighetsålder (15 år). (62) Han avled dock redan i augusti 1387, sedan han plötsligt insjuknat under en vistelse

3 According to Beaugrande (1982: 408) the participants do not necessarily have to be persons, the presence of any animate agent that has some force-possessing entity that can act and react with the world can meet the criterion of "story".

4 The storyworld can be interrupted, for example when the writer gives his/her comment on an event or a state. When the connection to the storyworld still remains, I take these as a part of the story.

på Falsterbohus. (63) Genast inträdde Margareta som regent i Danmark, och strax därpå även i Norge. (64) Hon antog titeln fullmäktig fru och rätt husbonde och framstod i detta läge som obestridd härskarinna i de båda rikena. (P4)

(60) In 1385 the towns and castles of the west Skanian members of the Hanseatic League were returned to the Danish Crown in accordance with the Stralsund peace agreement in 1370. (61) The same year Olof reached royal full age (15 years). (62) He died however as early as August 1387, having suddenly fallen ill during a stay at Falsterbohus. (63) Immediately Margareta succeeded as ruler of Denmark, and soon afterwards also of Norway. (64) She assumed the title of authorized mistress and acknowledged master and in this position appeared as undisputed ruler of both kingdoms. (P4)

In the first example there is no series of events described; nor does it include any two events (in event clauses) in temporal sequence. Example 2, on the other hand, forms a part of a longer series of events. The example includes three event clauses, which recapitulate events in temporal sequence, i.e. their order cannot be changed without changing the inferred sequence of events in the original semantic interpretation. I have underlined the narrative heads in event clauses, i.e. finite verbs, which carry the tense marker[5] of the clause (see Labov/ Waletzky 1967). The chronological order is established by assigning sequential symbols (the year 1385, the same year, August 1387, immediately) through the story. Besides event clauses there can be non-event clauses (i.e. state clauses that encode states of affairs, which persist over some interval of time in the storyworld, see Polanyi 1982) included in a story. However, non-event clauses cannot alone form a story. After finding out the series of events presented in event clauses I will describe them with regard to their placement and length. I will also discuss the roles that the stories have in the articles on the basis of rhetoric and the writers' own indications.

According to rhetoric, stories can be used in different discourses to fulfil different functions. Thurén (2000), who has analysed popularised texts, claims that a story is the most effective device that writers have at their disposal when popularising a scientific text. Stories are both entertaining and informative in their nature. Also, stories have good proof value, although they cannot alone function as proof of a

5 The possible tense in an event clause is simple past or simple present; no modals, present perfects or past perfects can act as a narrative head.

scientific fact. Besides entertaining and informing they may, however, act as a part of argumentation to support a claim. Regardless of the function, most often stories lighten the presentation, because it is easier for a reader to understand the information given in the form of a story than in some other form (Hellspong 2001; Thurén 2000). Stories may illustrate a train of thought and a writer can, after presenting a story, discuss some more advanced and theoretical topic. It is easier for the reader to take in the heavier theoretical discussion after reading a concrete story. When existing in the middle of the theoretical discussion, stories often serve to explain and concretise some abstract phenomena (Thurén 2000).

3. Stories in my material

I start by describing the series of events / stories that the material includes in relation to how long they are and how they are located in the articles. For example, the first academic article (A1) consists of 354 sentences in all. There is one story included in the article, starting at sentence 66 and ending at sentence 74. The following table shows all the stories found in my material.

Article	Placement in sentences	All sentences
A1	66-74	354
A2	6-12, 156-159, 174-176	240
A3	71-73, 78-80	132
A4	140, 187-231	305
A5	129-130, 145-148, 236-238, 275-281	394
P1		118
P2	45-48, 74-76	105
P3		83
P4	16-96	100
P5	28-176	217

Table 1. The placement and length of the stories.

As Table 1 shows there are two popularised articles (P1 and P3) that do not include stories at all, i.e. at least two event clauses in sequence.

In the remaining eight articles there can be found different kinds of stories. In the following, I aim to describe the different kinds by giving examples from my material.

3.1 Stories covering (almost) the whole article

The writer can start his/her text by presenting the first event and end the text by presenting the last event of the series. This kind of mode of presentation is possible especially in the popularised articles, because the reader does not expect to find (so much) academic discussion here as in corresponding academic articles (Hellspong 2000; see however Bloor 1996). The academic articles are also more bound to genre[6] conventions, which means that they cannot as easily be formed as stories (Koskela 1997). The academic articles can, however, include parts that can be compared to stories, but they are more clearly parts of the whole, not forming the whole text.

According to my material the supposition above seems to be true. There are only two articles, both popularised, which use stories that are placed (almost) through the whole article (P4 and P5). In these articles the events carry forward the contents and have as a function the giving of information.

The aim of article P5 is to discuss the possibility of marrying for love during a certain period of time in Sweden. The writer has chosen to discuss the subject by describing the social life of one young woman. The writer also expresses explicitly that she wants to 'get better acquainted with people in the past' (*för att komma människor i det förflutna närmare [...]*) and that is why she chooses to concentrate on one case. The instructions for popularised writers say that the writer should push forward people instead of scientific facts when popularising, and against this background the writer has made a good choice (compare Fjaestad 1993; Koskela 2002).

6 The term "genre" is used here to describe intertextual differences, that is the difference between academic articles and popularised articles (see Koskela 1995: 104).

In the article, the writer describes four different relationships the woman has with four different men. The last relationship ends with a marriage. On the grounds of the four relationships, the writer tries to analyse why the fourth one ended with marriage and the other three did not. In my opinion this is possible only in a popularised article, where the reader can be expected to be interested in one concrete case. The theoretical discussion and conclusions drawn on the basis of that one case do not have to be as thoroughly motivated as in a corresponding academic article. The nature of history as a branch of knowledge has been discussed many times because of the impossibility of producing generalised knowledge (Halldén 1983; Hellspong 2000; Kristensen and Schmidt 1995). As an idiographic discipline history does not concentrate on attaining generalised knowledge, but in this popularised article the writer expresses in the beginning that she wants to find out if it (in general) was possible to marry for love (see sentence 1 in Ex 3). Then she presents the case of one woman without expressing the fact that the knowledge gained on the basis of one case does not have much academic truth-value, i.e. cannot be generalised. Because the writer does not bind the concrete case in question to any general discussion about the topic, the reader sees the one case as an answer to the question raised at the beginning of the article.

(3) (1) Hur ofta kunde man följa sina känslor när man gifte sig för tvåhundra år sedan? [...] (17) För att komma människor i det förflutna närmare kan vi ta hjälp av deras korrespondens, om den sparats till våra dagar. (18) Privata brev avslöjar en hel del av känslor och tankar. [...] (26) En av kvinnorna vi möter hette Bernera Santesson. (27) Hon var dotter till brukspatronen och grosshandlaren Nils Santesson och hans hustru Margareta. (28) Bernera föddes 1781 och var den tredje dottern i familjen, där det också fanns en äldre son. [...] (149) För Bernera hade hennes förhållande med Niclas varit allvar. (150) Hon anförtrodde en av sina väninnor att hon visste att Niclas haft andra kvinnor, men att hon beslutat överse med det, eftersom det ändå var så vanligt bland män. (151) Uppgivet konstaterade hon med tanke på kvinnans möjligheter i livet. (152) "Huru sällan ser vi icke uppfyllandet af våra önskningar, och qwäfvia och nedtysta wår öfvertygelse är i de flesta cas (fall) vår lott". [...] (157) Under 1808 gifte sig Bernera, som då hunnit bli tjugosju år, med den fyra år äldre Johan Ulric. (P5)
(1) How often could one act on one's feelings when one was married two hundred years ago? [...] (17) In order to get better acquainted with people in the past we can make use of their correspondence if it has been preserved to our day. (18) Private letters reveal a good many feelings and thoughts. [...] (26)

One of the women we meet was called Bernera Santesson. (27) She was the daughter of the foundry proprietor and wholesale dealer Nils Santesson and his wife Margareta. (28) Bernera was born in 1781 and was the third daughter of the family, which also contained an elder son. [...] (149) For Bernera her love affair with Niclas had been serious. (150) She confided to one of her lady friends that she was aware that Niclas had had other women, but she had decided to connive at this, since it was still very common among men. (151) Resigned she reflected, considering woman's possibilities in life. (152) "How seldom we see our wishes come true, and suppressing and silencing our conviction is in most cases our lot." [...] In 1808 Bernera, who had then reached the age of twenty-seven, married the four year older Johan Ulric. (P5)

The function of the story in the example above is to give information. There is no academic discussion included that the writer binds the story to.

3.2 Short stories in the middle of an article

Besides the stories that are placed (almost) throughout whole articles, there are also stories in my material that exist as a part of a whole. At the minimum the stories consist of only two to three event clauses, as in the following example.

(4) (65) Skansens midvinterfest, som var ett av spelens fasta inslag, exemplifierar hur förhärligandet av hjältekungar och landets historia kunde te sig. (66) Vid spelen 1901 hade hela området försetts med marschaller och två alternerande musikkårer som underhöll med nationella musikstycken. (67) Vaktposter i svensk 1600-talsmundering höll ett vakande öga över området. (68) Det var inte utan sinne för skådespel och effekter det hela sattes i verket. (69) Plötsligt bröts nämligen lugnet när en av vakterna ropade: (70) " I gevär!", varpå Gustav II Adolf kom ridande i full galo (71) Flera andra svenska kungar fanns också närvarande. (72) Gustav Vasa var naturligtvis representerad. (73) Den här gången gömd i ett hölass och åtföljd av sina dalkarlar. (74) Kvällen avslutades med ett fyrverkeri. (A1)
(65) The Skansen midwinter celebration, which was one of the standard features of the games, exemplifies what form the glorification of hero kings and the history of the country could take. (66) During the games in 1901 the whole area had been provided with torches and two alternating bands which entertained by playing national pieces of music. (67) Sentinels in Swedish 17th – century equipment kept a sharp eye on the area. (68) It was not without a sense of play and effects the whole pageant was executed. (69) For suddenly the peace was broken when one of the sentinels cried out: (70) "To arms!", whereupon Gustavus II Adolphus came riding at full gallop. (71) Several

> *other Swedish kings were also present. (72) Gustavus Vasa was of course represented. (73) This time hidden in a loaded hay-cart and accompanied with his Dalecarlians. (74) The evening was finished off with a firework display. (A1)*

In example 4 above the first sentence includes an expression that reveals the function of the story. The writer has explicitly suggested that the story serves as an example of some element in the contents of the article; it illustrates a given fact. The writer wants to evaluate the role that royalties had in sporting events and has chosen to tell the readers a story about an occurrence where the king arrived on the scene of the event. The story also serves to support the writer's argument, i.e. that the kings were important. In my material there are several corresponding stories, one of them in a popularised article (P2). In all cases the writer does not explicitly state that the story serves as a concrete example; it can, however, be understood on the basis of the context.

In the academic articles, the writers state in several cases that they want to describe practice in addition to the theoretical discussion. The concrete cases are often described in event clauses, as in the following example. In most cases the writer also explicitly states that he/she aims to describe practice.

(5) (145) I mitten av 1950-talet <u>inlämnades</u> ett mycket värdefullt förslag som också uppmärksammades stort. (146) Nils Marklund hade konstruerat en ny kokillbearbetningsmaskin, och ersättningen blev mycket stor – 10 000 kr. (147) Det <u>anmäldes</u> till en riksomfattande förslagstävling där det vann första pris. (148) Det <u>valdes</u> även ut tillsammans med sex andra "bra" förslag att ingå i en film om förslagsverksamhet. (A5)
(145) In the middle of the 1950s a very valuable suggestion was delivered which was also paid great attention to. (146) Nils Marklund had designed a new mould processing machine, and the compensation was very great – 10 000 Swedish crowns. (147) It was entered into a nation-wide proposal competition where it won the first prize. (148) It was also selected togther with six other "good" suggestions to be included in a film on competition activity. (A5)

In the same article (A5) there are several short series of events that are all located in the latter part of the article. The writer has discussed in general how workers submitted proposals dealing with their work and how they succeeded in making their working place better. According to the writer, the theoretical discussion does not say much about what the concrete propositions looked like ("säger inte mycket om vilka konkreta förslag som arbetarna inlämnade"), and that is why he wants to describe some concrete cases. The writer reveals that he wants to give the reader the possibility of seeing practice in addition to the abstract academic discussion.

There are several similar stories in the academic articles, and in most cases the writer explicitly expresses the need for describing practice. In my opinion this could be something that is characteristic of the discipline. Because of the discussion of whether historical research can be considered as reliable and objective (see, for example, Collin/Køppe 1995; Kristeller 1961), historians – especially in academic articles – want to offer the reader the possibility of drawing their own conclusions. Because the contents of the concrete examples in academic articles often (if not always) come from the research material that the historians use, they can be considered as true (compare Thurén 2000). That is why they have more truth-value than fictitious examples that are made up just to give a concrete example of some abstract phenomena. In other disciplines, the concrete examples presented in the form of a story do not have to be true, although truth-value is otherwise important in all academic discourse (Bloor 1996; Koskela/Pilke 2001).

3.3 Stories at the beginning / at the end of an article

The story in the following example (Ex 6) is from an academic article (A2). It is located at the beginning of the article. The writer starts her text by talking about Elvida Jansson, a female worker who was interested in politics but who, because of her sex, had few possibilities of acting in the political arena in Sweden at the beginning of the twentieth century. The role of this story is to concretise the discussion that follows, in which the writer defines the political possibilities of female workers in Swedish society in general.

(6) (6) År 1919 fick skofabriksarbeterskan Elvida Jansson för första gången rösta i ett kommunalt val och två år senare i ett riksdagsval. (9) För en arbetare gick vägen till den politiska arenan via fackföreningen, och under 1920-och 1930-

talen kandiderade Elvida gång på gång till poster i Sko- och Läderindustriarbetareförbundets avd 17 i Örebro, men utan någon större framgång. (10) Samtidigt ägnade hon mycket kraft åt att bygga upp Skoarbeterskornas klubb och Stugföreningen, där kvinnliga skoarbetare diskuterade arbetsförhållanden, mötesteknik, kvinnans likställdhet med mannen, fredsfrågor, nattarbetslagen och sexualhygien – frågor som aldrig kom upp på dagordningen i fackföreningen eller i den socialdemokratiska arbetarkommunen. (11) Någon politisk karriär gjorde Elvida Jansson inte förrän hon år 1932 gick in i den av hemmafruar helt dominerade socialdemokratiska kvinnoklubben, men då gick det snabbt. (12) Efter ett år var hon klubbens ordförande, året därpå blev hon stadsfullmäktigeledamot och efter ytterligare ett par år invald i arbetarkommunens styrelse. (A2)
(6) In 1919 Elvida Jansson, who worked in a shoe factory, was for the first time allowed to vote in a local government election and two years later in a general election. (9) For a worker the path to the political arena went through the trade union, and in the 1920s and 1930s Elvida stood time and again for posts in the Shoe and Leather Industry Workers' Union, department 17 in Örebro, but without any greater success. (10) At the same time she devoted a great deal of energy to build up the Club for Women Shoe Workers and the Cottage Association, where female shoe workers discussed working conditions, meeting technique, sex equality between women and men, questions regarding peace, the law of night-work and sex hygiene – questions that never came up for discussion in the trade union or in the local branch of the Swedish Social-Democratic party. (11) Elvida Jansson never made any political career until in 1932 she became a member of the Social Democratic women's club, totally dominated by housewives, but then she made rapid progress. (12) In a year she was the chairperson of the club, the year after that she became a member of the city council and after a further couple of years she was selected as a member of the committee of local branch of the Swedish Social-Democratic Party. (A2)

Considering the length and placement, the story presented in Ex 6 is not central, but from the content point of view it summarises (by concretising) the central contents of the whole article. The writer explicitly expresses this by saying that she will in this article concentrate on discussing whether the concept of differentiated citizenship can help to understand Elvida Jansson's acting in the political arena (see Ex 7). When compared to the stories in popularised articles (see Ex 3) the story of Elvida could form the contents chosen for the corresponding popularised article.

(7) (88) I mitt eget pågående avhandlingsarbete om kvinnors kollektiva handlande under åren 1900-1950 använder jag medborgarbegreppet för att undersöka sambanden mellan kvinnors politiska deltagande och deras ställning i arbetsli-

vet. (89) Jag prövar också att tolka kvinnorörelsens agerande som en förhandling om innehållet i kvinnors medborgarskap. (90) *Här ska jag dock begränsa mig* till den fråga som skisserades inledningsvis: (91) Går det att med hjälp av ett differentierat medborgarskapsbegrepp förstå skoarbeterskan Elvida Janssons agerande på de fackliga och politiska arenorna? (A2)
(88) In my own on-going thesis work on women's collective activities during the period 1900-1950 I use the concept of citizen to study the connections between women's political participation and their position in working life. (89) I also propose to interpret the women's lib. as a negotiation concerning the substance of women's citizenship. (90) Here I will, however, concentrate on the question raised in the beginning of the article: (91) Is it possible with the help of a differentiated concept of citizenship understand the shoe-factory worker Elvida Jansson's acting in the union and political arenas? (A2)

The writer wants to concretise, as in example 4, and support her claims by offering a reader the possibility of becoming acquainted with one concrete case. This story differs, however, from the story in example 4 in the sense that while it concretises some smaller details by describing an instant moment, the story in A2 summarises a longer period in time.

At the same time the story in A2 lightens the presentation by giving a face to the abstract discussion. According to Hellspong (1998: 107) an academic writer can use stories to convince the reader of a controversial thesis. This may be one reason for the story in A2, because it is somewhat controversial that female workers have suffered because of men, as the article claims. Because the series of events is placed at the beginning of the article, it can also act as a rhetorical device to catch the reader's attention (see Rydstedt 1993).

There is another similar story in another academic article (A4) with the difference that the story is placed at the end of the article. The role of the story is still the same; the writer wants to summarize the contents of the article by describing a concrete case that supports the academic discussion. The writer also expresses it explicitly when she says that she wants to show how the law concerning children born out of wedlock worked in practice after discussing the topic on a more general level ("att få en inblick i hur lagen om barn utom äktenskap fungerade i praktiken"). This story also functions as support for the writer's arguments.

4. Conclusions

In this study I have examined the stories (series of past-time events presented in event clauses) that academic and popularised articles in the field of history include. My aim has been to find out to what extent the articles in my material include story-like parts. On the basis of the study it can be concluded that all the academic articles and three of the five popularised articles include story-like parts. Two popularised articles, somewhat surprisingly, do not include event clauses that could form a story.

However, the other two popularised articles include series of events that are placed almost throughout whole articles. These kinds of stories do not exist in the academic articles. The function of these stories is to carry forward the contents and at the same time give information. As I claimed at the beginning of this chapter, the three functions of stories in academic/popularised discourses are, according to rhetoric, to entertain, to inform or to support a claim. In popularised articles in history the stories are used to inform or to support a claim. It is somewhat surprising that there are not any stories included that exist only to entertain, although the popularised magazine in question, *Populär Historia*, aims to publish both entertaining and informative articles[7].

In the academic articles there can be found stories that are located at the beginning or at the end of the article. These stories summarize the whole content of the article by concretising the theoretical discussion with the help of one concrete case that presumably exists in the research material that the historian has used. Besides these, the academic articles in my analysis include shorter stories that give a concrete example of some part of the contents. In most cases they consist of a few lines in the middle of the academic discussion. All stories included in academic articles can be seen as a support of the theoretical arguments and claims included in the article. Also, the writers often explicitly state that they want to describe practice as well. This function can be motivated by rhetoric; concrete things are

7 Oswalds, E. 1998. Personal letter to Tiina Haapakangas.

easier to understand than abstract ones. Besides this function the shorter stories can often be seen as evaluations of some part of the contents, i.e. the writer wants to emphasize the importance of these details of the contents and chooses to illustrate them in the form of a story.

When comparing the academic and popularised articles analysed, the most visible difference is that only the popularised articles contain stories that have as their function the giving of information, to carry the whole text forward. In academic articles, stories do not have this role; they are therefore not as important as corresponding stories in popularised articles as parts of the whole text. As stories in academic articles function to support a claim by concretising or summarising, these stories could be left out without totally losing some part of the contents.

Stories, as defined in this study, are, however, only one type of narrative presentation. Besides the series of events that come up in this study, the articles studied include many so-called generic narratives, where the writer describes something that often happens or something that is generally true (Polanyi 1982)[8]. In the future it would be interesting to examine to what extent these narratives are used in academic and popularised articles on history. It would also be interesting to examine whether corresponding material in some other discipline makes use of stories in a similar way, i.e. whether articles in other disciplines introduce a storyworld which is described in event clauses, to fulfil different functions.

8 As Polanyi (1982: 18) puts it, any given event, agent or object in a generic narrative stands for a class of such events, agents, or objects, since the world of the narration is not a unique world, but rather a class of words in which the activities and circumstances described generally obtain.

References

Beaugrande, R. de 1982. The story of grammars and the grammar of stories. *Journal of Pragmatics* 6, 383-422.

Bloor, T. 1996. Three Hypothetical Strategies in Philosophical Writing. In Ventola, E. / Mauranen, A. (eds) *Academic Writing. Intercultural and textual issues*. Amsterdam/Philadelphia: John Benjamins, 19-43.

Collin, F. / Køppe, S. 1995. Indledning. In *Humanistisk videnskabsteori*. Copenhagen: Danmarks Radio, 10-35.

Fjæstad, B. 1993. *Välkommen som medarbetare i Forskning och Framsteg!* Brochure.

Fleischman, S. 1990. *Tense and Narrativity. From Medieval Performance to Modern Fiction*. London: Routledge.

Halldén, S. 1983. *Behövs det förflutna? En bok om det gåtfulla vardagslivet*. Stockholm: LiberFörlag.

Hellspong, L. 1998. *Argumentationens retorik*. Stockholm: Almqvist and Wiksell International.

Hellspong, L 2000. *Retorik och vetenskap*. Stockholm: Almqvist and Wiksell International.

Herodotos historia. 2000. C. Lindskog (*trans.*). Bendz, G. / Lindskog, A. (eds) Stockholm: Nordstedts Förlag.

Koskela, M 1995. Variation of Thematic Structure within a Text. In Hokkanen, T. / Leinonen, M. / Shore, S. (eds). *Suomen kielitieteellisen yhdistyksen vuosikirja*. Helsinki: Suomen kielitieteellinen yhdistys, 103-123.

Koskela, M. 1997. Vetenskap populärt – att göra det omöjliga möjligt? *Finsk Tidskrift* 1, 52-57.

Koskela, M. 2002. Ways of Representing Specialized Knowledge in Finnish and Swedish Science Journalism. *LSP and Professional Communication* 2 (1), 27-40.

Koskela, M. and Pilke, N. 2001. Exempel på exempel – en studie i populärvetenskapliga texter. In Järvi, O. (ed.). *LSP and theory of translation. 21st VAKKI Symposium*. Vaasa, 152-166.

Kristeller, P. O. 1961. Some problems of historical knowledge. *The Journal of Philosophy* 58, 83-110.

Kristensen, J. E. / Schmidt, L-H. 1995. Da humaniora ville være videnskab. Humanioras historie indtil år 1900. In Collin, F. / Køppe, S. (eds) *Humanistisk videnskabsteori*. Copenhagen: Danmarks Radio, 37-53.

Labov, W. 1972. *Language in the Inner City. Studies in the Black English Vernacular.* Philadelphia: University of Pennsylvania Press.

Labov, W. / Waletzky, J. 1967. *Narrative analysis: oral versions of personal experience*. Seattle.

Laurén, Ch. / Myking. J. / Picht, H. 1997. *Terminologi som vetenskapsgren.* Lund: Studentlitteratur.

Martin, W. 1987. *Recent theories of narrative.* Ithaca: Cornell University Press.

Melander, B. 1987. Något om populärvetenskapliga texter och populärvetenskapligt språk. In Gunnarsson, B-L. (ed.) *Facktext.* Malmö: Liber, 104-124.

Myers, G. 1990. Making a Discovery: Narratives of Split Genes. In Nash, C. (ed.). *Narrative in culture. The uses of storytelling in the sciences, philosophy, and literature.* London: Routledge.

Polanyi, L. 1982. Linguistic and social constraints on storytelling. *Journal of Pragmatics* 6, 509-524.

Polanyi, L. 1989. *Telling the American Story. A Structural and Cultural Analysis of Conversational Storytelling*. Cambridge, MA: The MIT Press.

Rydstedt, R. 1993. *Retorik*. Lund: Studentlitteratur.

Steinmetz, H. 1995. History in Fiction – History As Fiction: On the Relations between Literature and History in the Nineteenth and Twentieth Centuries. In D'haen, T. / Bertens, H. (eds). *Narrative Turns and Minor Genres in Postmodernism*. Amsterdam: Editionas Rodpi, 81-103.

Thurén, T. 2000. *Populärvetenskapens retorik. Inte bara att förenkla.* Stockholm: Liber.

Research material

Bergman, H. 1999. En familj som andra. Barnavårdsmän och genuspolitik i den tidiga välfärdsstaten. *Historisk Tidskrift* 2, 227-250. (A4).

Björk, G. 1998. Det bekönade medborgarskapet. Skoarbeterskor, fackförening och parti under 1920- och 30-talen. *Historisk Tidskrift* 2, 314-334. (A2).

Frånberg, P. 1997. Spriten och staten. Svensk alkoholpolitik började med förbud mot hembränning. *Populär Historia* 1, 36-41. (P1).

Furuhagen, B. 1997. När kyrkan skulle stoppa folkets fester. *Populär Historia* 3, 20-22. (P2).

Hjelm, J. 1999. Kreativitet på arbetsgolvet: Förslagsverksamheten vid Rönnskärsverken. *Historisk Tidskrift* 3, 509-536. (A5).

Ljungren, J. 1997. Tradition eller tävling? Nordiska spelen och kampen om vad idrott är. *Historisk Tidskrift* 3, 351-374. (A1).

Rydström, J. 1998. Tidelagaren och den homosexuelle mannen. Två typer i den svenska rättshistorien. *Historisk Tidskrift* 4, 510-521. (A3).

Skansjö, S. 1998. Kampen om Skåne på 1300-talet. Landskapet blev en bricka i förspelet till Kalmarunionen. *Populär Historia* 1, 23-27. (P4).

Ulvros, E. H. 1998. Att följa sitt hjärta. En kvinnas brevväxling om kärlek och äktenskap för tvåhundra år sedan. *Populär Historia* 3, 40-44. (P5).

Zander, U. 1997. Jubileum med förhinder. Intresset för unionsfirandet var svalt 1897. *Populär Historia* 2, 48-51. (P3).

Part Three
Dichotomies in LSP Research

The vibrancy of a discipline can be gauged by its capacity to engage with apparent or real dichotomies. LSP studies are no exception. Hence, in Part 3 of this volume, a number of chapters are presented covering issues such as scientific and literary texts, concepts and objects, novice and expert views of a discipline, emotion and applied science, culture and technical translation, and precision and vagueness. In terminology research, for example, there has always been a tension between the Platonists/neo-Platonists, who argue that concepts have a primacy over language, and the quasi-Aristotelian view that our senses, and indirectly language, is at least on a par with concepts, if not dominant. In Part 3, the reader is therefore challenged to consider a number of dichotomies which in some cases remain just that, and in others, are resolved for particular contexts.

Focusing on terminology as "a discipline addressing categorisation and epistemology", the first chapter by Johan Myking outlines a number of dichotomies at the heart of the growing scholarly literature, at the same time suggesting that "renegotiation" is both productive and necessary in order to move beyond a structuralist either / or view which risks oversimplification of the complex issues involved, at best setting up false Aunt Sallys, at worst creating barriers to progress. The second dichotomy addressed is that of LSP and literary texts: the chapter presented by Christer Laurén argues for credible links between these two types of writing. Adopting a historical approach, Laurén takes the reader through oriental "polythematics", the classical Greek tradition, the early novel and observational science, French realism and Darwin, and modern trends. His main argument is that writers of science – with only a few exceptions – do not dare to manipulate their own text traditions, whereas "literary writers have always been bold in relation to their conventions". Hence, LSP authors (specifically writers of science) have followed in literary traditions. The third chapter explores alternative – but ultimately interdependent – sign systems in a communicative framework. From this intersemiotic perspective, Heribert Picht explores the conversion of signs between different semiotic forms of representation particularly in relation to objects and concepts. Stressing the importance of both linguistic and non-linguistic signs, as well as their interactions and potential interchangeability in LSP texts, he argues that adequate specialist knowledge is a necessary pre-condition for the successful conversion of signs, at least from a communicative perspective.

In the fourth chapter, the perspective shifts towards the role of concepts and terms in academic/educational seminar discussions. Analysing the transcripts of three academic levels of seminars concerned with the discipline of terminology, Nina Pilke concludes that at the lowest "proseminar" level terms and concepts are barely discussed, whereas in doctoral seminars nearly 40% of terms identified are concerned with such issues, reflecting in all likelihood the crucial role of concept development in doctoral theses and novice-expert differences. The seminar itself is presented as a bi-partite locus of equality on the one hand and authority of knowledge on the other hand.

One aspect of texts which has until recently been largely ignored as irrelevant to LSP, is that of emotional expression. Arguing for a different perspective, Klaus-Dieter Baumann presents an interdisciplinary analysis of text-based data from a communicative-cognitive point of view. He concludes that emotion and cognition are closely linked, promising new avenues of LSP research. Michael Wittwer continues this theme in the following chapter with a case study, examining what he calls the "emotionality" of popularising medical texts in paediatrics in a translation context. He proposes three strategies to support the translation process and argues for further case studies in this neglected area, for which, it seems, texts aimed at children are particularly suitable. A further unusual aspect of LSP studies can be found in the chapter by Guadalupe Aguado de Cea and Inmaculada Álvarez de Mon y Rego who consider the role of culture in technical translation in the field of information technology. Using a functional approach, they identify a number of changes in the Spanish translations of articles from the US *Byte* magazine, ranging from a different choice of terminology in order to avoid transferring source-language connotations, to the omission of references to culture-specific US phenomena. While legal language is conventionally held to be precise, its use in international treaties can be purposely vague, according to Giuditta Caliendo in the concluding chapter on intercultural traits in legal translation. Legal translators as mediators between legal systems must find solutions which balance the requirements of both vagueness and precision. Some of the problems faced are illustrated on the basis of a trilingual English/French/Italian glossary of criminal law and human rights.

The chapters in Part 3 present a number of challenges to the discipline of LSP studies. Such challenges can be enriching in the sense that they are a sign of a discipline maturing by becoming more self-reflexive.

JOHAN MYKING

Dichotomies: Impossible and indispensable?

1. Introduction

Like most other fields of research, terminology has been constituted by a set of dichotomies, such as, for instance: *general and special language(s), terminology and linguistics, terminology and lexicography, words and terms, semasiology and onomasiology, motivation and arbitrariness*, and so on. It is generally agreed that the research traditions of LSP and terminology largely rest upon a number of such dichotomies.

In recent years a meta-discussion and criticism of dichotomisation was carried out within a number of social sciences (Miegel/ Schoug 1998) and also in linguistics, notably by Robert de Beaugrande (1997a, b). Further, traditional terminology is currently being questioned and criticised by proponents of new trends in terminology and terminography, and this criticism tends to take the central dichotomies as their point of departure.

As a discipline addressing categorisation and epistemology, terminology cannot escape these trends of rethinking. The study of scientific dichotomies forms part of the study of the metadiscourse of a science. The study of the dichotomies of terminology as important features of the metadiscourse of this discipline might contribute to a better understanding of the state-of-the-art within the field of terminology as well as current tensions and development trends.

2. The project

My chapter is part of the joint project "Semiotic theses (and paradoxes) about terminology as part of special communication" with Christer Laurén and Heribert Picht (see Laurén this volume, Picht this volume). Under the heading "The impossible task of dichotomisation", I take as my point of departure the following two theses:

- There are no fixed boundaries between specialised communication and other forms of communication, and, consequently,
- there are no fixed boundaries between terms and the rest of vocabulary and phraseology.

However trivial and obvious they may seem, these theses represent a criticism of traditional positions which imply that terminology "is something else" than linguistics, that special language "is something else" than general language, that terms are subject to "other laws" than words, and so on.

The idea behind this project is to explore contrasting pairs from texts on terminology as lexical evidence of patterns of thought, and thus start the analysis from a semasiological angle. By combining a semasiological study of some of the central dichotomies of terminology with a historical approach, I hope to demonstrate that a central set of terminological dichotomies at present may be perceived as pseudo-dichotomies due to epistemological progress.

My thesis is that this perception is interest-driven (externally, from the viewpoint of other disciplines, as well as internally, from within the discipline), and that dichotomies are inherently subject to "(re)negotiation". Some dichotomies of terminology have already been renegotiated, others still wait to be put on the agenda, and a number of new dichotomies seem to be appearing.

3. The core dichotomies of terminology

Taking Wüster's *Einführung* (Wüster 1985) as the starting point, we will see that even in the short chapter 1 on the particularity of terminology (1985: 1-5) a number of contrasting pairs occur. They are easily recognisable as well-established meta-terms of the Wüsterian tradition, expressing basic tenets of this tradition:

Terminologielehre	*Sprachwissenschaft*
Sprachzustand	Sprachentwicklung
(das Reich der) Begriffe	(das Reich der) Benennungen
Begriffe	Wortinhalte
Sachbedeutung	Mitbedeutung
Ist-Norm	Soll-Norm
Sprachrichtigkeit	Zweckmässigkeit
(systematische) Anordnung	(alphabetische) Anordnung
einsprachig	mehrsprachig

Table 1. Dichotomies in Wüster (1985).

Not all of these pairs can be assigned the status of stable and conventional dichotomies. For example, it is true that the pair '*monolingual*'/'*multilingual*' (*einsprachig/mehrsprachig*) expresses some sort of binarity and complementarity. It is not so obvious, however, that one member of this pair expresses a property typical of terminology and thus creates a contrast to something that is *not* equally typical, whereas "demarcation" is probably the main function of dichotomies (see below).

The following tables list a number of well-known dichotomies, based not on frequency lists but on interpretation from reading the works of terminology. The lists will, for reasons of space, not be fully documented with bibliographical references, but the reader will easily recognise and identify the dichotomies with respect to specific authors and works. Based on interpretation I think we can easily distinguish the following three types of dichotomies:

3.1 Dichotomies of demarcation

These dichotomies demarcate and identify terminology as a discipline or domain of research, and indicate that it is a distinct discipline by contrasting it with other disciplines. It is possible to distinguish two subgroups of demarcation dichotomies (Tables 2 and 3):

Terminology	Linguistics
Terminology	Lexicology
Terminology	Lexicography
Terminology/-graphy	Specialist lexicography

Table2. External dichotomies – with respect to neighbouring or competing disciplines.

"traditional"	sociocognitive terminology
Terminology	Socioterminology

Table 3. Internal dichotomies – with respect to directions within terminology.

3.2 Parametrical dichotomies

These dichotomies outline basic tenets, principles and methods as well as data and objects of study. Parametrical dichotomies of course also serve demarcation purposes:

term	word
onomasiology	semasiology
arbitrariness	motivation
special language (LSP)	general language (LGP)
subject specialist	layperson
(pertaining to) subject	(pertaining to) language
subject specialist	terminologist
specialist communication	* general communication?

Table 4. Parametrical dichotomies.

At least one dyadic pair is incomplete; the counterpart of 'specialist communication' is redundant or less acceptable, as this term is coined by analogy to one member of the 'special language' dichotomy.

3.3 Dichotomies of (internal) specialisation

Certain contrasting pairs and/or collocations express important conceptualisations and distinctions within the scientific tradition, i.e., they do not express any antagonism towards something "outside" or "inside" the discipline as in the previous sets. Rather, the lexical relationship between the members might be grasped by categories such as hyponymy or part-whole (Table 5):

special language (LSP)	Terminology
terminology	Terminography

Table 5. Dichotomies of (internal) specialisation.

3.4 Identification by clusters of dichotomies

By interpretation and scientific common sense, I find that the following set of dichotomies should be considered the core cluster of dichotomies: these are the dichotomies by which terminologists lay claim to and/or are assigned their scientific status and the dichotomies "by which terminologists live" or, at least, by which they allegedly live (2 demarcational, 4 parametrical):

terminology	*linguistics*
terminology	*lexicography*
term	*word*
onomasiology	*semasiology*
arbitrariness	*motivation*
special language (LSP)	*general language (LGP)*

Table 6. Identification by clusters of dichotomies.

Such lists may indicate a co-variation (disputed or agreed) between members of dichotomies, and the list itself may appear as a cluster. Within terminology, there has been a tendency to define terminology in contrast to lexicography and linguistics by apparent oppositions such as "term" vs. "word", "onomasiology" versus "semasiology", and so on. The combination of scientific preferences for "term", "onomasiology" and other members on the left hand side thereby indicating membership in the community of terminologists.

4. Dichotomies – features and functions

The concept of 'dichotomy' belongs to philosophy and theology rather than to lexical semantics, which does not use 'dichotomy' as a precise analytical category. As dichotomies are instances of the general principle of binarism, a plausible assumption would be that they share properties with other forms of lexical opposites, whether termed contrast, antagonism, antithesis, antonymy, dyad, binarity, opposition, counterparts, or polarity. Opposites are a heterogeneous class, as discussed by, amongst others, Cruse (1987).

The philosophers Miegel and Schoug define 'dichotomy' in the following way: (see Greek *dicha-* 'two' and *temnein* 'divide' or 'cut'):

> A conceptual division of a category in two subcategories. A dichotomy can be considered a dualism that organises thought in separate classes which tend to have a binary relationship. This binarity can be of a principled logical nature, one member per definition excluding the other (Miegel/Schoug 1998: 14, *translation by JM*)

Within structuralism and semiotics, the works of Lévi-Strauss and markedness theory initiated by Roman Jakobson in particular have dealt extensively with binarism as a salient pattern of thinking and categorisation. Charles Sanders Peirce writes in an unpublished paper:

> Two is the number of hard common sense, of the stern moralist, of the practical man. "Yes or no? Answer me categorically," says such a man. Heaven and hell, right or wrong, truth and fiction, gain and loss, agent and patient, living or dead, – on such distinctions our practical life turns (Peirce, unpublished ms. Jørgensen 1997: 227)

This does not mean, however, that there is something "unethical" associated with binary thinking, only that it organises perception and action along different lines from other forms of thinking. We might argue that dichotomies (like all forms of contrasts) have three basic functions which all are parts of scientific discourse:

- First, a *cognitive* or epistemological function, including classification and ordering, which makes new insights possible;
- second, a *didactical* function, including a rhetorical – which facilitates focussing, often on the 'positive' pole in particular and corresponds to the stylistic figure of antithesis;
- third, a *sociological* function, demarcation of membership in particular groups or settings, in the extreme form political – "friend or foe".

Miegel/Schoug (1998: 14) emphasise that binarities often are the product of concrete contexts. Dichotomies are context-bound but also context-negotiable. They may be praxis-bound and are not (always) stabilised and lexically coded opposites. Many opposites often have an important cultural significance and are difficult to reduce into simpler oppositions ("yin : yang", "heaven : hell", "body : soul"). According to Cruse, almost "anything" may obtain a dichotomy-like status or a binary choice given the appropriate contextual restrictions, see Cruse's examples "coffee : tea" or "gas : electricity" (1987: 198) (which are not good examples of lexical(ised) opposition, but relevant to many terminological settings). At the surface level, it is difficult or even impossible to distinguish dichotomies from mere collocations on the basis of linguistic criteria.

Two co-hyponyms which share a common superordinate is a binary pair if only the subordinate level is considered. It seems, however, that in culturally salient dichotomies no such superordinate concept may be found except by metalinguistic construction – there is no "natural" lexicalised superordinate of the "yin : yang" or "body : soul" types.

Cruse (1987: 262) lists a set of criteria for 'good oppositions'. Due to the context-specificity of scientific dichotomies it does not seem plausible to demand a very powerful analysis, for example. that all or most criteria should be met. If a weaker analysis is adopted the following three criteria seem possible to apply:

- *Binarity*, on the logical basis of negation: 'p' vs. 'not p' (Harris 2001: 163). Binarity is the essential and indispensable feature.
- *Neutralisation* (Cruse 1987: 255ff) occurs for instance if a lexical unit which participates in an opposition has a co-lexemic superordinate (for example *dog/bitch : dog*). This co-lexemic member is then neutralised.
- *Semantic markedness*: Following Cruse (1987: 257), the unmarked term is the neutralised, co-lexemic superordinate term, for example *dog* in the *dog/bitch* contrast. Following Harris (2001: 163), one member of the pair is 'marked' by a plus or 'positive' value, the other 'unmarked' by a minus or negative value as it lacks the feature in question. Thus, the neutralised term *dog* lacks the marked or positive feature of <female>.

If there is any point in taking a semasiological approach, it would be because the lexical meaning conveyed in a dichotomy very often corresponds to a commonsense analysis that distinguishes "insiders" from "outsiders". "Outsider" is of course a very ambiguous and non-scientific notion, which refers to the interested friendly-minded colleague or layman as well as colleagues who are proponents of different scientific approaches. So, common-sense semasiological analyses should only be used/explored as far as they reach.

In some cases it does seem possible to analyse some of the dichotomies of terminology within the framework of co-lexemic neutralisation and markedness, by inserting a superordinate:

	lexicography
lexicography vs. terminology →	lexicography vs. TERMINOLOGY
	lexicography
lexicography vs. terminography →	lexicography vs. TERMINOGRAPHY
	terminology
terminology vs. terminography →	terminology vs. TERMINOGRAPHY
	words
words vs. terms →	words vs. TERMS

Figure 1. Proposed co-lexemic superordinates for hyponymic lexical units.

Within such an analysis, the tests for neutralisation, markedness and co-lexematic superordinates easily lead to the conclusion that the members to the right, *terminology*, *terminography*, and so on, bear the "positive" value, for example they are the "marked", "unusual" or "noteworthy" members. When we speak of "terminology", we speak of something more distinct and specific than of the broad field of "lexicography", hence: *terminology* is the "marked" member. Similarly, within the context of terminology, *terminography* is the specific, distinct and "marked" member with respect to the broader field of terminology. Depending on world-view, intentional depth and degree of *Fachlichkeit* (see below) such analyses will probably make some sense in certain contexts, but there is of course nothing "objective" about them: Some kind of world-view is expressed, and in some cases a world-view might suit non-terminologists and at the same time correspond to a common-sense understanding ("because terms are some sort of word, terminology must be some sort of lexicography"). In other cases, the focus on the "positive" member is a point of departure for disputing the whole distinction.

In other cases it is all too evident that the co-lexemic subordinate is only potential. To comply with the general scientific understanding of the matter, the subordinate cannot do without a specifier which makes the hyponymy unambiguous:

language
**language vs. special language* → *general language vs. special language*

linguistics
linguistics vs. terminology → *sociolinguistics vs. terminology*

Figure 2. Proposed superordinates with additional specification.

Finally, in a number of dichotomies this kind of analysis does not hold. It seems very difficult to establish a superordinate concept of *motivated : arbitrary* or *semasiology : onomasiology* except by learned construction.

The principles according to which dichotomies are organised can then be summarised as:

a) (an idea of) *difference* and
b) *antagonism*, combined to form an internal hierarchy of

c) *normality* – one of the categories of a dichotomy is considered more "normal" than the other. This is
d) a powerful strategy of *focussing* on the relevant object (in casu: of study), and this, in turn, corresponds to such aims as
e) *identity marking*, in casu: in building cohesive research communities and gaining general acceptance from the broader research community. This would also mean that dichotomies are
f) *interest-driven*: Whatever merits the label of "normal" obviously must depend upon point of view.

One last point should be noted: a number of dichotomies from linguistics would probably be very hard to analyse in terms of neutralisation and markedness. A natural and/or co-lexemic common superordinate is lacking in pairs such as *langue* : *parole*, *signifiant* : *signifié*, "intension : extension", "semasiology : onomasiology", and so on, and assigning a "plus-value" to one of the members in each pair seems difficult.

5. Criticism of dichotomies

The logic-based view of binarity typical of structuralism is, according to Harris (2001: 163), controversial and has within semiotics and cultural studies acquired a negative reputation because it inculcates the "values favoured by current establishments and suppress[es] dissidence or alternative views". The marked members in a semantic sense consequently acquire a superior status in a social sense. Further, dichotomisation implies a static perspective that is not open to the analysis of dynamic processes, which is a focal point in Beaugrande's criticism (see below). In the cultural sciences there is, according to Miegel/Schoug, a strong de-dichotomising tendency, inspired by deconstructionists and post-structuralists. As examples, ethnology, religion, gender studies and economics are mentioned (Miegel/Schoug 1998: 14ff). Influences from recent directions in linguistics, such as prototype theory and system theory, are also parts of this trend, which is also present in terminology.

Within linguistics, this type of criticism has been conducted notably by Robert de Beaugrande (1997a: 51, 84-85, 1997b, especially in his discussion of Saussure.) According to Beaugrande, the dichotomising tradition of the structuralist tradition is incapable of grasping the complex reality in dichotomies. Instead, Beaugrande calls for integrative approaches:

> We can lay to rest our stony dichotomies and schemes for fragmenting language and freeing theory from practice. Our science can shift from confrontational rhetoric over free-standing formal theories and notations over to cooperative projects for describing real data and addressing social issues of discourse. (Beaugrande 1997a: 51)

Beaugrande proposes to convert the static dichotomies into dynamic dialectics controlled by the indeterminacy principle (1997b: 357, see below, section 7.2). In short, critics claim that dichotomisation is something static and may be associated with reductionism, whereas anti-dichotomisation or deconstruction is associated with dynamism and also with holism. The anti-reductionist attitude, too, is a feature of current criticisms of traditional terminology (Myking 2001: 53).

6. Negotiation and renegotiation – some semasiological sketches

The following sketch aims at indicating how a number of positions well-known from the research literature fit into a framework constructed by semantic categories. This sketch is preliminary and needs to be discussed in depth in later work.

6.1 'p' vs. 'not 'p'

The disjunctive criterion of 'p' – 'not p' applies to incompatible complementaries: whatever falls into one class, cannot fall into another. Applied mechanically to a number of "classic" dichotomies the result would be as follows:

- Terminology is not linguistics
- Terminography is not lexicography
- Terminography is not special lexicography
- Terms are not words
- Semasiology is not onomasiology

The newly introduced socio-cognitive terminology (Temmerman 2000) fits into this formula:

- Socio(-cognitive) terminology is not traditional terminology

Similarly, the results of or attempts at renegotiation may produce results that are analysable also in semantic terms.

6.2 Suggesting identity (compatibility)

- Terminography is identical to (shares the same parameters as) special lexicography (Bergenholtz 1995, Svensén 1998)
- "Socioterminology" equals "terminology" (Louis Guespin, *Avant-Propos* to Gaudin 1993: 9)

6.3 From co-hyponym/antonym to superordinate

The criterion of 'p' – 'not p' not only applies to antonyms or opposites, but also to co-hyponyms, i.e. complementaries with a common superordinate term. The result is a change of "world-view":

- Terminology is a branch of (i.e., a hyponym of) linguistics (Laurén, Myking and Picht 1998 (1997), ch. 12

- Terminology is a branch of (i.e., a hyponym of) lexicography (possibly a layman's view)
- "Classic terminology" is a branch of (and so on) terminology (Louis Guespin, *Avant-Propos* to Gaudin 1993: 9)
- All terms are words, terms form a subgroup of the lexicon (various)

The possible co-lexemic superordinates are neither natural, current nor generally accepted. The scale of applicability ranges from 'none' to 'possible'. Some of them are likely to provoke charges of imperialism, at the least, they risk being ignored as expressing the view of an outsider.

6.4 Tri-chotomisation

- The fusion of lexicon and grammar to "lexico-grammar" (Halliday)
- Bergenholz/Engberg's (1995: 184) model of general vs. special language and intersection
- Sager's distinction of "words, terms and standardised terms" (1980, 1990)

6.5 Abandoning the one-dimensional and logical approach

- All terms are words, term status is a matter of communicative behaviour (Kageura 1995, Pearson 1998)
- Special language is natural language used in particular communicative settings (Sager 1980); such settings are a matter of degree (Kalverkämper 1990)

7. Possible solutions

A number of dichotomies discussed in this chapter have been the subject of discussion for quite some time. It is possible to outline three levels of renegotiation and agreement.

7.1 Renegotiated dichotomies

General and special language

For many years solutions which outline hyponymy and inclusion have been proposed. Since Kalverkämper's introduction of the concepts of *Fachlichkeitsgrad* and *Fachsprachlichkeitsgrad* (Kalverkämper 1990) based on prototypicality and graduality it appears that the idea of a strict dichotomy between LGP and LSP has been drastically weakened.

Terminology and linguistics

This dichotomy was introduced by Wüster but was also maintained and discussed by writers such as Rondeau (1982) and Kocourek (1981), who both demonstrated efforts to overcome it. The solution proposed in Laurén/Myking/Picht 1998, chapter 12, is based on inclusion and hyponymy combined within an extended conception of the superordinate concept of LINGUISTICS: when terminology is viewed co-hyponymously with other subdisciplines of linguistics, the superordinate concept of LINGUISTICS is defined in a broader and more liberal sense than has usually been the case.

7.2 Negotiable dichotomies

Words and terms

A number of traditional disagreements have to be addressed in order to account for this dichotomy in a satisfactory way, starting with the fundamental: Is a term a representation only, or is it a sign? At least, there seems to be a consensus that most terms belong to natural language and as such are words, at least from a morphological point of view (disregarding for a moment the issue of multiword units). A number of authors seem to argue in favour of a multifaceted view based on "discourse". They perceive terms as pragmatic units and "termness" as a matter of pragmatic status irrespective of morphology. "Terms" become subordinate to "words in general" or co-hyponymous to the notion of "other words".

Semasiology and onomasiology

There seems to be little dispute about the conceptual status of this dichotomy, that is, the two members referring to complementary and opposite directions of the concept-term relationship. There is, however, a dispute as regards its parametrical function, whether or not the onomasiological approach merits its dominant status within terminology (the "classical" approach) or whether semasiology deserves upgrading (notably Temmerman 2000: 42).

The solution might lie in Beaugrande's recommendation to transform static dichotomies into dialectic procedures whereby the members control each other within the indeterminacy principle (Beaugrande 1997b: 357, see above). This would mean recognising that the two principles are applied dialectically within the working processes of terminography, a position held by Laurén/Myking/Picht (1998: 218; see also Laurén/Myking/Picht 1997) . The consequence would be a weakening of the parametrical status of this dichotomy with respect to "schools".

Motivation and arbitrariness

It is worth noting that the dichotomy of motivation and arbitrariness has not been a very prominent dichotomy in traditional writings. Rather, it has acquired an important parametrical status by the criticism from socio-cognitive terminology (Temmerman 2000, see Myking 2001: 56-57). In addition, it bears an inherent ambiguity as regards its semiotic vs. communicative status. A more conscious understanding of this dichotomy is needed, and probably the dichotomy operates at three levels, in order for the members to be compatible (which, of course, means that the dichotomy is dissolved).

From the point of view of the *communicative* function of terms, motivation has been an important recommendation within a number of "classical" approaches to terminology. The principle of arbitrariness refers to Wüster's *semiotic* separation of "das Reich der Begriffe" and "das Reich der Benennungen", which is considered functional by Wüster-oriented terminologists but dysfunctional by socio-cognitive terminologists. From the point of view of communicative function, there seems to be a considerable degree of agreement that 'motivation' is functional (see Temmerman 2000: 44 compared to Laurén et al. 1998: 258). As regards the *morphological* classification of terms, on the other hand, I have argued elsewhere (Myking 1997) that it is difficult to maintain the dichotomous classification of terms into motivated and non-motivated. A more inferential and relevance-oriented view seems necessary, based on prototypicality and graduality.

7.3 Difficult negotiation topics

Discussions on two demarcation dichotomies seem particularly difficult.

Terminography and special lexicography

This topic borders on being non-negotiable; the outcome seems uncertain. The problem may be formulated in terms of complementarity vs. identity. In Laurén et al. 1998 (see also Laurén et al. 1997) the dichotomy is maintained (within the wider co-hyponomy of terminology as a branch of linguistics). Svensén (1998) comes close to suggesting identity, a position also more or less suggested by Bergenholz (1995).

Classical/Wüsterian/traditional vs. sociocognitive terminology (and also socioterminology)

This dichotomy is the organising principle of Temmerman's work on sociocognitive terminology (Temmerman 2000) and is also, but less explicitly present in French socioterminology, as exemplified by

Gaudin (1993). While these works have generated a substantial discussion on parameters, negotiations are at best in an initial phase.

8. Conclusions

Dichotomies are important because they enable identification of the object of study as well as theoretical and methodological tenets. The price, however, is (over-)simplification. From this discussion it seems plausible to formulate a set of theses about the central dichotomies of terminology:

- They have been or are subject to a remarkable renegotiation that is not yet concluded.
- As a result, none of the core dichotomies have by now become generally accepted as unique and unambiguous properties of terminology.
- This tendency towards de-dichotomisation is necessary and valuable in order to avoid scientific isolationism.
- Renegotiation does not, however, mean absence of conflict.

In addition, some dichotomies have been recontextualised in new directions, notably recent trends which are opposed to established or “traditional” terminology.

References

Beaugrande, R. de 1997a. *New Foundations for a Science of Text and Discourse: Cognition, Communication, and the Freedom of Access to Knowledge and Society*. Norwood, New Jersey: Ablex.

Beaugrande, R. de 1997b. *Linguistic Theory*. London/New York: Longman.

Bergenholtz, H. 1995. Wodurch unterscheidet sich Fachlexikographie von Terminographie? *Lexicographica* 11/1995, 50-59.

Bergenholtz, H. / Engberg J. 1995. Tendenser inden for den nyere fagsprogsforskning i Danmark. *Hermes* 15/1995, 179-206.

Cruse, D. A. 1987. *Lexical Semantics*. Cambridge: Cambridge University Press.

Gaudin, François 1993. *Pour une socioterminologie. Des problèmes semantiques aux pratiques institutionnelles*. Rouen: Publications de l'Université de Rouen No 182.

Harris, R. 2001. Binarism. In Cobley, Paul (ed.). *The Routledge Companion to Semiotics and Linguistics*. London/New York: Routledge, 163.

Jørgensen, K. Gall 1997. Lingvistik og semiotik. [...] og der var én, og der var to [...]. In Jørgensen, K. Gall (ed.) *Anvendt semiotik*. Copenhagen: Gyldendal, 213-233.

Kageura, K. 1995. Toward the theoretical study of terms – A sketch from the linguistic viewpoint. *Terminology* 2/2, 239-258.

Kalverkämper, H. 1990. Gemeinsprache und Fachsprachen – Plädoyer für eine integrierende Sichtweise. In Stickel, G. (Hg.) *Deutsche Gegenwartssprache*. Berlin/New York: Gruyter.

Kocourek, R. 1981. Prerequisites for an applicable linguistic theory of terminology. In Savard, J.G and Faforge, L. (eds) Pr*oceedings of the 5th Congress of AILA*. Québec: Université Laval.

Laurén, Ch. / Myking, J. / Picht, H. 1997. *Terminologi som vetenskapsgren*. Lund: Studentlitteratur.

Laurén, Christer / Myking, Johan / Picht, Heribert 1998. *Terminologie unter der Lupe. Vom Grenzgebiet zum Wissenschaftszweig.*

IITF-Series 9. Wien: IITF. (German edition of Laurén/Myking/ Picht 1997).

Laurén, Ch. (this volume) The interdependence of LSP text and literary text.

Miegel, F. / Schoug, F. 1998. *Dikotomier. Vetenskapsteoretiska reflektioner*. Lund: Studentlitteratur.

Myking, J. 1997. The concept of "motivation" in terminology. In Lundquist, L. / Picht, H. / Qvistgaard, J. (eds) *LSP. Identity and interface. Research, knowledge and society.* Proceedings from the 11th European Symposium on LSP, 1997. Copenhagen: Copenhagen Business School, 328-338.

Myking, J. 2001. Against prescriptivism? The "socio-critical" challenge to terminology. *IITF Journal, 12/1-2,* 49-65.

Pearson, J. 1998. *Terms in Context.* Amsterdam/Philadelphia: John Benjamins.

Picht, H. (this volume) Konversion zwischen verschiedenen semiotischen Repräsentationsformen für Gegenstände und Begriffe.

Rondeau, G. 1982. *Linguistics and terminology*. Unpublished manuscript.

Sager, J.-C. 1980. *English Special Languages*. Amsterdam/ Philadelphia: John Benjamins.

Sager, J.-C. 1990. *A Practical Course in Terminology Processing.* Amsterdam/Philadelphia: John Benjamins.

Svensén, B. 1998. Terminografi och lexicografi – blir det samma sak nu när ordböckerna blir databaser? *LexicoNordica* 5/1998, 77-90.

Temmerman, R. 2000. *Towards New Ways of Terminology Description; the sociocognitive approach.* Amsterdam/Philadelphia: John Benjamins.

Wüster, Eugen ^{2}1985. *Einführung in die allgemeine Terminologielehre und terminologische Lexikographie*. Copenhagen: Copenhagen Business School.

CHRISTER LAURÉN

The interdependence of LSP text and literary text

Innovations in scientific text traditions may originate from literary texts. New forms, new text traditions, give new possibilities of thinking and, at the same time, are expressions of a different style of thought. Thus the formal metamorphoses of literature also influence scientific thinking and scientific text traditions. Let us take a look at this process in a very long perspective in order to get a view of the development of this relation; that is, creating a distance in order to reach an overview.

In the following we will in pairs compare one literary text exemplar or tradition with one LSP exemplar and try to find representatives of the metamorphoses and innovations mentioned. Let us begin with a very different perspective.

1. "Polythematics" in the orientalist tradition

Orientalists at work on Persian and Arabic literature have shown that Persian and Arabic poetry differs from European poetry by often being illogical and non-continuous, as they sometimes experience it themselves. One description by a well-known Orientalist, William Jones, who lived in the 18th century, expresses this in the following way: "Oriental Pearls at Random Strung" [*sic*].

The polythematic ancient Arabic lyrical form *qasida* has a basic schema which, according to the German orientalist Jacobi (1971) consists of the following three parts: a) an elegiac-erotic prelude or love lament; ending with a connection to b) an enthusiastic description of the poet's camel; ending with a connection to c) a finishing part (self-praise or a panegyrical song of praise to the addressee). This is the most perfect and unique creation in early Arabic poetry, and it has, naturally enough, also had a strong influence on Persian literature (Kronholm 1995: 70). A European will react more or less in the same way as William Jones did in the 18th century.

Western thinking proceeds in comparison with this in a linear, logical way. Hence, from Johann Wolfgang von Goethe to Roman Jakobson the phenomenon has been noted in the poetical texts of Orientalism. Interestingly enough this polythematic style also appears to emerge in non-fictional and LSP texts.

Orientalists have shown that the discontinuity which characterized an early classic like the Persian poet Hafiz (14th century) has also become part of later prose, even of modern newspaper prose (Lentz 1952).

When a journalist writes a text he can without much ado pass from theme A to theme C. Having concerned himself for a while with theme C he may begin to deal with theme D, to return to A but only to soon pass on to F, which is by no means connected with the theme of the article. The motivation could be described in such a way that if A and B are metaphorically related, one can freely exchange them with each other. These different themes within polythematics may nevertheless be even logically conflicting.

A Finnish Orientalist and semiologist, Henri Broms, who for a couple of years at the beginning of the 1980s on the instruction of the Saudi government compiled scientific data bases in Riad, has stated that one half of OPEC's oil ministers at that time published their reports in verse (Broms 2003: 72). This is mentioned here as a parenthesis.

Broms discusses his time at the Saudi-Arabian National Center of Science and Technology and the sometimes seven-hour-long address of the head of the department at the department meetings, which could have a polythematic character. Broms could sit listening for hours without becoming sure of what theme was actually being discussed (Broms 2003: 75).

We should perhaps bear in mind that the concept of art in European tradition and in European languages also included what we today call science (Kukkonen 1989: 100-111). There was formerly no clear dividing-line between literature and science. We should also at the outset emphasize the importance of metaphorical thinking for creativity; the purely linear thinking that the computer manages so eminently has nothing to do with creativity.

2. Drama and Plato's philosophy

We can say that Plato developed the first European science in the form of philosophy. In order to find possibilities for making use of argumentation and to avoid any cultural transfer from preliterary society, which appealed to the emotions of the type the singing and playing blind poet Homer's Iliad and Odyssey represented, Plato had made use of the literary form of drama.

There are many advantages of dialogue. Plato could with its help present arguments for and against, he could simulate the teacher's and the pupil's pedagogical conversation, and the dramatic dialogue should according to tradition lead to a result. But from the dramaturgist's point of view (Ödeen 1988: 12), Plato's dialogues are examples of anti-dramatic narration. He deliberately toned down the drama. The audience should not emotionally be drawn into the action. The dialogues were intended to persuade through reasoning. Plato strives for the objective and rational truth, not the subjective and emotional, but the form, the external dramatic form needed, was brought in from literature. Here we have to remember that Plato lived at the crossroads between literary and oral cultures. Therefore he used the means of a well-established oral tradition, the means of drama.

The analogical thinking that Plato makes Socrates use is a sharp metaphorical thinking. The difference between similarity and identity is essential to scientific language (Holmgaard 1998: 263). Through Aristotle's *Per genum proximum et differentiam specificam* similarity and difference were combined with each other (Holmgaard 1998: 269).

Plato was not the only one to develop LSP communication on the basis of existing literary traditions, but he was a pioneer in his rejection of versified language (Havelock 1986: 29). Titus Lucretius Carus *De rerum natura* is a scientific thesis, and in verse. The textual genres have slowly crystallized in the course of centuries and millennia. The Latin grammar, *Donatus*, was written and learnt for centuries in hexameter before it was thought that the time demanded alexandrines.

3. The early novel and the scientist as observer

In the 18th and 19th centuries there emerged a strong European tendency towards realism in literature. It could be said here that as Aristotle belittled the genres that merely dealt with what had in fact taken place, in this realistic epoch of the new bourgeoisie that which was merely imagined was disparaged. It was a question of new readers emerging, new to literature, a middle class (Hawthorn 2001: 27) who felt more at home with colloquial language and reality effects. It was important for them to believe that human beings existed in concrete life (Holmgaard 1998: 212), "that sense of 'real life' – of recognizable everyday existence […]" (Hawthorn 2001: 10).

The early novel with its realism was characterized by a narrative causality which was very clearly visible, for example in Samuel Richardson's (1689-1761) *Pamela, or Virtue Rewarded* (1740-1741), even in the title. His next letter novel was *Clarissa or the History of a Young Lady* (1748; published in eight parts). Clarissa describes in her letters with a sense of detail her fate day by day, yes, often hour by hour. Lovelace, the seducer, harasses Clarissa and this is described in sharp psychological portraits. Clarissa is credulously willing to believe the seducer's honest intentions but is time and again disappointed. As a result of the seducer's attacks she is driven into illness and hysterics. Lovelace has many suspect assistants, linguistically very realistically characterized, and Clarissa is made the victim of many evil plots. The story ends with Lovelace drugging Clarissa and raping her. Clarissa flees from her family and ends her life alone but proud. She is a saint but she has lost her virtue. A strict Christian moral marks the whole book and Clarissa herself. Even though Lovelace repents and wants to marry her, she cannot consent. For she is violated.

Both Clarissa and the other novels provide detailed pictures of the age and can be read with profit for that reason alone by anyone who has an interest in cultural history.

A scientist who in many ways creates his science corresponding to popular realism and is on the same lines as Richardson and a great number of others, is Carolus Linnaeus or Carl von Linné (1707-78). His monumental work is of course *Systema Naturae* of 1735, which consists of the parts *regnum lapideum, regnum vegetabile* and *regnum animale*. He wanted to show the richness of creation: "God created, Linné organized", it was said. No wonder. His father, a priest used to sit in his garden with his little son Carl on his lap reading from Genesis about how the Almighty created the garden of Eden and allowed Adam to become the very first gardener. Carl loved the story, and the passage of Genesis probably from then on stayed in his mind: "So the man gave names to all the livestock, the birds of the air and all the beasts of the field". Linné was later called the King of the Flowers but also the Second Adam, possibly both names his inventions.

With the aid of logic and abstract concepts he arranged the hosts of plants and animals. The foundation of botany was to him *dispositio* and *denominatio*, i.e. classification and name giving. It is true that he was looking for a natural system which placed the groups of plants in their spontaneous kinship with one another as determined by nature, i.e. he was looking for the divine plan of creation. Still, he had no more exact idea of this natural system. He did discover hybrids between species of plants and animals, but he could not find any reasonable explanations of them. It has been said that he was a representative of a past age, a very successful scholastic.

The rare talent of Linné consisted of his powers of observation, the wealth of detail in his descriptions and his fantastic ability to arrange synchronically what he had seen and described. The sexual system of plants was the means of assistance for the arrangement he had discovered. A discoverer or explainer he was not, however. Instead he was a true Christian, a counterpart to Richardson.

His first journey as scientist and observer in Sweden was made as early as 1735 and started from Uppsala northwards through Lapland and down along the coast of what is now Finland. *Iter Lapponicum* is a masterpiece of observations (see, for instance, his Latin description of midges (2003: 157) in *Iter Lapponicum*). Of course there are attempts at explanations or reasons, but there is no question of there being any successful one: see, for example, the explanations of why people in Hälsingland are big and the Laplanders short in stature (2003: 110-111) or why Laplanders are so healthy (2003: 111).

The world Linné described and arranged he himself experienced in a highly emotional way. The driest details prove to the intense observer the omnipotence and the sense of beauty of the Creator. When he retired from his post as Rector of Uppsala University, he made a speech with the symptomatic theme *Deliciæ naturæ* (1773).

A Swedish historian (Lindroth 1978: 209) assumes that Linné's highly successful classification work and influence both internationally and in Sweden may have delayed modern developments in Swedish botany.

But in literature we gradually pass over to another type of explanation other than the divine one.

4. Balzac, Zola and Darwin

Honoré de Balzac (1799-1850) is a representative of French realism. He is an exposer of human vices, burlesque, and wallows in the boundlessly chaotic ruthlessness of human society. He paints an immense panorama of the French society of his day, maps it out piece by piece, social class by social class, in all its genuine materialism and careerism. He collected his works in *La comédie humaine* and systematized them in various series, for example, *Études de mœurs, Études philosophiques, Études analytiques,* and so on. Still, the classification was only an apparent one, since he occasionally classified one and the same work under one title, sometimes under a different one. But his descriptions are at least as detailed as pictures of the age as Richardson's, the difference being that he does not moralize. When he, for instance, in the brief novel *Ferragus* (1833), the first part of the *Histoire des Treize,* describes the streets of Paris, he is highly realistic and does not shrink back from the worst environments. He wants to penetrate what is genuinely human.

Balzac's clarity was first felt as a gain but then, in time, began to be felt as irritating naïve empiricism.

Towards the end of the 19th century it was increasingly realized that reality was not so simple (Holmgaard 2001: 232). From Balzac to Zola the novel was developed simultaneously with science; there was a mutual strengthening of the will to build up a rational narrative causality (Holmgaard 2001: 234). The early 18th century novel has detailed explanations even of individual actions. The novel has therefore been of importance for spreading this way of thinking. Popular realism and consequently the novel paved the way for similar innovations in science, as well as in the linguistic sciences. There is a very clear and deliberate departure from Christian-didactic predecessors which had a different type of causality, by the nature of punishment and reward (Holmgaard 1998: 236).

A following period of science, also connected with the development of this literary realism of Balzac, Zola and many others, including the central concept of causality, includes Charles Darwin's five-year long voyage which, like Linné's journeys included diligent observations of details which, however, formed the basis of a new theory of development in nature.

When the modern novel at last achieves its accepted form around 1800, it is also natural that modern science will find space and opportunities with Darwinism as its exponent. It will now simply be possible to recount the long development in prose and to interpret it. When Charles Darwin started his journey in 1831 on the Beagle, he had grown up in times when prose literature had long been characterized by realism in observations. His *Journal and remarks*, 1832-1836, published in 1839, is not as central to science as the later *On the origin of species by means of natural selection, or the preservation of favoured races in the struggle for life* (1859). To realism had also been added the demand for explanations.

But already Darwin's *Journal* and the popularized version *A naturalist's voyage* contain, in addition to detailed observations, constant speculations about causal connections. This does not mean that he lacked a feeling for the poetry of nature. When he mentions newly formed ocean islands and their fauna, he says that he is afraid the poetry will disappear if dung-eating insects and parasitic spiders were the first inhabitants.

In linguistic and literary sciences similar thinking leads to comparative currents and we get for instance historical and comparative linguistics. Parallel with the species and types one begins to divide natural languages into species and families and to explain the reasons behind processes.

From the middle of the 19th century there emerged a growing awareness of unambiguousness as a goal to reach in philosophy and science (the realization among novelists that reality was not so simple!). The development of symbolic logic led to puristic purges. At the same time literature struck new paths which implied that ambiguity was deliberately exploited. Various sciences have seen it as their task to impose strict limits for themselves while literature has the freedom of fiction (Holmgaard 1998: 396).

5. Modern poetry and modern science

In the 19th and 20th centuries elements of a style reminiscent of the Persian-Arabic style we mentioned in the very beginning was discovered in European modernism. The linear style which passed from one conclusion to the next was rejected. Modernists of the 20th century passed over to a metaphorical way of thinking which they gave expression to in their texts. When Henri Broms translated Hafiz's poetry into Finnish, he says himself that he did this in the modernistic style of the 20th century, with deliberate 'jumbledness' (Broms 2003: 70), and he was praised by Finnish modernists who found Hafiz's texts to be real poetry.

Broms, the Orientalist, points out in a study (1968) that European modernism in the 19th and 20th centuries through innovations by Mallarmé, Valéry and others developed text traditions where continuity is achieved solely through psychological associations. He and others have also pointed out that the Russian symbolists of the 19th century show influences from Hafiz and, hence, from polythematic thinking. The Russian symbolists were important for modern poetry in the West as well. The circle seems to be closed.

It can be said that scientific thinking during the last few decades has approached this modernism or realized the advantages of theories concerned with a modernistic way of formulating theories about our complicated mode of existence.

As time went on, towards the end of the 20th century, it became increasingly obvious that logical positivism and logically oriented linguistic philosophy did not meet the demands one had made on them to reach reliable knowledge. In particle physics the researcher himself was allowed to choose if he wanted to believe in a super string theory or some other theory, in theoretical biology if he wants to believe in some theory of order or in some Darwinian development theory of the first, second or third type or in some complexity theory of some sort. Even if this researcher seemed convinced that he had made a rational choice, he found himself in the same situation as the person who a hundred years earlier had read modernistic literature. Various kinds of causalities were conceivable and the researcher had to make a choice which could not be rationally motivated (Holmgaard 1998: 370).

6. The wall has fallen down

What I have presented here consists of a few glimpses of a comparative history of texts and ideas which is not yet written down as well as certain central hypotheses related to this history. A great deal of empirical work still remains to be done. There exists quite a lot of knowledge about the development of literary texts but only some knowledge of the history of LSP texts. Therefore, the work that remains to be done is to combine these two and to investigate closely the textual history of scientific texts.

The hypothesis that the literary text has played a primary role in relation to LSP texts – or should we rather say the scientific text – seems highly credible. There are few scientists, apart from some few innovators (Laurén/Nordman 2003), who dare to manipulate their own text traditions. On the other hand, literary writers have always been bold in relation to their conventions.

References

Broms, H. 1968. *Two studies in the relations of Hafiz and the West.* Studia Orientalia 39. Edidit Societas Orientalis Fennica. Helsinki.

Broms, H. 2003. *Saudisampanjaa. Suomalaisena islamin maailmassa.* Helsinki: Terra Cognita.

Havelock, E. A. 1986. *The Muse learns to write.* New Haven & London: Yale University Press.

Hawthorn, J. ^{4}2001. *Studying the novel.* London: Arnold.

Holmgaard, J. 1998. *Teoriens topik.* Aalborg: Medusa.

Jacobi, R. 1971. *Studien zur Poetik der altarabischen Qaside.* Veröffentlichungen der orientalischen Kommission. Akademie der Wissenschaften und der Literatur zu Mainz 24. Wiesbaden.

Kronholm, T. 1995. *Spegelbilder. Den arabiska litteraturens historia.* Stockholm: Natur och Kultur.

Kukkonen, Pirjo 1989. *Från konst till vetenskap. Begreppet vetenskap och dess språkliga uttryck i svenskan under 400 år.* Meddelanden från institutionen för nordiska språk och nordisk litteratur vid Helsingfors universitet A 5. Helsingfors: Helsingfors universitet.

Laurén, Ch. / Nordman, M. 2003. *Två sociologer och två idiolekter.* Språkvetenskap 42. Vasa: Vasa universitet.

Lentz, W. 1952. *Beobachtungen über den gedanklichen Aufbau einiger zeitgenössischer persischer Prosastücke. Der Islam* 1952: 2/3.

Lindroth, S. 1978. *Svensk lärdomshistoria. Frihetstiden.* Stockholm: Norstedts.

Linnæus, C. 2003. *Iter Lapponicum. Lappländska resan 1732. I. Dagboken.* (eds) Hellbom, A. / Fries, S. / Jacobsson, R. Umeå: Kungl. Skytteanska Samfundet.

Ödeen, M. 1988. *Dramatiskt berättande. Om konsten att strukturera ett drama.* Stockholm: Carlsson.

HERIBERT PICHT

Konversion zwischen verschiedenen semiotischen Repräsentationsformen für Gegenstände und Begriffe

1. Einleitung und Hypothese

Es ist eine altbekannte Tatsache, daß in jeder Form von Kommunikation mehrere semiotische Systeme gleichzeitig zum Einsatz kommen, sich ergänzen und sich in ihren Repräsentationsformen überschneiden. Ein Witz mag dies illustrieren. Im Autobus hängt eine Verbotstafel: *Es ist strengstens untersagt, zu reden mit dem Chauffeur. Der Mann braucht seine Hände zu Chauffieren.*

Unter Konversion verstehen wir die Austauschbarkeit der Repräsentationsform einer Botschaft dargestellt in einem Zeichensystem durch die Repräsentationsform eines anderen Zeichensystems.

Grundlegende Voraussetzungen für eine erfolgreiche Konversion ohne Informationsverlust sind:

1. Die Kommunikationsteilnehmer müssen die Zeichensysteme kennen, zwischen denen eine Konversion stattfindet.
2. Ferner ist es erforderlich, daß die verwendeten Repräsentationsformen mindestens einem der menschlichen Sinne zugänglich sind.
3. Außerdem müssen die Kommunikationsteilnehmer über ausreichendes Fachwissen verfügen, das durch die angewendeten semiotischen Systeme repräsentiert wird.

Mit Ausgangspunkt in der Definition und den Voraussetzungen haben wir folgende Hypothese aufgestellt: *Die Konversion zwischen Reprä-*

sentationsformen ist theoretisch grundsätzlich möglich, führt jedoch nicht immer zu dem angestrebten Kommunikationsergebnis.
Folgende vier Themenkreise sollen hier behandelt werden:

- Denkbare Konversionsmöglichkeiten nach der Sinneswahrnehmung
- Systeminhärente und pragmatisch bedingte Beschränkungen
- Repräsentationsformen für Abstrakta
- Folgen des Konventionsverlustes.

2. Konversionsmöglichkeiten nach der Sinneswahrnehmung

Gehen wir von den nicht-sprachlichen Repräsentationsformen aus und untersuchen die Möglichkeiten, sie in sprachliche Formen zu konvertieren, ergibt sich folgendes Bild (in Anlehnung an Nöth 1985: 206).

2.1 Die visuelle, graphische Repräsentationsform

Zu diesen Repräsentationsformen gehören Fotos, Zeichnungen verschiedenster Art, Gemälde, Diagramme, Symbole, Piktogramme, Noten, Satzzeichen, diakritische Zeichen und dergleichen. Rein theoretisch lassen sich diese Zeichen sprachlich wiedergeben; ein Blick auf die Praxis der Kommunikation jedoch macht deutlich, daß eine sprachliche Repräsentation eher selten ist und in einer Reihe von Fällen auch auf praktische Grenzen stößt, z.B. wird die sprachliche Wiedergabe von Noten nicht zu Musik führen oder eine Beschreibung der Mona Lisa kaum genau das Bild in der Vorstellung eines Botschaftsempfängers hervorrufen, der das Bild nicht kennt.

Voll konvertierbar in eine sprachliche Repräsentationsform ist jedoch das Zeichensystem der Taubstummensprache.

2.2 Die auditive Repräsentationsform

Bei weitem nicht alle Geräusche können als Zeichen gelten; sie sind Anzeichen, Repräsentationen von Eigenschaften eines Gegenstandes, z.B. das Quietschen meiner Küchentür. Zum Zeichen werden Geräusche erst durch Konvention, die auch eine gewisse Systematik voraussetzt. Ist einem Geräusch oder Ton jedoch eine bestimmte Bedeutung zugeordnet, kann von einem Signal gesprochen werden, das ohne Bedeutungsvariation in ein anderes Zeichensystem überführt werden kann.

Ein auditives Zeichen kann sprachlich wiedergegeben werden, sei es in Form eines Wortes, einer Benennung oder einer Aussage, die wiederum verschiedene Formen haben können:

Hornsignal (Halali) – "die Jagd ist beendet"
Tonfolge (Melodie) des Handy – "jemand ruft an"
Tonfolge einer Sirene – "Alarm"

Ein auditives Zeichen kann auch in ein anderes nicht-sprachliches Zeichen konvertiert werden. Die zwei verschiedenen Tonfolgen an einer Verkehrsampel repräsentieren "rot" bzw. "grün", die außerdem durch ein Piktogramm (stehendes und gehendes Männchen) oder durch das geschriebene Wort (dänisch: *gå* (‚gehen') und *vent* (‚warten')) für Farbenblinde verdeutlicht werden. Es liegt also eine doppelte visuelle Repräsentation vor.

Ein auditives Zeichen kann in ein taktiles Zeichen konvertiert werden, z.B. wird durch das Vibrieren des Handys ein Anruf angekündigt.

Musik kann durch elektronische Einrichtungen in Diagrammform sichtbar gemacht werden, allerdings entsteht dadurch keine Musik.

2.3 Die olfaktive Repräsentationsform

Auch in diesem Falle muß, wie bei den auditiven Formen, zwischen dem Geruch als Eigenschaft eines Gegenstandes und dem Geruch als

Signal unterschieden werden. In beiden Fällen ist eine Konversion in sprachliche Zeichen möglich. Wird eine Eigenschaft sprachlich wiedergegeben, besteht das Problem, daß das gewählte Wort einen Geruch nur ungenau beschreiben kann und individuelle Abweichungen eher die Regel sind, da Menschen Gerüche verschieden auffassen und damit auch unterschiedlich sprachlich realisieren.

Wird ein Geruch dagegen als Signal verwendet, ist eine eindeutige Konversion in sprachliche Zeichen dank eben dieser Konvention möglich. Einem an sich geruchlosen Gas wird ein unangenehm riechender Stoff als olfaktives Zeichen hinzugefügt, das einen Gasaustritt anzeigt und somit als Warnung vor Vergiftung oder Explosionsgefahr fungiert.

Eine Konversion in andere nicht-sprachliche Repräsentationsformen ist eher selten, obwohl gerade ein Gasaustritt auch durch auditive und visuelle Alarmsysteme vermittelt werden kann.

2.4 Die gustative Repräsentationsform

Für diese Repräsentationsform gilt das über die olfaktive Formen Gesagte analog – Geschmack als Eigenschaft und als Signal. In seiner Eigenschaft als Signal tritt der Geschmack zumeist als Warnung auf, z.B. durch den Zusatz von 0,2%–2% Pyridin, Benzol, Methanol, Petroläther etc. wird Äthylalkohol denaturieret (vergällt).

2.5 Die taktile Repräsentationsform

Auch für diese Repräsentationsform gelten ähnliche Grundbedingungen wie für die zwei vorhergehenden, allerdings mit einer nicht unwesentlichen Erweiterung. Die olfaktiven und gustativen Repräsentationsformen bilden kaum größere Kommunikationssysteme, die taktile dagegen hat in der Blindenschrift Braille ein voll ausgebildetes Kommunikationssystem, das dem Zeichensystem der Taubstummensprache vergleichbar ist. Beide Systeme sind individuellen Interpretationen entzogen, sie leiden also nicht an den Schwächen, die die sprachliche

Wiedergabe von Eigenschaften hat, wenn es darum geht, gustative, olfaktive und taktile Sinneswahrnehmungen zu verbalisieren.

3. Beschränkungen der Konversion

Die Konversion, obwohl theoretisch möglich, unterliegt zwei wesensverschiedenen Beschränkungen:

1. Beschränkungen, die im Zeichensystem angelegt sind und von ihm nicht überwunden oder kompensiert werden können; also systeminhärente Beschränkungen.
2. Beschränkungen, die auf pragmatische Faktoren zurückzuführen sind, z.B. wird einer Repräsentationsform der Vorrang gegenüber einer anderen gegeben, weil sie unter bestimmten Kommunikationsbedingungen und -zwecken ein größeres Ausdruckspotential hat oder einen höheren Sicherheitsgrad gewährleistet.

3.1 Systeminhärente Beschränkungen Unmögliche Konversion

Musik, die bekanntlich auditiv wahrgenommen wird, kann wohl in Noten oder Diagramme konvertiert werden, die visuell erfaßt werden können. Allerdings sind diese Konversionsformen nur sekundär und der gehörten Musik nicht vergleichbar. Das Lesen der Noten oder der Diagramme vermittelt keinen musikalischen Eindruck. Auch kann kaum eine Parallele zum gelesenen und gesprochenen Wort gezogen werden.

Ganz sicher ist, daß Musik nicht in sprachliche Zeichen konvertiert werden kann. Die Beschreibung oder Besprechung eines Konzerts ist nicht vergleichbar mit dem Musikerlebnis selbst (Laurén et al. 1998: 199).

Unvollständige Konversion

In diesem Abschnitt seien alle Arten von Unzulänglichkeiten zusammengefaßt, die einem semiotischen Zeichensystem innewohnen und eine vollständige Konversion ohne Informationsverlust a priori unmöglich machen.

Olfaktive, gustative und taktile Sinneswahrnehmungen können zwar sprachlich repräsentiert werden, sie sind aber doch nur Annäherungen an das individuell Aufgefaßte. Oft werden Metaphern als sprachliche Repräsentationen herangezogen, die schon an sich einen Vergleich oder eine Parallelität mit etwas anderem beinhalten. Ein Wein kann z.B. süffig, vollmundig oder samten sein; ob diese Adjektive aber trotz einer gewissen Konventionalisierung von allen Mitgliedern einer Sprachgemeinschaft mit genau derselben Bedeutung verstanden werden, muß bezweifelt werden. Auch ist es wohl eher ungewöhnlich, daß eine Frau ein ihr unbekanntes Parfüm nur nach einer verbalen Beschreibung in einem Katalog kauft.

Eine weitere systeminhärente Beschränkung besteht bei einer graphischen, nicht-sprachlichen Repräsentation darin, daß z.B. Dimensionen, Formen, Maße, Farben, Proportionen, Lage etc. mit großer Genauigkeit wiedergegeben werden können. Materialeigenschaften, Funktionen, Besitzverhältnisse, Alter und dergl. aber nur bedingt oder gar nicht repräsentierbar sind und folglich durch andere semiotische Systeme – in den meisten Fällen durch Sprache – wiedergegeben werden müssen.

Beschränkungen der Systembildung

Inwieweit nicht-sprachliche Zeichensysteme die Eigenschaft besitzen, komplexere Begriffssysteme wiedergeben zu können, ist noch wenig erforscht. Eine erste Sichtung des Analysematerials läßt jedoch erkennen, daß erhebliche Unterschiede zwischen Fachgebieten bestehen (Picht 1999). Die Kommunikation in Fachgebiete wie Architektur, Anatomie, Technik, Wirtschaft u.a. bedient sich zu einem großen Teil nicht-sprachlicher, graphischer Repräsentationsformen, im Recht und einigen anderen Geisteswissenschaften ist diese Repräsentationsform weit seltener anzutreffen.

Es ist jedoch eine Tatsache, daß selbst in Fachgebieten mit ausgeprägter Anwendung von graphischen, nicht-sprachlichen Zeichensystemen, diese nicht imstande sind, den gesamten Begriffsapparat systematisch zusammenhängend zu repräsentieren. Kurzum, es können nur Teile der Begriffsapparate nicht-sprachlich wiedergegeben werden.

Hierzu einige Beispiele:

- Die drei visuellen Zeichen einer Verkehrsampel bilden ein System, das jedoch in seiner auditiven Form nur durch zwei Zeichen (die "grün" und "rot" repräsentieren) wiedergegeben wird. Hier liegt also eine Systemreduktion vor.
- Olfaktive und gustative Zeichen bilden kaum größere Systeme, sie weisen eher auf Einzelbegriffe hin – vor allem Warnungen und Hinweise ohne eigentlichen Systemzusammenhang. Allerdings macht der Teil der Weinterminologie, der sich auf die Beschreibung der gustativ und olfaktiv auffaßbaren Eigenschaften bezieht, ein System aus.
- Zwar können z.B. alle Teile einer Fachwerkkonstruktion graphisch dargestellt werden, nicht aber die statischen Eigenschaften oder die Eigenschaften der verwendeten Hölzer.

3.2 Pragmatisch bedingte Beschränkungen

Im Gegensatz zu den inhärenten Beschränkungen, die dem Zeichensystem eigen sind, ist bei den pragmatisch bedingten Beschränkungen eine Konversion grundsätzlich möglich, in der Praxis aber wenig oder gar nicht gebräuchlich. So ist es durchaus denkbar, eine technische Arbeitszeichnung oder eine Bauzeichnung in eine rein sprachliche Repräsentationsform zu konvertieren. In einem solchen Falle wird – bei gleichem Präzisionsgrad – ein äußerst komplizierter Fachtext mit höchstem Fachlichkeitsgrad entstehen, der wahrscheinlich auch die Kompetenz des fachlich geschulten Lesers übersteigt. Man stelle sich die rein verbale Beschreibung eines Rohbaus für einen Maurer vor. Abgesehen davon, daß eine solche Beschreibung mit einem Hohngelächter abgewiesen würde, würde sie weit mehr Platz als eine Zeichnung beanspruchen. Außerdem kann die Beschreibung nur linear sein, was der Verständlichkeit wenig zuträglich ist, zumal eine schnelle, selektive ja oft sogar „springende" Perzeption in solchen Kommunikationssituationen die Regel ist.

Pragmatisch bedingte Begrenzungen der verbalen Repräsentationsform gehören nicht nur zu den Zeichenkonventionen bestimmter Fachgebiete, sie können auch gesetzlich vorgeschrieben sein, so z.B. fordert die Baubehörde neben anderen Dokumenten eine Zeichnung des beantragten Neu- oder Umbaus, bevor die Baugenehmigung erteilt werden kann.

Etappen eines Konversionsprozesses

Die obigen pragmatisch bedingten Beschränkungen können aber durchbrochen werden, wenn man sich den Entstehungsprozeß eines Neubaus vor Augen führt. Die darin vorkommenden Kommunikationssituationen lassen Etappen des Konversionsprozesses sichtbar werden:

1. Der Bauherr beauftragt einen Architekten mit dem Bau und in den ersten Gesprächen vermittelt der Bauherr dem Architekten seine Wünsche und Vorstellungen in der Regel verbal.
2. Der Architekt fertigt eine erste Skizze des Grundrisses und der Ansichten aus verschiedenen Blickwinkeln an – eine zweidimensionale graphische Repräsentationsform mit relativ geringem Abstraktionsgrad, die die Grundlage für weitere Gespräche bildet.
3. Bei größeren Bauvorhaben werden eventuell dreidimensionale Modelle aus Holz, Gips oder anderen Materialien erstellt, die heute oft durch ebenfalls dreidimensionale Computersimulationen ergänzt bzw. ersetzt werden.
4. Nach Klärung aller grundlegenden Fragen fertigt der Architekt Bauzeichnungen für die Baubehörde und die Handwerker an.

An diesem Beispiel kann gezeigt werden, daß eine Konversion von der sprachlichen Repräsentation zur nicht-sprachlichen nach der ersten

Etappe stattfindet, die weiteren Konversionen sind 'interne' Konversionen innerhalb eines Zeichensystems, die sich vor allem auf den Fachlichkeitsgrad der Repräsentation beziehen.

4. Repräsentationsformen für Abstrakta

Unter Abstrakta verstehen wir Begriffe und Gegenstände, die keine materielle Form haben, z.B. elektrischer Widerstand, Gewissen, Vernunft, Zeus etc. Inwieweit mythologische und religiöse Gegenstände als Begriffe aufgefaßt werden können, soll hier nicht diskutiert werden (siehe hierzu Picht 2002).

In der Regel werden Begriffe und Gegenstände dieser Art durch sprachliche Zeichen kommunizierbar gemacht. In anderen semiotischen Systemen werden sie durch Ersatzgegenstände – Symbole – repräsentiert, die zumeist visuell erfaßt werden können, z.B. durch Bilder, Statuen, Personen, materielle Gegenstände, geschriebene Zeichen etc.

Oft bilden Symbole ganze Bezeichnungssysteme und die Bedeutung des Symbols erhält seinen semantischen Wert durch den Systemzusammenhang, z.B. repräsentiert der Hammer in der nordischen Mythologie den Gott Thor und das Prinzip, das er verkörpert, in kommunistischen Systemen war seine Bedeutung eine ganz andere und in der Freimaurerei wiederum hat er eine dritte Bedeutung, die mit den beiden ersten nichts gemein hat.

Das Omega-Zeichen als Symbol für den elektrischen Widerstand hat bedeutungsmäßig keinen Zusammenhang mit dem gleichen Zeichen im Christentum. Der Totenkopf mit gekreuzten Knochen ist einerseits eine Warnung vor giftigen Substanzen und andererseits ein Zeichen für die Vergänglichkeit.

Die Frage, warum eine nicht-sprachliche Repräsentationsform entwickelt wurde, läßt sich nicht immer eindeutig beantworten, sicher aber ist, daß z.B. technische Symbole eindeutig und kürzer und damit anwendungsökonomisch sind. Außerdem sind Symbole sprachunabhängig – nicht aber kultur- und systemunabhängig – und erlauben zum einen eine Kommunikation über Sprachgrenzen hinweg und zum anderen Analphabeten, Begriffe zu perzepieren, deren schriftliche Repräsentation ihnen nicht zugänglich ist.

Symbole können eine "innere" Konversion durchlaufen, die oft in einer Reduktion besteht, so wurde "Thor" z.B. als Bronzefigur mit dem Hammer, als stark stilisierte Zeichnung auf Runensteinen und durch den Hammer allein als Zeichnung oder als physischer Gegenstand in Miniaturausgabe dargestellt. Man könnte in diesem Falle von Metonymie (pars pro toto) sprechen (Picht 2002).

Die hohe Ikonizität des Symbols ist nicht gleichbedeutend damit, daß eine Abbildung des Begriffs oder Gegenstandes versucht wird, die ohnehin so gut wie ausgeschlossen werden kann. Metaphorische Elemente dagegen sind oft anzutreffen, ihr Erkennen jedoch, d.h. die Herstellung der Verständnisbrücke zwischen Symbol und Bedeutung, hängt von dem Systemwissen des Erkennenden ab.

Wir können also festhalten, daß eine Konversion zwischen verschiedenen Zeichensystemen auch bei Abstrakta möglich ist.

5. Folgen des Konventionsverlustes

In einer semiotischen Studie (Laurén/Picht 2000) wird die Frage gestellt, wie eine Botschaft über sehr große Zeiträume hinweg vermittelt werden kann – eine Frage, die auch andere Semiotiker beschäftigt hat.

Mit Ausgangspunkt in Wittgensteins Aussage, daß ein Zeichen erst seine Bedeutung durch die Anwendung erhält, d.h. im Diskurs, wurde der Begriff „kultureller Diskurs" geschaffen und so erklärt:

> Ein sehr genereller semiotischer Begriff, der Wittgensteins sprachlichem Diskurs entspricht. Dieser Diskurs enthält sprachliche und nicht-sprachliche Repräsentationsformen in unterschiedlichen quantitativen Konstellationen. Die Repräsentationsformen haben oft eine komplementäre Funktion und können auch austauschbar sein. (Laurén/Myking/Picht: *in preparation*)

Für unsere Überlegungen bedeutet diese Aussage, daß das Kennen des kulturellen Diskurses eine unabdingbare Voraussetzung für das Verstehen eines Zeichens ist. Geht das Wissen über die kulturelle Einbettung einer Kommunikation verloren, löst sich auch die saussuresche untrennbare Einheit von Ausdruck und Inhalt auf. Mit anderen Worten, das Wissen über die durch den kulturellen Diskurs begründete Konvention, die die Zuordnung von Repräsentationsform und Inhalt im Bewußtsein wachhält, entscheidet darüber, ob und wie lange mit den gleichen Zeichen über die zugeordneten Bedeutungen kommuniziert werden kann. Dies gilt sowohl für die Vergangenheit als auch für die Zukunft. Aus der Archäologie sind hinreichend Beispiele bekannt, wo Zeichen und Zeichensysteme gefunden wurden, die nicht mehr gedeutet werden können, da die Konvention verloren gegangen ist. Als Beispiel für den Konventionsverlust in der Zukunft können die Überlegungen in Posner (1990) dienen, wo gefragt wird, wie Menschen in 10.000 Jahren vor den Gefahren einer Atommülldeponie gewarnt werden können. Welche Zeichen könnten eine solche Ausdruckskraft haben, daß sie trotz Konventionsverlust eine so wichtige Botschaft, zumindest in der Form einer generellen eindringlichen Warnung, vermitteln können? Als Lösung wurde die Religion, eine Priesterschaft oder ein heiliger Ort, zu dem jeglicher Zugang verboten ist, vorgeschlagen.

Es ist aber nicht unbedingt erforderlich, den Begriff 'kultureller Diskurs' auf solche extreme, aber nicht unrealistische Beispiele zu beschränken. Für denjenigen, dem der kulturelle Diskurs unbekannt ist, besteht auch keine Konvention zwischen Zeichen und Inhalt; sie muß erlernt werden. Dies gilt in besonderem Maße für die Fachkommunikation, denn wer den kulturellen Diskurs eines Fachgebietes nicht kennt, kann auch die Konvention nicht kennen, d.h. er kann Zeichen und Inhalt nicht einander zuordnen und damit ist auch eine Konversion zwischen Repräsentationsformen für ihn nicht möglich.

6. Konklusion

Die eingangs aufgestellte Hypothese kann an sich weitgehend als haltbar angesehen werden, doch ist sie dahingehend zu erweitern, daß einige Konversionen aus systeminhärenten und andere aus pragmatischen Gründen nicht möglich bzw. höchst ungebräuchlich sind. Ferner muß hinzugefügt werden, daß ein Konventionsverlust die Konversion *a priori* unmöglich macht.

References

Laurén, Christer / Myking, Johan / Picht, Heribert 1998. *Terminologie unter der Lupe. Vom Grenzgebiet zum Wissenschaftszweig.* IITF-Series 9. Wien: IITF.

Laurén, Christer / Myking, Johan / Picht, Heribert *in preparation.*

Laurén, Christer / Picht, Heribert 2000. Att överföre budskap från en tid till en annan. En semiotisk studie. In Jauhola, Päivi / Järvi, Outi / Wilske, Detlef (eds) *Fackspråk och Översättningsteori.* VAKKI-symposieum XX. Vasa 11-13.2.2000. Vaasa, 215-223.

Nöth, Winfried 1985. *Handbuch der Semiotik.* Stuttgart: Metzler.

Picht, Heribert 1999. Einige Überlegungen zur nicht-sprachlichen Repräsentation von Gegenständen und Begriffen. *SYNAPS. Fagspråk, Kommunikation, Kulturkunnskap.* Arbeidspapirer. Institutt for språk, Norge Handelshøyskole, 3/99, 1-50.

Picht, Heribert 2002. Zur Repräsentation von immateriellen Gegenständen. Der Fall "Thor". In Björkelund, S. / Koskela, M. / Nordman, M. (eds) *Språk som formar vär(l)den. Festskrift till Christer Laurén på 60-årsdagen.* Språkvetenskap nr. 40. Vaasa: Vaasa University, 237-248.

Posner, Roland (ed.) 1990. *Warnungen an die ferne Zukunft. Atommüll als Kommunikationsproblem.* München: Raben-Verlag.

NINA PILKE

Thematic variation in academic seminars – student discussions of concepts and terms

1. Introduction

The number of people working with knowledge management continues to increase. The various duties in the different fields require new knowledge and new solutions, effective planning and excellent communication skills. Those who are experts in language and communication and have an academic education are one of the most central groups of experts in our society today. These language experts work everywhere; they are technical writers and terminologists, translators and information managers both in public administration and enterprises, interpreters, teachers, secretaries, journalists, researchers, and so on. The target group in my study is a group of future language experts, namely those who are studying Scandinavian languages (Scandinavian philology) at the University of Vaasa in Finland.

One of the most central aims of studying at university level is to learn academic ways of thinking. Facts (field-specific knowledge) are reconciled with knowledge concerning methods (research methods). In academic education, seminars in particular are the forum for learning to participate in academic discussion and giving and receiving academic criticism. Seminar discussions are one of the most student-centered modes of teaching in groups. The aim is to make the students familiar with knowledge within their own field (epistemic premises), academic thought and communication.

Earlier studies (Luukka 1996) have examined among other things the students' opinions of good seminar discussions. The results show that it is obvious that the expectations of good discussions in-seminars and direction are contradictory. On the one hand the students stress that the discussion should be equal and free, while on the other hand, they seek to establish strict control of the discussion, even resulting in the teacher forcing the participants to speak.

Consequently, the seminar meeting is clearly bipartite. The first part consists of the academic discussion that presupposes equality, and the second part is the educational discussion that requires authority of knowledge.

2. Objectives of the research project

The aims of my research project are to 1) examine what kinds of opinions university students and teachers have about learning through seminars, and 2) examine the characteristics of academic discussion in university seminars. The research is comparative in nature. My aim is to compare the interaction between students within one group and between groups consisting of students at different stages of their studies. The study focuses on seminars on three different levels in the Department of Scandinavian Languages at the University of Vaasa; Proseminars, Thesis seminars and Doctoral seminars. In the following I have placed the seminars studied into Luukka's (1996) figure, which shows that the seminar discussion lies somewhere between "academic discussion" and "educational discussion":

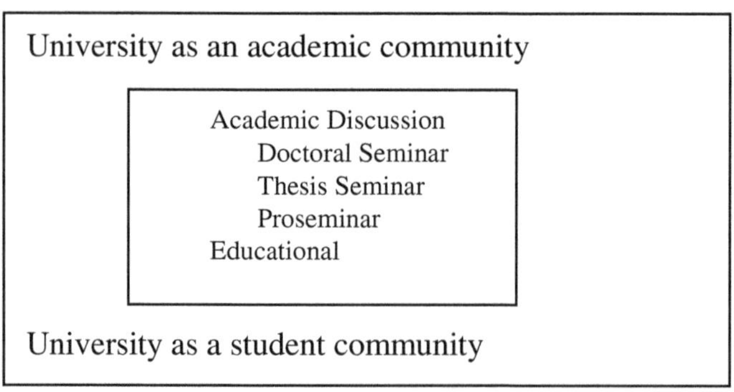

Figure 1. Three university seminars as objects of research (adapted from Luukka 1996).

Proseminar (ProS) is the first seminar for most students in the Faculty of Humanities (third study year). It therefore lies nearest to educational discussion; the students need on average a lot of advice and support from the advisor when they are doing their research, presenting the results and giving comments on each other's reports. The Proseminar plays an important role in the students' academic studies. The first seminar gives the students an introduction to research and academic discussion and it gives a picture of how a research project is carried out in the form of a "miniature research" project.

It is important that the students have experienced research work as a meaningful activity and that they have been socialized into the community when they take part in the following seminar, the *Thesis seminar* (TS). Those who participate in Thesis seminars are on the home stretch of their studies (fourth or fifth study year) and they already have knowledge of academic research work, discussion and argumentation. The functionality of the seminar plays an important role in the students' graduation and also for the university with respect to examination objectives.

Those who take part in a *Doctoral seminar* (DS) are aiming at a licentiate or doctoral degree. In many cases the participants already have some experience of doing research as well as of directing research projects. The discussion in Doctoral seminars can be assumed to be most suggestive of group discussion and therefore lies nearest to the ideal of academic discussion (see Figure 1).

In the present chapter the focus lies on the thematic variation in the seminars. An important aspect of the study is to examine how special concepts and terms are discussed in the three different seminars.

3. The material of the study

The research material consists of three parts. The first part consists of a questionnaire (written) addressed to the participants in the seminars chosen. The second part of the material consists of the recorded seminars (video + audio). The analyses in this chapter are founded on this part of the material, i.e. on a transcription of the tapes.

	ProS	*TS*	*DS*
Date	10.04.2001	22.02.2001	16.03.2001
Participants	10 + 1	10 + 1	10 + 1
Length	63 min	49 min	96 min

Table 1. Recorded seminars.

Table 1 shows that the three seminars were recorded during the spring of 2001. There are 10 participants plus the instructor in each seminar group and the length of the seminar varies from 49 to 96 minutes. The written seminar reports, which function as the base for the discussion in the seminars, form the third part of the material and are used when needed in the analysis of the recorded material.

4. Findings

In analysing the recordings I use the concept “turn” (Sv. ‘samtalstur’, see Norrby 1996; Persson 1997) as the point of departure. A turn starts when the speaker begins to speak and ends when somebody else takes over or when the speaker finishes an utterance by falling silent. A change of turns thus always implies a change of speaker, and a turn can comprise just occasional words or constitute a longish contribution to a discussion.

When counting turns during the three seminars, *conversational support* is also included in the numbers (see Adelswärd 1992; Norrby

1996: 131-132; Hakulinen 1998). Researchers who make a distinction between minimal response (*yes* as an answer to a question) and backings which do not demand the right to speak, do not grant the status of turns to interjections like *hm* and *mm* unless the silence between utterances can be interpreted as a pause (see Linell/Gustavsson 1987; Norrby 1996: 136). Conversational support in the form of particles are, however, an indication of active listenership and they are in my opinion important in seminars where one argues, states one's reasons and expresses one's point of view concerning different solutions. In my study I therefore think, in agreement with Hakulinen (1998), that dialogue particles even by themselves can constitute a turn.

	ProS (f=213) %	*TS (f=458) %*	*DS (f=812) %*
Thesis writer (W)	22	32	41
Opponent(s) (O)	28	16	45
Instructor (I)	46	42	12
Participants (P)	4	9	2

Table 2. Turns in the seminars (%).

In the Proseminar, the participants take 213 turns in 63 minutes. The instructor uses 46% of all turns (see Table 2). Table 2 shows that after the instructor comes the "opponent" – whose job is to challenge the views expressed by the author of the thesis – with a share of 28% and the writer of the thesis with a share of 22% of all turns. Of the other participants, three contribute with a total of 4% of all turns. In the Thesis seminar 458 turns in all are taken in 49 minutes. From Table 2 it appears that the instructor accounts for 42% of the turns in the seminar and the writer of the text for 32%. The opponent's share is 16% and that of the other participants 9% of all turns. In the research seminar 812 turns are taken in the course of 96 minutes. Engagement in the discussion is somewhat different compared with the other two seminars, the instructor's share of the turns being merely 12% compared with more than 40% for the other two. Judging the share of turns, the discussion seems to take place mainly between the opponents and the writers of the text. The share of the turns of the other participants is the lowest of all seminars, only 2%.

4.1 Thematic variation in the seminars

The informants in my investigation point out that it is important for the seminar to be rewarding from the point of view of its content. A particular wealth of angles of approach is seen as a sign of a successful seminar meeting (see Pilke 2003). In order to get a picture of what is discussed in the seminars and of how and to what extent this is done, I have studied the structure of the discussion in the light of main themes. By *main theme* (MT) I mean in this context the whole within which the content of a certain topic is discussed (see for instance Gunnarsson 1998). A survey of the transcriptions of the recorded seminars shows that the discussion moves between six main themes. The different themes with a brief description of their content are to be seen in Table 3.

THEME	*Examples of subjects discussed*
1) Concepts and terms	definitions of concepts; what is meant by a certain term, what term one should choose, relations between concepts and so on.
2) Disposition	sections; arranging, moving something in the text, subheadings and so on.
3) Literature	reliable sources, own text-adopted ideas, interpretation of literature, possible sources, references to relevant literature
4) Specifying and completing	fundamental questions concerning aim, material, method as well as the empirical approach
5) Technical details	*typography, references to sources (form), bibliographical list (arrangement), quotations and so on.*
6) Language	linguistic correctness, stylistic questions

Table 3. Themes of the seminars.

Table 4 below shows that the most discussed theme (measured in numbers of turns) in all three seminars is *Specifying and completing.* In the Proseminar this theme is the clearly dominant one with a share of 65% of the turns. Even in the Doctoral seminar the share of this theme is high since more than half of the turns concern this theme. In the Thesis seminar the share is somewhat lower, slightly over 30%.

	ProS %	*TS %*	*DS %*
Concepts and terms	1	12	39
Disposition	11	13	6
Literature	3	15	1
Specifying and completing	65	31	51
Technical details	13	24	2
Language	7	5	1

Table 4. Turns in the six main themes (%).

A clear difference between the seminars in my study is that the theme *Concepts and terms,* which is the focus of this chapter, is clearly given more space in the Doctoral seminar than in the other two seminars. In the Proseminar only 1% of the turns concern this theme. In the Thesis seminar the corresponding share is 12%. In the Doctoral seminar *Concepts and terms* is the theme to which the next greatest number of turns is devoted (39% of all turns) after *Specifying and completing.* This difference can at least partly be explained by the fact that the participants in the Doctoral seminar create new theories and thus need their own term systems. The new knowledge and the new terms always have to be related and defined with reference to previously existing systems, which is not always problem-free or unambiguous.

Within each main theme it is possible to distinguish a number of partial themes (PT). In the Doctoral seminar and the Thesis seminar the discussion comprises a total of 42 partial themes, while the number of partial themes in the Proseminar is somewhat lower, 31. Within the theme *Concepts and terms,* it is possible to distinguish only one partial theme in the Proseminar compared with seven in the Thesis seminar and 13 in the Doctoral seminar.

4.2 The Concepts and terms theme

An academic text always contains terms, and it is important to both define the concepts one uses and be consistent in the use of terms (see Strömquist 1988: 20). Such advice is given in all manuals which deal with academic writing, and all seminar instructors take up the question at some stage during the introductory lectures. Thus one can expect that terms and concepts form a conspicuous theme in the seminar discussions. In the Proseminar, as mentioned above, there is, however, only one partial theme concerned with concepts and terms. In the Thesis seminar, the proceedings are introduced by a discussion of concepts and terms, and these questions are returned to at the end of the seminar meeting. In the Doctoral seminar, questions concerned with concepts and terms are dealt with at regular intervals from the beginning, but stop during the last quarter.

An analysis of the content of what is discussed in connection with the theme *Concepts and terms* shows that the discussions in the seminars at the three different levels are not alike. In the Proseminar, the theme *Concepts and terms* is almost ignored since neither the instructor nor the other participants continue the discussion after the opponent's introductory comments on difficult linguistic terms in the text concerned. Instead of, for instance, asking what is felt to be difficult or whether one should possibly define the concepts differently, the instructor proceeds to discuss the reliability of the source (see example 1).

(1) Proseminar

O	[...] hard to understand as they are academic, linguistic terms
I	yes we can with satisfaction note that (W) has used the Swedish Academy grammar; and that is the grammar one should consult, from the proseminar stage on, in thesis and seminar connections [...]

In the Thesis seminar the questions related to the *Concept and terms* theme concern linguistic concepts, for example when it is a question of sense, when of meaning (see example 2) and what is the difference between emotively and contextually loaded and positively and negatively loaded expressions respectively.

(2) Thesis seminar

O1	I looked at page 22 after the example where you say that drinking hero gets a positive emotive meaning, is it meaning you study or is it sense or just something that somebody uses for for...
I	so you mean is it a term there?
O1	yes
I	mmm
W	well Andersson and Furberg use...
I	what do they mean by meaning there then, what do they mean... they talk about meanings earlier on, but here meaning is rendered by another word, here it is sense
O1	that was just what I thought about, so that
I	well, well it's a bit odd
W	problem
I	so don't use meaning here [...]

In the Doctoral seminar the discussions about conceptual questions and the selection of terms are more multi-faceted than in the two lower seminars. There are discussions about terms used for the categories of analysis selected, definitions of concepts, intensions of concepts and even whole conceptual systems with regard to super-, sub-, and co-ordinate concepts (see example 3).

(3) Doctoral seminar

O1	well, we were in fact just going to ask about the term acting or the concept acting, that is why we were in there – what do you understand by acting
W	well, that should of course be explained. Acting is all that one does while one sits doing simultaneous interpretation, that is, one writes down numbers one hears…
O1	Oh
W	[…] one turns over one's papers and so on. Acting can also be what one does in advance when one is preparing oneself.
O1	is it more like what is concrete as…
W	yes
O1	yes, not as a result of thinking,
W	exactly

Analyses concerning who takes part in the discussions involving the main theme *Concepts and terms*, who opens the discussions and how many turns are used in the discussions also show that there are differences between the three seminars. In the Proseminar it is the opponent who tries to shift the discussion to the theme of concepts and terms after some linguistic aspects have been dealt with. Since the instructor, who otherwise markedly steers the discussion, does not take part in the discussion about terms, this theme is passed over. In the Thesis seminar the main theme *Concepts and terms* is four times opened by an opponent, three times by the instructor. Once the writer of the thesis himself takes up a question related to a term in the title of the thesis. In the Thesis seminar the number of turns varies between 2 and 13 (on average 7 turns / sub theme) and in the Doctoral seminar the number varies between 7 and 77 (on average 24 turns / sub theme). In the discussion in the Thesis seminar both the instructor and the thesis writer practically always participate; three times it is a question of a dialogue between these two actors; three times one of the opponents participates and twice one of the other participants. In the Doctoral seminar the discussion about concepts and terms most often (5 times) involves the instructor, the thesis writer and both the opponents; thus four people participate. Four times in all either of the opponents and the thesis writer have a dialogue related to the theme; three times the instructor serves as the third participant in the discussion and once one of the other participants takes part in a discussion with the instructor, the thesis writer and one of the opponents.

In order to get a still more detailed picture of the participation in the discussion with regard to the selected theme, I have studied how many turns the various participants use within the theme in the Thesis seminar and the Doctoral seminar.

	TS %	*DS* %
Thesis writer	*35*	*41*
Opponents	*22*	*46*
Instructor	*39*	*13*
Participants	*4*	*1*

Table 5. Turns/participants concerning the *Concepts and terms* theme in the Thesis seminar and the Doctoral seminar (%).

Table 5 shows that the picture that Table 2 above presents of the participants' activity in the whole seminar is also true with regard to the *Concepts and terms* theme. In the Thesis seminar the instructor speaks more than in the Doctoral seminar, where the opponents use the majority of the turns. A difference with respect to the instructor's way of participating in the discussion on the *Concepts and terms* theme is that the instructor in the Thesis seminar most frequently provides a concluding comment which rounds off the discussion and gives the thesis writer a concrete solution to the problem discussed (see example 2 above). The instructor thus serves as the knowledgeable authority in a teaching situation. In connection with the *Concepts and terms* theme, the instructor in the Doctoral seminar most frequently participates in the discussion in the middle of the sub theme. He does not make straight recommendations but takes part in the discussion for instance by asking whether some concept should be further defined, by providing the theoretical background for a certain term or by confirming that the thesis writer and the opponents have reached a common solution to a terminological problem. In this way the discussion resembles an equal and free academic discussion where the thesis writer himself serves as the expert.

5. Discussion

The purpose of this chapter has been to describe and discuss thematic variation in academic seminars. In particular I have examined how special concepts and terms are discussed in seminars on three different levels in the Department of Scandinavian Languages at the University of Vaasa: Proseminar, Thesis seminar and Doctoral seminar.

The outcomes of the analyses concerning *Concepts and terms* show that terms and concepts are most discussed in the Doctoral seminar, where 39% of all turns are related to this theme. In the Thesis seminar, the corresponding share is 12% and in the Proseminar merely 1%. The outcome can at least partly be explained by the fact that those who take part in the Doctoral seminars are creating their own terms and concept systems, which demands that exact definitions and connections with already existing systems will have to be explicitly elucidated.

The seminars also differ from one another with regard to their content. In the Proseminar the theme *Concepts and terms* is passed over with a cursory comment on difficult terms. In the Thesis seminar there is a discussion about which terms represent certain linguistic concepts. In the Doctoral seminar the discussions of conceptual questions and the selection of terms is more multi-faceted. The discussion concerns terms used for the selected categories of analysis, definitions of concepts, the intensions of concepts and even whole systems of concepts in terms of super-, sub- and co-ordinate concepts. The results show that the field-specific socialization process is clearly at different stages with regard to discussions about concepts and terms in the three different seminars.

An analysis of the number of turns related to *Concepts and terms* shows that the instructor in the two lower-level seminars always participates in the discussion with concrete suggestions for solutions. In the Doctoral seminar, on the other hand, the instructor has a somewhat different role by asking clarifying/specifying questions, making the participants responsible for how the discussion develops. It is thus possible to see a distinction between an educational discussion where the students need a knowledgeable authority who controls the discussion on all levels and an academic discussion where the already more experienced researchers argue for and against on the basis of arguments typical of "science" in the sense of academic discussion.

References

Adelswärd, V. 1992. Kommunikativa stildrag – om tystnad och turtagande, skrattande och frågande. In S. Strömquist (ed.) *Tal och samtal.* Lund: Studentlitteratur, 127-149.

Gunnarsson, B-L. 1998. Spelet om den akademiska kunskapen. En studie av ämnesutvecklingen i forskarseminarier. *NyS* 24, 41-72.

Hakulinen, A. 1997. Vuorottelujäsennys. In Tainio, L. (ed.) *Keskusteluanalyysin perusteet.* Tampere: Vastapaino, 32-55.

Linell, P. / Gustavsson L. 1987. *Initiativ och respons. Om dialogens dynamik, dominans och koherens.* (Series *SIC,* 15). Linköping: Tema kommunikation.

Luukka, M-R. 1996. Seminaari-luokkahuoneviestintää vai ryhmäkeskustelua? In Laurinen, L / Luukka, M.-R. / Sajavaara, K. (eds) *Seminaaridiskurssi-diskursseja seminaarista.* Jyväskylän yliopisto / Soveltavan Kielitutkimuksen keskus, 39-84.

Norrby, C. 1996. *Samtalsanalys. Så gör vi när vi pratar med varandra.* Lund: Studentlitteratur.

Persson, A. 1997. *Diskursdeltagande-vilja och framgång på forskarseminarier.* (Series *TeFa*, 17). Uppsala: Uppsala universitet.

Pilke, N. 2003. "Akademiska diskussioner". In Sorvali, I / Rossi, P. (eds) *Svenskan i Finland 7.* Föredrag vid sjunde sammankomsten för beskrivningen av svenskan i Finland, Uleåborg 19-20 april 2002. Oulu: Oulun yliopisto, 169-178.

Strömquist, S. 1988. *Uppsatshandboken.* Uppsala: Hallgren & Fallgren.

Klaus-Dieter Baumann

A communicative-cognitive approach to emotion in LSP communication

1. Introduction

Since the end of the 20th century the shift of modern LSP research towards an interdisciplinary analysis of LSP texts has increasingly led to the exploration of their *emotional dimension* which can be regarded as the result of complex *appraisal processes* of LSP text author(s) and/or recipient(s).

As a result of this, theories of emotion which have been ignored by LSP research for a long time are of increasing methodological and methodical significance because they offer far-reaching strategic orientations for the communicative-cognitive analysis of information processing in LSP texts (Baumann 2001).

Finally, the development of different – sometimes even controversial – psychological theories of emotion makes it clear that there are varying ways of dealing with emotion, defining its fundamental relation to cognition and describing the complicated mechanisms of integration between emotion and cognition (Otto/Euler/Mandl 2000).

Therefore, we have considered the substance of all existing theories carefully in order to piece together those exponents that are undisputed and essential to an interdisciplinary approach to emotion in LSP communication.

In our LSP text analyses, we commenced from a multidimensional, interdisciplinary theory (Baumann 1992) that understands emotions as complex processes caused by cognitive appraisals of objects, processes and so on, that have varying intensities.

Undoubtedly, emotion and cognition are two complementary aspects of human activities.

2. An interdisciplinary approach to emotion in LSP communication

As a result of the cognitive turn of contemporary LSP research, the analysis of the correlation between emotion and LSP communication has become – especially from the point of view of information processing – one of the main fields of interdisciplinary research (Jahr 2000; Baumann 2001: 32).

In considering the findings of the emotional theories and of the extensive inductive-empirical German and English LSP text analyses, this research systematically deals with a) the realisation of emotions on the various levels of LSP communication (Baumann 1992; 1994; 2001) and b) the interrelation between emotion and LSP text comprehension.

The first phase of the interdisciplinary analysis is based upon an *inductive-empirical analysis of English and German LSP texts* – all belonging to one and the same text form, namely the *article* (articles from an encyclopaedia, scientific articles, popular science articles) – from the fields of medicine and linguistics. The corpus analysed comprises 27 paragraphs, 142 sentences and 3,022 words in English, and 32 paragraphs, 137 sentences and 2,330 words in German – with 92 paragraphs, 497 sentences and 9,419 words in total.

This limitation of the LSP text corpus was intentional because the seven texts were presented, together with questionnaires, to 80 test subjects – all of them students of applied linguistics / LSP communication at the University of Leipzig (Baumann 1995: 107-117).

The second phase of the interdisciplinary analysis of emotion in LSP texts is based upon the inductive-empirical analysis of English, German and Russian LSP texts, comprising 795 printed pages in total (Baumann 1992).

The *interdisciplinary* approach to the LSP text corpus is based on *descriptive, functional, structural, comparative, statistical and other methods* which unfortunately cannot be explained in detail here due to lack of space.

Finally, we found that fifteen different, hierarchically ordered dimensions determine emotion in LSP texts:

2.1 The cultural dimension of emotion

Since the 1990s, several contrastive LSP text analyses have demonstrated that LSP communication is largely culturally specific (Clyne 1981: 61-66; Baumann/Kalverkämper 1992).

The present integration of cultural determinants into the emotional analysis of LSP communication makes a considerable step further in the direction of a cognitive and cultural extension of contemporary LSP research.

According to most of the emotional theories, emotions can be regarded as culturally specific knowledge that is socialised, constructed, controlled and conventionalised (Vester 1991: 98).

As expected, it is especially the transfer of emotions in LSP text translations which opens up new prospects for research (Salnikow 1995). In the past few years, cross-cultural investigations have brought to light that there are many emotions which cannot be translated into other languages equivalently. In Japanese, for example, the rituals of spoken LSP communication are extremely relevant in avoiding non-adequate communicative behaviour between partners.

Furthermore, the field of complimentary language means in Japanese LSP is by far more extensive than in any other European LSP (compare the expression of social ranking by means of complimentary language depending on the relative junior/senior position of the communicative partners; the high frequency of hedging in LSP texts to avoid the impression of intellectual superiority or of self-confidence) (Krusche 1983).

Lastly, contrastive analyses of English, Russian and German LSP texts have shown that there are many culturally specific rituals of communicative interaction which have profound emotional effects (for example: phrases of routine, negative appraisal of silence in LSP discourses in western European scientific communities vs. positive appraisal of silence in Asian scientific communities; different strategies of respect towards LSP communicative partners in eastern/western Europe; existence of different communicative strategies to realize a specific self-image / to characterize other communicative partners in western, eastern and developing countries; use of culturally specific functions of overstatement/understatement in LSP texts, especially in UK/USA) (Baumann 1992).

2.2 The social dimension of emotion

In the last years, the psycho-social approach has opened up a promising method of relating the use of emotions to social characterristics of the communicative partners.

In LSP text analyses, we have concentrated on the dynamic relation between the social position of the communicative partner(s) and the use of emotions.

In this context, the concept of the 'emotional role' has been defined as a part of the social knowledge (or social competence) comprising the prototypical reactions, conventions and norms of the communicative partners (Averill 1996: 24-38). These have to be finely delineated in order to guarantee a communicatively adequate expression of emotion (conclusion of agreements / business negotiations / sales talks; communication between physician and patient; judicial hearings and so on).

Interestingly, socio-emotional analyses of business communication have unmistakably confirmed our assumption that there are complex interrelations between the cultural background of the communicative partner, his/her social position within the corporation and the realization of emotional behavior (Baumann 1991: 23).

From the methodological point of view, the concept of corporate identity is especially suitable for demonstrating the social character of emotional behavior on account of its complexity as a specific cultural, socio-economic, psycho-emotional and communicative-cognitive phenomenon (Baumann 1994: 105-125; 2001: 107-126).

2.3 The situational dimension of emotion

Without doubt, an interdisciplinary emotional analysis of LSP communication has to make use of all situational conditions which determine the production and reception of LSP texts (Baumann 1992: 171).

In LSP communication, these include the following aspects:

Elements of the technical situation of activity:

- constellation of the communicative partners,
- specific character of the (technical/social/natural-scientific) field,
- stage and speed of development in the science (see genetics, biotechnology, theory of information processing and so on),
- correlation between the primary specialized activity and the LSP communication and so on.

Elements of the social situation:

- scientific status of the communicative partner(s) (level of prior knowledge, (non-) symmetrical communicative relations),
- standards of value, social norms, traditions and thinking habits of the communicative partners,
- familiarity/social distance of the communicative partners.

Elements of the situation surrounding the communicative partners:

- quality of the interpersonal relations,
- scientific, professional and language competence,
- age, sex and so on (Baumann 1992: 170).

The concept of *feeling rules* has played a fundamental role in many emotional theories for some years. According to A. R. Hochschild (1979: 551-575) the category "feeling rule" is understood as a normative model of behaviour determining in what situation which emotion can be regarded as adequate (the situation-bound use of emotional variables in the LSP text form *necrologue* as a communicative part of memorial rituals, or *laudation* as a speech of praise about colleagues' scientific achievements).

LSP analyses have made clear that the situational dimension of emotion is aimed at directing the communicative partners' attention to selected information.

2.4 The cognitive dimension of emotion

We broadly agree with the exponents of the emotional theories who define emotion as a process of appraisal and a basic determinant of LSP communication. Clearly, emotions can influence the information processing of individual LSP communicative partners to a high degree because of the following reasons:

A. Emotions are the basic cognitive driving force of information processing, directing the focus of attention to specific information.
B. Emotions influence the ongoing integration of information into the long-term, temporary and immediate memory.
C. Emotions combine functionally equivalent cognitive elements and determine the hierarchical order of the contents of thinking.
D. Emotions i) restrict and ii) convey the wealth of cognitive information (Ciompi 1997).

From the point of view of LSP research strategy, the concept of LSP thinking styles has opened a promising avenue for analyzing the interrelations of cognition, emotion, science and subject matter systematically. Concerning the complexity of thinking styles, Fleck gives the following explanation:

> Vergleichen wir Denkstile untereinander, so bemerken wir ohne weiteres, dass die Differenzen zwischen zwei Denkstilen kleiner oder größer sein können. So ist im allgemeinen die Differenz zwischen dem Denkstil der Physiker und der Biologen nicht sehr groß, wenn letztere sich nicht gerade zum Denkstil der Vitalisten bekennen. Sie ist viel größer, wenn es sich um Physiker und Philologen handelt, noch viel größer zwischen dem Denkstil des modernen europäischen Physikers und eines chinesischen Arztes oder eines Kabbala-Mystikers: in diesem Falle ist die Divergenz der Denkstile so groß, dass ihr gegenüber

> diejenige zwischen dem Physiker und dem Biologen überhaupt verschwindet [...] .Je größer die Differenz zweier Denkstile, umso geringer der Gedankenverkehr [...] (Fleck 1994: 142-143).

In addition, Fowler (1977) tries to analyse thinking styles on a more comprehensive textual basis. Instead of using the term "thinking style" he prefers the expression "mental style" to refer to the cognitive dimension of emotion. In this context he remarks:

> Der Begriff des Mentalstils [...] verweist also auf den besonderen Aspekt der (unbewussten oder bewussten) Stilgebung, der [...] speziell auf Einstellungen, Attitüden, Meinungen, *Werthaltungen*, Weltanschauungen, *psychische Befindlichkeiten*, also *auf mentale (kognitive und emotionale) Einstellungen bzw. Befindlichkeiten,* der Charaktere/Sender zurückzugehen scheint (Fowler 1977 in: Nischik 1991: 3; italics – K.-D.B.).

Future analyses must be extended to other LSP thinking styles in order to systematically expand on the insights concerning the interrelations between *the emotional characteristics of LSP texts and the underlying cognitive processes of the communicative partners.*

2.5 The subject-specific dimension of emotion

In the last few years, LSP experts have become aware of the enormous significance of the subject-specific dimension for the emotional analysis of LSP texts. Most often when somebody has an emotion it is about an object, a state of affairs or a process. This means that emotions are undeniably object-directed. The quality and intensity of the emotions toward the object depend on the actual appraisal and the personal confusion of the communicative partners. As early as the beginning of 1990s, Skudlik emphasized the outstanding importance of the subject-specific determinants in the following way:

> Das undifferenzierte Vorverständnis sieht deutliche Unterschiede zwischen der Sprache der Naturwissenschaften und der Sprache der Geisteswissenschaften. Letztere scheint der Alltagssprache näher zu liegen, scheint sich eher durch eine terminologisch stärker festgelegte Verwendung der gemeinsprachlichen Begriffe und besonders auch durch *andere stilistische Gebräuche* als Wissenschafts-

> sprache auszuweisen. Bei ersterer dagegen denkt man sofort an einen umfangreichen terminologischen Apparat mit Ausdrücken, die der Laie nie gehört hat, an eine Unzahl von Formeln beziehungsweise die formelhafte Verwendung bestimmter sprachlicher Mittel (Skudlik 1990: 221; italics – K.-D. B.).

In reference to LSP texts in the social sciences, she continues:

> Die Geisteswissenschaften dagegen können sich nicht so gänzlich von der Gemeinsprache lösen. Denn Gegenstände der Geisteswissenschaften sind Werke, Taten und Geschehnisse, *in welche der Mensch Gehalte, Sinn und Absichten* bereits *gelegt hat*, die nun mit- und nachzuvollziehen sind (Skudlik 1990: 224; italics – K.-D. B.).

As a result of comprehensive LSP text analyses, it has become possible to differentiate the following aspects that determine the subject-specific dimension of emotion:

A. the differentiation of the totality of sciences into *natural, social and technical sciences,*
B. the institutionalization of scientific findings as special branches of knowledge,
C. the degree of subjective orientation (psychological nearness) of the LSP author to the text contents (rational vs. emotional; distant vs. close; objective vs. subjective and so on),
D. the attitude of the LSP text author to the (individual /social) significance of the text contents,
E. the degree of authenticity of the contents (real vs. fictitious) and
F. the accentuation of methodological positions of specific scientific schools of thought.

Further LSP text analyses still have to make clear the actual relevance of the subject-specific dimension for an interdisciplinary theory of emotion in LSP communication.

2.6 The functional dimension of emotion

The analysis of the functional dimension of emotion demonstrates how important it is to regulate adequately the intensity of the exchange of ideas, thoughts and information from one communicative partner to the other. After all, the functional dimension can be regarded as the key to the communicative development of social relations among partners who are linked by a common communicative activity.

As a result of the interdisciplinary LSP text analyses, the following functions of emotion have been discovered:

A. the regulative function: this is directed at adapting the communicative behavior of the partner to the norm of LSP communication (see communicative signals of acceptance, refusal, exclusion of a partner from the scientific community) (Baumann 2001: 9-34).

B. the directive function: the influence of emotions on the processes of planning, preparing and realizing communicative activities. The communicative procedures stimulating (requesting – appealing), demanding, instructing and commanding are appropriate for expressing different degrees of emotional engagement (Michel 1985: 92).

C. the informative function: this gives information about the extent to which the communicative purpose of the LSP text author has been realized through emotions (emotional way of informing LSP text recipients) (Schmidt 1981: 24).

D. the function of information retention refers to the existence of an emotional memory, for example emotions help in bringing about a higher sentimental value of LSP information and

E. the function of making information processing more effective aims at making LSP text comprehension easier by integrating emotions into communication (use of communicative procedures: vivid description, narration in LSP texts of historiography).

The functional differentiation of emotions has clearly shown the methodological relevance of this dimension for an interdisciplinary approach to emotion in LSP communication.

2.7 The textual dimension of emotion

One of the most challenging tasks of LSP research, cognitive science and emotional psychology is to develop an interdisciplinary theory of LSP text production and LSP text reception that illustrates the transfer from the mental reflection of the objective reality into language structures.

Communicative-cognitive LSP text analyses have clearly shown that the reception of LSP text structures is based on information processing that comprises all components of the communicative knowledge system (Baumann 2001: 83). Clearly, LSP text reception is not only a data- and knowledge-controlled process, but is also a process of appraisal activating the consciousness of the recipient(s). The textual dimension of emotion manifests itself in the sequence of macro-structural units of LSP texts, the so-called "text construction plan". The text construction plan can be defined as linear-sequentially and hierarchically arranged basic cognitive patterns of subject matter transferred to language on the different levels of LSP communication. The concept of the text construction plan has proved to be appropriate for demonstrating the principles of information transfer on the level of LSP text.

Interestingly, the analyses of social scientific LSP texts especially have shown that not each individual LSP text form has a strictly conventionalized text construction plan (for example scientific essay, popular-scientific article, non-fiction book, guide and so on). Additionally, some of the compositional units of LSP text forms can vary depending on the branch of science (for example the text construction plan of historiography vs. psychology) (Baumann 1992).

As a result of our analyses, we have found the following reasons for the macro-structural variability of social scientific LSP texts:

- the (non-)binding character of the LSP text contents (for example hypothesis, law of nature, rule and so on),
- the sort of background knowledge (for example expert knowledge, layman knowledge),
- the individual scope of experience of the communicative partners,
- the orientation of the LSP text to a specific group of recipients,
- the specific communicative context in which the LSP text is embedded,
- the ease or difficulty of comprehension of the LSP text,
- the integration of appraisal in the LSP text,
- the institution where the underlying transfer of knowledge is realized (for example, school, college, university, open university and so on),
- the communicative transfer strategy of knowledge (for example, digression, glossary and so on) and
- the integration of the LSP text in a pragmatic context (theory / practice).

The following paragraph from the English LSP text form *monograph of historiography* clearly demonstrates how the above-mentioned aspects work together to transfer information. Those textual elements which have been italicized express an emotionally-colored appraisal by the LSP text author:

> - Of the two, I should say that Gladstone was the *more unforgettable* as a personality. I take as the test what one would have thought of each if one had met him in a train without knowing who he was. In such circumstances Gladstone, I am convinced, would have *struck me* as one of the *most remarkable* men I had ever met, and would have soon *reduced me* to a *speechless semblance of agreement*. Lenin, on the contrary, might, I think, have seemed to me at once a *narrow-minded fanatic* and a *cheap cynic* [...] (Text Number (T-Nr.) 11, Target Text (TT) 12).

Undoubtedly, the textual dimension of emotion decisively contributes to the communicative structuring of the information transfer.

2.8 The stylistic dimension of emotion

The analysis of the stylistic dimension of emotion opens up new epistemological perspectives in making the correlation between contents and form and between LSP text style and emotion more transparent (Baumann 1996: 355-388). From the point of view of interdisciplinary-oriented LSP research, the stylistic dimension of emotion refers to the structural and functional aspects of stylistically relevant elements and relations that contribute to the interpretation of LSP text content.

Our LSP text analyses have shown that there are numerous influences of stylistic devices on the aesthetic colouring of LSP texts which are closely connected to the following aspects:

A. Stylistic elements can make LSP text recipients understand the facts and processes better by building bridges between communicative partners' different presuppositions. In addition, stylistic elements can improve LSP text comprehension because they transfer information in a highly activated cognitive state (for example, parenthesis, parallelism, antithesis and so on):

> - Afterward he described him as the 'uprightest and most conscientious man' in his three kingdoms *(England, Scotland and Wales)* (T-Nr. 8, III, TT 14/H 2: parenthesis).

B. Stylistic elements can contribute to the realization of specific partner-related LSP texts by breaking up monotonous sentence structures (for example, chiasmus where the main sentence elements are reversed) (Baumann 1992: 58):

> - [...] our concepts develop as we organize the environment to which we respond and we organize our environment through developing our concepts; *we know ourselves through knowing the world and we know the world through knowing ourselves* (T-Nr. 3, 2, TT 20/58).

C. Specific stylistic elements can help to bridge a socially asymmetrical relationship between the communicative partners by varying, deepening and repeating facts in LSP texts (for example, repetition, synonymy, emphasis and so on):

- The flame was *glorious-radiant* with the colours of antique knighthood and the flashing gallantries of the past; but no substance fed it; *flaring widely*, it *tossed to and fro in the wind*, it was suddenly put out (T-Nr. 36, TT 2/11: characterization of Elizabeth I.).

D. The so-called mind-style elements (for example, amplification, syllogism, isologue as mental parallelism, antithesis, simile, allegory, irony, hysteron/proteron and so on) can help to explain the effects of emotion in the processes of LSP text production and reception. Mind style elements significantly activate the attention and receptiveness of the communicative partners so that they are able to perceive the objects and processes in an intensified way.

The mind-style elements have the following emotional potentialities:

- the intensification of impressiveness:

The author wants to emphasize mental relations in order to achieve an enduring effect in the argumentation by using pictorial comparisons, metaphors, personifications and epithets.

- The Leveller challenge was altogether dispersed – although the *spectre of a Leveller revival* was often conjured up, as the *Scylla to the Charybdis of Papists and Jacobites between which the good ship Constitution must steer her course.* (T-Nr. 1, I, TT 12/18) (pictorial comparison).

- As the *gulf* between monarch and people widened the lonely King turned to his French Catholic wife for comfort and advice. (T-Nr. 8. 18, TT 8/52) (metaphor).

- the focusing of clearness:

- *You can* put rats in mazes and men in barbed wire cages, and observe their methods of escape. *You can* administer drugs and observe their effect. *You can* turn a male rat into a female [...] (anaphora + parallelism) (T-Nr. 11, 9, TT 22/37-39).

The author tries to make the LSP text comprehension easier by using emotional schemata.

- an increase in clarity of LSP text contents by inserting/post-poning examples:

  - In the first place, language serves for the expression of the content: it has a representational, or, *as I would prefer to call it*, an ideational function (*This is sometimes referred to as the expression of 'cognitive meaning', though I find the term 'cognitive' misleading; there is after all, a cognitive element in all linguistic functions)* [...] (parenthesis, colon + explication) (T-Nr. 12, 14, TT 8/38-39).

  - In spite of this conservatism, however, legal language has changed, *even if slowly.* (postponed information) (T-Nr. 9, 8, TT 48/29).

The inserted/postponed information is typical of an associative mind style.

- the support of text reception by the interplay of general and particular information principles:

  - [...] and English is still a major language for international communication in many scientific and technical fields. (The language of air traffic control, for instance, is largely English). (T.-Nr. 2, TT 18/199-200).

These interplays of information can offer a pause to reflect on the text content (syndetic/asyndetic repetition, synonymy). Stylistically coloured (sub-)titles of texts can function as text-structuring devices and as important sources of information. In social scientific LSP texts especially, it seems to be common to introduce into the text aphorisms or good pegs used as a base for argumentation:

  - The Great Rebuilding: A Reassessment (In: Past & Present No 77/Nov. 1977, 33).

Our interdisciplinary LSP text analyses have clearly shown that the stylistic dimension of emotion has an important epistemological function. We have also discovered that stylistic elements point to information processing in a very effective way.

2.9 The syntactic dimension of emotion

The complex cognitive structure of the special knowledge which has to be materialized in the communicative process needs a specific syntactic modification. In this respect, our interdisciplinary LSP text analyses have shown that emotions are transferred by the following text-syntactic categories:

- use of tenses (historical present),
- use of mood indicating what the LSP text author is doing with a proposition in a particular communicative situation,
- functional sentence perspective indicating the information structure (theme–rheme),
- formation of ellipses,
- use of syntactical stereotypes (as a kind of emotional prejudice) in specific LSP text forms (for example, in law),
- use of reference and predicate structures (pro-forms, deictics, indefinites, proper names, appellatives),
- syntactic coherence of LSP text and visual code,
- paratactic and hypotactic sentence configurations,
- sentence cohesion referring to specific features that link different parts of the LSP text,
- forms of speech or writing: monologue, dialogue, polylogue,
- literal repetition of speech/writing in form of quotations, and
- text-constituting function of word order (Baumann 2001: 57).

According to the linguo-statistical analyses carried out by Hoffmann/ Piotrowski (1979), the above-mentioned text-syntactic phenomena have different relevance to the communicative process, but all the categories have the same function: to express emotion. This is realized by the following strategies:

A. accentuation of relevant information by foregrounding:

- *This is not a humor of* hostility or resentment, *it is a humor of* superiority and condescension (T-Nr. 4, TT 8/25 initial sentence; negation in front position of the sentence + repetition)

- *The joke-tellers themselves* often recognize that the butts of their jokes about stupidity are a closely related people who are perceived as flawed and ambiguous rather than alien and disliked (T-Nr. 4, TT 9/39 initial sentence).

B. intensification of the conspicuousness of relevant text information by topicalization (theme-rheme-interaction, inversion, emphasis):

- *What is critical is not* what each measurement culture does, but in what it prioritizes (T-Nr.5, TT 53/48).

- *What should be a force* for internationalism has in reality become an isolationist force (T-Nr. 5, TT 25/29).

C. focusing of LSP text content by re-structuring communicative activities (adopting other points of view by: reporting, quotations, question-answer sequences, contrast and repetition of facts):

- *Welche Kenntnisse erlauben die Dekodierung der Metapher?* (T-Nr. 3, TT 12/54 – initial sentence; answers from sentence 55)

- "Yes, science and technology have changed the nature of power. We are living […]"(T-Nr. 6, TT 25:. 21, quotation)

D. modification of the LSP text author's communicative intention (for example mood: subjunctive, imperative):

- Consider the following ethnic jokes [...] (T-Nr. 4, TT 14/79; imperative)

- We *would like* now to examine the working hypothesis more closely. (T-Nr. 5, TT 43/94; subjunctive in the initial sentence).

To sum up, text-syntactical categories offer a wide range of possibilities for expressing emotion.

2.10 The punctuation dimension of emotion

This dimension refers to those graphic signs (for example exclamation, question and quotation marks) signaling certain attitudinal or appraisal qualities of the LSP text author(s). This can be demonstrated by the following example:

> - Später führt der Weg des Symbols in die Gegenwart: Es wird zum Firmenzeichen der Shell Oil Company, die Reisende mit Öl versorgt! (T-Nr. 1, TT 24/130; use of exclamation mark / emphasis).

Our interdisciplinary LSP text analyses have clearly shown the enormous emotional potentialities of punctuation.

2.11 The lexico-semantic dimension of emotion

The lexico-semantic dimension of emotion concentrates on the analysis of the emotional circumstances under which lexical items are selected and used in LSP texts.

Our interdisciplinary LSP text analyses have confirmed that the lexico-semantic dimension of emotion is closely connected with the cognitive contents of the LSP text (Hoffmann 1986; Baumann 2001). Consequently, the complex approach to the lexico-semantic dimension of emotion has to consider the proportion of connotative and denotative meaning elements in LSP texts carefully.

In this connection, we start from the following methodological positions:

- From the point of view of *semantics,* the extraordinarily complex interrelations between *cognition and emotion* have to be described functionally and structurally (Schippan 1984).

- The connotative meaning elements can be understood as the emotionally determined image of facts or processes in our mind. They also make clear the personal associations of the individual LSP communicative partner. In this respect, connotative elements open a possibility for analyzing the process of cognizing more efficiently.
- The meaning of LSP texts is firmly embedded in the concrete practical activities of the people functioning as the basis of mental processes. Interestingly, both kinds of activity are closely interrelated with denotative and connotative meaning elements of LSP texts.
- The differentiation between LSP text meaning and LSP text sense corresponds to the differentiation between denotation and connotation.

In analysing the lexico-semantic dimension of emotion, *connotative-semantic equivalences* play a central role. They illustrate specific emotional recurrences repeatedly connecting specific sequences of events in LSP communication. The connotative-semantic equivalences are demonstrated in the following paragraph:

> - Among eminent philosophers, excluding men still alive, the most personally impressive, to me, was William James. This was in spite of a complete naturalness and absence of all apparent consciousness of being a great man. No degrees of democratic [...] (T-Nr. 11, 11/TT 3, 11-13).

A positive appraisal is being expressed by the connotative-semantic equivalences: eminent, most personally impressive, complete naturalness, absence of all apparent consciousness of being a great man. The individual standard of appraisal is being expressed by: “to me”.

Obviously, the mental picture of an object can decisively be determined by the subject of communication (Wotjak 1977).

2.12 The morphological dimension of emotion

It refers to those morphemes capable of conveying expressive meaning (for example prefixes: *ant-*, *counter-*, *extra-*, *mis-*, *non-*, *sub-*, *super-*, *ultra-*; suffixes: *-ful*, *-hood*, *-able*, *-ish* etc.) (Hansen/Hansen/Neubert/Schentke 1982).

2.13 The phonetic dimension of emotion

This dimension refers to spoken LSP texts and comprises those emotions which can be expressed by intonation, articulation, pauses and so on.

2.14 The semiotic dimension of emotion

This dimension can be sub-classified into two groups:

- The kinesics dimension of emotion dealing with the use of facial expression and body gesture to communicate meaning in spoken LSP texts (Mole 1999).
- The visual dimension of emotion referring to the effects which are caused by the integration of visual code into written LSP texts (Stöckl 1997).

3. Summary

Our interdisciplinary LSP text analyses have shown that a great amount of the emotional dimension of an LSP text is intimately bound up with the complexity of cognition. This outcome creates new prospects for further communicative-cognitive description of LSP communication and broadens the cognitive dimension of LSP research in general.

References

Averill, J.R. 1996. Intellectual emotions. In Harre, R. / Parrot, W.G. (eds) *The emotions. Social, cultural and biological dimensions.* London: Sage, 24-38.

Baumann, Klaus-Dieter 1991. Die Fachlichkeit von Kommunikation und ihre Bedeutung in der Entwicklung einer Unternehmensidentität. In Bungarten, Theo (ed.) *Konzepte zur Unternehmenskommunikation, Unternehmenskultur & Unternehmensidentität.* Tostedt: Attikon (Beiträge zur Wirtschaftskommunikation Bd.2), 23-25.

Baumann, Klaus-Dieter 1992. *Integrative Textlinguistik.* Tübingen: Narr (Forum für Fachsprachen-Forschung 18).

Baumann, Klaus-Dieter 1994. *Fachlichkeit von Texten.* Egelsbach/ Frankfurt am Main/Washington: Hänsel-Hohenhausen (Deutsche Hochschulschriften 1023).

Baumann, Klaus-Dieter 1995. Die Verständlichkeit von Fachtexten. Ein komplexer Untersuchungsansatz. *Fachsprache* 17/3-4, 107-117.

Baumann, Klaus-Dieter 1996. Fachtextsorten und Kognition – Erweiterungsangebot an die Fachsprachenforschung. In Kalverkämper, Hartwig / Baumann, Klaus-Dieter (eds) *Fachliche Textsorten.* Tübingen: Narr (Forum für Fachsprachen-Forschung 25), 355-388.

Baumann, Klaus-Dieter 2001. *Kenntnissysteme im Fachtext.* Egelsbach/ Frankfurt a.M./München/New York: Hänsel-Hohenhausen (Leipziger Arbeiten zur Fachsprachenforschung 16).

Baumann, Klaus-Dieter / Kalverkämper, Hartwig (eds) 1992. *Kontrastive Fachsprachenforschung.* Tübingen: Narr (Forum für Fachsprachen-Forschung 20).

Ciompi, L. 1997. *Die emotionalen Grundlagen des Denkens. Entwurf einer fraktalen Affektlogik.* Göttingen: Vandenhoeck and Ruprecht.

Clyne, Michael 1981. Culture and discourse structure. *Journal of Pragmatics* 5, 61-66.

Fleck, Ludwik 1994. *Entstehung und Entwicklung einer wissenschaftlichen Tatsache. Einführung in die Lehre vom Denkstil und Denkkollektiv.* Frankfurt am Main: Suhrkamp (Suhrkamp-Taschenbuch Wissenschaft 312).

Fowler, Roger 1977. *Linguistics and the Novel. New Accents.* London: Methuen.

Hansen, Barbara / Hansen, Klaus / Neubert, Albrecht / Schentke, Manfred 1982. *Englische Lexikologie. Einführung in Wortbildung und lexikalische Semantik.* Leipzig: Bibliographisches Institut.

Hochschild, A.R. 1979. Emotion work, feeling rules, and social structures. *American Journal of Sociology* 85, 551-575.

Hoffmann, Joachim 1986. *Die Welt der Begriffe. Psychologische Untersuchungen zur Organisation des menschlichen Wissens.* Berlin: Deutscher Verlag der Wissenschaften.

Hoffmann, Lothar / Piotrowski, R.G. 1979. *Beiträge zur Sprachstatistik.* Leipzig: Verlag Enzyklopädie.

Jahr, Silke 2000. *Emotionen und Emotionsstrukturen in Sachtexten.* Berlin/New York: Walter de Gruyter.

Krusche, Dietrich 1983. *Japan, konkrete Fremde. Dialog mit einer fernen Kultur.* Stuttgart: S. Hirzel Verlag.

Michel, Georg (Hrsg.) 1986. *Sprachliche Kommunikation. Einführung und Übungen.* Leipzig: Bibliographisches Institut.

Mole, John 1999. *Mind your Manners. Managing business cultures in Europe.* London: Nicholas Brealey Publishing.

Nischik, Reingard M. 1991. *Mentalstilistik. Ein Beitrag zu Stiltheorie und Narrativik.* Tübingen: Narr.

Otto, Jürgen H. / Euler, Harald A. / Mandl, Heinz (eds) 2000. *Emotionspsychologie. Ein Handbuch.* Weinheim: Psychologie Verlags Union.

Salnikow, Nikolai (ed.) 1995. *Sprachtransfer – Kulturtransfer. Text, Kontext und Translation.* Frankfurt a.M./Berlin/Bern/New York/ Paris/Wien: Lang (FASK/Johannes-Gutenberg-Universität Mainz, Reihe A, Abhandlungen und Sammelbände 19).

Schippan, Thea 1984. *Lexikologie der deutschen Gegenwartssprache.* Leipzig: Bibliographisches Institut.

Schmidt, Wilhelm (ed.) 1981. *Funktional-kommunikative Sprachbeschreibung.* Leipzig: Bibliographisches Institut.

Skudlik, Sabine 1990. *Sprachen in den Wissenschaften. Deutsch und Englisch in der internationalen Kommunikation.* Tübingen: Narr (Forum für Fachsprachen-Forschung 10).

Stöckl, Hartmut 1997. *Werbung in Wort und Bild. Textstil und Semiotik englischsprachiger Anzeigenwerbung.* Frankfurt am Main/Berlin/Bern/New York/Paris/Wien: Lang (Europäische Hochschulschriften Reihe 14, Angelsächsische Sprache und Literatur 336).

Vester, H.-G. 1991. *Emotion, Gesellschaft und Kultur: Grundzüge einer soziologischen Theorie der Emotionen.* Opladen: Westdeutscher Verlag.

Wotjak, Gerd 1977. *Untersuchungen zur Struktur der Bedeutung*. Berlin: Akademie Verlag.

MICHAEL WITTWER

Emotion and translation: Using the example of popularising medical texts in paediatrics

1. Introduction

In this chapter we study the possibility of the translation of emotions and emotional expressions that can be found in popularising medical texts in paediatrics. First of all we look at the emotionality of the source text, but we also try to consider the role of the emotions of the translator within the translation process as well as the influence of the recipient's emotions to the understanding of the translated text. Hence we try to answer the following questions within this study:

1. What is the emotionality of the source text and how it can be determined by the translator?
2. What kind of categorization of emotions of the source text can be undertaken and is itself emotionality measurable?
3. How should the translator accommodate to the emotionality of the source text or what influence has the emotionality on the translation process?

We consider understanding as a precondition for the linguistic-cognitive processing of the source text. In our study we aim to show possible strategies that can help the translator to reach the linguistic-cognitive and emotional processing of the source text. At the same time we outline which productive processes are started up by these strategies within the cognition of the translator.

2. Emotionality of text

The starting point of the study is the determination/definition of the emotionality of text. We proceed on the assumption of a complex analysis because several dimensions have an influence on emotionnality in the world of emotions of the respective recipient (see Wittwer 2002: 171).

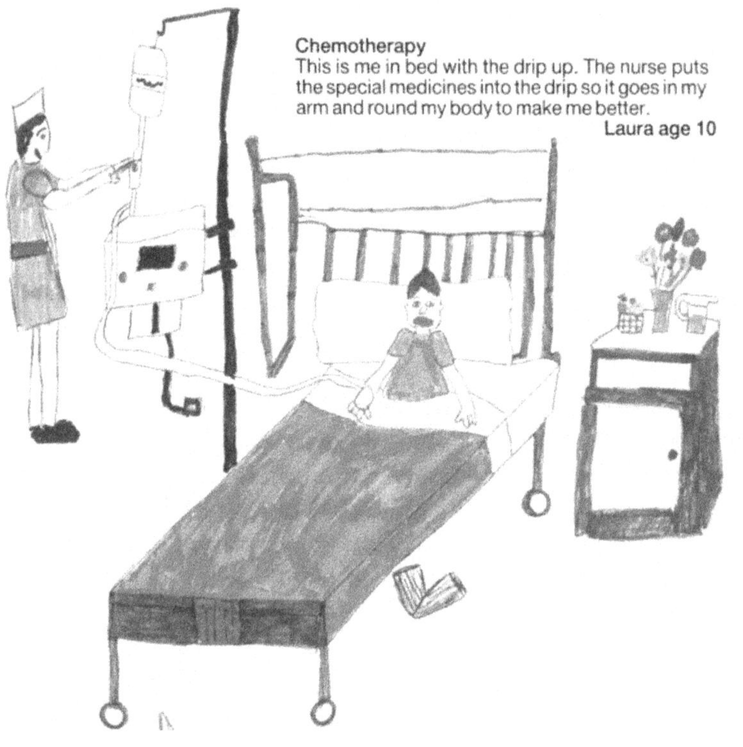

Picture 1. *Our Cancer*: 16.

As seen in Picture 1, the situation "hospital" which is unknown and strange for the child is depicted by a drawing of a child. The picture shows a social interaction between the nurse and the patient as well. Since the text deals with a small child the translator can estimate its cognitive abilities. The dimension of content is delimited by the subtitle *chemotherapy*. The translator evaluates the technical information from the terms *special medicines* and *drip*. The phrase *to make me better* can be understood as a linguistic expression of emotions and the countenance of the child can be seen as an extra-linguistic expression of emotions.

Hence, the emotionality of a source text is represented to the translator as a reflection of the cultural, social and cognitive characteristics of the respective situation of communication within the dimension of content which is characterized by professionality and understandability using appropriate language, as pointed out in Wittwer (2002). The comprehension of the source text means for the translator at the same time that he perceives the emotions contained in the text and anticipated by the author.

As Schmidt (1981) has pointed out, the change of the recipient's relationship to reality can be obtained by a conscious arousal or amplification of emotions that are based on a positive or negative assessment. The following example underlines his statement:

> When I was told I had cancer I was upset, but I thought well I've got it and there's nothing I can do about it but get on with it and try to get better. – Colin, 10 (Our Cancer:10)

The term *cancer* predetermines the emotional state of grief, sorrow, worry, despair ("I was upset"). Nevertheless, in a later clause, the author consciously uses the positive emotion of hope ("try to get better") to induce the recipient to assist in the treatment of the disease.

In other words, the author of the text (and a translator is to some extend an author) wants to induce the recipient to motivate their cognition emotionally. This is also pointed out by Kintsch (1998):

> The continuous flow of emotions in interpersonal interactions, but undoubtedly also in less direct interactions, such as occur in reading a story, functions as a modulator and motivator of cognition (Kintsch 1998: 22).

Hence, the comprehension of the source text can be understood as a cognitive process which is reflected within the linguistic-cognitive and emotional processing of the source text.

It follows from this that the translator has to take into consideration the following three main strategies:

2.1 Strategy I: Understanding the emotions of the source text as a whole

This strategy starts up a few constructive processes within the cognition of the translator. These processes include the analysis of the social situation of communication of the source text, the activation of specific cultural patters, the classification of the emotions and the evaluation of the cognitive abilities of the group of recipients of the target text.

The analysis of the social situation of communication of the source text contains the investigation of the author-recipient-relationship as well as the estimation of the situation in which the reception of the target text will take place. At the same time there is an analysis of the emotional situation of communication by the translator.

> We are between the ages of 3 and 13. We are part of the Children's Cancer Unit at the Royal Victoria Infirmary. Newcastle. (*Our Cancer*, inside cover)

The authors of the source text are child cancer patients and the recipients are children with cancer as well. This special situation of text reception is represented by the serious disease which has been diagnosed and the hospital's everyday routine, meaning that the situation is strange for the child; it is frightening for the child, the child is helpless and this is the same for the most part for the people to whom the child relates, the parents.

Accordingly we agree with the following statement of Fries (2000) concerning the emotionality of the situation of communication:

> The semantic-conceptual complexity of words which express our emotions enables us to conceptualise in a finely honed way emotional scenarios relating to our sensibilities, their expression and the objects involved. This seems to be a useful premise for our social behaviour. (Fries 2000: 84; *translation MR*)[1].

The following example elucidates this "picking our emotional concepts out as a central topic" (original example including the "errors" in the source text):

(1) Example:

My fears of Leukaemia By Beverly age 10	*Meine Furcht vor Leukämie* Beverly, 10
Sitting in hospital feeling unhappy, waiting, A doctor came over, He talks to us, mum listens carefully, The doctor goes away, Mum talks to me, Hot then cold, shivering with fear, Then I went to sleep, I kept wakening, Sweating. [...] (*Our Cancer*: 8)	Sitze im Krankenhaus, fühle mich unglücklich, und warte. Ein Arzt kommt. Er spricht mit uns und Mutti hört genau zu. Der Arzt geht wieder. Mutti spricht mit mir. Erst heiß, dann kalt, zitternd vor Furcht. Dann ging ich schlafen, wachte ständig auf, schweißgebadet. [...] (*Translation by the author*)

In turn, our social behaviour activates specific cultural patterns in our cognition. The activation of specific cultural patterns in the cognition of the translator is executed by recognizing and understanding the cultural systems used in the source text. In this connection Gerzymisch-Arbogast (1994) makes the following statement:

> The recognition of these systems and their differences is, of course, dependent on the knowledge of the reader/translator or on their ability to understand such cultural systems in an objective way.
> (Gerzymisch-Arbogast 1994: 84; *translation MR*)[2].

1 "Die semantisch-konzeptuelle Komplexität unserer Gefühlswörter ermöglicht eine ausgefeilte Thematisierung unserer emotionalen Szenenentwürfe, die sich auf unser Empfinden, dessen Ausdruck und die involvierten Gegenstände beziehen. Das scheint für unser soziales Verhalten eine brauchbare Voraussetzung zu sein."

2 "Dabei ist das Erkennen dieser Systeme in ihrer Differenziertheit natürlich

The relevant literature gives various concepts for the understanding of emotionality. Mees (1983) distinguishes three categories of emotions – the emotion of relationships, empathy and purpose that are again subdivided into 13 classes. Ulich/Mayring (1992) arrange emotions in 4 groups: affection (like), aversion (dislike), well being and discomfort (Ulich/Mayring 1992: 138). Another concept thoroughly acceptable for translators is provided by Wierzbicka (1999). Within her concept the emotions are arranged into the following categories (see Table 1):

Category	**Example**
Something good has happened.	Joy and fun, luck and happiness, satisfaction, pleasure, delight, relief, excitation, hope, love
Something bad has happened.	Sadness, bad luck, grief, distress, sorrow, pain, despair, disappointment, frustration, hate
Bad things may happen.	Fear, dread, fright, horror, concern, panic, anxiety, excitement, anger, worry
I do not want that such things happen.	Grudge, displeasure, disappointment, fury, rage, indignation, bitterness, shock
Thinking about other people.	Envy and jealousy, regret, mercy, compassion and self-compassion, gloating, admiration and self-admiration, contempt
Thinking about ourselves.	Shame, pride, regret, guiltiness, embarrassment, thoroughness

Table 1. Categories of emotions according to Wierzbicka (1999).

Another constructive process is the evaluation of the cognitive abilities and facilities of the group of recipients of the target text. That means for the studied translation of popularising special texts in paediatrics that the translator has to carry out an exact analysis of the recipient's age. With reference to emotionality, Battacchi/Suslow/ Renna (1996) determine in that connection cognitive processes as a base of emotional reactions, proposing that there is always a cognitive process at the beginning of an emotional situation, the realization of the situation which releases an emotional reaction (Battacchi/Suslow/Renna 1996: 42).

At that point we go back to the poem quoted above. The first two lines ease the realisation of the situation even though utilized un-

vom Kenntnisstand der Leserin/Übersetzerin bzw. von ihrer Fähigkeit, sich solche Kultursysteme sachlich zu erschließen, abhängig."

knowingly by the author and at the same time they verbalize the emotional reaction "to be unhappy".

Sitting in hospital feeling unhappy, waiting,	Sitze im Krankenhaus, fühle mich unglücklich, und warte.

(*Our Cancer*: 8)

Hence the translator has to think himself or herself into the emotions of the author of the source text and to represent these emotions according to the cultural specification of the target group, taking into consideration the recipient's cognition. That, of course, depends on the cognitive abilities as well as on the social and cultural knowledge of the translator.

Seen in a more abstract way, he strategy presented above can be viewed as a strategically constructive process of comprehending the source text.

2.2 Strategy II: Production of adequate emotional words matched with the cultural, social and cognitive particularities of the target text recipients

The production of the target text follows constructive processes, in which the dimension of content and the linguistic dimension of the source text are linked together taking into consideration the situation of communication and all elements of text construction.

The translator's task is to convey the source text and its information with regard to contents and professionality to the recipient of the target text avoiding conflicts of communication. The communicative functions and grammatical structures are closely linked to the dimensions of understandability but also to the dimension of the professionalism of the translation.

In an earlier study of grammatical structures and communicative functions of the comics used in paediatrics, we stated that professionalism and professional knowledge can be conveyed to the recipient by means of linguistic skill together with a high-level understandability, taking into account the emotionality of the recipient (see Wittwer 2001: 207).

It goes for the translator as well as for the author of the source text as stated by Jahr (2000) that an emotional style as a piece of circumstantial evidence for the "presence" of the self and the mental sympathy of the text writer can encourage the vested interest of the recipient (Jahr 2000: 230). He will understand the content of a text much more easily if his thought process is tied up to his emotional world. In the studied popularising special texts of external communication in paediatrics, this attendance of the self is basically presented by the partly autobiographical character of the texts and also by the fact that the recipient is addressed in person.

> We decided to tell you our stories. We hope they help you to understand. We send you our love.
> (*Our Cancer*: 1)

The translator represents the highest level of comprehension of the source text – the clarity about it – as a mental and linguistic representation of the source text within the target text, which is related to practice.

2.3 Strategy III: Suppression of own emotions

A particularity of that mental and linguistic representation of the source text is the suppression of one's own emotions that may occur during the comprehension of the source text (for example, the consternation of the translator). It is impossible for the translator himself to proceed with the reception of the source text without emotional sympathy in particular since the popularising special texts of external communication in paediatrics deal with the topic "Diseases in children". However the translator's own sensibility has to be suppressed while creating the translation to eliminate the misrepresentation of the emotionality of the source text.

3. Measurability of emotions

At this point it seems reasonable to discuss the measurability of the emotions expressed in the source text. We will analyse the linguistic dimension as well as the content dimension of the text. The specialist source text, as a popularising text aimed externally at non-experts in paediatrics, can be classified as an emotional text according to its topic and to the relevant target group. But such an intuitive classification is not at all sufficient to identify the degree of emotionality.

In our study we estimate the general degree of emotionality based on the relationship of sentences with emotional phenomena to the overall number of sentences and constituents of a sentence within the text. (see Table 2). We do not distinguish between stylistic, lexical, syntactical or contextual encoding of emotions.

	Simon	*Our Cancer*
Overall number of sentences and constituents of a sentence:	177	244
Sentences with emotional phenomena:	49	78
Percentage:	27.,68	31.97

Table 2. Example for the estimation of the degree of emotionality.

Another starting point is the analysis of the emotions used in the source text in detail. In popularising special texts of external communication in paediatrics there can be detected emotions of the categories "well-being", "relationship", "calming down", "expectation/hope", "sorrow/grief", "anger/discomfort", "fear", "pain" and "pleasure/ gladness". The following table shows these emotions including some examples (Table 3).

well being (4)	relationship (6)
It was nice to be home. … feel much better … made me feel much better … felt alright	I couldn't be bothered with myself or anyone else. Louise as feeling left out. … friends … made friends … help each other … help you
calming down (6)	expectation/hope (5)
... not to worry about it I would not feel any pain. … that it wouldn't hurt. It did not hurt (2x). It didn't hurt.	My hair will grow back. … last treatment … celebrate … back at school … hair is back I hope my story will help you.
sorrow/grief (8)	anger/ discomfort (9)
Mum looked worried. We wondered what was going to happen to us. … being upset … be upset … had worried … this might happen … felt sad … we all worry	I felt like crying. I felt cross. I was cross. ... felt sick and tired I didn't like it. ... felt miserable ... made me sick ... be naughty ... felt angry
fear (7)	pain (3)
I was frightened. … being frightened I was scared. … a bit scared … felt frightened It frightened me. … treatment … horrible	... my leg started hurting ... felt the pain again The pain kept coming back.
pleasure/gladness (1)	… have lots of fun

Table 3. Emotions in the corpus *Our Cancer* (analysing approximately 30% of the corpus).

4. Results

In general it can be noticed that there will be no difficulties in decoding the linguistic expressions of emotions if the translator applies the above-mentioned strategies for comprehension as a precondition for the linguistic-cognitive processing of the source text. Nevertheless, it seems necessary to point out that popularising special texts in paediatrics aimed at external communication relies in particular on emotionality and therefore reproducing the emotional expressions precisely and accurately is essential. Hence the role of emotions within the process of translation cannot be underestimated and it should accordingly be a subject of further studies to proceed with the clarification of the general translatability of emotions.

References

Battacchi, M. W. / Suslow, T. / Renna, M. 1996. *Emotion und Sprache*. Frankfurt a. M.: Peter Lang Verlag.

Fries, N. 2000. *Sprache und Emotionen.* Bergisch Gladbach, BLT Mensch & Wissen, Bd. 25, Verlagsgruppe Lübbe.

Gerzymisch-Arbogast, H. 1994. *Übersetzungswissenschaftliches Propädeutikum.*, Tübingen/Basel: A. Francke Verlag (UTB für Wissenschaft; Uni-Taschenbücher; 1782).

Jahr, S. 2000. *Emotionen und Emotionsstrukturen in Sachtexten: ein interdisziplinärer Ansatz zur qualitativen und quantitativen Beschreibung der Emotionalität von Texten.* Berlin/New York: Verlag Walter de Gruyter.

Kintsch, W. 1998. *Comprehension: a paradigm for cognition.* Cambridge, Cambridge University Press.

Mees, U. 1985. Was meinen wir, wenn wir von Gefühlen reden? Zur psychologischen Textur von Emotionswörtern. *Sprache und Kognition*. 1/1985, 2-20.

Schmidt, W. 1981. *Funktional-kommunikative Sprachbeschreibung.* Leipzig: Bibliographisches Institut .

Ulich, D. / Mayring, Ph. 1992. *Psychologie der Emotionen.* Stuttgart: Verlag Kohlhammer.

Wierzbicka, A. 1999. *Emotions across languages and cultures : diversity and universals.* Cambridge: Cambridge University Press. (Studies in emotion and social interaction : Second series).

Wittwer, M. 2001. Grammatische Strukturen und kommunikative Funktionen in der Fachtextsorte Comic in der Pädiatrie. In Vogel K. (ed.) *Grammatik in Fremdsprachen, Fremdsprachen und Hochschule* (FuH) 62/2001, Bochum: Ständige Kommission des Arbeitskreises Sprachenzentren, Sprachlehrinstitute und Fremdspracheninstitute (AKS).

Wittwer, M. 2002. Emotionalität bei der Fachübersetzung von Comics in der Pädiatrie. In Kovtyk, B. / Wendt, G. (eds) *Aktuelle Probleme der angewandten Übersetzungswissenschaft. Sprachliche und außer-sprachliche Faktoren der Fachübersetzung*. Frankfurt a. M:, Peter Lang Verlag.

Corpus:

Our Cancer. A collection of drawings and writings from young children who share the experience of cancer. Compiled and Edited by Avril Trapp. The Royal Victoria Infirmary, Queen Victoria Road, Newcastle upon Tyne, NE1 4LP, 60 pages, 770 sentences, 8825 words.

Simon has Cancer. Written by Lisa Brazier, Avril Trapp, Nancy Yates. Illustrated by Pauline Joyce. Victoria Publications, The Royal Victoria Infirmary, Queen Victoria Road, Newcastle upon Tyne, NE1 4LP, 35 pages, 180 sentences, 1,918 words.

GUADALUPE AGUADO DE CEA AND
INMACULADA ÁLVAREZ DE MON Y REGO

Cultural aspects in the translation of texts in the domain of information technology

1. Introduction

Translation studies is no longer limited to a purely linguistic approach. The importance of cultural implications for translation is increasingly emphasized and experts have been highly interested in cultural aspects, especially in the field of literary translation as many publications of the 1990s show (Snell-Hornby 1995; Toury 1995; Hatim/Mason 1997; Hatim 1997; Nord 1997; Bassnett/Lefevere 1998). Bassnett/Lefevere (1998: 132) even claim that translating can be defined as an "intercultural transfer".

When compared to literary translation, technical translation is usually considered to be free from cultural information. Technical texts are thought to be mainly informative and addressed to an international discourse community that share the same knowledge and values. Nearly 20 years ago, Newmark (1988: 151) stated that technical translation is "potentially [...] non-cultural, therefore 'universal'". However, he also specified that it is far from "actually non-cultural". Since then, the importance of culture for technical translation has greatly increased especially in the field of information technologies (IT). Nowadays, the users of these technologies are a large and varied group that cannot be labelled solely as subject experts. Technical knowledge is no longer restricted to the workplace and has become part of our daily lives. This fact is reflected in texts and therefore affects the process of translation. Many of the translations concerning this domain are not addressed exclusively to a specialized audience but to the general public. At present, there are many IT magazines published for readers who cannot be described as theoretical experts belonging to an international community but as sophisticated computer users from a language community located in a geographical area at a specific time. Moreover, the social and cultural background of the writer or the country of publication exert a strong influence on how technical information is provided.

The aim of this chapter is to analyse several examples of technical translations that illustrate the way in which the information is adapted to the cultural background of the new audience. The source texts are selected from *Byte,* a computer magazine published in the United States; the target texts correspond to its European edition in Spain. The articles found in this American computer magazine usually present a new product, which is compared to others in the market and both its advantages and disadvantages are taken into account. The main purpose of these articles is informative and the text type is expository. The intended reader is a computer user that knows quite a lot about these machines and is highly interested in the constant innovations brought about by technology, but this prototype reader is neither a theoretical expert nor an intellectual belonging to an international discourse community[1].

The examples selected make clear the need for cultural adaptation, as the intended audience are European Spanish speakers. From a theoretical point of view, the functional theory of translation, also known as the theory of *skopos* (Reiss/Vermeer 1991/1996) and relevance theory (Sperber/Wilson 1986; Gutt 2000) provide a sound theoretical basis to justify the adaptations exemplified in this chapter.

2. A brief overview of technical translation

Technical translation refers to the process of translating those texts belonging to what are called specialized languages and is usually clas-

1 Some of the linguistic features of *Byte* articles, which classify them as a specific genre of computer discourse, are discussed in Posteguillo (1996).

sified along with other varieties such as legal translation, scientific translation or the translation of medical texts. But an exact definition is a moot point. For a well-known expert like Newmark (1988: 151), technical translation is distinguished from other forms of translation by the presence of terminology. In a recent study of technical translation by Gamero (2001: 23), the key feature is the type of texts this form of translation deals with, technical texts. However, it is sometimes difficult to specify which texts to include under that label. On the one hand, the difficulty stems from the real meaning of the adjective "technical"[2] which does not imply the same in "technical terms" and "technical texts". While "technical terms" can pertain to every subject field, "technical texts" are usually identified with those related to engineering. On the other hand, technical texts include many types of discourse and many genres, which are continuously being created[3]. This constant emergence of new genres is evident in the IT domain where a great variety of "cybergenres" has appeared.

3. The theoretical framework

Functional theories of translation, which have been so successful in the German context, are not totally new. As early as1974, Nida and Taber talked about "dynamic equivalence" which represented an important development from the previous notion of formal equivalence. In later works, Nida emphasized the importance of the target reader and the cultural aspects involved in translation. Nevertheless, his theories were strongly influenced by Chomsky and his approach to language.

2 For a thorough discussion on the usage of the adjectives "technical" and "scientific" for qualifying language or texts both in Spanish and English, see Álvarez de Mon (2001).

3 Gamero (2001) distinguishes 30 different genres for technical translation in German.

Later, other linguistic theories such as Halliday's systemic functional grammar also influenced translation theorists who became attracted by the communicative approach. Hatim/Mason (1990: 10) distinguished three dimensions for the translation process: the communicative, the pragmatic and the semiotic dimension.

But for translation specifically, the functional approach corresponds to what is known as *Skopostheorie,* which was developed by Reiss/Vermeer (1991/1996). For these authors, translation is not simply a linguistic activity but a human action and the prime principle determining any translation process is the purpose, *skopos* in Greek, of the translation action. As Vermeer (2000: 221) explains:

> Any form of translational action, including therefore translation itself, may be conceived as an action, as the name implies. Any action has an aim, a purpose [...] The word *skopos*, then, is a technical term for the aim or purpose of a translation. [...] Further: an action leads to a result, a new situation or event, and possibly to a "new" object.

To that idea of purpose, Nord, also a functionalist, adds the notion of "loyalty", which she describes as the "responsibility translators have toward their partners in translational interaction" and, as she explains, "loyalty means that the target-text purpose should be compatible with the original author's intentions" (Nord 1997: 125).

The implications for translation of the functional approach seem also to coincide with the explanations[4] on the process of translating provided by the application of Relevance theory (Gutt, 2000). Relevance theory (Sperber/Wilson 1986) is an attempt to elaborate on Grice's maxim that most human communication is the expression and recognition of intentions, presenting at the same time a cognitive core which is central to all human communication efforts. When people communicate following the principle of relevance they achieve the most benefit for the least cost, being the benefit the effect on the receiver and the cost, the amount of mental processing required. Applied

4 Gutt (2000: 203) makes it clear that his relevance-theoretic study of translation intends to explain "how the phenomenon of translation works. It does not constitute or advocate a particular way of translating".

to translation, this means that the translator must take into account the readers' assumptions in order to achieve the same effect as the source text. This perspective is especially attractive for translators and with it the importance of cultural knowledge comes to the fore. As Gutt (2000: 238) himself states translators

> [...]realize that language differences are only one of the barriers that stand in the way of communication across languages; the other, and sometimes more formidable, barrier is that of differences in contextual background knowledge.

4. Cultural problems in technical translation: the Spanish version of *Byte*

The analysis of the source texts and the target texts used in this study reveals that cultural problems can be grouped into four categories:

- The presence of the American way of life and real events that are closely linked to the development and changes in computer technology in the United States.
- Politeness and stylistic features that are different in Spanish technical articles.
- Specialized terms which have different connotations in the target language.
- Source language metaphors that do not have an exact equivalent.

The examples chosen belong to different sections of these articles, which are clearly affected by cultural implications. Firstly, headlines; secondly, the sentences in the articles whose purpose is to exemplify and clarify the information given by means of examples based on the cultural reality of the source reader; thirdly, the sentences in which the writer involves the reader. Finally, some lexical and terminological problems derived from the different use or connotations of the terms in English and Spanish are considered.

4.1 Headlines in articles

Headlines in articles can be compared to titles in books as they make clear the importance of cultural differences. For the literary genre, Nord (1990: 153) states that titles of books illustrate both the need and the possibility of a functional translation. Titles are independent units of meaning and closely linked to factors such as the time, the place or the purpose of the message of the source text. Besides, titles are highly conditioned by the effect they should produce on the audience, and therefore they should play a specific role in the target culture. In technical magazines, the effect they produce is especially important because the headline functions as a sort of decoy that draws the reader's attention towards the article. In the following example (Example 1), the translator does not maintain the original headline because it is not appropriate for the new audience.

Example 1

Source Text	Target Text
When will E-cash jingle in your e-pocket?: Already successful in Europe, e-cash is hitting the U.S. – with answers and questions	*En Europa ya funciona... ¿y en EE.UU.?* *El dinero electrónico suscita preguntas y respuestas en los Estados Unidos, mientras que en Europa ya funciona satisfactoriamente*

For the European readers of the target text the question in the source text, *When will E-cash jingle in your e-pocket?*, would be irrelevant as electronic money is already in use in Europe. For that reason, the translator has chosen for the first sentence of the headline a question that could attract a European reader who can feel curiosity about the idea that Europe is ahead of the United States in technology, *Already in use in Europe; What about the U.S.?* The second sentence restates and explains the question making the topic explicit, *E-cash raises questions and answers in the U.S. while in Europe it is already working satisfactorily*. For the Spanish reader, the informative interest lies in the unknown future of electronic money in the United States. In this way, the technical translator acts as a mediator and facilitator of the informative content and therefore plays the role of writer or even editor of the target text (Cabré 1999: 188).

4.2 Different cultural reality

In technical texts it is possible to find references to the culture of the source text. In literary translation, these *culture-specific items*, as Franco Aixela (1996: 70) calls them, can be eliminated from the target texts or, otherwise, they can be explained in a footnote. But footnotes are neither common in *Byte* nor in similar publications; therefore, these cultural references are usually adapted or eliminated as in the following examples.

In example 2, the author of the ST supposes that the reader can visit New York and experience its way of life. The European readers of the target text may know about Manhattan but probably they would not feel included by the proposal of buying a paper or a hot dog since it is not probable they will visit New York in the near future. The changes carried out by the translator can be justified from a functional perspective. The statement in the target text fulfils the same rhetorical function as the imperative in the ST: to convince the reader of the advantage of choosing New York as the first city to try e-cash in the States. Few Spanish readers would feel involved if the text were to suggest this unlikely individual experience: *intente comprar un periódico o un perrito caliente en Manhattan con un billete de cincuenta dólares*. This would not be a successful way of achieving the communicative purpose. However, a generalising sentence restricted to those who have already visited the city would also sound adequate for those readers who may feel the appeal of visiting New York some time (Example 2).

Example 2

Source Text	Target Text
It shouldn't come as a surprise that the first major U.S. trial of electronic cash is taking place in New York City. <u>Try buying a newspaper or a hot dog in Manhattan with a $50 bill</u>	*No es de extrañar que los intentos más serios para implantar el dinero electrónico en los Estados Unidos se estén llevando a cabo en la ciudad de Nueva York. <u>Cualquier persona que haya estado allí sabe lo difícil que resulta conseguir un periódico o un perrito caliente con un billete de cincuenta dólares</u>*

The translation proposed (backtranslated from Spanish: 'anyone who has visited New York knows how difficult it is to buy a paper or a hot dog with a fifty dollar note') includes only those people that have visited New York and therefore results more appropriate for a European audience. Finally, the shift from Manhattan to New York as the place where the hot dog or the paper is paid for is highly suitable following relevance theory. For the Spanish reader, New York "is" Manhattan and the choice of a smaller geographical context only would be required if there were other boroughs such as Brooklyn or the Bronx also mentioned in the text.

Example 3

Source Text	Target Text
While trials are just beginning at the U.S., approximately 50 e-cash systems are already operational around the world	*Aunque en Estados Unidos las pruebas no hayan hecho más que empezar, en el mundo ya funcionan aproximadamente 50 sistemas de dinero electrónico. <u>En España, por ejemplo, ya conocemos las tarjetas monedero del sistema Visa Cash, adoptado por numerosas entidades bancarias como la Caixa y Caja de Madrid), y los modelos 4B y Euro6000, impulsados por la filial europea de Mastercard</u>*

Example 3 presents a situation similar to the previous one, but solved inversely. In this case, the translator adds new information, which is relevant only for the reader of the target text. For a Spanish readership, the information in the source text would be too general and therefore it could even lead to wrong conclusions as it is not sufficiently updated for the target reader's background knowledge. For this reason, the translator considers it relevant to add some information concerning the systems used in Spain. In this way, the target text fulfils the same informative purpose as the source text and provides information congruent with the general knowledge of the target reader.

4.3 Different writer and reader's involvement

Byte, in its original version in English, is characterized by an informal style that is generally achieved by the explicit presence of the writer and the reader in the text. However, Spanish expository writing favours an impersonal style. Therefore, in the Spanish version of *Byte,* neither the writer nor the readers are present in the text in an explicit manner and informality is attained by a different strategy: the use of informal and colloquial words.

There are several reasons for the different involvement of the writer and reader in the source text and target text. Apart from Spanish expository style, the translation process itself contributes to impersonality. The translator does not comply with the strong statements of the original author and being only a mediator of the writer in the transmission of the source text information prefers to be less direct. Impersonality also derives from a linguistic feature of the Spanish language, which does not require subject pronouns in front of verbs.

Example 4

Source Text	Target Text
Here's why today's PCs are the most crash-prone computers ever built – and how you can make yours more reliable	*Algunas razones que explican por qué los actuales PC son los ordenadores más proclives a las averías...y algunos trucos para mejorar su fiabilidad*

In example 4, the literal translation of "how can you make yours more reliable", *cómo puede hacer el suyo más fiable*, does not conform to the more impersonal style of technical articles in Spanish where explicit mention of the reader is usually avoided. For this reason, the translation proposed is successful. The Spanish word, *trucos*, which in this use could be paraphrased as "skilful ways to solve a problem", implies a reference to the target reader since the reader would be the one to apply those *trucos*. Besides, the Spanish word *truco* is also equivalent to the English word "trick" and thus it brings to the target text the colloquial flavour of the source text maintaining at the same time the technical purpose of explaining how to solve a problem[5]. Besides, the choice of the Spanish word *truco* by the translator supposes that the target reader is an expert or at least skilful enough to carry out the action successfully. The definition of the word in the

5 Frequently, the articles of *Byte* include a section under the heading of "Tip" where the reader can find a useful way to avoid the negative consequences of a certain action or an explanation of how to solve specific problems. This section is equivalent to the "Troubleshooting tables" typical of "Instruction Manuals".

Spanish dictionary makes clear those connotations of skilfulness acquired through practice and time. The Spanish dictionary (*DRAE*, 2001) defines the word as *cada una de las mañas o habilidades que se adquieren en el ejercicio de un arte, oficio o profesión*[6].

Example 5

Source Text	Target Text
Readers of <u>my column</u> know that <u>I'm wildly excited</u> about the uses of HTML-aware e-mail and conferencing.	*Los lectores habituales de <u>esta revista</u> se habrán percatado de que <u>existe un gran revuelo</u> alrededor de las posibilidades del correo electrónico y los sistemas de noticias con soporte HTML*

Again the more impersonal style of the Spanish version of *Byte* is revealed in example 5. Now, it is the writer who is the one that is left out of the target text. Firstly, "my column", is translated as *esta revista* to avoid the presence of the original author, as the Spanish edition is not an exact version of the whole magazine and does not always include the same sections as the original. Secondly, the translator avoids the first person pronoun in "I'm wildly excited" by using an impersonal expression, *existe un gran revuelo* – something like 'there is a great commotion' or 'a great stir was caused'. This translation successfully transfers the two main features of the source text expression "wildly excited": the reference to an emotional state and the familiarity of the writer. *Revuelo* implicitly conveys the verbal process of feeling an emotion as its definitions show. The Spanish dictionary (*DRAE*, 2001) defines *revuelo* as *turbación y movimiento confuso de algunas cosas* ('disturbance and confused motion of some things') or *agitación entre personas* ('stirring of people'). The word implies the idea of emotion or excitement of the English expression but now it is not a personal feeling of the writer but a feeling of a group of people. In journalistic language, the idea of causing *revuelo* is nowadays a very popular stylistic device used in order to emphasize the importance of something.

6 Knack or skill achieved in the practice of a craft, trade or profession.

4.4 Terms in the source text with a different range of use and different connotations in the target text

In specialized languages, terminology plays a key role and designates a concept or an object that is known across different cultures. However, new terms are not created out of nothing; more often than not old words receive new meanings. Consequently, when used in a text, specialized terms are not always free from the connotations of that word in the general use and writers play with that usage, and these connotations are not easily transferred to the target readers[7]. In the texts analysed, it is possible to distinguish two types of terms that reveal these cultural problems. They can be domain specific terms as in example 6 or metaphorical expressions used by the author as in examples 7 and 8.

Example 6

Source Text	Target Text
But ADSL remains vulnerable to rival technologies in the single family-home, because incumbent <u>telcos</u> control the <u>local "copper loop"</u> where their own DSL equipment would be located.	*Sin embargo, ADSL sigue siendo vulnerable en el terreno de los edificios unifamiliares, donde las <u>compañías concesionarias</u> controlan <u>el tendido</u> en el que debe colocarse el equipo DSL.*

In example 6, two specific telecommunications terms "telcos" and "local loop" have been avoided, as their presence in the target text would cause confusion for the Spanish reader. "Telco" is a truncation of *telephone company*. In Spanish, a similar abbreviated term *las telecos* is already being used but its meaning is broader as it refers to any telecommunications company, not only telephone companies. Even the expression *compañías telefónicas* would not be adequate in Spanish. *La (compañía) telefónica* was the name of the only Spanish telephone company working in the country until a few years ago. Consequently the use of this expression to refer to any telephone company does not seem appropriate. For that reason, the solution *compañías*

7 For a detailed account of many of the problems of computer terminology and its translation into Spanish see Aguado (1994/1996)

concesionarias ('licensed companies') manages to convey this general idea of any telephone company.

Concerning "local loop", "loop" is the term used to refer to the subscriber's line, that is, the telephone line that links the subscriber's telephone to the central exchange. Consequently, the translation chosen *tendido*, which could be paraphrased as 'those lines that are laid out', is suitable as this is the physical realization of the telephone lines.

Recently, in the Spanish news about the liberalization of local calls, the term "loop" was literally translated by *bucle*, but except in this case, in the field of telecommunications, the usage and connotations of the word *bucle* make it unsuitable for the Spanish reader of *Byte.* Besides, in Spanish, the collocation, *bucle de cobre,* is not used at all. *Cobre* collocates with the superordinate *cable* and the usual term is *cable de cobre.*

Cultural problems in the translation of *Byte* into Spanish also come from the use of metaphors in the source texts. These metaphorical expressions, rather than being created by the writer of the article, are lexical metaphors used in order to obtain a more attractive prose and a brighter style As they do not have an equivalent in Spanish the translator frequently chooses to omit them.

Example 7

Source Text	Target Text
No other technology has taken our Web-<u>driven</u> world <u>by storm</u> the way Java has	*Ninguna otra tecnología <u>ha conmocionado</u> tanto este mundo, <u>obsesionado</u> con el Web, como Java.*

The metaphorical expression "take the world by storm" in example 7 is not created by the writer, but could be described as a lexical metaphor as it is possible to find it in a general purpose dictionary such as *The Oxford Advanced Learner's Dictionary* (1995). In Spanish there is not an exact equivalent metaphor reflecting this idea of success by means of a physical phenomenon like a storm. Thus, the Spanish translator prefers to express the metaphor differently and uses a verb that implies a personal feeling *conmocionado* ('shocked').

A similar solution is the one adopted for the translation of the term "driven". This participle also refers to a physical process and makes the reader imagine a world controlled or guided by the Internet. However, the translator has preferred to express the great importance of the Internet by using a verb that describes its effect on people. The world is *obsesionado* ('obsessed'). These two examples show that now it is the Spanish text, which is more personal as the translator prefers to use verbs denoting emotion instead of physical processes.

Example 8

Source Text	Target Text
Enter message-based queuing (MBQ), middleware for different applications to share store-and-forward transactions with each other, sending the intermediate steps of the transactions back and forth via messages. It's a delicate dance – decrementing an item in inventory before the purchaser's credit has been checked is probably not a good way to go –but MBQ is close enough to real time that scores of businesses are checking into it anyway	*Aquí entra en juego la cola basada en mensajes (Message-Based Queuing o MBQ), un middleware que permite que diferentes aplicaciones compartan el almacenamiento y envío de transacciones, transmitiendo los pasos intermedios mediante mensajes. Se trata de un asunto delicado, ya que retirar un artículo del almacén antes de comprobar la disponibilidad de saldo o de crédito no parece una buena idea, pero MBQ es lo suficientemente parecida al tiempo real como para que las empresas estén tomándola en consideración.*

Example 8 also shows the preference of the source text for visual metaphors that the Spanish translation omits. In the target text there is a more neutral style focusing mainly on transmitting content. The target text maintains the expression "steps", *pasos*, but does not play with its meaning of "dancing steps", conveying only the meaning of "stage". As the target text does not translate "back and forth", the allusion to a dance is lost and for that reason the "delicate dance" turns into un *asunto delicado* ('a delicate matter').

5. Conclusions

It is important to stress that technical translators working in the field of information technologies have to face several problems that deal with cultural aspects, which traditionally were not typically considered as characteristic of technical translation.

Among the main cultural aspects that affect the translation into Spanish of the magazine *Byte* we can mention the following:

- American customs and way of life that illustrate technical developments.
- Different information content adapted to the interests of the new target audience, as technology does not reach society at the same pace and in the same way in Europe and the US.
- Stylistic conventions specific to the target community as Spanish expository writing does not favour the explicit involvement of the reader
- Fossilized metaphors typical of the source language which do not have an equivalent in the target language
- Different connotations that English terminology has in Spanish. In order to translate successfully, IT technical translators need to know about the technology and the society of the language community of the writer or the publication, the textual characteristics and stylistic conventions of the specific genre being translated, the background knowledge, the norms of politeness and the expectations of the target audience, the words, expressions and metaphors typical of the language community of the writer of the source language and their equivalence in the target language and, of course, the specific terminology and also its variations in usage and its connotations in the target language.

Consequently, translators "become experts in cross-cultural communication" (Pym 2000: 182) and act as intercultural mediators who do not merely translate[8]. If technical translation is seen as intercultural mediation, the translator is allowed to adapt the source text to satisfy both the publisher and the target reader. As stated in Nord (1997: 86) when referring to thc changes carried out when translating technical texts, the following words of Sager (1993: 113) should be given attention:

> Any modification of a text is carried out in the perceived interest of an improvement of the text as part of a specific message. It involves making texts more effective for and in a particular communicative situation.

References

Aguado, G. 1994 / 1996. *Diccionario Comentado de terminología informática*. Madrid: Paraninfo.

Alvarez de Mon, I. 2001. Problemas en torno a la denominación del lenguaje científico-técnico: Ciencia, técnica, tecnología e ingeniería, *Ibérica* 3, 31-42.

Bassnett, S. / Lefevere, A. 1998. *Constructing cultures*. Clevedon/ Philadelphia: Multilingual Matters.

Cabré, Mª T. 1999. *La terminología: Representación y comunicación*, IULA: Universidad Pompeu Fabra.

Franco Aixela, J. 1996. Culture-specific items in translation in Alvarez, R. / Vidal. A. (eds) *Translation, Power, Subversion*. Clevedon/ Philadelphia: Multilingual Matters, 52-78.

Gutt, E.A. 2000. *Translation and Relevance. Cognition and Context.* Manchester/Boston: St. Jerome Publishing.

Hatim, B. 1997. *Communication across cultures. Translation theory and contrastive text linguistics*. Exeter: University of Exeter Press.

Hatim, B. / Mason, I. 1990. *Discourse and the translator.* London/ New York: Longman.

8 This intercultural mediation is even more important in the IT domain, in what is known as software localization.

Hatim, B. / Mason, I. 1997. *The translator as communicator*. London/ New York: Routledge.

Newmark, P. 1988. *A textbook of translation*. New York: Prentice Hall.

Newmark, P. 1991. *About translation*. Clevedon: Multilingual Matters.

Nida, E.A. / Taber, Ch.R. 1974. *The theory and practice of translation*. The United Bible Society (Translated into Spanish by de la Fuente Adánez, A. 1986. *La traducción: Teoría y práctica*. Madrid: Ed. Cristiandad.)

Nord, Ch. 1990. Funcionalismo y lealtad: algunas consideraciones en torno a la traducción de los títulos. In Raders, Margit and Cones, Juan (eds) *II Encuentros Complutenses en torno a la traducción* (12-16 diciembre 1988). Madrid: Universidad Complutense de Madrid, 153-162.

Nord, Ch. 1997. *Translating as a purposeful activity*. Manchester: St. Jerome Publishing.

Oxford Advanced Learner's Dictionary 1995. Oxford: Oxford University Press.

Posteguillo, S. 1996. Is *Byte* popular science? In Barrueco, S. / Hernández, E. / Sierra, L. (eds) *Lenguas para fines específicos V* Alcalá de Henares: U. de Alcalá, 425-432.

Real Academia Española [22]2001. *Diccionario de la lengua española*. DRAE Madrid: Espasa.

Reiss, K. / Vermeer, H. 1991. *Grundlegung einer allgemeinen Translationstheorie*. Tübingen: Niemeyer Verlag (Translated into Spanish by García, S. / Martín, C. / Witte, H. (coord.) 1996. *Fundamentos para una teoría funcional de la traducción*. Madrid: Ed. Akal.)

Sager, J.C. 1993. *Language Engineering and Translation: Consequences of Automation*. Amsterdam/Philadelphia: John Benjamins.

Snell-Hornby, M. 1995. *Translation as Intercultural Communication*. Amsterdam/Philadelphia: John Benjamins.

Sperber, D. / Wilson, D. 1986. *Relevance*, Oxford: Blackwell. (Translated into Spanish by Leonetti, E. 1994. *La Relevancia*. Madrid: Visor.).

Toury, G. 1995. *Descriptive translation studies and beyond.* Amsterdam/Philadelphia: John Benjamins.

Vermeer, H.J. 2000/1989. Skopos and Commission in Translational Action. In Venuti, L. (ed.) *The Translation Studies Reader.* London and New York: Routledge, 221-232 (Translated into English by Andrew Chesterman).

Corpus used in this research

Flohr, U. / Rupnik, J. When will e-cash jingle in your e-pocket? *Byte*, January, 1998: 85.

Flohr, U. / Rupnik, J. En Europa ya funciona...¿y en Estados Unidos? *Byte*, Enero, 1998: 149.

Joch, A. Call control, for the rest of us *Byte*, January, 1998: 86.

Joch, A. Controlar las llamadas de los mortales *Byte*, Enero 1998: 150.

Linthicum, D. S. Java Evolves, *Byte*, January, 1998: 60.

Linthicum, D. S. Java evoluciona *Byte*, Enero 1998: 123.

Mace, S. Broadband goes guerrilla, *Byte*, January, 1998: 78.

Mace, S. La guerrilla de la banda ancha, *Byte,* Enero 1998: 141.

Mace, S. Getting the message *Byte*, January, 1998: 87.

Mace, S. Mensaje recibido *Byte*, Enero 1998: 152.

McGraw, G / Felten, E. Avoiding hostile applets, *Byte*, May 1997: 89-92.

McGraw, G / Felten, E. Evitar applets hostiles, *Byte,* Mayo 1997: 102-104.

Montgomery, J. The next Windows *Byte*, January, 1998: 56.

Montgomery, J. El próximo Windows *Byte*, Enero, 1998: 120.

Udell, J. HTML Groupware, *Byte*, January, 1998: 73.

Udell, J. Groupware HTML *Byte*, Enero, 1998: 133.

Udell, J. Stop the insanity *Byte*, January, 1998: 64.

Udell, J. Detener la locura *Byte*, Enero 1998: 126.

Yager, T. E-mail servers for the enterprise *Byte,* April, 1998, 114-118.

Yager, T. Servidores de correo electrónico para la empresa *Byte,* Abril, 1998, 146-150.

GIUDITTA CALIENDO

Intercultural traits in legal translation

Il n'est chose en quoi le monde soit si divers qu'en coutumes et lois *[...]*
Montaigne, Essais, II, 12

This chapter relates to a national research project on interculturality in LSP[1] and investigates, through a comparative approach of different legal systems, the problems related to the translation of legal texts in multilingual and multilegal organizations.

After an introductory analysis on the aspects of precision and ambiguity that coexist in international law texts, the study takes on an intercultural slant in illustrating the translation strategies and choices used to transfer legal messages across different cultures and legal systems, namely English and Italian. To this end, the last section presents the results gleaned from a previous study on comparative law, which led to the creation of a legal glossary on human rights and criminal law. This terminological work, compiled for the translators of the European Commission in Brussels and Luxembourg, is entirely based on a source corpus of international criminal law: a judgment of the European Court of Human Rights (*Case of Rowe and Davis vs. the United Kingdom*[2]).

1 *Intercultural Discourse in Domain-specific English*: <http:/www.unibg.it/cerlis/progetti.htm>.

2 <http://www.echr.coe.int/Eng/Judgments.htm> (16/02/2000, REF00001380, Application n. 00028901/95).

1. Introduction

Recent developments in the fields of judicial cooperation, human rights and war crimes have gradually enhanced the role played by international organizations within the political arena. After the Second World War, the appearance of these institutions on the world stage fuelled the consequent spread of multilingualism in transnational politics and diplomacy. This also coincided with the issue of providing an accurate and official translation for those legislative acts which, being legally binding in target countries, needed to be unequivocally translated into different legal systems (Taylor 1998). Since then, translation and language services have been increasingly recognized as the axis of global and interinstitutional communication as greater efforts have been made to guarantee accurate and homogeneous application of the law throughout different judicial systems.

With regard to the linguistic and technical difficulties that legal translation entails, international institutions are often placed on the same footing as bilingual and trilingual countries. However, it is important to stress that in countries like Switzerland, Belgium or Finland the translators' burden is considerably alleviated by the presence of a common judicial background, what Šarčević describes as a shared legal system of reference:

> The chances that the receivers will attach the same meaning to the parallel texts of a plurilingual instrument are greatest when all the texts derive their meaning from the same legal system irrespective of the language. The fact that the receivers share the same knowledge base means that they also use a common system of reference, thus greatly simplifying the interpretation process. (1997: 68)

In the case of international organizations, such "common ground" is replaced by a mosaic of divergent legal systems. Legal translation is not simply confined to matters of linguistic discrepancy, but intrinsically bound to the numerous recipient cultures and legal orders. The complexity of text production at international level will therefore increase in proportion to the Member States involved: a higher number of official languages will correspond to more legal systems to be taken into account in the translation process.

Today, the number of official languages in international bodies may vary from two, as in the case of NATO (English and French), to six, as for the UN and the WHO (English, French, Spanish, Russian, Chinese and Arabic). The judgments of the European Court of Human Rights (ECHR) are only delivered in English and French although complaints may still be lodged with the Court in one of the official languages of the "contracting states" (those which have signed and ratified the European Convention of Human Rights). The most linguistically crowded is the European Union, which now counts 20 official languages following the fifth wave of enlargement which has opened the doors to new countries from central Europe and the Mediterranean. Multilingualism thus leads to "multilegalism": on one hand there is the need to produce a plurilingual legislation and, on the other, the intricacy of adjusting specific concepts to different judicial settings like common and civil law, the two principal and most contrasting legal systems in the western world today.

A further difference between bilingual countries and international organizations is that the latter lack co-edition procedures in their legislative drafting process. Legal documents are not drafted simultaneously in different languages, as would happen in the Canadian administration, but are translated from one "original" source and subsequently recognized as official and equally authentic. The absence of a "pivot" language is asserted by Article 33 of the Vienna Convention on the Law of Treaties ("Interpretation of treaties authenticated in two or more languages"), which precludes any reference to an original and dominant text. Specifically, in cases of misinterpretation or inconsistencies between different languages, the Article states that the interpretation that best reflects the intention of the whole text will prevail:

> When a treaty has been authenticated in two or more languages, the text is equally authoritative in each language [...].
> The terms of the treaty are presumed to have the same meaning in each authentic text [...].
> [...] when a comparison of the authentic texts discloses a difference of meaning which the application of articles 31 and 32 does not remove, the meaning which best reconciles the texts, having regard to the object and purpose of the

treaty, shall be adopted. (Vienna Convention on the Law of Treaties, Article 33)

2. Vagueness and diplomacy in international law

Vagueness and ambiguity are some of the key features generally attributed to legislative writing. Hiltunen (1990: 82-84) agrees on the need for legal language to be vague and inclusive enough to cover a "maximally wide variety of different circumstances", also because the deliberate use of flexible meanings can safeguard the legislator's position should the interpretation of the law be questioned.

At the international level, the use of broader expressions and definitions responds to the double need to find a political compromise between different countries and leave the text open to different interpretations. The lack of specificity in international law also favours all-inclusiveness, which helps accommodate legal rules to different judicial systems and varying circumstances. Translators thus find themselves in the difficult position of maintaining a fair balance between different orientations. In addition, their margin of manoeuvre remains extremely limited since "strategic" ambiguities cannot be interpreted in one way or another but need to be left unbiased in the target text.

An example attesting the importance played by vagueness in instruments of international law is the United Nation Council resolution 1441 (November 2002), which proved to be a crucial step in the outbreak of the Second Gulf war. From the outset, the wording of the resolution was at the centre of heated negotiations and kept on fuelling debates on a global level in the months that preceded and followed the military attack in Iraq. The first draft of the resolution initially authorized Member States to use "" to restore international peace and security in the area. This document, produced jointly by the United States and the UK, led to tumultuous negotiations, particularly with Russia and France. The latter, threatening to veto the document, questioned the phrase "all necessary means" and stated that any material breach found by the inspectors should not automatically lead to war. These objections ultimately led to the final draft of the resolution adopting a much vaguer stance: the formulation was removed and replaced by a warning stating that Iraq would face "serious consequences" *as a result of its continued violations*.

The tensions and disagreements that accompanied the drafting of resolution 1441 also stemmed from the lingering influence of the language used in previous resolutions, as if it had set some sort of precedent in the history of the relations between the UN and its members. Specific reference can be made to the UN Security Council resolution 678 which, adopted in response to the Iraqi occupation of Kuwait in 1990, authorized the USA-led forces to intervene and restore security in the region. The text contained the same reference to "all necessary means", which, given the historical and political circumstances, meant war. Twelve years later, in the light of this "precedent", resolution 1441 had to be cautiously worded to avoid any particular formulas which, used in previous occasions, would engender "automaticity" and trigger an authorization to use force.

In terms of its general content, the amended version of resolution 1441 also turned out to be extremely vague. It clearly evaded any direct specification as to what "serious consequences" would follow in the event of Iraq's continued violations of its obligations. In this respect, Melinkoff (1963: 22) interestingly lists "serious" amongst the law adjectives deliberately used for their flexible meaning and vagueness.

One of the reasons behind this highly diplomatic wording was the attempt to reach a wide political accord among the parties involved. A watered-down version was in fact the easiest way to obtain majority support from the full 15 members of the Security Council and avoid any veto from the five nations that possessed such power. Having failed to give an explicit consent or proscription, the text remains still open to conflicting interpretations and can be placed in what Hart (1961: 119) describes as "a penumbra of uncertainty".

3. Standardization in international legal instruments

The elusiveness and ambiguity that typically distinguish legal language are equally widespread in instruments of international legislation (Šarčević 1997). However, many scholars have underlined how such features paradoxically clash with the conditions of certainty and precision that are stringently required for texts imposing obligations and conferring rights (Covacs 1982; Gibbons 1994).

One of the means employed in international law to minimize ambivalence and confusion is the use of fixed formulas and repetitive patterns that contribute to setting out the structure and progression of text contents. Conservatism includes not only the choice of lexical constructions but also the entire layout, the manner by which different sections are arranged and hierarchically ranked within a text.

Judgments of the European Court of Human Rights are a clear example of texts adhering to a standardized format and style. With direct reference to the *Case of Rowe and Davis vs. the United Kingdom* (§ 4), introduced here as a representative example of ECHR judgments, it is possible to recognize separate and numbered paragraphs, in turn divided into various subsections:

a. The introductory unit. It includes the title of the judgment, the case application number and date of delivery, followed by the list of judges composing the Chamber.
b. "Procedure". This section provides information concerning the identity of the parties involved, together with their representatives and advisers. When the official title of a body or a party is mentioned for the first time, a shorter name is given in brackets and then used throughout the entire text (Alcaraz/Hughes 2002), for example "European Commission of Human Rights (the Commission)", "The United Kingdom Government (the Government)", "Rowe and Davis (the Applicants)".
c. "The facts", comprising two subcategories:
   i. "Circumstances of the case", which reports on all the details concerning the applicants and, diachronically, the circum-

stances that generated the offence and led to the first trial before a domestic court;

ii. "Relevant domestic law", which offers an overview of the rights and obligations provided under the relevant national legislation. It also illustrates the practice followed according to different juridical circumstances.

d. "The law". This section is entirely based on the Convention for the Protection of Human Rights and Fundamental Freedoms and develops into two subparagraphs opening with the following formulas:

i. "Alleged violation of Article *X* of the Convention", which refers to the applicants' claim of a presumed breach of a Convention Article;

ii. "Application of Article 41 of the Convention", immediately followed by the relevant quotation:

> If the Court finds that there has been a violation of the Convention or the Protocols thereto, and if the internal law of the High Contracting Party concerned allows only partial reparation to be made, the Court shall, if necessary, afford just satisfaction to the injured party.
>
> (Article 41 Convention for the Protection of Human Rights and Fundamental Freedoms)

The section continues with an exhaustive list of the pecuniary and/or non-pecuniary damages claimed by the defendants.

e. The final formula "For these reasons, the court unanimously holds [...]". It anticipates the summarizing conclusions of the case: "The Court holds that there has been a violation of Article *X* of the Convention". The respondent State is therefore to pay the applicants, within an established period of time, a certain amount of money in respect of pecuniary/non-pecuniary damages, costs, expenses and interests.

Throughout the whole text, paragraphs are invariably numbered to facilitate reading and cross-reference with parallel texts in different languages. Uniformity is also respected in terms of punctuation and capitalization that help to keep the flow of the text "under control" (Hiltunen 1990: 83-87).

4. A case-study on comparative criminal law: translation as cultural transposition

In an era of expanding communication across nations and intensified contacts between different legal systems, international law is acquiring a growing weight over domestic legislations. The international legislator is constantly faced with the need to overcome cultural divergence and make legal instruments fit multiple recipient countries. In the European Union for example, Community law is directly applicable in all Member States, where it is guaranteed primacy over national law. Decisions and Regulations enacted by the Council of the European Union are directly applicable and legally binding in all EU countries. Likewise, judgments delivered by the European Court of Human Rights can affect the legal status of all contracting states. On the subject, Tebbens (1982) recalls the *Case of Marckx vs. Belgium*[3], a famous ECHR judgment which had immediate legislative repercussions in Europe and laid the foundations for later jurisprudence on legal relationships between parents and children. The Court found that Belgian law unreasonably limited the rights of unmarried mothers and discriminated against "illegitimate" children with regard to inheritance rights. Still today, the decision is considered as a major achievement in European legislation for equal rights between children born in and out of wedlock.

This closing section starts from another ECHR judgment with the intent to put forward some practical solutions to the terminological problems arising in the area of comparative criminal law, with specific reference to the English and Italian legal systems. The analysis originates from a previous lexicographic work, a comparative glossary on

3 <http://www.echr.coe.int/Eng/Judgments.htm> (13/06/1979, REF00000119, Application n. 00006833/74).

criminal law and human rights (Caliendo 2001), written within the framework of a collaboration with the Translation Service of the European Commission.

The project originally started with the translation of a case brought before the European Court of Human Rights (*Rowe and Davis vs. the UK*) concerning a series of violent robberies that led to the arrest of three men, convicted of murder and sentenced to life imprisonment. The trial caused wide uproar in the UK since, although the victims reported that two of the attackers were white, three black men were finally convicted. The text of such controversial judgment proved particularly prolific from a linguistic point of view and was thus selected as the source corpus of the glossary itself. Dealing with criminal law, one of the most incompatible and therefore interesting fields in legal translation, the text also offered solid grounding for a cultural and linguistic analysis of the two systems of common and civil law.

From the outset, the general aim of the glossary coincided with the production of a specialized lexicographic work that could find functional and recipient-oriented solutions to transfer legal messages across cultural contexts, even when the target language lacked parallel concepts or an appropriate specialized terminology. The terms were translated resorting to flexible parameters, according to which translation could detach itself from the original text and introduce an analogous notion representing the "closest natural equivalent of the source language message" (Nida/Taber 1969: 12), always respecting the legislator's original intent (Garzone 1999).

The glossary followed a semasiological structure (starting from the sign to explain its content), although it was conceived and compiled according to an onomasiological approach (analysing the content and then naming it with a sign). Due to the enormous discrepancies between common and civil law, a comparative evaluation of the two concepts was the essential first step in identifying common content and then finding parallel signs in the target language. Before moving on to the practical analysis of the structural and lexical differences existing between English and Italian criminal law terminology, it is important to underline that the examples selected represent only a limited number of the translation strategies adopted during the drafting: Amplification, Diffusion and Divergence (Fawcett 1997; Taylor 1998).

4.1 Amplification

This strategy is particularly suited to meeting the requirements of precision and accuracy. It is generally employed for those terms that do not seem to pose any particular translation problems and are wrongly "taken for granted". In some cases in fact, words are morphologically parallel but not semantically so. Amplification makes the reader aware of the existing contrasts in semantics and content by adding extra elements to the texts, generally footnotes or bracketed additions. By doing so, the translator can provide all the explanatory comments that emerged from his research work and comparative analysis, as shown in the examples below:

(1) Appeal ~ *Appello*

The translation of "appeal" might deceitfully look like an example of equation, for example an automatic equivalence based on a one-to-one correspondence. In spite of their morphological parallelism, the two terms are given a different semantic interpretation in their respective legal systems:

- in English law, an appeal refers to the mere correction of the questions of law considered to be wrong in the judgment, whilst the Italian *appello* can imply the entire re-examination of all the questions of law and questions of fact that had already been decided on;
- unlike common law, the Italian system suspends the effects of the decision being contested;
- common law does not guarantee the same principle of appealability: a specific decision can be declared "final" and therefore incontestable.

From a diachronic perspective, de Franchis (1984) also remarks that, up to 1907, the right to appeal did not even exist in English criminal law.

(2) Grievous bodily harm ~ *Lesione personale grave*
This legal term denotes a serious injury that can constitute an element of several offences (such as burglary) and takes on different semantic nuances in the two languages. Interestingly enough, while the English term places emphasis on the purely physical aspect of the violence, the Italian translation *lesione personale grave* also encompasses the possible mental injury that can be caused by the offence.

(3) Criminal records ~ *Precedenti penali*
The "note of previous crimes for which someone has been convicted" (Collin 2000: 95) represents an additional example used to describe different procedures in common and civil law. In Italy, it is incumbent upon a citizen to prove the absence of previous criminal records. A *precedente penale* can also affect the gravity of the penalty or compromise the chance to be placed under probation order. In English law, on the contrary, criminal records cannot influence the jury and they are not unveiled before the defendant is found guilty by the jury.

4.2 Divergence

As for divergence, the strategy consists in choosing a terminological option from a range of possible alternatives according to the context in which the term is translated:

(4) Conviction ~ *Sentenza di condanna / Verdetto di colpevolezza*
The English term "conviction" can correspond to two possible translations into Italian: *verdetto di colpevolezza* and *condanna*. Considering the jury's participation in the trial, the two alternatives indicate, respectively, the finding of guilt by the jury ("verdict of guilty"), and the imposition of the penalty by the judge ("sentence"). Although related, the two concepts remain independent as the judge can still decide to order the defendant's discharge in spite of the jury's verdict of guilty.

(5) Defendant ~ *Imputato / Convenuto*

Another example of divergence is represented by the word *defendant*, which can be translated by both *imputato* in criminal law and *convenuto* in civil law cases (de Franchis 1984: 627).

(6) Compensation ~ *Indennizzo / Risarcimento*

"Compensation", the payment made to cover the cost of damage or hardship caused to another person, has a wide meaning in English law and can be expressed by the Italian *indennizzo*. However, when the damage is the result of a wrongful act, it is then called *risarcimento*. The term *compensazione* is a "false friend" and corresponds to the English "set-off".

4.3 Diffusion

In the case of diffusion, the lexical relation between source and target text can be summarized as a "1: >1" ratio. The following example shows how the original concept is conveyed through a longer lexical elaboration in the target version.

(7) Burglary ~ *Furto aggravato con violazione di domicilio*

From a comparative analysis of English and Italian criminal law, it emerges that "burglary" covers a wider semantic area than *furto*. The latter lacks the intrinsic idea of "trespass" and needs to be lexically stretched into *furto aggravato con violazione di domicilio* (here the lexical ratio is 1:6), which encompasses the aggravating circumstances of *furto con scasso* and *violazione di domicilio* (Caliendo 2003).

5. Concluding remarks

The post-war establishment of supranational organizations has contributed to expanding governments' views on foreign policy and external relations. A broader platform of exchange on commercial and political grounds has called for an institutionalization of international relations between countries, especially from a legal perspective. As a consequence, an intense network of conventions, treaties and joint agreements has started to consolidate and acquire a dominant position vis à vis national legislations.

Upholding the idea that no legal system can be eradicated from its social and cultural substrata (Pigeon 1982), the study draws attention to the challenges facing these institutions to simultaneously represent different legal traditions on a global stage. In order to be democratically representative, international bodies must be able to give a single voice to the different languages and to the divergent interpretation of the law that unfolds across national courts. Such linguistic and cultural equality is also guaranteed by the adoption of a multilingual regime, which can be described as a neutral forum where different judicial systems converge in spite of their diversity.

A great share of the task is fulfilled by the work of linguistic services, which are steadily growing and offering their contribution to make international legal instruments available to an ever-increasing number of nations. Hence, translation becomes the herald of interculturality, the instrument to interpret single identities and harmonize the different needs dictated by national legislative settings.

Linguists working for European and international organizations are faced with the same linguistic difficulties as national legal translators: ambiguous messages to unravel and extremely rigid types of text to handle. In addition, they have to play into the legislators' hands and "respect" the vagueness that often lies behind multilateral political agreements. Target texts have to maintain just as diplomatic, all-inclusive and unbiased a tone as the original document, also in view of the fact that they are vested with the same legal value.

The contribution culminates in a presentation of the outcomes of a practical terminological work drawn up in the field of comparative law within an international environment. Based on the dichotomous relationship between common and civil law, today's most representative and conflicting legal systems, the analysis of the translation strategies applied aims at exemplifying how conceptual and semantic differences are practically faced and solved in a professional context.

References

Alcaraz E. / Hughes B. 2002. *Legal Translation Explained.* Manchester: St Jerome Publishing.

Caliendo, G. 2001. *Glossario EN/FR/IT. Diritti dell'uomo e Diritto Penale.* Bruxelles: Centro Informazione e Documentazione Italiano – AGL01, SdT, Commissione europea.

Caliendo, G. 2003. Translating legal English: The challenge of diversity. In Lima, M. (ed.) *Language, culture and politics: issues and debates in political science.* Napoli: CUEN, 37-50.

Covacs, A. 1982. La réalisation de la version française des lois fédérales du Canada. In Gémar, J.-C. (ed.) *Langage du droit et traduction. Essais de jurilinguistique.* Brossard, Québec: Linguatech, 83-100.

Fawcett, P. 1997. *Translation and Language. Linguistic Theories Explained.* Manchester: St Jerome Publishing.

Garzone, G. 1999. The Translation of Legal Texts. A Functional Approach in a Pragmatic Perspective, *Textus* XII/2, 391-407.

Gibbons, J. (ed.) 1994. *Language and the Law.* New York: Longman.

Hart, H. L. A. 1961. *The Concept of Law.* Oxford: Oxford University Press.

Hiltunen, R. 1990. *Chapters on Legal English: Aspects Past and Present on the Language of the Law.* Helsinki: Suomalainen Tiedeakatemia.

Melinkoff, D. 1963. *The Language of the Law.* Boston: Little, Brown & Co.

Nida, E. A. / Taber, A. 1969. *The theory and practice of translation.* Leiden: Brill.

Pigeon, L. P. 1982. La traduction juridique – L'équivalence fonctionnelle. In Gémar, J.-C. (ed.) *Langage du droit et traduction. Es-*

sais de jurilinguistique. Brossard, Québec: Linguatech, 271-281.

Šarčević, S. 1997. *New Approach to Legal Translation*. The Hague: Kluwer Law International.

Taylor, C. 1998. *Language to Language. A Practical and Theoretical Guide for Italian/English Translators*. Cambridge: Cambridge University Press.

Tebbens, D. H. 1982. Le dictionnaire juridique néerlandais-français: un exercice de droit comparé. In Gémar, J.-C. (ed.) *Langage du droit et traduction. Essais de jurilinguistique*. Brossard, Québec: Linguatech, 175-184.

i) Dictionaries

Collin, P. H. 2000. *Dictionary of Law*. London: Peter Collin Publishing.

de Franchis, F. 1984. *Dizionario giuridico* , 1 Milano: Giuffré.

ii) Electronic Sources

Convention for the Protection of Human Rights and Fundamental Freedoms 1950. Available: <http://www.echr.coe.int/ Convention/webConvenENG.pdf> [accessed September 25, 2003].

European Court of Human Right. Available: <http://www.echr.coe.int> [accessed September 25, 2003].

UN Security Council Resolution 678, 1990. Available: <http://www.fas.org/news/un/iraq/sres/sres0678.htm> [accessed September 25, 2003].

UN Security Council Resolution 1441, 2002. Available: <http://www.un.org/Docs/scres/2002/sc2002.htm> [accessed September 25, 2003].

Vienna Convention on the Law of Treaties, 1969. Available: <http://www.un.org/law/ilc/texts/treaties.htm> [accessed September 25, 2003].

Part Four
Terminology and Knowledge Management

Part 4 of this volume concerns terms, traditionally the basic building blocks for the LSP of a specific domain. The study of terms and terminologies can play an important role in the newly emerging subject of "knowledge management", a term coined to assert the fact that the knowledge within an organisation is as important a resource as land, labour and capital, or arguably more important than these traditional assets. In a knowledge-based economy, innovation and change are critical to the survival of organisations, societies and nation states. The pioneers of knowledge management (Nonaka and Takeuchi 1995) were keen to emphasise that the dissemination of knowledge such as best practice and "knowledge of doing" within an organisation, across departmental and technological boundaries, is essential for successful competition. And it is often in texts that knowledge is stored and disseminated across a range of genres: organisation-specific memoranda, reports, manuals, as well as journals (experts communicating with experts) and textbooks (experts communicating with novice experts).

Rather surprisingly, in books and journals concerned with knowledge management there is seldom any discussion of the language in which knowledge is disseminated. While linguists such as Herbert Clark (1996) have contributed to one important aspect of knowledge management, namely communities of practice, by discussing how people with different experience and from different backgrounds attempt to form a "common ground" for communicating effectively, no mention of specialist terminology is made. For the LSP community, the understanding of terms across disciplines and occupational boundaries, as well as the mapping of knowledge spaces within domains and languages, are major factors in the management of knowledge.

Terms and the concepts they represent in the highly-specific domain of cattle disease in Cameroon are shown by Bassey Antia, Yaya Mahamadou and Tioguem Tamdjo in the first chapter of Part 4 to be variously understood by veterinary personnel professionally trained in French on the one hand and nomadic cattle farmers typically speaking Fulfulde on the other hand. The fact that the knowledge is mapped differently – veterinary personnel, for instance, list nine diseases, the farmers 13 – can lead, the authors point out, to dangerous false assumptions on the part of the farmers about relevant treatments, which can in turn cause public health problems by allowing diseased animals into the food chain. The conceptual differences are also overlaid with linguistic mismatches within the local language, for example, different relations of synonymy, and between languages, where equivalences remain unclear. It is concluded that terms and their predications provide access to knowledge structures and that studying terms as understood by different but mutually interested discourse communities can therefore make a contribution to knowledge management. In the following chapter, Giuseppina Cortese picks up the theme of problems in multilingual communication, which could be exacerbated by the challenges of multiculturalism. Cortese discusses LSP implementation policies and challenges the "hegemony of English", suggesting ways of dealing with this. In management sciences, for instance, she argues that the influence of English is pervasive with profound effects across the globe. Hence, English has become the linguistic tool for managing knowledge. So, in her view, it is important to understand how to manage knowledge *across* disciplines, languages and cultures.

Dictionaries can also be seen as a kind of knowledge management, attempting to systematise and codify a body of knowledge, or, as in the case of the Czech-English law dictionary described by Marta Chromá, two systems which are themselves codifications with the aim of regulating human behaviour. The conceptual approach outlined by Chromá is realised in the inclusion of '"explanations" (chosen to avoid the strict interpretation of "definition") to facilitate transfer between two different legal systems, or seen from a different perspective, to manage the transfer of knowledge and its application in particular cases. In managing knowledge, assumptions can and are made about the level and scope of knowledge possessed by different interlocutors in the communication process.

Focusing more on the phraseological level, in the penultimate chapter in Part 4, Stanislaw Goźdź-Roszkowski aims to link "restricted combinability in legal language" with genre. This study is based on a subcorpus of contract law taken from a 3-million word corpus covering a range of legal subdomains and genres. The genres investigated in relation to the chosen domain are contracts, judgements, text books and reports. Goźdź-Roszkowski's detailed analysis of the phraseology of the legal term/concept of "consideration" – a kind of compensation or recompense – reveals examples of genre-specific patternings.

In the final chapter, an analysis of the little researched "lecture note" (*Vorlesungsskript* in German), Hans Lechleiter describes a corpus-based study related to German for chemistry students. Of particular interest in Lechleiter's chapter is his case-study analysis of how a particular student has annotated his/her lecture notes. It is shown that the verb plays a crucial role in the student's understanding, even in LSP, that syntax and lexis form "parts of a unity", and that metaphors can lead to learning problems. The study provides interesting insights into one student's attempt to map the domain of chemistry through a second language.

This fourth Part encompasses many domains and different perspectives on aspects of what can broadly be called knowledge management, indicating widening research possibilities in particular for terminology studies and its applications. In such attempts to understand and thereby potentially to improve the quality of professional communication, modern knowledge management shares at least one goal with the early 20th century pioneers of terminology science.

References

Clark, Herbert 1996. *Using Language.* Cambridge: Cambridge University Press.

Nonaka, Ikujiro / Takeuchi, Hirotaka 1995. *The Knowledge-Creating Company*. New York & Oxford: Oxford University Press.

BASSEY ANTIA, YAYA MAHAMADOU AND TIOGUEM TAMDJO

Terminology, knowledge management and veterinary anthropology

1. Introduction

The economic and other costs of recent epizooties such as bovine spongiform encephalopathy (BSE) and foot-and-mouth disease have been huge. At the end of its efforts to contain the latter disease, the UK had spent some 10 billion euros. The ensuing blame game suggests that broader sections of society need to take an active interest in what happens in certain professional spheres, especially those activities that directly impinge on society (safety, food safety, and so on). One is reminded here of those definitions that view public health as the concerted action of society in assuring health.

This chapter discusses the role of communication in discussions on animal health. The importance of communication is underscored by the following description of the challenges by the League for Pastoral People (LPP):

> In the implementation of a support project for camel pastoralists in Rajasthan/India, one of the major challenges for L.P.P. and its partner-NGO has been to act as an interface between pastoralists on the one side and project staff with academic backgrounds in animal science and veterinary medicine on the other. We have observed that, due to a lack of reference points and concepts, communication between them is very problematic. (Köhler-Rollefson/Bräunig 1998: 1).

This chapter illustrates how the different knowledge configurations of veterinarians and livestock raisers can create problems of communication and, *ipso facto*, concerns of food safety and public health. From the analysis it should be obvious that communication in this sector requires some of the same kind of care and management as communication in other safety-critical areas such as aviation or weapons manufacturing. It should also be evident that assuring food (animal protein) safety and public health is not just the responsibility of veterinarians and animal scientists, but also of scholars of language for special purposes (LSP). A related point has been made elsewhere (Antia/Yassin 2001; Antia 2002) in respect of the management of childhood diseases.

2. Framework

The analysis offered rests on the tripod of veterinary anthropology, knowledge management and terminology. Veterinary anthropology is a term coined in the 1980s to refer to an approach to animal health care that: (a) realises that to reach the animal you cannot circumvent the owner who, like his animal, is embedded in a cultural context; (b) requires observing, interviewing and participating in the activities of the owner. For this study, therefore, understanding and facilitating communication assumes some preparedness to do anthropology.

All anthropology is, in some sense, the beginning of knowledge management (KM). We take a view of KM as the explicitation of implicit or tacit knowledge typically undertaken in order to facilitate sharing and reuse. While anthropology shares with KM the idea of explicitation, KM tends to be additionally concerned with application or operationalization of unlocked knowledge. We may therefore say that in doing KM we are doing an "audit of intellectual assets" (*sensu* Grey 2003) possessed by both livestock raisers and veterinarians who provide advisory services in order to determine what resources are available, how they are deployed and what the bottlenecks are.

Terms have been described as "a means of acquiring, retrieving, creating, communicating, storing, representing and operationalising specialised knowledge" (Antia 2000: xv). Terms designate units of specialist knowledge and are therefore the building blocks of specialist knowledge and communication. In this sense, terminology is an obvious ancillary to unlocking the ontology of knowledge possessed by actors in the pastoral world. The use of terms as heuristic is therefore appropriate for this exercise in veterinary anthropology and knowledge management.

3. Study background and method

Data for the study was obtained in the Far North Province of Cameroon, a region that shares borders with north-eastern Nigeria. Both regions have the highest livestock population in the respective countries. Cattle farmers are typically nomadic (as opposed to sedentary), speak Fulfulde (severally referred to as Fulani, Peuhl, and so on) and have available as relevant intellectual assets traditions of animal husbandry. Veterinary personnel (doctors, particularly assistants) typically speak Fulfulde as well, but have received western veterinary education in the medium of the French language. In providing extension services, veterinary personnel use Fulfulde and mentally translate between French and Fulfulde, back and forth. It is this mental translating activity that explains question (b) shown below.

Focus group discussions were organised for each of three groups of actors in the pastoral world: livestock raisers (n=12), veterinary doctors (n=3) and veterinary assistants (n= 4). The agenda for discussion revolved around establishing a list of the most prevalent cattle diseases in the community (thus, terms) and obtaining descriptions of these diseases (aetiology, symptomatology, pathogenesis, therapy, and so on). In a second round of discussions, the terms for diseases mentioned were to be sorted in descending order of perceived gravity.

4. Study questions

a. In the knowledge of livestock farmers as well as of veterinary personnel, what is the term-concept relationship like?
b. Do French terms which veterinary personnel say are equivalent to Fulfulde terms refer to the same concepts?
c. Do farmers and veterinary personnel have the same view of the epidemiological significance of diseases as may be revealed by a term-sorting task?
d. What are the consequences of asymmetrical knowledge evident in any of the questions above?

The last question is answered in the context of answers to the preceding questions.

5. Results

As can be seen in appendices 1 and 2, cattle farmers list and describe thirteen diseases (that is, terms) while veterinarians list nine. As they are extremely compatible, data obtained from veterinary doctors and from veterinary assistants are conflated. The following analysis is based on diseases (n=9) appearing on both the livestock-raisers' list and that of the veterinarians.

On term-concept relationships, the data showed instances in which a term (for a disease in one language) corresponded to more than one term in the other language. Examples:

(1) i. (French) *charbon symptomatique* (*blackquarter*. Syn: *black leg*) = (Fulfulde) *Gaouyel* and *Boutou*
ii. (Fulfulde) *douslaré* = (French) *trypanosomiase* et *constipation* (*trypanosomiasis* and *constipation*)

To comment on example (i), for instance, in their listing and description of diseases, cattle farmers present *Gaouyel* and *Boutou* as different diseases. However, veterinary personnel, when asked to provide French equivalents of all terms mentioned by cattle farmers, assign *charbon symptomatique* ('black quarter') to both *Gaouyel* and *Boutou.* They, in other words, consider these two terms as synonymous. In descriptions provided of diseases mentioned, it is apparent that the presence of oedema in charbon symptomatique, *Gaouyel* and *Boutou* may suggest some similarity, but this is hardly sufficient basis as oedema is present in other conditions (*Boumsoude, Boudi, Baccalé, Foulokké*).

Imagine, therefore, a scenario in which veterinary personnel (who have *charbon symptomatique* in mind) tell farmers not to let into the food chain animals that have *Gaouyel.* They might use the term in the erroneous belief that its synonymic relationship to *Boutou* is well known. Farmers, in whose nosology *Boutou* and *Gaouyel* are different, would obviously not consider that advisory as applying to cattle with *Boutou,* which thus ends up on our dinner plates. From a communication standpoint, it is clear that providers of veterinary services need to understand the nosology or disease ontology of their client communities in order to pass on knowledge effectively.

With respect to the second question on the conceptual intension of French and Fulfulde terms described by veterinary personnel as equivalent, the degree of (a) symmetry is provided in Table 1. To arrive at the degree of similarity, we use the description that has more symptoms as denominator. We have also taken an extremely flexible or modulation view (*sensu* Vinay/Darbelnet, 1995) of the descriptions, which allows us for instance to consider a description of a cause in one language as equivalent to a statement of an effect in the other.

Kikoyel a. Animal is weak b. Lags behind herd c. When touched animal jumps, falls then dies d. (Autopsy) Enlarged spleen	Pasteurollosis a. Weight loss b. Constant diarrhoea c. Oedema of the throat d. Whizzing respiration e. Animal may appear healthy on leaving the ranch in the morning, only for it to die in the evening
a=a; **1 symptom of 5 shared, i.e. 20%**	
Mbalki a. Appetite loss b. Inability to walk c. Refuses to drink until it dies	Fascioliasis a. Foul-smelling diarrhoea b. Weight loss c. Constant weakness
a=b; b= c; **2 symptoms of 3 shared, i.e. 66%**	
Damal a. Initial appetite loss b. Refusal to eat for 3 –4 or even more days preceding death c. (Autopsy) Rotten spleen	Anthrax a. Non-pitting oedema which, on excision, looks dark
No symptom shared, i.e. 0%	
Mborou/Djobou a. Excessive salivation through mouth and nos-trils. b. Injury to the nail area c. Animal releases foul-smelling odour d. When severe, may lead to loss of tongue e. NB: Djobou has all of the above symptoms + ulcers around the neck	Foot-and-mouth disease a. Affects all oxen, but calves have highest number of deaths. b. Excessive salivation c. Pustules in the mouth d. Nail and interdigital injuries Ulcers on the udders
a=b; b=d; e=e **3 symptoms of 5 shared, i.e. 60%**	
Boutou a. Muscle enlargement b. Animal unable to go out in search of pasture	Black quarter/ black leg a. Pitting oedema in the muscle groups (shoulder or thigh) b. When oedema is excised there is a foam surrounding dark spot
a=a; **1 symptom of 2 shared, i.e. 50%**	
Boumsoudé a. Enlargement of the abdomen b. Difficult breathing c. (Autopsy) Rotten lungs	Contagious bovine pleuropneumonia a. Lungs affected b. Pleura becomes thick c. 1 lung more affected than the other d. Difficult breathing e. Productive cough f. Catarrh g. Marked weight loss

a=b; b=d; c=a/b; **3 symptoms of 7 shared, i.e. 42%**	
Douslaré a. Affects only calves b. Looks like malaria c. Sudden death if animal drinks water within 2 days of onset of disease d. Occurs once in an animal's life time	Trypanosomiasis + constipation a. Constant fatigue b. Excessive lacrymation c. Loss of tail hair d. Weight loss and anaemia e. Loss of appetite
No symptom shared, i.e. 0%	
Baccalé a. Animal limps b. General body swelling c. Animal's ill health does not prevent reproduction	Brucellosis a. Joint swelling
a/b=a; **2 symptoms of 3 shared, i.e. 66%**	
Gaouyel a. Inexplicable + dangerous disease because an animal that is apparently healthy in the morning may die while grazing b. Often body swelling and when touched swollen parts make noise. These parts appear black.	Black quarter/ black leg a. Pitting oedema in the muscle groups (shoulder or thigh) b. When oedema is excised there is a foam surrounding dark spot.
b=a/b; **1 symptom of 2 shared, i.e. 50%**	

Table 1. Conceptual correspondence of Fulfulde-French terms considered to be equivalent by Veterinary Assistants.

Of the nine term pairs, there is less than 50% conceptual symmetry in four, with two of these five actually having 0% symmetry. Admittedly, further symptoms could have been mentioned that might have had the effect of increasing the percentage of symmetry. However, it is conceivable that symptoms mentioned are the ones perceived as most pathonomic. It is also conceivable that the stated degree of symmetry could reduce if divergent views on therapy were factored in. *Damal, Mbalki and Mborou* are said to be incurable, whereas their putative French equivalents (*charbon bactéridien, douve, fièvre aphteuse* respectively) are curable. Factor into the foregoing the observation that in some cases (for example, *Baccalé* vs. *Brucellose*) the descriptions are contradictory (does not prevent reproduction vs. induces abortion). and the picture that emerges is one of a perfect recipe for dysfunctional communication, with far-reaching consequences.

The veterinary extension worker, who for self-serving reasons chooses to base his diagnosis on cattle-owner reports, as opposed to physical examination, would process a complaint of *Kikoyel* as *pasteurollosis*. He would probably prescribe sulphadimidine or broad-spectrum antibiotics. Suppose that this diagnosis is incorrect and that the animal has *la douve* (*fasciollasis*) which, though sharing certain characteristics with pasteurollosis, is treated with Nitroxymil or Rafoxonide. This wrong treatment would have had a number of effects. There is the spectre of resistance to sulphadimidine when later the animal does in fact have *pasteurollosis*. There are cost implications of developing alternative drugs. There is the issue of toxicity, given that every medication contains toxic material which over time can affect vital organs.

With respect to the third question on the epidemiological significance of diseases mentioned, the results of the term-sorting task are presented in Table 2 below. The table presents (in the left column) diseases which cattle farmers say belong to class one and (to the right) the only diseases which veterinary personnel mentioned (and which they believe to be the only ones worth worrying about).

Cattle farmers	Veterinary personnel
1. *Bodewu* or *petou* (rinderpest)	1. *Contagious bovine pleuropneumonia – CBPP* (Boumsoudé)
2. *Boumsoudé* (CBPP)	2. *Rinderpest* (Bodewu) – already eradicated
3. *Damal* (anthrax)	3. *Anthrax* (Damal)
4. *Gaouyel* (black quarter)	4. *Black quarter* (Gaouyel/Boutou)
5. *Kikoyel* (pasteurollosis)	5. *Pasteurollosis* (Kikoyel)

Table 2. Term-sorting task.

There is a large measure of agreement in the ordering of these five diseases, which therefore suggests that perception of epidemiological significance is extremely compatible. The only instance of incongruence is *Bodewu – peste bovine* ('rinderpest'). Although veterinary personnel mention it, for them its significance is more historical than contemporary. Rinderpest is believed to have been eradicated. Cattle farmers, however, hold a different view. There could be several explanations. Firstly, a disease can be said to have eradicated, even with an

80% success rate (which is adequate to guarantee generalised immunity). Secondly, from a cognitive linguistics standpoint, it would appear that for cattle farmers rinderpest is the cattle disease par excellence, or something of a prototype for assessing diseases. The hypothesis here is that this functional role and memories of the devastation caused by this disease inadvertently make real what is presumably a conceptual device for ordering and recollection.

6. Conclusion

We have used a term-driven approach to unlock some of the ontology of knowledge possessed by livestock raisers and veterinarians. The exercise has shown areas where there is disarticulation between the knowledge possessed by actors in the pastoral world and what the threats to communication and to public health are. It is obvious that for optimal communication to take place veterinary extension providers need to understand knowledge possessed by their client communities, and to negotiate between that knowledge and that which they seek to pass on. Just as pilots must come to terms and be at home with a great variety of accents of English (possibly as many accents as they are control towers), veterinary personnel, because they are also involved in safety-critical communication, need to gain familiarity with the emic knowledge which they seek to supplant, complement, reinforce or augment. We have shown that much of this knowledge resides in terms and in their predications.

References

Antia, B.E. 2000. *Terminology and Language Planning: an alternative framework of discourse and practice.* Amsterdam/Philadelphia: John Benjamins.

Antia, B.E. 2002. A Development Agenda Perspective to Language for Special Purposes. Plenary lecture at the 13th European LSP Symposium. In Koskela, M. / Laurén, C. / Nordman, M. / Pilke, N. (eds) *Porta Scientiae II. Lingua specialis. Proceedings of the 13th European LSP Symposium.* Vaasa: University of Vaasa Press, 429-452.

Antia, B.E. / Yassin, K. 2001. Coming to terms with the patient's terms on the patient's terms: terminology in public health. In Mayer, F. (ed.) *Language for Special Purposes: Perspectives for the New Millennium.* Vol. 2. Tübingen: Gunter Narr, 871-881.

Grey, D. 2003. What is knowledge management? Available: <http://km-forum.org/what_is.htm> [accessed: July 11, 2003].

Köhler-Rollefson I. / Bräunig, I. 1998. Anthropological veterinary medicine: the need for indigenizing the curriculum. Paper presented at the 9th AITVM Conference in Harare, 14th-18th September, 1998. Available: <http://www.vetwork.org.uk/ilse2.htm> [Accessed: July 15, 2003].

Vinay, J.P. / Darbelnet, J. 1995. *Comparative stylistics of French and English.* Amsterdam/Philadelphia: John Benjamins.

Appendices

Appendix 1. Names and descriptions of diseases, according to livestock raisers

Name of disease	*Symptoms*	*Cause, treatment, prevention*
1. Bodewou ou Petou	a. Bloody diarrhoea b. Eyes very red	(a) Break two (a white and a red nut of cola) into seven pieces; read verses (112) of the Holy Koran on the pieces of cola. Boil the pieces in a pot that has just been used in cooking the evening meal. Make the sick animal and the rest of the herd drink the mixture the following morning. (b) Pound millet that is two seasons old, and administer on sick animal and rest of the herd.
2. Kikoyel	e. Animal is weak f. Lags behind herd g. When touched animal jumps, falls then dies h. (Autopsy) Enlarged spleen	(a) Apply red hot metal to the joints of sick animal (b) boil the bark of a cailcedra plant, and give the animal to drink (c) very contagious disease
3. Mbalki	d. Appetite loss e. Inability to walk f. Refuses to drink until it dies	cannot be cured
4. Damal	d. Initial appetite loss e. Refusal to eat for 3 –4 or even more days preceding death f. (Autopsy) Rotten spleen	(a) No traditional therapy; (b) refer to Veterinary authorities (c) very dangerous
5. Mborou / Djobou	g. Excessive salivation through mouth and nostrils. h. Injury to the nail area i. Animal releases foul-smelling odour j. When severe, may lead to loss of tongue NB: Djobou has all of the above symptoms + ulcers around the neck	(a) apply honey on the surface of infected parts (b) disagreement as to whether there is a western cure, with five farmers answering in the negative (c) does not prevent reproduction

Appendix 2. Names and descriptions of diseases, according to veterinary doctors and assistants

Name of disease	*Symptoms*	*Cause, treatment, prevention*
1. Pasteurollosis	f. Weight loss g. Constant diarrhoea h. Oedema of the throat i. Whizzing respiration j. Animal may appear healthy on leaving the ranch in the morning, only for it to die in the evening	Tetracycline Prevention : pasto-vax® vaccine
2. Black quarter/black leg	c. Pitting oedema in the muscle groups (shoulder or thigh) d. When oedema is excised there is a foam surrounding dark spot	Antibiotics Prevention : symptovax vaccine
3. Anthrax	Non-pitting oedema which, on excision, looks dark.	Antibiotics
4. Contagious bovine pleuropneumonia	h. Lungs affected i. Pleura becomes thick j. 1 lung more affected than the other k. Difficult breathing l. Productive cough m. Catarrh n. Marked weight loss	Antibiotics Prevention : Perivax vaccine
5. Tuberculosis	a. Weight loss b. Cough c. Inflammation of the ganglions d. Diarrhoea	Treatment should not be attempted. Animal should be slaughtered as soon as possible and disposed off.
6. Trypanosomiasis	f. Constant fatigue g. Excessive lacrymation h. Loss of tail hair i. Weight loss and anaemia j. Loss of appetite	Trypanocidal drugs - Berenil - Trypamidium - Novidium Prevention : Trypanocidal drugs
7. Fascioliasis	d. Foul-smelling diarrhoea e. Weight loss f. Constant weakness	Fascioliasis drugs
8. Foot-and-mouth disease	e. Affects all oxen, but calves have highest number of deaths. f. Excessive salivation g. Pustules in the mouth h. Nail and interdigital injuries i. Ulcers on the udders	Self-resolving benign disease
9. Brucellose	a. Joint swelling (hygroma)	Antibiotics

GIUSEPPINA CORTESE

LSP: Multilingual deficiency, multicultural ambiguity*

1. Aims

The world of work, as well as linguistic heritage and recent sociolinguistic modifications in local environments, are increasingly demanding multilingual and multicultural competence. Instead, the educational sphere conservatively seems to emphasize a monolingual approach geared to ESP in a perspective of narrow practicism. Whilst paying lip service to "the importance of languages", those responsible for educational policy all too often stick to an "English only" attitude, supine to an opportunistic, utilitarian view of the predominance of English. The current negative phase in the economic cycle is often invoked to justify limited provisions for languages and, further, to restrict domain-specific English to the "service courses" of old. Such negligence hardly leaves room to foster and to apply current research into multicultural and pluritextual domain-specific literacies (Candlin/Hyland 1999; Bhatia 2002: 49-53) which are crucial to a knowledge-based society and, more specifically, to communities of practice which construct and disseminate knowledge through synergy with educational institutions and agencies.

This chapter explores both the sociocultural practices and the epistemic persuasions nourishing ambiguous stances on multiculturalism as well as deficiencies of choice, that is to say limited learning opportunities with regard to multilingual specialized discourse, focussing on local manifestations (in the region of Piedmont and the city of Turin) of a more general trend. The chapter claims that: a) language

*National research project MIUR 2002, prot. 2002104353.

teachers need to work on perceptions and representations of languages; b) the LSP profession needs to endorse a policy of domain-specific multilingualism; c) LSP scholars should promote appreciation of their concerns amongst the wider public.

2. History and histories: linguistic heritage and sociolinguistic repertoire

> For good or ill, at the end of the second millennium AD and the fifth full millennium since recorded history began, English is unique. No language has ever before been put to so many uses so massively by so many people in so many places – on every continent and in every sea; in the air and in space; in thought, speech, and writing; in print on paper and screen; in sound on tape and film; by radio, television, and telephone; and via electronic networks and multimedia. It is also used as mother tongue or other tongue – fluently, adequately, or haltingly; constantly, intermittently, or seldom; happily, unhappily, or ambivalently – by over a billion people. (McArthur 1998: 30)

A region never "speaks" a single history. Particularly in border areas, language policies reflect the vicissitudes of neighbouring nation states, their alliances or antagonisms, as well as changing circumstances/ideologies in domestic affairs. Current toponomastics in the Italian region of Piemonte, for example, shows a return to ancient French place names for which Fascist autarchy had imposed a transliteration into Italian: thus, Salabertano or Salice d'Ulzio are again officially named Salbertrand and Sauze d'Oulx. Parallel to this, there has been the spread and primacy recognition of the Italian standard, though the local Patois and its variants specific to valleys and villages along the alpine border have survived to a degree. On the French side, remarkable Italian migration since Word War II has produced enclaves of Italian usage which have not escaped the attention of sociolinguists.[1]

1 See for example Lucci/Millet (1992: 85) on the linguistic repertoire and linguistic attitude emerging from the names of shops in Grenoble: whereas the "banlieue blanche" has an exclusive preference for English, the "banlieue

The language map traced by official policy is constantly blurred by the flow of human beings following the basic human drive to seek a better station in life. Thus my great-great-grandfather, Guillaume Humbert, left his home town of Château Queyras, on the French side, and crossed the Alps to find a new niche for himself in the shade of the fortress which, beautifully restored, still towers over my grandfather's home village of Exilles. A skilled knife grinder, he found plenty of work with the bayonets of the army garrison populating the fort, and also developed some medical skills which, so the legend goes, were highly appreciated in the village. His descendants became firmly rooted in the new local and then in the new national identity, till post-world war scarcity led some to migrate back to France.

Such hints of family history would hardly deserve any attention; the fact that my mother's grandmother, known in her village as "Tante Pauline", had received her primary instruction in French and never quite mastered standard Italian is no special memory, for a large number of families native of the region share such linguistic precedents. Yet anecdotal evidence, dating back to the early 1970s, sets the picture in a different light. I distinctly remember a young English-language graduate trying to convince my mother that she was mispronouncing her own family name, for, surely, Humbert is to be pronounced /'h^mbə(:)t/. How off-putting, this rash denial of her own roots coming from another Piedmontese: was Nabokov's *Lolita* so popular as to make people forgetful of their own linguistic heritage? In terms of language consciousness, this episode was the "tip of the iceberg" – besides replacing French as the dominant second language, English was effacing linguistic memory from our regional identity.

American English was gaining popularity with young adults, who liked the language for ideological and symbolic reasons. Such reasons were, however, very different from those of our wartime

rouge" only rarely uses English and shows an orientation, though not an exclusive preference, for Italian.

predecessors[2]; North American literature, music and culture no longer represented the (elitist) nourishment they had been for the imagination of the Resistance heroes, supporting them in their effort to create "another country" of courage and honour. Whilst the city of Turin turned into one of the major poles of immigration from our rural South, American texts were nourishing contestation and sociocultural criticism of the very consumer society which was attracting southern labourers and white collar workers. Fluently spoken by relatively few[3] amongst the affluent and the progressively-minded, English was at the same time growing into a prerequisite for career advancement, with in-house language courses mushrooming in mid to top-level companies. It firmly gained the position of first foreign language in the school system and made its ingress in non-literary university curricula.

Nearly thirty years later, and with several generations of learners, teachers and teaching methods involved in this English-first policy, what are the tangible results? Most school leavers with five to eight years of English complain that their knowledge of the language is of little use in actual interaction. Parents observe with perplexity the swings of the pedagogical pendulum and voice their complaints: from too much to too little grammar. They encourage their offspring to pursue international certification and make substantial investments in study-abroad programmes.

Are people really motivated to use and learn the language? Do they perceive language-learning as a lifelong process? A most eloquent answer comes from an anonymous native speaker, who was recorded in the course of field research: "I am tired" – goes the revelation – "of teaching *people who have no desire to learn the language*" (my emphasis). Thus, explicit recognition of a need to learn the language often goes hand in hand with a deep-seated indifference to it:

2 Whilst North American literature started acquiring a "mythical" aura as the carrier of alternative values to the regime in the early 1940s, what needs to be stressed here is that the dominant pedagogical model in EFL, till very late in the century, remained "British" English.

3 An Italian-speaking US news commentator commemorating the late Senator Agnelli included amongst the reasons for his excellent relations with the US political and financial elites the fact that he was one of the few Italian industrial leaders who could speak English fluently.

awareness is not the same as willingness. The comment identifies ambivalent and resistant attitudes to language power, nourished, I suspect, by sociocultural representations associating mastery of the English language with social promotion and hierarchy[4] – a form of prejudice and a stereotyped belief which only the recent increase in transnational mobility has seriously started to erode. Fluency in English is a socially sensitive topic.

Thus, in spite of "early bilingualism" (initiation to English in primary/pre-primary education) and of whole colonies of native speakers (for the myth of the native-speaker dies hard) teaching learners from all walks of life, access to the language as a daily affair is still an opportunity and a competence reserved to the few. At the same time, in this city which used to be French-speaking, dwellers no longer seem to recognise French street names[5]: the culture loss is a *fait accompli*. Further, this divorce from past linguistic heritage seems paralleled, as regards young people, by a loss in their own "crib language" – the vocabulary of Italian adolescents being down to about half the expected size.[6]

The many histories of the region and of its main city, especially migration history but also industrial history, labour history and intellectual history, chart the course of a complex linguistic heritage and changing sociolinguistic repertoire. The context now appears to be largely monoglot in the sense that the majority are actually "native" (though not "uncontaminated") speakers of Italian sociolects, with

4 "The expansion of English has brought about a sociologically profiled gradient of social presence and exclusion", writes Duszak (2002a: 17), who also notes, and her point is indeed crucial, that the gap between people's assumptions about their knowledge of the language and their actual language skills needs investigating (2002a: 228). It is worthwhile noting that, according to recent research at the University of Turin, learners may underestimate their own EFL competence (Solly 2003).

5 In his regular column on *La Stampa,* well-known specialist in English world literatures Gorlier has often reported on this cultural loss; for example (see for example Gorlier 2002), he reports local speakers using the English tonic stress for such historically significant names as Cavour.

6 For recent comments by psychologists and linguists concerning Italian adolescents within this widely attested, transnational trend in the language of youth, see *La Stampa*, 14 Jan. 2003: 15.

northern Italian prestige features tinged by more or less marked traits from the local as well as various other dialects.[7] As argued above, there is evidence of language oblivion as regards French, with a clear predominance of English as a foreign language. Further, like many other European metropolitan areas, Turin is now coping with a highly diversified non-EU immigrant population: 32% of the newborn in 2002 had a "multiethnic ribbon" (Minucci 2003), with one or both parents of a foreign nationality.

In terms of their linguistic repertoire, the fragile newcomers speaking alien idioms, from eastern European to Chinese, South American and African tongues, are truly multilingual. Forming ethnically cohesive networks and neighbourhoods, they may practise more than one native language and often extend the repertoire through marriage with other foreign nationals. Their shop-windows, fashion, produce and "culture scripts" (Wierzbicka 1998) are revitalising our ethnolinguistic urban landscape (Landry/Bourhis 1997) as much as identifying specific spaces of marginalisation: all too often, the perverse effects of cultural impermeability make *this* multilingualism into a barrier and a curse.[8] Whilst educationalists, social workers and the police try to implement local programmes for the negotiation of mutual fears and mutual boundaries into feelings of solidarity, full citizenship will eventually involve heavy curtailment of this multilingual repertoire in the complex transformation of social identities.

7 For an accurate, statistically documented sociolinguistic appraisal of dialects – their current revival, positive perception and re-positioning in the local repertoire of Italian speakers, with code-switching and code-mixing phenomena occurring now in all regions and in ordinary conversation – see Berruto 2001; for the "quaint" usage of dialect as part of a fashionable revisiting of "the old ways", see Telmon 2002 on the catering business (restaurant names reveal both a retrieval of dialects and a taste for plurilingualism).

8 For a discussion of hate speech and a view of multiculturalism as a coverup for the fear of a hybrid society, see Fish 1997.

3. EFL: heyday and beyond

The multilingual situation amongst the old and new disenfranchised, in their native lands as well as in their refugee contexts, demands language policies that will not force them into a linguistic and cultural no man's land, alien to their own culture.[9] Only a fine-tuned agenda of intercultural dialogue can avoid these risks, and if such dialogue is diversified instead of being channelled exclusively through the major international language, a wider range of participants will become involved and take responsibility: would the petitions from Italy that saved Safya from death by lapidation in Nigeria have been so successful if the texts had been in English?

Moreover, the spread of English throughout the world has led to a backlash on the language itself, increasingly manipulated by different indigenous identities. An advertising campaign in Italy during the 2002 Christmas season, for example, clearly exploited linguistic "domestication" in a striking hybrid. The phonemes of famous Christmas carols had been turned into sequences of Italian morphemes, reproducing the sounds of English captured by an Italian ear, for example

(1) GINGOL BEL
GINGOL BEL
GINGOL OL DE UEI[10]

Such cross-cultural graphics are the creative side of a process which more often consists of an ambiguous misappropriation of English especially by the media, as in the job advert below (Figure 1):

9 On language programmes in developing countries that will valorise the mother tongue and on other key issues of multilingualism that will be only marginally mentioned in this paper, such as language maintenance within migrant communities and multilingualism in the construction of a "European public sphere", see contributions in the *International Journal of Bilingual Education and of Bilingualism* 2002, 5/6.

10 More recently, a Valentine poster by the same jewel factory: AI LOVIU BEIBI. Notice that Happy Valentine cards and Valentine celebrations are less popular in Italy than in anglophone cultures.

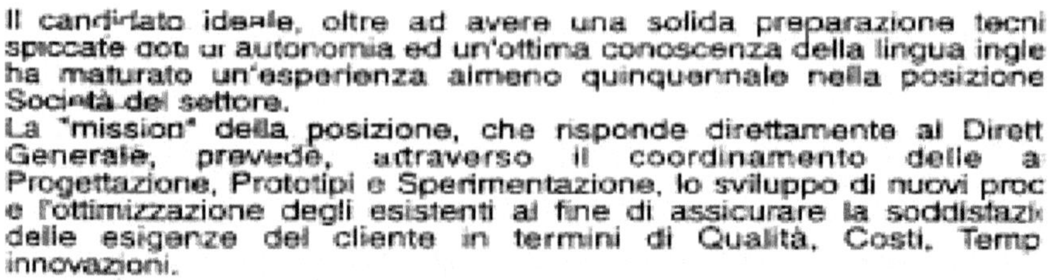

Il candidato ideale, oltre ad avere una solida preparazione tecni
spiccate doti di autonomia ed un'ottima conoscenza della lingua ingle
ha maturato un'esperienza almeno quinquennale nella posizione
Società del settore.
La "mission" della posizione, che risponde direttamente al Dirett
Generale, prevede, attraverso il coordinamento delle a
Progettazione, Prototipi e Sperimentazione, lo sviluppo di nuovi proc
e l'ottimizzazione degli esistenti al fine di assicurare la soddisfazi
delle esigenze del cliente in termini di Qualità, Costi, Temp
innovazioni.

Figure 1. Source: *La Stampa*, February 2002.

Italian job advertising makes lavish use of English to identify work positions (*manager* and so on), so the reading public is familiar with such loanwords (Duszak 2002b also stresses this with regard to the Polish media). However, one may wonder here what readers will make of *La "mission" della posizione.* The "false friend" *position* is a rather bizarre instantiation of the Italian *posizione,* which usually applies to a secure or settled job / successful career and consequent good station in life (*una buona posizione*)[11] and certainly sounds odd in the context of job descriptions. Even more awkward is the occurrence of "*mission",* which in English advertising or job announcements usually refers to company ethics and pro-social commitment (see the last two lines in Figure 2 below). But *mission* is now frequently used in Italian in-house language (or rather, the jargon of *linguaggio aziendale*) to mean the specific tasks/competencies involved in a job.

11 For an authoritative literary source see for example C. Levi, *Cristo si è fermato a Eboli*: "Il ragazzo voleva entrare ora al corso per sottufficiale dei carabinieri, e sarebbe partito tra poco. Non sognava che la divisa. Non era questo l'avvenire che il padre aveva sperato per lui, ma era tuttavia *una buona posizione*" (Torino: Einaudi, 53, my emphasis).

onveniently located near the Metro. Qualified candidates should send
ı resume outlining their employment history with salary requirements
ınd a cover letter describing their superior ability to sell over the
elephone and provide examples of successful sales strategies.

The Washington Post

Attn: Personnel/TSR/AB
1150 15th Street, NW
Washington, DC 20071

We are committed to diversity in the workplace and promote a drug-free environment.

Figure 2. Source. *The Washington Post,* August 1998.

Such deviance from the standard collocation in the English genre pattern, like other distorted echoes and citations, seems to be common currency in the Italian media and may well be an embodiment of the advertiser's power, as in this case, to filter out potential applicants who are unfamiliar with the current business language. These loanwords, then, are more than manifestations of an "anglomanie paresseuse et aveugle" (Galisson 2002: 502); they are socially loaded forms of linguistic manipulation, which discursively construct new lines of social discrimination (see Duszak 2002a: 6 on similar strategies in Polish media).

The Italian government, even, is producing major examples of this "outgroup" rejection strategy. Recent guidelines concerning research in science and technology include statements like the following,

(2) impiego di *venture capital* per *spin-off* della ricerca e di capitale di rischio per lo *start-up* di nuove imprese

as well as numerous other English noun phrases or premodifiers (*knowledge intensive*, *knowledge based*, *turn over*, *reverse market)* freely imported into the Italian register of science and technology.[12] One is tempted to say that English works here to don an image of competitive efficiency to research marketing policies which carbon copy “international” standards and procedures. This linguistic and textual “sell-out” to Anglocentric models in important sectors such as business, the print media and the production of knowledge smacks of the hegemonic “center”-“periphery” relationships eloquently discussed in Canagarajah’s (2002) study of geopolitical inequalities – a study which is of much interest to my present topic, particularly its analysis of ethnocentric mystification and silencing of ways of producing and textualizing domain-specific knowledge outside predominant canons.[13]

This is not to predict a “decay” of Italian, nor a “balkanisation” of English. It seems that Italian firms have started to realise that the promotion of their products draws an advantage from the parallel promotion of a strong sense of identity carried through language, so a reduction of this anglicising trend is likely to occur. As for English, the very history of the USA mainstream is a massive example of one culture being “done” differently by various groups. Rather, it is interesting to note how the variegated geography of EFL/ESL contexts increasingly shows a drop in competence standards everywhere, often coupled with a more or less subterranean resistance to the language. This would seem an expected outcome in postcolonial situations, or in contexts where the language may dramatically symbolize the very opportunities which are denied to the local populations. However, one does not need to travel such cultural distances to perceive the problem; the anonymous EFL teacher quoted in part 2 above shows how, even in western countries, the higher the compulsion the lower the

12 From “Linee guida per la politica scientifica e tecnologica del governo”, available on the site of the Ministero dell’Istruzione, dell’Università e della Ricerca. Quoted in G. Autino, “La dimensione internazionale del discorso scientifico in lingua inglese: la questione dell’egemonia linguistica”. Tesi di laurea, supervisor G. Cortese. Università di Torino, academic year 2003.

13 See also Canagarajah (2001: 117) on the need for new approaches to the pedagogy of ESL academic writing, which will help language-minority students “negotiate a place for for their local discourse conventions, intellectual traditions, cultural practices and the vernacular”.

disposition to learn the language, especially as regards mature learners with an instrumental motivation. The concern in language pedagogy to differentiate objectives and approaches, well-exemplified in the volume edited by Candlin/Mercer (2001), shows how the linguistic profession has become deeply aware of the need for practitioners to place themselves on the same contextual wavelength as their learners and to negotiate methodologies in terms of local representations of the language.

Whilst English celebrates its heyday as the primary international language, on the European continent the recognition is spreading that empathy and mutual cognitive environments are built on more secure foundations when "intercomprehension" across the respective languages is possible: young graduates initiating their work experience within mobility schemes; students leaving the home cocoon and discovering different lifestyles through Socrates exchanges; travellers growing aware that tourism means more than a "cultural gaze"; the sick pursuing advanced care protocols in highly specialised institutions abroad – all these are newcomers to the value of plurilingualism.

At the start of the new millennium, the citizens of Europe seem to be perceiving a public space which is no longer a distant entity in the hands of the "Eurocrats" but rather an arena where individuals are responsible actors in the definition of a new balance between unity and heterogeneity[14]. This new balance requires equitable recognition of needs and opportunities, for which expanding intercultural competences are a prerequisite. Whilst regional sociolinguistic landscapes are being incisively modified by migration and immigration, regional identities are reworking cultural schemata, particularly the perception of multilingual/multicultural social groups, hopefully toward the defeat of xenophobia and anti-foreigner discourse. At the same time, ethnocentric and linguistically self-defeatist prejudice viewing the appropriation of foreign languages as something meant only for the upwardly mobile elites is another attitude that is beginning to change.

Such ambiguities in folk ideologies of multilingualism/ multiculturalism identify relevant dimensions on the agenda of the linguis-

14 For a discussion of an "active" European identity and cultural/linguistic pluralism, see Murphy-Lejeune/Zarate (2003).

tic profession,[15] indicating that important work needs to be done on representations of languages, on "impression management"[16] concerning national/ethnic/racial affiliation – in one word, the ineliminable component of social identity which Duszak (2002a) calls "Othering" – and on their implications in terms of social distance.[17]

4. Tertiary education: plurilingual or anti-languages?

Thus, civil society is spontaneously – though not quite straightforwardly – moving towards an appreciation of multilingual practices. Expert guidelines issued by the Council of Europe and investing all stakeholders, from Ministries of Education to families, are disseminating the notion that acquisition of "the other" second language is a timely and necessary educational bonus. Clearly then, for job market entrants to be enabled to face the world of work with plurilingual competences, it is crucial that tertiary education address the issue.

Does the question of providing opportunities to cope with academic and professional demands in more than one language appear to be a substantial concern for academic institutions? The current scenario looks disheartening. Although official reports, Ministry guidelines and the grey literature issuing from international agreements all stress "the importance of foreign languages", the facts show a dramatic setback. In Italy the new university reform, carrying an aura of managerial practicism, seems to be producing a threefold regression: first, a growing intolerance for LSPs which are seen as "stealing" space from the core academic or professional subjects that qualify the specificities of curricula; secondly, a return to the "English-only" policy, mostly as a face-saving operation to show that at least one foreign language is offered; thirdly, a revival of the notion of ESP as a "ser-

15 On language ideologies and language myths, see Milroy 2000.
16 On "impression management" and the fear of conveying racist sentiments, see Condor 2000.
17 Early plurilingual education is key to these issues (Cortese 2003).

vice" to be provided with minimum expenditure of human and financial resources.

The main reservations concerning LSP seem to be: a) there has been a decline in the native language competences, therefore teaching more than one foreign language may be unrealistic; some provision should be made instead for improvement in the standards of the national language, especially as regards writing skills; b) outsourcing for minimal language competence can be a more efficient, practical and above all cheaper way to "solve the problem"; c) credits "spent" on language study reduce or limit the specific formative content of the degree curriculum.

Following this agenda, and giving it further credibility on the assumption that "languages are expensive" as teaching may require laboratory equipment besides posts and salaries, an "English only" policy is often pursued, using the left-over credits from the assignment of degree credits to the various disciplines, for example two credits, for this ESP "course". In numerous cases, one lecturer is facing hundreds of students with heterogeneous levels of language competence – situations invariably justified by a scarcity of funds. Finally, international certification is turning into a formidable excuse (Solly 2003) to do without LSP courses: an engineering student with PET is considered to have sufficient "languages" to face the profession! Once again, lip service has come to mask an ideology effacing cultural and linguistic pluralism as an objective in higher education.

Obviously there are exceptions to this situation, but in the main the "renovated" academic setup has involved a negative turn for languages in special domains. This is both the manifestation and the consequence of a political disequilibrium in the decision-making arenas, where linguists are all too often a powerless minority.

We, as a professional community of linguists, need to renegotiate our *Lebensraum* in our local sphere of action, and to argue for a valorisation of language education in specific domains. Experience suggests that such a conspicuous lack of fit between declarations of intention at policy level and actual scarcity at implementation level cannot be corrected by individual negotiation – indeed it may, but at a formidable cost in terms of individual energy and emotional investment. It is therefore high time for the profession to take a stand and to produce authoritative policy statements to be disseminated to decision-makers, from Rectors' Conferences to Faculty Deans, so as to shake up the current lack of disposition to hear, when it comes to local realisation of national and international directives on plurilingual education.

5. Academic language planning and "epistemic oligarchies"

Who are, then, the potential addressees of an effective LSP implementation policy? Academic and research institutions in general have developed de-territorialised epistemic communities characterised by subgroupings. These "schools of thought" nourishing different theoretical/methodological persuasions are now increasingly networked, with a remarkable degree of knowledge transfer through researcher mobility that is no longer predominantly bound to English-speaking contexts; the scientific community is aware of the increase of human and social capital connected with the accumulation of experiences of work and life in *different* countries.

Whilst transnational, plurilingual activity is more and more ingrained in the actual practices of scientific communities, allocation of space for language study in higher education institutions is a different story altogether and is bound to local administration. From the interlocking of knowledges with the corporate world sponsoring research, and from local power relations within the institutions, new "epistemic oligarchies"[18] are emerging locally and deploying the mundane strategies which affect, and are affected by, economic policy in the increasing characterization of education as a marketplace. In spite of the fact that a very large share of the new start-ups as well as large corporations are concerned with communications, these local oligarchies, I believe, prefer to ignore the principal dimension of *human* communication, that is to say multilingualism. It is these oligarchies, then, that

18 Frankly, I cannot remember whether this is a label I myself devised, or whether it comes from my intertext.

need to shake off what seems to be an ambiguous[19] and short-sighted attitude on multiculturalism/plurilingualism within the academy and the professions. They are the key interlocutors for linguists, since they are the ones who wield the power to curtail and deviate the financial flows from the Ministrics or central Administrations: whilst governments decide to support language-learning / teaching, locally these power structures may well decide to prioritise outsourcing instead of enabling the university to implement diversification of language learning.

When the ascendancy of English as *the* international language became an obvious process, many a voice was raised[20] to warn that anglicisation would involve linguistic loss by foreignising great national traditions of scientific writing. Lexical, syntactic and rhetorical assimilation of English patterns would equally involve – indeed, both processes were considered to be well underway – increasingly anglicised ways of *doing* science. The impending risk was an impoverishment of cultural pluralism. Such alarms proved perhaps excessive, at least as regards Mediterranean Europe, for its scientists do not appear to be prone to "submit" to the English language (Carrio 2002) or too interested in seeking excellence in its use; rather, it would seem that they ambiguously stick to the old preconception equating language use in specific domains with a "toolbox" of specific terminology (Nuccorini 2002).

19 The development of projects such as *Tuning* is highly significant in this respect. This European inter-institutional academic programme is pursuing an open debate on issues of quality, effectiveness and *transparency in the educational structures* (Gonzalez Ferreras/Wagenaar 2003, my emphasis).

20 Such concerns were expressed by scientists from different fields during a panel on the question of ESP/EAP translation from/into Italian (Cortese 1996) and are very well argued by the late mathematician De Giorgi in an interview discussed in Cortese (1999). For a more recent and thoroughly linguistic treatment, see Laurén, Myking/Picht (2002) for their discussion of the dynamics of domain loss / renouncement / conquest and reconquest / expansion / cultivation, in connection with anglifying tendencies and language planning policies. See Laurén (2002), for a discussion of linguistic hegemony in connection with the risk of truncated identities. For the case of the Norwegian oil industrry, a relevant instance of language planning in connection with cultural identity, see Sœbøe (1997), Rangnes (1997), Laurén (2002).

Now, it is precisely this persuasion which is guiding the myopic policies on LSP at tertiary level described above. According to this view, language is the linear sequencing of discrete units; a "specialist language" is characterised by specialised vocabulary; special vocabulary is the heart of the "vehicular" role of languages in special domains. Thus goes the syllogism centred on the idea that language is a mere container – "a conceptual *other*, which linguists, on the contrary, argue can legitimately be seen in *the first place* as a *linguistic construction*" (Cortese 2002: 369). Nothing has done more damage to LSP pedagogy and caused so much misunderstanding about language education in specific disciplines and professions than this notion of language as mere vehicle.[21] It is easy to see how, within this reductive equation of LSP with special lexicon, two credits are deemed to be enough for a language course; it is just as easy to see how, in conservative quarters, testing is again predominantly seen to consist of word-for-word translation (Cortese 2002: 371).

We are then entitled to speak of a deficiency in the academic interpretation of multilingualism: at the local policy level, provision of a diversified language pedagogy is increasingly seen as unnecessary; at the level of language awareness, ignorance of the communicative focus of language pedagogy and research leads to a commodity view of languages, as a mere utility grafted on a specific body of learning. The paradox is clear when one considers the increasing plurilingual experience both in society at large and in the epistemic communities themselves: hence "epistemic oligarchies", inasmuch as they fulfil the role of local gatekeepers, are deploying a deliberate avoidance strategy. The plurilingual/pluritextual nature of our knowledge-based economy is simply left alone: let the young researchers or job-market entrants cope on their own. If they do not possess the language competences to cope, there is always some handy scapegoat: teachers, teaching methods, lack of adequate technology and so on.

21 Recent CLIL experimentation also seems to put a premium on, or to highlight, students' gratification in the 'incidental' acquisition of specialised lexicon.

6. Conclusions

What we need to set out to do, then, is negotiate the common ground with the professions which Bhatia (2002: 41) finds lacking. Show the gatekeepers how linguistic education consists above all in the development of a culture of texts. Show how academics and professionnals constantly engage in the production and consumption of documents pivoting on different genres and text-types, addressing different interlocutors for different purposes. Show how interpretive and critical skills are the very foundation of LSP, whose formative role makes the "special vocabulary" view of language appear to be a naïve, "efficient" but ultimately ineffective reduction of LSP research and pedagogy: "*la dérive instrumentaliste actuelle, qui fait de certains enseignants les monteurs (pressés) d'une langue rudimentaire, pratico-pratique, à usage strictement professionnel*" (Galisson 2002: 498, my emphasis).

Here, Fairclough's (2001: 234) emphasis on the centrality of discourse in the constructs of "knowledge economy" and "knowledge society" is crucial:

> Of course knowledges (science, technology) have long been significant factors in economic and social change, but what is being pointed to is a dramatic increase in their significance. The relevance of these ideas here is that "knowledge-driven" amounts to "discourse-driven": knowledges are generated and circulated as discourses, and the process through which discourses become operationalized in economies and societies is precisely the dialectics of discourse.

Such dialectics involves the projections of "possible worlds" as well as materialization of discourses into actual work tools and into discoursal genres which may or may not be eventually "owned" by those who apply the related speech styles, but certainly entail a positioning of subjects, a dialectic of identity (Fairclough 2001: 235-36). In this sense, even the most technical discursive formation and communicative genre involves semiotic activity – reflective practices, values and awareness. It involves, therefore, culture-bound phenomena and world-views which, when given a voice, indeed make the knowledge-based economy/society mean much more than the western economy and the western way of knowing prevalently textualized in NS-NNS English.

It needs to be persuasively argued that the literacy activities and genres within epistemic communities are diverse, and also differentiated from those characterising communication in the respective work-sites/professional arenas. A pluralist view of the author function, of such crucial factors as identity and positioning in writing practices, and awareness of the complementarity of literacy with spoken communication, needs to be conveyed. As shown by Riley (2002), this "culture of texts" in special domains proceeds from the epistemological framework of a knowledge-based society wherein written/spoken/multimedia communication evolves from shared knowledge: but knowledge is differently constructed, valued and exercised in discourses by academics, professionals, specializing apprentices, industrial leaders, policy-makers, trade unionists and other social actors.

At the same time, key aspects of writing as social action, such as the imbrication of the social and the epistemological in the actual texture of spoken and written communication, need highlighting in order to show that social practices are differently perceived and conveyed in different cultural systems, so that it is profitable for today's highly interconnected, transnational firms to acquire a consciousness of "languaging" skills extending to a plurality of texts in more than one foreign language and literate tradition.

The issue is no longer, or is not simply that the hegemony of English needs to be contained, but rather that there is much to be gained from a culturally pluralistic perspective obtained by tapping knowledge resources and discourse traditions in their own linguistic embodiments.

Arguing for genuine and widespread plurilingualism in LSP is no quixotic defence of languages against academic authority. There are advantages to be gained in plurilingualism: for a less opportunistic approach to English as a foreign language; for the re-appropriation of the local multicultural heritage and, last but not least, for a re-appropriation of fine-tuned literacy in the "crib language". Within the framework of "universalistic contextualism" so well illustrated by

Martinelli (2002), intercultural dialogue through multilingual communication is a fundamental prerequisite for self-reflexivity, the critical self-awareness of local identities which provides the cornerstone for overcoming particularised behaviours and for the diffusion of equity in socioeconomic relations. These goals should be priorities in tertiary education everywhere – in universities as well as other formative agencies which make up systems of learning, synergistically producing and disseminating knowledge.

It is no coincidence that the Turin School of Engineering, which has a long-standing tradition of excellence also outside national boundaries, recently published guidelines for dissertation writing. This reveals the degree of concern within the profession about the decline of writing standards in the national language. However, to revive those standards it is not sufficient to recommend that the language of engineering documents bear no frills. The blueprint would have been much more effective if linguists had been involved, maybe with a view to providing a comparison of text types across a number of languages which are of primary importance in terms of our School of Engineering's strategic collocation in Europe and in the Alpine ecosystem. Here, to return to my familiar context of Piedmont in which I have grounded my discussion, is a "rhetorical affordance" gone lost; discursive investigation of the genres used in engineering (besides the well-researched "engineering report") across different institutions and their respective languages would usefully promote intercultural attitudes and literate skills much needed by engineers who are out to face the requirements of transnational professional practice.

I have outlined, with particular reference to the region I know best in sociolinguistic terms, a two-tiered multilingual situation – one level referring to the new configuration of ethnolinguistic space due to migration, and one referring to the intensifying transnational mechanisms of the knowledge-based economy. Both are ridden by ambiguities and misrepresentations which the linguistic profession is called upon to investigate and to make manifest to decision makers for a viable policy of multilingualism. As regards the future of LSP, a strong commitment to the formative value of pluritextuality is needed. Academic and corporate gatekeepers should be led to understand that the responsible exercise of the professions today is geared to the capacity to use and to produce a plurality of text types in more traditions of writing. The present provision of plurilingual services in educational institutions and in the world of work presents crucial deficiencies in this respect.

Besides intensifying work on "impression management" concerning multilingualism, the LSP community needs to elaborate a forceful statement endorsing language diversification, especially in higher education and in the publishing industry, spelling out very clearly that the construction and dissemination of knowledge is a discursive enterprise with a multilingual/multiliterate communicative focus and pluritextual realisations.

To conclude, I would again like to recall Bhatia's claim for "more meaningful and collaborative initiatives to integrate LSP and professional practice in what might be considered a shared vision" (Bhatia 2002: 41). This gap with the extra-mural world can also be filled, in my view, by efforts to "popularise" the specialist knowledge of the linguistic profession, following the example of the natural scientists. Exhibitions and events such as "science parks" for the lay public – using media, cinema, theatre and public shows *besides* public lectures – are successfully spreading a positive approach, and consequently substantial support, for research in contemporary science:

> It is necessary for public opinion and politicians alike to develop an understanding not only of the facts, but of the methods in science. Public communication by scientists is turning into one of the most relevant factors of democracy in what has been called "the society of knowledge". (Fasolo 2003; my translation)

Why not promote communication between LSP scholars and the general public? Outside and beyond the "ivory tower" of cultural institutions, the knowledge-based economy needs to understand in order to negotiate: to promote a pluralist culture and a critical pedagogy of texts, and to find support for it, we also need to make it more widely appealing.

References

Andersen, Ø. 1997. Textual Variation in A Professional Setting. In Lassen, I. (ed.), 59-66.

Berruto, G. 2001. Parlare dialetto in Italia alle soglie del Duemila. In Beccaria, G.L. / Marello, C. (eds) *Dalla parola al testo. Scritti per Bice Mortara Garavelli.* Alessandria, Edizioni dell'Orso, 33-49.

Bhatia, V. 2002. LSP and Professional Practice: Negotiating Disciplinary Conflicts. In Gotti, M. / Heller, D. / Dossena, M. (eds) *Conflict and Negotiation in Specialized Texts*. Bern: Peter Lang, 41-57.

Canagarajah, A. S. 2001. Addressing Issues of Power and Difference in ESL Academic Writing. In Flowerdew, J. / Peacock, M. (eds) *Research Perspectives on English for Academic Purposes.* Cambridge: Cambridge University Press, 117-131.

Canagarajah, A. S. 2002. *A Geopolitics of Academic Writing*. Pittsburgh, Pa.: University of Pittsburgh Press.

Candlin, C.N. / Hyland, K. (eds) 1999. *Writing: Texts, Processes and Practices*. London: Longman.

Candlin, C.N. / Mercer, N. (eds) 2001. *English Language Teaching in Its Social Context. A Reader*. London and New York: Routledge, in association with Macquarie University and the Open University.

Carrio, M.L. 2002. The Use of Phrasal Verbs by Native and Non-Native Writers in Technical Articles. In Cortese, G. / Riley, P. (eds), 233-246.

Condor, S. 2000. Pride and Prejudice: identity management in English people's talk about "this country". *Discourse & Society*, 11/2, 175-205.

Cortese, G. (ed.) 1996. *Tradurre i linguaggi settoriali*. Torino: Edizioni Libreria Cortina.

Cortese, G. 1999. Translating Science Texts: Issues of Representation and identity. *Parallèles*, Université de Genève, 21, 7-32.

Cortese, G. 2002. "My Doxy" is not "Your Doxy": Doing Corpus Linguistics as Collaborative Design. In Cortese, G. / Riley, P. (eds), 367-414.

Cortese, G. 2003. "The shipment kind salutes". 'Marry Christmas!' Aspects de l'acquisition du plurilinguisme à l'écrit», *Le Français dans le Monde*. Numéro Spécial: Recherches et Applications, *Vers une compétence plurilingue*. Paris: CLE International, 67-85.

Cortese, G. / Riley, P. (eds) 2002. *Domain-specific English. Textual Practices across Communities and Classrooms*. Bern: Peter Lang.

Duszak, A. 2002a. Us and Others: An Introduction. In Duszak, A. (ed.) *Us and Others. Social Identities across Languages, Discourses and Cultures*. Amsterdam/Philadelphia: John Benjamins, 1-28.

Duszak, A. 2002b. Words and Social Identities. In Duszak, A. (ed.), 213-231.

Fairclough, N. 2001. The Dialectics of Discourse. In Cortese, G. / Hymes, D. (eds) *"Languaging" in and across Human Groups. Perspectives on Difference and Asymmetry. Textus. English Studies in Italy* XIV/2, 231-242.

Fasolo, A. 2003. "E" la settimana del cervello. *La Stampa, Tutto Scienze e tecnologia*, 5 march.

Fish, S. 1997. Boutique Multiculturalism, or Why Liberals Are Incapable of Thinking About Hate Speech. *Critical Inquiry* 23, 378-505.

Galisson, R. 2002. Didactologie: de l'éducation aux langues-cultures à l'éducation par les langues-cultures. *éla. Etudes de linguistique appliquée* 128, 497-510.

Gonzalez Ferreras, J. / Wagenaar, R. 2003. Tuning educational structures in Europe: opportunities, possibilities and obstacles, paper to be published in the Conference Proceedings *Working on the European Dimension of Quality*. Circulated by e-mail.

Gorlier, C. 2002. Dimenticare il francese. *La Stampa*, 8 January, 22.

Landry, R / Bourhis, R.Y. 1997. Linguistic Landscape and Ethnolinguistic Vitality. An Empirical Study. *Journal of Language and Social Psychology* 16/1, 23-49.

Lassen, I. (ed.) 1997. *Interactional Perspectives on LSP, Language and Cultural Contact* 27. Aalborg:Aalborg University Press.
Laurén, C. 2002. The Conflict between national languages and English as the language of arts and sciences. In Cortese, G. / Riley, P. (eds), 87-97.
Laurén, C. / Myking, J. / Picht, H. 2002. Language and domains: a proposal for a domain dynamics taxonomy. *LSP & Professional Communication* 2/2, 23-29.
Lucci V. / Millet, A. 1992. Les noms des magasins ont-ils un sens? *Lidil*, Décembre, 63-112.
Martinelli, A. 2002. Markets, Governments, Communities and Global Governance. Presidential Address, ISA, XV Congress, Brisbane. *International Sociology* 18, 2.
McArthur, T. 1998. *The English Languages*. Cambridge: Cambridge University Press.
Milroy, L. 2000. Two nations divided by the same language: contrasting language ideologies in Britain and the United States. Plenary paper, ESSE 2000 Conference, Helsinki, August 27th.
Minucci, E. 2003. Il nuovo "baby-boom" viene da lontano. *La Stampa*, 5 January, 33.
Murphy-Lejeune, E. / Zarate, G. 2003., L'acteur social pluriculturel: évolution politique, positions didactiques. *Le Français dans le Monde*. Numéro Spécial: Recherches et Applications, *Vers une compétence plurilingue*. Paris: CLE International, 32-46.
Nuccorini, S. 2002. The Role of Dictionaries in Non-native Academic Writing. In Cortese, G. / Riley, P. (eds), 207-231.
Rangnes, O.K. 1997. The Mother Tongue as a Threat To Professional Identity: Norwegian Oil Workers' Attitudes to Norwegian Oil Terminology. In Lassen, I. (ed.), 52-58.
Riley, P. 2002. Epistemic Communities: The Social Knowledge System, Discourse and Identity. In Cortese, G. / Riley, P. (eds), 41-64.
Sœbøe, R. 1997. Language Use, Language Planning and Cultural Identities. A Sociological Analysis. In Lassen, I. (ed.), 42-51.
Solly, M. 2003. *English Language Learning in Domain-specific Contexts: A Case Study*. Torino: Edizioni Libreria Cortina.

Telmon, T. 2002. Regresso culturale e recupero modaiolo dei dialetti locali del Piemonte. Una lettura sociolinguistica dell'onomastica della ristorazione. In Silvestri, D. / Marra, A. / Pinto I. (eds) *Saperi e sapori mediterranei. La cultura dell'alimentazione e i suoi riflessi linguistici* II. Napoli: Università degli Studi di Napoli "L'Orientale", 335-350.

Wierzbicka, A. 1998. German "cultural scripts": public signs as a key to social attitudes and cultural values. *Discourse and Society* 9/2, 241-82.

MARTA CHROMÁ

A Czech-English law dictionary with explanations: A conceptual approach to dictionary-making

1. Introduction

Building specialised bilingual dictionaries has always been intricate and subtle work; while usually produced by linguists (and only exceptionally by domain experts) they are intended to serve multiple user groups such as specialists in and students of the respective subject area, translation and interpretation practitioners and students, and other potential users of varying subject-areas, linguistic backgrounds and experience. A specialised bilingual dictionary should be the outcome of extensive comparative research and using such methods as are applicable in specialist-language lexicography and terminography[1].

Modern jurisprudence in the developed world has interlinked with, and been based on, social sciences (Knapp 1995: 4-5); therefore law always depends on the political environment of the society to which it applies. Unlike other social sciences, law is a normative discipline formulating rules binding on members of the respective society. So that they are observed by the members of this society, the rules should be written in a language which allows for a uniform interpretation within that society. Each system of law, as well as the language through which the law is communicated to those on whom it is binding, is determined by, and often limited to, the history, traditions and culture of the society in question. A bilingual law dictionary which covers two different languages (such as Czech and English in our

1 Surprisingly, the term *terminography* has not yet been included in the Oxford English Dictionary, CD-ROM, [3]2002.

case) and two different legal systems (i.e. Anglo-American law based on common law and continental law based on Roman law) should facilitate adequate "cross-understanding" and reasonable "cross-interpretation" of legal rules existing within the two different social contexts[2].

The definition of the user group is widely recognized as one of the most influential factors at the pre-lexicographical stage (Atkins 1993: 12). It may be admitted, however, that potential users of the dictionary would constitute a group diverse in motivation, and heterogeneous in the aggregate of their previous experience in language and law.

The primary objective of the Czech-English Law Dictionary has been to assist those who deal with Czech legal texts when trying to understand and transfer them into (legal) English. Potential users can be generally subdivided into two major sets of individuals: those primarily educated as linguists and usually without any legal background (primarily translators and interpreters, but also Czech teachers of legal English); and graduates of or students at law schools, usually lacking formal linguistic education. In addition there are numerous dictionary users who are neither linguists nor lawyers, such as journalists. For such users, their educational background may be unrelated to either law or the English language but their professional careers have brought them into contact with a field relating to and dealing with law.

The most common reason for a Czech lawyer to consult the Dictionary would be his or her need to explain relevant details of Czech law to a client or colleague from another country who speaks English. Teachers of legal English would use the Dictionary with the same motivation (i.e. explaining Czech law), but to make such explanation to a different audience (students of law). Translators and interpreters would use the Dictionary when translating a Czech legal text into English, trying to be as precise and accurate in their communica-

2 See research carried out by the Canadian Department of Justice concentrating on the intersystemic transposition of common law terms into civil law terminology within one language–English–and one country. The results are available at <http://canada.justice.gc.ca/en/ps/bj/harm/liste.html> as *Bijural Terminology Records*.

tion as possible. Journalists may search for specific information when they need to understand particular legal facts and comment on them. Whichever subgroup a potential user of the Dictionary belongs to, he or she will look for more than mere law taxonomies. Specific contexts of individual branches of law, larger syntactical units, explanations of polysemic (or polysemous) terms and concepts, and so on, are useful tools in assisting their orientation in the language of law.

Therefore a comparative legal and linguistic study was carried out to primarily analyse three main aspects forming the basis for the writing of the *Czech-English Law Dictionary with Explanations*:

1. the language of law in the Czech Republic (legal Czech) and major English-speaking countries (legal English),
2. approaches to the translation of legal texts, and
3. approaches to dictionary-writing in the area of bilingual special-purpose lexicography.

This chapter will concentrate on some selected items in each of these areas.

2. The language of law

Language for Legal Purposes (LLP)[3], as an LSP variety, is used to facilitate interaction within legal discourse. It is a variety of language strongly determined by the respective discourse event and context. Research of this subsystem of the general language system consists of describing and analysing the selection, combination and use of existing morphological, lexical and syntactic units, structures and patterns

3 Unlike the Czech language, which uses only one term, *odborný jazyk,* to denote the language of specialized domains of knowledge, an English speaker can choose from a few: *language for special/specific purposes, sub-language, scientific language, specialized language* (Pearson 1998: 28) or *domain-specific language* (Meyer/Skuce7Kavanagh/ Davidson 1997).

that would best serve the specific stylistic, genre and discourse functions of a text in a concrete subject area, and specific social context. Specificity of the discourse seems to be primarily a pragmatic category reflecting the communicative purpose and needs of the users – professionals in the respective subject field and, possibly, lay (or paralegal) persons charged with legal assignments.

Pearson (1998: 31) lists six factors which help to characterize an LSP variety:

(a) limited subject matter (such as law);
(b) lexical, semantic and syntactic restrictions (such as the use of terminology);
(c) "deviant" rules of grammar (such as the English legal term "an information", which preserves in procedural meanings the status of countable noun, which is considered obsolete and rare in general language; see, for example, *OED*, electronic edition);
(d) a high frequency of certain constructions (such as highly formalized sentence patterns in statutory texts);
(e) text structure (such as legislation or contracts), and
(f) the use of special symbols.

The first three features as applied to the Czech and English languages when used for legal purposes were included in our study; items d) and e) were beyond its purpose. The last feature, although limited in appearance, deserves to be mentioned here primarily in relation to translating citations of various legislative sources or translating laws. A substantial difference between Czech law and Anglo-American law exists in the use of the symbol "§" (read as "section" in English). Whereas Czech statutes are subdivided into "sections" each of which starts with the symbol "§" and a respective Arabic numeral, British legislation[4] is completely free of the symbol although it subdivides its statutes into "sections" too. Visual discrimination in British statutes is made using in bold type the respective Arabic numeral followed by a

4 The symbol "§" can be found in US legislation; however, its occurrence and purpose do not correspond with legislative drafting rules applicable to Czech law.

dot. Sections in both systems are further subdivided into subsections (C. *odstavec*), paragraphs (C. *písmeno*), and subparagraphs (C. *věta*[5]). Thus a citation of a provision in a Czech statute may appear as: *§12, odst. 3, písm. a, věta třetí*. The same citation of a British statute would be: *s. 12 (3) (a) (iii)*. For a translator or any other person dealing with the two texts and unaware of the differences in the designation of the parts of a law, the situation is more complicated in a translation from English to Czech. While a literal translation of the whole of the Czech citation into English would be odd but, in principle, comprehensible to an English lawyer, our experience suggests that a literal transposition of the English citation into Czech would be hardly understandable even to a lawyer (with no previous knowledge of the British legal system).

2.1 Legal framework

There are many potential problems in the translation of legal information from Czech into English, which should be somehow reflected upon by the bilingual law dictionary; these problems, in summary, can be seen as resulting from the three issues explained below:

(a) Czech legal terminology, as well as the whole legal discourse, has been unstable, developing, expanding, exposed to substantial foreign law influence, and out of strict legal and linguistic control for at least the last eleven years;

(b) systemic and conceptual differences between continental law, from which Czech law has been derived, and common law, one of the main sources of the Anglo-American system of law, should induce translators not only to intersemiotic (translation) analysis but also necessarily to intrasemiotic analysis (Tomášek 1991: 153), i.e. legal interpretation of the source text (ST); and

5 The English *subparagraph* is visually structured and preceded by small Roman numbers. The Czech *věta* is set out in a simple order of individual sentences making a complex statement without any visual structuring or numbering.

(c) the Anglo-American system of law comprises five major legal systems – those of the USA, the UK, Ireland, Canada and Australia – and dozens of others which employ English as an official language and whose legal systems have been based on common law (such as former and present members of the Commonwealth, or Scotland): thus an extensive synonymy and polysemy of English legal terms may be expected.

European Community and European Union law and the *acquis communautaire*[6] written in English have been another source of equivalents in law as well as language. However, due to the fluctuating quality of translations, this source has not always been reliable or trustworthy.[7]

Limited reliability of Czech in law

One factor which partially affects the research of discourse in Czech law, with a special emphasis on legal terminology and upon which the writing of the Dictionary was based, is the question of the validity of legislative acts and the reliability of their language. According to Kořenský/Cvrček (1999: 32-33) almost nothing has been done since 1918 to purify Czechoslovak, and later (since 1993) Czech legislation or make it transparent in this respect. Among the 30,000 texts published in the Collection of Laws since 1918, one sixth are not legislative acts (for example various editorial announcements and comments, resolu-

6 *Acquis communautaire* is a French term widely used in all EU languages. It means all written documents, whether legally binding or not, passed by the EU institutions.

7 Moreover, the terminology of European law has not yet been fully standardized within the system of Czech law. The standardization process, undertaken by a specialized department within the Office of the Government of the Czech Republic, has primarily been aimed at fixing, reducing or expanding the existing meanings of *Czech* legal terms and terminological phrases, or coining new legal terms corresponding to the reality of European law; Czech in this context serves as the target language. In contrast to the above project, the main task of the Czech-English Law Dictionary has been to find English equivalents of existing Czech legal terminology reflecting the national legal system; Czech has been the source language.

tions and so on). About 10,000 acts have been expressly repealed. The remaining 15,000 can be subdivided, with respect to their validity, as follows:

(a) one third is hardly to be classified due to a "legislative muddle" (i.e. over the years some parts have been repealed, some amended, and no accounts of such changes have been kept); in contrast, for example, any new or amended law passed by the Australian Parliament is accompanied by an exhaustive list of all laws or regulations adopted earlier which have been affected by the new law, and the changes to the respective provisions are included in the list (for example the Corporations Act 2001);

(b) the second third consists of laws still in force but obsolete (not implemented, such as the State Budget statutes where a new statute is passed every year but the previous one is not repealed);

(c) the remaining 5,000 legislative acts create the core (more or less) of our legislation which is in force.

Generally, the first ("muddled") group has a tendency to expand.[8] Naturally, every legislative amendment represents a change in the scope and quality of concepts used. The changes after 1990 (the collapse of the communist regime) and 1993 (the split of former Czechoslovakia into the Czech Republic and the Slovak Republic) have been unique within Czech history with respect to the quantity of adopted legislation, and we can justifiably assert that it has led to a quite chaotic situation not only within the legal order itself but also within the sphere of legal terminology and language, which is our main concern[9].

8 Since 1990, despite a few affirmative resolutions of the Government, no attempts have been made to free the valid legislation of all provisions affected by hidden derogation or otherwise; therefore, the legislative confusions and irregularities have become more solid and somehow "standardized".

9 Five major Czech codes have been materially affected by that process, namely, the Civil Code, the Civil Procedure Code, the Criminal Code, the Criminal Procedure Code, and the Commercial Code. The Civil Procedure Code, adopted in 1963, was amended 5 times before 1990 and 36 times between 1990 and 2002; the Commercial Code, adopted in 1991, has been

Moreover, the accession of the Czech Republic to the European Union, accompanied by the legislative "flurry" by the Government and Parliament since 1996 to quickly approximate Czech laws to those of the EU, have substantially contributed to uncertainty in the language of Czech law, followed by its obscure and ambiguous interpretation. Unlike in Anglo-American legislation, in Czech statutes a section in which the terms used in the respective law are defined or otherwise contextualized, is usually absent. Essentially, neither legal tradition, culture or customs (see, for example, Knapp 1998), nor legislative practice (see the Rules of Legislative Drafting 2000) allow for such a part to be inserted into a statute; however, due to the recent hectic and chaotic situation in Czech legislation there are some laws equipped with an interpretative part – not necessarily reducing the general confusion.[10]

Differences between legal systems

The existing material differences between Czech law as a continental law derivative on the one hand, and the Anglo-American systems of law based on common law on the other, create a large area of potential discrepancies in finding semantic English equivalents of Czech terms, terminological phrases and larger syntactical units. Zgusta calls equivalent such a lexical unit of the target language (TL) which has the same lexical meaning, i.e. designation, connotation, and/or range of applications as the respective lexical unit of the source language (SL) (1971: 312). Looking for a suitable equivalent requires an in-

amended 22 times; the Trade Licensing Act, adopted in 1991, has been amended 50 times. As an example, among those 22 amendments of the Commercial Code, there have been three "big" changes in basic terminology; what was mostly changed however was the form (designans, signifiant) and not the content (designatum, signifié) of the respective concepts.

10 For example, terms such as *consumer* or *supplier*, and their rights, are defined in a slightly different manner in two laws (the Civil Code 40/1964 Sb. as amended, and the Consumers' Protection Act 634/1992 Sb. as amended). One can think of situations such as when a person makes a complaint about defective goods sold by a retail shop: the shop assistant would insist on the regulations of the Civil Code whereas the client would rely on the Consumers' Protection Act which is more beneficial to him: both positions would be right.

quiry into the system of Anglo-American law in order to find an identical, similar, or close in meaning legal concept rather than following the pure lexical meaning of the word or phrase.

We tend to uphold Šarčevič's distinction between three basic degrees of (semantic) equivalence (2000: 238) (referring to research on the conceptual analysis of legal terms pursued by the "Internationales Institut für Rechts- und Verwaltungssprache" in Berlin, Germany):

(a) *near equivalence*, where concepts in the SL and TL expressed by the respective terms share all of their essential elements and most of their accidental characteristics;
(b) *partial equivalence* where concepts in the SL and TL share most of their essential elements and only some of their accidental characteristics; and
(c) *non-equivalence* where concepts in the SL and TL share a few or none of their essential elements and no accidental characteristics.

It should be added, however, that both *essential elements* and *accidental characteristics* of concepts in different legal systems under analysis should be considered with regard to *issues (questions, matters) of* law and *issues (questions, matters) of* fact. Equivalence (near or partial) of concepts occurs only if both corresponding legal and corresponding factual elements can be traced. For example, the English term *birth certificate* has a near Czech equivalent: 'rodný list'. In both jurisdictions the terms denote a sheet of paper issued by an official authority to prove the date and place of birth and the child's parents: this is the *factual* aspect of the concept. *Legally*, the certificate may entitle the person in whose name it was issued to benefit from the social security system, succession laws, and so on.

On the other hand, the lack of an equivalent legal term in the Anglo-American system of law requires a certain degree of explanation, and the creation of what Arntz (1993: 16) calls an "equivalent paraphrase". The explanatory paraphrasing of a source-language term previously unknown in the target language may be demonstrated, for example, in translating the Czech legal term *přestupek* into English.

As a matter of fact, *přestupek* in general Czech means any violation of any rule; in Czech law, it denotes a specific transgression of *administrative* law by an individual – Czech law does not consider such acts to be of sufficient gravity to constitute a criminal offence and necessitate entering in criminal or police records. The Anglo-American system of law classifies unlawful acts based on identical facts as crimes, for example *traffic offences* or *breaches of the peace*. In this sense the two systems correspond with regard to the question of fact, but no correspondence exists with regard to the question of law; therefore neither near nor partial semantic equivalence may be found. In order to precisely translate both legal and factual requisites of the Czech *přestupek* into English an explicative term such as *administrative infraction* may be used : "administrative" suggests the *legal* aspect of an act, "infraction" denotes its *factual* substance.

Differences between individual English-speaking countries

Differences between Anglo-American law terminology among individual English-speaking countries constitute another problem for translation. For example, the British legal term "company", as defined in the Companies Act 1985, is identical in its legal meaning and effect to the US "corporation", defined by the (Revised Model) Business Corporation Act 1984; thus, considering their linguistic features, one may assume these terms are synonyms. However, the two terms should not be used interchangeably within the British or US legal systems since the term *company* in US law usually denotes an unincorporated entity[11], whereas *corporation* in original British legal texts regularly means an entity established not primarily for profit-making but to provide public services under the authority of public administration.

Similarly, the British term *frustration* (as a kind of discharge of contract) has its US counterpart *impossibility*; the British *theft* (defined by statute in The Theft Act 1967 as a proper legal term) is termed *larceny* in US legislation; the British word *jail* is a popular

11 The latest edition of *Black's Law Dictionary* admits the term *company* as being synonymous with *corporation*; however, the latter remains the statutory term.

name for a prison; *jail* in American English[12] denotes a place for pre-trial temporary confinement, close in its usage to a *police cell* or *holding cell*; and dozens of others. Consequently several questions arise: which of two or even three terms should be suggested as the best equivalent of a Czech term in a Czech-English law dictionary: British *statutory instrument*, US *executive/regulation*, or Australian *legislative instrument* for the Czech *podzákonný právní předpis*? Should there be any preference at all? Should there be as a part of the dictionary instructions on how to translate legal texts? The answers to these questions are fully dependent on the linguistic, subject-field and social contexts, as well as the publisher's policy. We are inclined to claim that no specialist bilingual dictionary may precisely instruct users in such or a similar situation: the choice of equivalents will depend on the purpose for which the dictionary is consulted (translating a legal text, informing a client, teaching legal language), the linguistic and legal competence of the users themselves, the addressees (or recipients of the target text), and the genre of the legal text in the SL and its counterpart in the TL, and so on. It would be rather impractical to produce instructions or guidelines due to the wide range of legal topics and genres, the large scope of legal texts to be translated, and the extensive coverage of functions to be met by the translated legal texts.

2.2 Linguistic framework

Although Newmark (1987: 160) suggests that terminology makes up perhaps 5-10% of a text, it is traditionally considered the basis of a LSP variety. It is the part of vocabulary for specific purposes that has been profoundly described, analysed and standardized (ISO R 1087 1990). Our experience has suggested, however, that lawyers without sufficient linguistic background use the concepts *terminology* and *LSP variety* indiscriminately, thus mistakenly reducing the language of law to a mere set of legal terms.

12 The term *jail* in the USA denotes a confinement established and run by a local authority such as a county; prison is a penitentiary institution established and operated by a State or the federal government.

Law terminology encompasses a wide range of special-purpose expressions, phrases and higher syntactic units that can be subdivided into five groups:

(a) Terms of art, or "pure" law terms including legal Latin; it is a somewhat limited in number group of words or phrases that are not used outside the branch of law unless stylistically marked. For example, the Czech term *cedent* and its English counterpart *assignor*.

(b) Terms "generalized" in everyday non-legal communication; these are words with related legal meaning (such as Czech *pozemek*, *nedbalost* and their respective English translations *land* and *negligence*).

(c) Expressions of general import acquiring specific legal meaning if so defined by legislation; one example can be mentioned – that of a British law called the Welfare of Pigs Act 1998 which provides a definition of a *pig* for the purposes of that law (i.e. only "an animal of the porcine species of any age, kept for breeding or fattening" is a *pig* within the ambit of the Act). In Czech law, the Family Act introduced the Czech word *zodpovědnost* as a legal term in an unprecedented context of *rodičovská zodpovědnost* ('parental responsibility'): this is the only occurrence of the prefixed *zodpovědnost* whilst the essential legal term is *odpovědnost*.

(d) Phraseological and semi-syntactical units; (i) so-called phrasemes are multi-word terms usually formed by elliptical nominalization (for example, Czech *zákonná domněnka svědčící manželu matky* translated as *statutory presumption of paternity of husband of mother*, or English *maliciously damaging the property of another*, translated into Czech as *úmyslné poškození majetku jiného*); (ii) repeatedly-used stipulating clauses hardened into terminological units, such as Czech *pokud zákon nestanoví jinak* and its English counterpart *unless the Act provides otherwise*; and (iii) clauses such as *má-li soudce za to, že* (translated as *where it appears to the judge that*), or *žalovaný měl způsobit škodu* (in English *the plaintiff is alleged to have caused damage*), where the legal usage has shifted their function from a simple assumption without significant implications to the determination of circumstances that would create legal consequences.

(e) Jargon creates a significant portion of terminology in both legal Czech and English. Jargon may not be confined only to the lexicon of a subject-field; as a subvariety of language it also covers morphology and syntax. The elliptical language in everyday legal and judicial practice tends to condense and economize the legal speech (and unofficial writings), thus shifting to jargon. One example of this dichotomy can be given: the Czech Code of Criminal Procedure provides for *peněžitá záruka* (English *pecuniary security*) to be granted under certain circumstances to remand the defendant's attendance before court. In Galinski's understanding (1982: 189) it is a prescriptive term declared as such by law. In legal practice, however, the term *kauce* (English *bail*) is widely used. Whereas the Anglo-American legal system employs the term *bail* in both statute and everyday legal practice, Czech law practitioners use the two terms discriminately according to the formality of the situation (such as an attorney approaching the judge in a courtroom asking for *peněžitá záruka* for his client, and the attorney talking to his client explaining what *kauce* is).

Conceptual analysis is considered a cornerstone of terminography (Meyer/Skuce/Kavanagh/Davidson 1997). It should be pursued whenever an identical term in the target language does not exist or its equivalent is in doubt. The more general the legal term that is in question, the higher the degree of probability that can be presumed with respect to the existence of a terminological counterpart in the TL. Dealing with terms denoting more particular concepts means that conceptual analysis need always be undertaken in order to determine the boundaries of the SL and TL concepts, and to decide the manner in which the SL term should be transposed to the TL term, preserving the maximum of the characteristics of the former. Conceptual analysis helps decide whether *semantic* equivalence suffices to adequately transfer legal information in a particular case, or whether *functional* equivalence should be employed. Conceptual analysis usually leads to finding a suitable *functional* equivalent, i.e., an expression, phrase or a larger unit not necessarily semantically equivalent, which serves the same function in the target text (TT) as the SL term in the ST. The term *functional equivalence* is used in general translation theory (for example Newmark 1987: 83) and in comparative law (Šarčevič 2000: 236); Šarčevič admits (2000: 238), and our own experience supports her conclusion, that most functional equivalents are only partial semantic equivalents.

3. Legal translation

There are at least three interlinked questions to be considered when talking about legal translation:

(a) what it is,
(b) by whom it is pursued,
(c) for what purpose it is carried out and to whom it is addressed.

The first two questions will be briefly dealt with here; the third reaches beyond the scope of this study.

Law belongs to a wider category of the humanities, the vocabulary of which is based on abstract words and expressions which, however, bear quite precise meaning. Legal terminology consists primarily of abstract terms deeply and firmly rooted in domestic culture and intellectual tradition, remaining first and foremost a national phenomenon (Šarčevič 2000: 13). However legal language is not just composed of technical terms, of a specific terminology. It is rather a formalized language at all levels: lexical, syntactic, textual (Reed 1993: 81) and also with respect to genre (see Chromá 2003: 70).

The primary objective of legal translation is that the target recipient should be provided as explicit, extensive and precise legal information in the target language as is contained in the source text, complemented (by the translator) with facts rendering the original information fully comprehensible in the different legal environment and culture, and serving the purpose of translation.

Legal translation should be based primarily on comparative genre analysis in order to ensure the transfer of legal information is as precise, accurate and comprehensible as possible, and to shape TT in a manner adequate to its purpose.

Since legal information contained in the ST is often (slightly) ambiguous and indefinite it should be interpreted within the SL first, then translated into the TL, and finally conformed to the purpose of translation and genre of the TT.

Tomášek (1990: 113) points out that legal translation is a procedure based on both linguistic and legal comparative approach. He asserts that the content of legal information should be fully preserved and transposed into the TL so that the TT corresponds with usage in the target legal environment. What is denoted as "intralingual" translation by Beyer/Conradsen (1995: 175), Tomášek (1991: 147) calls "intrasemiotic" translation and describes as the transfer of information from the first to the second semantic level – i.e. the interpretation of law by means of the transfer from legal language to legal metalanguage. "Intersemiotic" translation then means the translation of a legal text from one language to another.

We can go a bit further: legal translation can *only* be based on (legal) interpretation of the original text in the SL and its transposition into the language and legal culture of the recipient. Reasonable interpretation of the ST and its adequate transposition into the TT may be practicable only if we know the respective legal topic in both systems. For example, a British statute translated into Czech will never have the same degree of normativity for a Czech national living in the Czech Republic; in many cases such translation would be done to inform a Czech recipient (for example to inspire a Czech legislator). Moreover, the purpose of translating a Czech law into English for a Briton living and working in the Czech Republic will also be only informative: if the British person needs to rely on such a statute before a Czech court he or she should refer only to the Czech text of the law officially published in the Collection of Laws of the Czech Republic. On the other hand, a private contract made between British and Czech parties will most likely be written in English and Czech, both versions being considered equal counterparts, and parties might rely on either language version in the case of conflict; so although the legal systems differ the purpose of both texts is identical: to bind parties and provide them with agreed and/or statutory rights and obligations.

The process of legal translation can be generally visualized as follows:

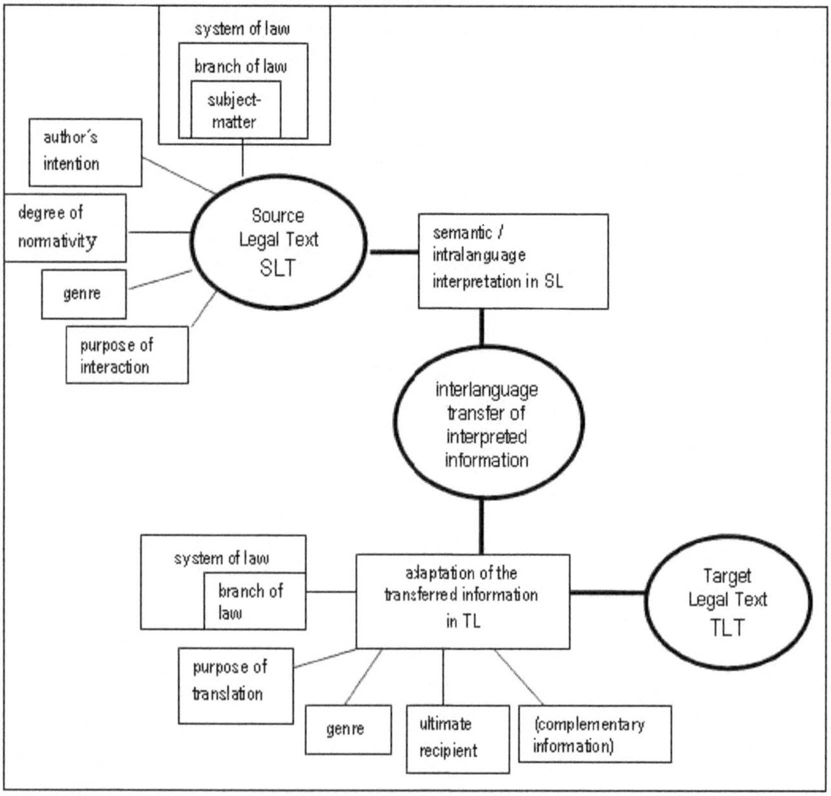

Figure 1. Process of legal translation.

The competence of translators (and interpreters) of law[13] is a crucial issue in quality legal translation. As Picht/Draskau (1985: 20-21) em-

13 Translators' excellent bilingual competence is a matter of course.

phasize, the acquisition of the relevant language for specific purposes is compulsory for those employed in the special field and mediators of texts with a professional content (for example translators). They extend Picht's earlier demand that translators should have been trained in terminology (Picht 1982: 172), which forms only a minor portion of a specialist language. Thus, Beyer and Conradsen's (above) assumption that legal translation requires both linguistic skills and *some basic* understanding of legal concepts seems to be rather an underestimation.

The three prerequisites which exist for successful translation of legal texts (a basic knowledge of the legal systems, familiarity with the relevant terminology, and competence in the specific legal writing style of the target language) constitute practical rules which should be respected by each translator. This is supported by our own experience: translation of legal texts should not be done without quite an extensive knowledge of the respective legal topic in both the SL and TL, i.e. the knowledge of concepts, terms denoting these concepts, sentence patterns visualizing the information, genre classification of the text, and knowledge of legal culture, and so on, in both languages, linked by the purpose of the concrete translation.

It should also be noted that translators and interpreters form a user group of a specific type and ultimate significance for a lexicographer writing specialized dictionaries. As Varantola (1998: 189) argues, translators try to find non-dictionary type information in dictionaries because it is not readily and systematically available from other sources; they also need information relating to longer stretches of text than a single lexical item. Supporting such an opinion, Rogers/Ahmad (1998: 195) maintain that "translators might justifiably expect specialised dictionaries to codify the conceptual, grammatical and pragmatic information which is observable in language use by experts, technicians, marketing specialists, and so on, and in some cases, to normalise their use". We tried to at least partially satisfy such expectations in our *Czech-English Law Dictionary with Explanations*. It should be noted that, however underestimated and disregarded by lawyers, translators and interpreters assist and influence the process of transposing one legal system (or its elements) into another legal language and system, and thus facilitate international collaboration among individuals or entities[14]. Many in the Czech Republic act under the state licence of “court interpreter”[15] granted by the Ministry of Justice of the Czech Republic. The round seal they affix to their work should be a guarantee that the translation is linguistically and legally correct and accurate[16].

4. The writing of the dictionary

The main theoretical resources for the writing of the dictionary were two books bearing identical titles, *Manual of Lexicography / Manuál lexikografie*. The first was written in English by Zgusta in 1970 and became a lexicographer’s bible worldwide; the second was written in Czech by Čermák and Blatná in 1995 and reflected recent developments in dictionary-making including corpus linguistics and lexicography.

A dictionary which helps its users to produce legal texts in the TL as well as adequately translate source legal texts into the TL must be founded upon a profound comparative legal and linguistic study that would (a) determine (semantic or functional) equivalents at the levels of vocabulary, syntax and genres, and (b) select the appropriate lexicographic material to be included in the dictionary. A bilingual

14 Our own recent expert experience showed that the bad translation of official procedural documents had substantially contributed to the decision of a foreign court not to extradite a criminal (Czech citizen) from a foreign country to the Czech Republic.

15 There are more designations of these licensed translators: sworn interpreter, certified translator or interpreter, and forensic interpreter. All the names suggest that a certain official procedure must have been taken for that person to have been so appointed.

16 It should be admitted, however, that such guarantee is quite frequently unjustified and unreasonable: the Ministry has not provided for a uniform system of qualifications to be required from translators applying for the licence; as a result each regional court in charge of registers of court translators has set its own requirements thus sometimes admitting translators with inadequate competence in legal translation.

law dictionary should contain not only the SL terminology but also syntactic units that are relevant to the language of law. Since Czech law is derived from continental law based on written codes and statutes, the SL and TL corpora, facilitating conceptual and functional analyses, should encompass essential legislation relating to private and public law, materials based on the legislation, such as annotations and textbooks or authentic documents, and law dictionaries. Case law will play an important role in searching for relevant conceptual equivalents in legal English. A user-friendly approach should be chosen for the formatting of the dictionary (for example, the repetition of examples should be higher) as a strong linguistic background cannot be expected of all users.

The title of the dictionary *Czech-English Law Dictionary with Explanations* is meant to suggest that the dictionary contains more than simple equivalents of Czech legal terms. Fillmore (1978: 167) claims that law has its own sort of semantic principles; the semantics of the technical stratum of legal language are founded on stipulative definitions. Such assumptions, however, would not apply to dictionary-making since the purpose of definitions contained in bilingual dictionaries is rather different.

Defining can have different discoursal functions (Swales 1981: 111), and our intention was to provide as much conceptual information as may be permitted by the scope and size of the dictionary (and by the publisher) and needed by translators in deciding what equivalent to selected for their particular purpose. The term "explanation" was chosen to avoid an authoritative connotation of the word "definition". However we maintain Swales' conclusion that the function of definitions "is more to furnish explanations of terms than to establish axioms which form part of a logical system of postulates and theorems" (1981: 107). Pearson (1998: 117) supports this assertion, claiming that dictionaries are *rephrasing*, i.e. clarifying usage, rather than *defining* in the sense of *prescribing,* and that dictionary definitions are merely *reporting* rather than *defining* for the first time.

Dictionary-writing in the era of electronic media cannot dispense with reliable hardware and efficient software. Most publishing houses which concentrate on lexicography possess prodigious corpora and databases worked on by efficient teams of lexicographers. Since our task was much more modest and the "team" consisted only of one member we had to choose reliable software that would help us fulfil our objective. Paradox 5 for Windows is the database software used for storing and processing excerpts; the database consists of more than 80,000 records. The OUP software "Wordsmith Tools" was selected to set basic statistical data about the corpus: the database of Czech excerpts consists of approximately 167,000 words, of which approximately 145,000 were selected either to serve as headwords or for the exemplification of use on the Czech side of the dictionary; the database of English equivalents of headwords and examples of use consists of approximately 253,000 words, of which 215,000 were selected to be included in the dictionary. Corel WordPerfect 8 was used as a word-processor for the ultimate processing of individual entries; the final version of the dictionary consists of approximately 9,200 Czech headwords, 29,000 Czech terms, terminological phrases and semi-sentences, and about 46,000 of their English contextualized equivalents.

References:

Arntz, R. 1993. Terminological Equivalence and Translation . In Sonneveld, H. S. / Loening, K. L. (eds) *Terminology: Applications in Interdisciplinary Communication.* Amsterdam/Philadelphia: John Benjamins.

Atkins, S. B. T. 1993. Theoretical Lexicography and Its Relation to Dictionary-making. *Dictionaries. Journal of the Dictionary Society of North America* 14, 1992/1993, 4-43.

Beyer, V. / Conradsen, K. 1995. Translating Japanese Legal Documents into English: A Short Course . In Morris, Marshall (ed.) *Translation and the Law. American Translators Association Series* Volume VIII. Amsterdam/Philadelphia: John Benjamins, 145-178.

Čermák, F. / Blatná, R. (eds) 1995. *Manuál lexikografie*. Praha: H+H.

Chromá, M. 2003. The Language of Arbitration: From Intent to the Act . In Bhatia, V. / Candlin, C. / Gotti, M. (eds) *Legal Discourse in Multilingual and Multicultural Contexts*. Bern: Peter Lang, 63-86.

Fillmore, C. J. 1978. On the Organization of Semantic Information in the Lexicon . In Farkas, D. / Jacobsen, W. M. / Todrys, K. W. (eds) *Papers from the Parasession on the Lexicon*. Chicago: Chicago Linguistic Society, 148-173.

Galinski, C. 1982. Standardization in Terminology – an Overview. In Nedobity, Wolfgang, (ed.) *Terminologies for the Eighties, Infoterm Series 7*. Munich: K. G. Saur, 186-226.

ISO R 1087 1990. *Terminology and Vocabulary*. Paris: ISO.

Knapp, V. 1995. *Teorie práva*. Praha: C.H.Beck.

Knapp, V. 1998. *Tvorba práva a její současné problémy*. Praha: Linde.

Kořenský, J. / Cvrček, F. / Novák, F. 1999. *Juristická a lingvistická analýza právních textů. Právněinformatický přístup*. Praha: Academia.

Legislativní pravidla vlády ('The Rules of Legislative Drafting'). Resolution of the Government of the Czech Republic 596 of 14th June 2000..

Meyer, I. / Skuce, D. / Kavanagh, J. / Davidson, L. 1997. Integrating linguistic and conceptual analysis in a WWW-based tool for terminography. Available: <http://www.cs.queensu.ca/achallc-97/papers/p021.html> [accessed: August 4, 2003].

Newmark, P. 1987. *A Textbook of Translation*. London: Prentice Hall Int.

Pearson, J. 1998. *Terms in Context*. Amsterdam/Philadelphia: John Benjamins.

Picht, H. 1982. Reflexions on Training in Terminology in the 1980s. In Nedobity, Wolfgang (ed.) *Terminologies for the Eighties (Infoterm Series 7)*. Munich: K. G. Saur, 172-185.

Picht, H. / Draskau, J. 1985. *Terminology. An Introduction*. Guildford: University of Surrey.

Reed, D. 1993. Some Terminological Problems of Translating Common Law Concepts from English to French . In Sonneveld, H. S. / Loening, K. L. (eds) *Terminology: Applications in Interdis-*

ciplinary Communication. Amsterdam/Philadelphia: John Benjamins, 79-86.

Rogers, M. / Ahmad, K. 1998. The Translator and the Dictionary: Beyond Words? In Atkins, B.T.S (ed.) *Using Dictionaries* (*Lexicographica Series Maior* 88). Tübingen: Niemeyer, 193-204.

Šarčevič, S. 1989. Conceptual Dictionaries for Translation in the Field of Law . *International Journal of Lexicography* 2/4, 277-293.

Šarčevič, S. 2000. *New Approach to Legal Translation.* The Hague/ London/Boston: Kluwer Law International.

Swales, J. 1981. Definitions in Science and Law – Evidence for Subject-Specific Course Components? *Fachsprache* 3/3-4, 106-112.

Tomášek, M. 1990. K vybraným problémům překladu právního jazyka. *Translatologica Pragensia IV*, Acta Universitatis Carolinae Philologica 4/1994 , 113-120.

Tomášek, M. 1991. Právo – interpretace a překlad. *Translatologica Pragensia V*, Acta Universitatis Carolinae Philologica 4-5, 147-157 .

Varantola, K. 1998. Translators and their Use of Dictionaries. In Atkins, B.T.S (ed.) *Using Dictionaries* (*Lexicographica Series Maior* 88). Tübingen: Niemeyer, 179-192.

Zgusta, L. 1971. *Manual of Lexicography.* Praha: Academia / The Hague: Mouton.

STANISLAW GOŹDŹ-ROSZKOWSKI

Legal terms in context: Phraseological variation across genres

1. Introduction

It is no accident that the title of this chapter bears some resemblance to the now classic book by Jennifer Pearson *Terms in Context*. Pearson's book belongs to those invaluable studies in which it was demonstrated that corpora can be successfully used in terminology work. What may seem to be an established practice in general language lexicography is not necessarily so in specialised lexicography. Pearson (1998) has pointed out the lack of appropriate corpora and a reluctance on the part of "traditional" terminologists to rely on "authentic" texts as the possible reasons for the discrepancy. The situation has apparently been constantly improving along with the increased ,availability of electronic text and linguistic tools to create one's own specialised corpora.

The present study has been premised on the necessity of studying terms in context and on placing particular emphasis on usage by means of real texts used as a primary source of data. Retrieving relevant contextual fragments can have a disambiguating function in the case of related lexical units. In legal English there is, for example, the notorious abundance of terms used to refer to court decisions in disputes which have the meaning of "revoke" such as: *annul*, *cancel*, *dismiss*, *overrule, recall, reverse, set aside* and so on, LSP users and translators alike would greatly benefit from linguistic tools that could deal systematically with the troublesome area of synonymy. The access to ample contextual information is particularly important for non-native LSP users whose tasks include specialised text production in English. In Poland, for instance, translating into non-native tongues, especially into English is a common occurrence due to the acute shortage of qualified native speakers of foreign languages who would know Polish well enough to translate. The situation might improve in view of Poland's entry into the European Union but it is not likely to be entirely remedied in the foreseeable future. Other Polish LSP users, such as, for instance, legal professionals are also expected to write texts where fluency and accuracy of expression are vital. It is in such context that the issue of correct use of word combinations in specialised texts strikes one as particularly important. The existence of this problem in the context of LSP had been noted (Bergenholtz 1995). In the general process of language learning, it is very characteristic for language learners, even at a fairly advanced stage, to produce sentences which conform with the grammar rules but which tend to sound unnatural. A special-language user with inadequate linguistic knowledge and a rudimentary grasp of a particular domain appears to be in a somewhat similar situation to that of the child or student of language (Bergenholtz 1995: 17). He or she may know a term but has little idea of how to use it. The LSP user might also face the problem of not knowing or not being certain whether certain word combinations conform with their standard usage in a field of knowledge, i.e. if they are acceptable by a particular LSP community. In the author's view, this issue is particularly pronounced in legal texts because legal systems exert a varying degree of influence on the writer's choice of words. Indeed, in extreme cases, failure to employ word combinations according to specific formulations prescribed by law could result in the entire text being invalidated (Kjaer 1990a). Other, less harsh penalties for disregarding restricted combinability in legal language could include affecting the legal force of a text, affecting the stability of the law or rejecting the text by a particular LSP community if this text fails to include routine conventional phrases which are widely recognised as preserving the generic integrity.

Unfortunately, most specialised mono-, bi- and multilingual dictionaries do not very often provide explicit contextual information on word combinations. The exception are some dictionaries with encyclopaedic information or those few which apart from providing definitions include example sentences (a recent example is the

Słownik Prawa/English Law Dictionary published by Peter Collin Publishing).

In this chapter it is argued that any terminological resources providing information on combinability of terms should take into account a genre or genres in which a given term appears. Sometimes, it might not be enough to produce a list of possible collocations. If, for example, we take a set of lexical collocations of a basic, widely used term, such as *contract*: (reproduced here from Alcaraz/Hughes 2002: 167) *void contract, voidable contract, binding contract, exclusive contract, breach of contract, terms of contract, the law of contract, rules of contract,* it would be extremely useful to know the distribution of those items across legal genres within the domain of contract law. It would be interesting to find out, for example, if the term *voidable contract* appears only in textbooks, or also in statutes, judgements, law reports and contracts. It might appear only in two or three genres or in all of them. Equally, data on frequency of a term and its combination in different genres could be of real help. It is suggested in this study that there seems to be a strong correlation between restricted combinability of a term and a genre in which it appears and such information could be of great importance to the LSP users working with legal language.

2. The case of *consideration*

To illustrate the point made above, we shall look at the term *consideration*. It is a basic term in the Anglo-American common law of contract. In the legal lexicon *consideration* belongs to the category of semi-technical terms. Apart from its general meaning, it designates "whatever is given or accepted by each party in return for the other party's reciprocal meaning"(Alacaraz/Hughes 2002: 160). *Black's Law Dictionary* defines *consideration* as

> That which is actually given or accepted in return for a promise. The inducement to a contract. The cause, motive, price, or impelling influence which in-

> duces a contracting party to enter into a contract. Some right, interest, profit or benefit accruing to one party, or some forbearance, detriment, loss or responsibility, given, suffered, or undertaken by the other. (*Black's Law Dictionary*).

Clearly, there exist different schools of phraseology and various ways of classifying word combinations. A very useful overview of word combinations in language for specific purposes can be found in Kjaer (1990) and in Thomas (1993). Below, we shall examine the collocational patterns of the term *consideration* based on frequency, that is, attention is drawn to lexical items which display a significant co-occurrence within the specified co-text. Adopting the frequency criterion means that one is provided with raw output yielded by the concordancing programme. It is raw in the sense that the combinations are of different form and nature. Some will be collocations or terminological phrases (usually of the verb + noun form, the noun being a term) some still phraseological terms (especially multi-word terms) characterised by restricted commutability. Both types are relevant for the group of LSP users specified above. In the author's belief, the following are the most crucial questions for the user:

1) Is the distribution of a particular term restricted to a particular genre or genres, or does it appear universally in a given domain?
2) In which most frequent combinations can a term be found?
3) Are these combinations unique to a particular genre or genres?

2.1 The legal corpus

The corpus, which has recently exceeded 3 million running words, comprises texts from different branches of law, for instance, contract law, family law, constitutional law, and so on, and it contains a range of different legal genres. For the purpose of this study, a subcorpus of contract law was isolated with texts grouped in four different samples representing the genres of contract, judgement, textbook and report. The contract sample contains standard-form commercial contracts. The judgements are those handed down by the House of Lords in their capacity as the highest court of appeal in the UK. The textbook sample contains a random selection of different texts concerning the theory of contract law. The texts were culled from various standard textbooks on this subject. Finally, the reports are papers of the Law Commission working on the reform of law in England. The samples are of roughly equal size of 60,000 words, which can be assumed to be sufficiently representative of each genre. The analysis was aided by the Wordsmith Tools software.

2.2 The analysis

Table 1 below represents some simple descriptive statistics, which are nevertheless quite interesting because they show that there is a neat division between the four genres with respect to the raw frequency of the term in question. *Consideration* appears in the textbook and the report with a similar frequency, which is markedly higher than of its frequency in the contract and the judgement genres, where the difference between the two is negligible.

Genre	*%*
Textbook	0.12
Report	0.10
Contract	0.05
Judgement	0.04

Table 1. Raw frequency of the term *consideration* in four legal genres.

It is interesting to note that *consideration* is strikingly more frequent in genres that represent "juristic" language, that is the metalanguage of the law, than in contracts and judgements – the language in which law is actually laid down.

Before we look at the examples of the actual use of *consideration* in the texts, in Table 2 we can see the most commonly found (in dictionaries) adjective + noun forms with *consideration* as the head.

standard/institutional terms
concurrent consideration
executed consideration
executory consideration
good consideration
inadequate consideration
(il)legal consideration
past consideration
sufficient consideration
valuable consideration

Table 2. Most commonly found actual uses of *consideration.*

It is interesting to note that the adjectives (except one) are not past participles, which is very common for such compounds in most special languages (Thomas 1993). These are standard, institutionalised terms in the sense that they can be commonly found in mono- and bilingual dictionaries of law as well as in textbooks on contract law. As a side issue, it will be interesting to see if those terms actually appear in legal texts. If so, do they appear in all the four genres or is their occurrence in any way restricted?

Contracts

Let us, however, see in what combinations we can find *consideration* in contracts. The phrases in bold preceded by bullets have been placed according to their frequency in descending order. Almost half of all the occurrences of *consideration* in this genre appear in the prepositional phrase *in consideration of* as exemplified below:

1) *NOW, THEREFORE, in consideration of the mutual covenants and conditions herein, the parties agree as follows: [...]*

The use of this phrase implies the reciprocal nature of the transaction. Its sense is "in return for" or 'in exchange for'. The distribution of this phrase seems to be restricted to virtually one point in contract documents where the parties' commitments are introduced. In the sample under consideration, *in consideration of* has not been found anywhere else in the documents, although the corpus evidence did admit of possible, however slight, variations such as, for example, the one below:

2) *It is therefore agreed, in consideration of the mutual promises and covenants hereinafter as follows:*

Here, *in consideration of* seems to appear in a fairly restricted environment of a specific formulaic statement.

The second most frequent combination demonstrated in (2) and (3) can be found in a variant indicated by the brackets. Both, *good consideration* and *valuable consideration* are terms in their own right, as shown in Figure 2. But only *good consideration* can appear in the combination *for good consideration*, no instances of *for valuable consideration* have been found in the contracts section of the corpus. As we shall see below, this restriction does not necessarily hold true for other genres.

3) *For good and valuable consideration, the Seller has agreed to sell and the Buyer has agreed* to buy the Property upon the terms and conditions set forth in the Contract

Now, therefore, for good consideration, the receipt and sufficiency of which is hereby acknowledged, the parties hereto hereby agree as follows: [...]

Both *in consideration of* and *for good and valuable consideration* are to be found at precisely the same point in a contract. They are part of a sentence which introduces probably the most essential part of any contract in which the parties' obligations are laid out. It is a characteristic feature of legal genres to exhibit distinctive macrostructural features (Goźdź-Roszkowski 2000, Alcaraz 2002). Contracts are no exception in this respect. Even though the principle of freedom of contract entails a considerable degree of flexibility, the flexibility concerns the content rather than the form. The subject matter of a contract can be virtually anything depending on the intentions of the parties. In practice, contracts tend to preserve standard formats and employ tried and tested conventional formulas. The two phrases are part of such standard, conventional formulas. An immediate implication of a pedagogic nature is that it is absolutely essential that translators grappling with legal texts or generally anyone writing legal texts should know them.

The Adj + N combination (example sentences 4 and 5 below) has been included because of its relatively high frequency. It is most probably not an institutionalised standard term but an example of a free word combination, a collocation. It seems to be characteristic of contracts to refer to the entirety of *consideration* by means of this particular adjective. As we shall see later, this is not necessarily the case in other genres. Yet, in contracts no other related adjective could be found. So, for example, one does not tend to come across combinations such as: *absolute consideration* or *complete consideration*.

4) *As total consideration for the purchase and sale of the Corporation's Stock, pursuant to this Agreement, the Purchaser shall pay to the Seller the sum of [...] such total consideration to be referred to in this Agreement as the "Purchase Price".*

5) *The total consideration and method of payment thereof are fully set out in Exhibit "A".*

Sentences 6 and 7 below show what seems to be an alternative way of expressing the totality of consideration by means of the adjective *aggregate*. There are, however, only seven instances of this combination in the whole sample corpus.

6) The Purchaser shall pay to the Vendor the *aggregate* amount of the purchase *consideration* calculated in accordance with the provisions of Clause 2 hereof.

7) *The transaction hereby effected does not form part of a larger transaction or of a series of transactions in respect of which the amount or value or the* aggregate *amount or value of the* consideration *exceeds five hundred pounds*

There is a standard clause in many contracts which could be called "discretionary" in the sense that it empowers a named agent to make a decision concerning the amount or value of consideration. In such a case, one typically comes across the phrase *for such consideration.* Its strong co-occurrence with *as X may think fit* (or its variant shown in example (9) has prompted the author to think of the two as forming one unit. A similar clause can be found in Power of Attorney documents, which might suggest that this instance of legal phraseology is not confined to the genre of contracts. Still, it does not appear in any other genre under consideration in this study.

8) *To sell or dispose of or grant options over the undertaking of the Company or any of the assets of the Company, or any part thereof, movable or immovable,*

in any such manner and for such consideration as the Company may think fit *and in particular for shares, debentures, [...]*

9) For the purposes of or in connection with the business of the Company to mortgage and charge the undertaking and all or any of the real and personal property and assets, present and future, and all or any of the uncalled capital for the time being of the Company, and to issue at par or at a premium or discount, and for such consideration and with and subject to such rights, powers, privileges and conditions as may be thought fit, debentures or debenture stock [...]

10) To sell the property situate at [...] Poland for such consideration and on such terms and conditions as the Attorney shall think fit.

Finally, this combination has a similar function to the first two (*in consideration of, for good and valuable consideration*) considered above in indicating the mutual nature of a given transaction. This is not to say that *in consideration of, for good* (and *valuable consideration*) and *for the consideration named* mean exactly the same and are freely interchangeable. Statistically, *for the consideration named* is by far the least frequent. All three, however, have a restricted distribution within the documents and a very specific function.

11) *WITNESSETH, that the Contractor and the Owner* for the consideration named *agree as follows [...]*

Judgements

The combination *for valuable consideration* is reminiscent of of the one that we examined in sentences 2 and 3 above. Contrary to what we saw in contracts, *valuable consideration* is never preceded by *good.* It not part of a formulaic expression. Here, it appears in its strict technical sense, while in contracts it tended to be part of a larger unit, where the meaning of *valuable* was included in the meaning of *good,* i.e. in the sense of a consideration legally valid.

12) *I cannot doubt that a contract for valuable consideration to grant an easement over Blackacre would be a contract for the disposition of an interest in land [...]*

In this genre, all the occurrences of the standard multi-word term *failure of consideration* which have been retrieved are preceded by *total*. As we will see below, this term can be also preceded by by *partial* or it can appear without any modifiers.

13) *It follows that a claim that there was a total failure of consideration cannot succeed.*
Since the tapes were never delivered in accordance with the contract as varied, there had been a total failure of consideration and they were entitled to the return of the $ 12,000

Sentences 14 and 15 show some affinity to those numbered 5 and 6 because all of them seem to refer to *consideration* in its entirety. However, one should be wary of using the phrases interchangeably. Those in 14 and 15 refer to consideration in its strictly pecuniary sense, which is emphasized by the words *paid* and *payable* used in the immediate context of this term.

14) *The licence only became effective when the whole of the consideration had been paid*

15) *The rights referred to in the first part of the contract, vested in the plaintiffs at the latest when the whole of the stated consideration of $$$ payable for those rights had been paid by the plaintiffs to the defendants.*

Agreed consideration is again an example of an Adj + N combination with a high frequency (second most frequent in this genre) but restricted to the genre of judgements.

It is listed in an *English-Polish Dictionary of Legal and Economic Terms* with its Polish equivalent of 'uzgodniona zapłata'.

16) *The plaintiffs paid the agreed consideration of $ 12,000 for the licence and then requested the defendants to insure and send by recorded delivery to the plaintiffs' nominee in Munich video tapes of the films [...]*

Textbook

Failure of consideration means that consideration, which was legal and agreed upon originally, no longer exists or "has been extinguished partially or entirely" (*Black's Law Dictionary*). The term frequently appears without any modification in this genre.

17) *Rejection of goods, therefore, usually produces a total failure of consideration.*

18) *It has been shown by McElroy and Williams that discharge for impossibility and discharge for failure of consideration had different historical roots.*

The situation with the *for good consideration* phrase is analogous to that described in the section on judgements above about *for valuable consideration. For good consideration* in textbooks does not appear in the formulaic, solemn statements which introduce the parties' obligations. Let us however note that in sentence 19 the original denotation of this phrase remains the same but in pragmatic terms it is very different.

19) *Thus, if B owes money to X, he may make a contract with A, whereby A agrees,* for good consideration *to discharge this debt.*

20) *Where a man,* for good consideration, *gave a note expressed to be "for money borrowed which I promise never to pay", the word "never" was rejected.*

The combination *for valuable consideration* has not been found in the entire corpus of contracts. Nor has *valuable consideration* for that matter. It might be hypothesized that *valuable consideration* is a term that belongs to the theory of contract and it is extremely unlikely to appear in highly operative texts such as contracts.

21) *Lord Cairns went further and said, if parties, for valuable consideration, with their eyes open, contract that a particular shall not be done, all that a Court of Equity has to do is to say, by way of injunction, [...]*

22) *Valuable consideration for this purpose may consist in any consideration sufficient to support a simple contract, or an antecedent debt or liability.*

Consideration must move from the promisee is a fine example of legal phraseology often referred to as "maxims" (Bergenholtz 1995). Sentences (23) and (24) below show a fairly straightforward use of it, that is, the maxim is produced in its full and original wording. But sentence (25) differs in that respect by containing a truncated version of the original maxim yet retaining the collocation of *consideration* and *move*. It can be argued that sentence (25) could not be in fact fully understood if one was ignorant of the exact wording and meaning of the original maxim.

23) *It is one of the best-known axioms of the common law of contract that consideration must move from the promise*

24) *If the rule that consideration must move from the promisee were abolished, it would help C only if A had made his promise to C.*

25) *The facts that no promise was made to the daughters and that the alleged consideration did not move from them are simply ignored.*

If we refer back to Table 2 which shows a selection of the most common standard institutionalised terms, we can notice that some of them can be found below. In fact, it is in the textbook genre that one can come across most of the standard, institutionalised terms from Table 2.

1. executed consideration

26) *Here it is to be stressed that the right does not arise out of any contract (for there need be none), but from the fact of* executed consideration *by the plaintiff at the defendant's request.*

2. executory consideration

27) *The writ also came to be used where money had been paid under a mistake or upon* executory consideration *which had wholly failed and where also it had been extorted by fraud or duress.*

3. past consideration

28) *Where a guarantee was expressed to be given to the plaintiffs 'in consideration of your being in advance' to J.S., it was argued that this showed a* past consideration

4. sufficient consideration

29) *A promise by the buyer, however, to confer upon the seller some independent benefit, actual or contingent, may constitute* sufficient consideration *for the acceptance of the smaller sum.*

These four terms presented immediately above appear to be restricted to one genre only. Not a single occurrence of any of them has been found outside the textbook sample.

2.3 Report

Reports seem to show a rather limited range of word combination possibilities for *consideration*. The two most frequent are listed below. They do not differ from what we have seen in judgements and textbooks, except for *partial* as another possible adjective that co-occurs with *failure of consideration*.

30) *There has been no total failure of consideration, and money paid cannot be recovered on a partial failure of consideration*

31) *A new contract made for good consideration after coming of age, notwithstanding that it may do the same thing as intended by an earlier contract made during minority, is not a ratification of that earlier contract.*

Table 3 lists the most frequent combinations in which *consideration* appears and shows how each combination is distributed across the four genres.

	contract	*judgement*	*textbook*	*report*
in consideration of	+			
for good (and valuable) consideration	+		+	+
total consideration	+			
for such consideration ...as X may think fit	+			
for the consideration named	+			
for valuable consideration		+	+	
total failure of consideration		+	+	+
the whole of consideration		+		
agreed consideration		+		
consideration must move from the promisee			+	
executed consideration			+	
executory consideration			+	
past consideration			+	
sufficient consideration			+	

Table 3. Most frequent combinations in which *consideration appears.*

3. Conclusions

The data presented above has shown that adding a genre dimension to the analysis of terms in context can greatly enrich our knowledge about the lexical environment of terms. For example, in the case of *consideration* it is possible to point to a unique set of combinations in which this term appears in contracts. The phrases *in consideration of*, *for good and valuable consideration* and *for the consideration named* as well as the combination *for such consideration ...as X may think fit* tend to be fairly frequent in contracts but not a single instance has been found in judgements, textbooks or reports. We have noticed that the reason for this could be the macrostructural features of contracts and the existence of conventional routine phrases. Similarly, for instance, the use of *total* before *consideration* appears to be idiosyncratic. Despite the existence of other synonymous adjectives, one is far more likely to come across the combination of *total consideration* and not for example *complete consideration* in contracts. On the other hand, in textbooks, there are certain standard terms, for example, *executory consideration* or *past consideration* not appearing at all in contracts or the other genres for that matter. We are not at this point concerned with why this is so but merely recording the facts. A genre-oriented corpus search can also demonstrate that certain combinations can have a wider distribution. This was the case with *failure of consideration* appearing in judgements, textbooks and reports. In pedagogic terms, it seems essential that students be familiar with such restraints on term combinability if they are to produce effective highly specialised texts. Clearly, frequency-based enquiries are meant only as first-point reference for those unfamiliar with the contextual environment of terms.

References

Alcaraz, E. / Hughes, B. 2002. *Legal Translation Explained.* Manchester, UK: St. Jerome Publishing.

Bergenholtz, H. / Tarp, S. (eds) 1995. *Manual of Specialized Lexicography*, Amsterdam/Philadelphia: John Benjamins.

Goźdź-Roszkowski, S. 2000. Using parallel corpora to analyse the language of contracts in English and Polish. In Lewandowska-Tomaszczyk, Melia (ed.) *PALC'99: Practical Applications in Language Corpora* Bern: Peter Lang, 553-565.

Kjaer, A.L. 1990a. Context-conditioned word combinations in legal language. *IITF Journal* (Journal of the Institute for Terminology Research) 1/1-2, 21-32.

Kjaer, A.L. 1990b. Methods of describing word combinations in language for specific purposes *IITF Journal* 1/1-2, 3-20.

Pearson, J. 1998. *Terms in Context.* Amsterdam/Philadelphia: John Benjamins.

Thomas, P. 1993. Choosing headwords from language-for-special-purposes (LSP) collocations for entry into a terminology data bank (term bank). In Sonneveld, H. / Loening, K. (eds) *Terminology. Applications in Interdisciplinary Communication*. Amsterdam/Philadelphia: John Benjamins, 43-68.

Dictionaries consulted:

Black's Law Dictionary, [6]1990.
Dictionary of Law, L.B. Curzon, [5]1998, Financial Times, Pitman Publishing.
Słownik Terminologii Prawniczej i Ekonomicznej Angielsko-Polski (An English-Polish Dictionary of Legal and Economic Terms), Jaślan J, Jaślan H. Wiedza Powszechna Warszawa.
Słownik Prawa (English Law Dictionary), P.H. Collin, K. Bartnicki, Peter Collin Publishing / Wydawnictwo Wilga, 2001.

HEINZ LECHLEITER

Lecture notes and how they are read by foreign students: A case study

1. Introduction

At a time when student exchanges between countries become more and more widespread, it seems important to look at a text type which students are exposed to more than any other in the course of their studies: the lecture note (or *Vorlesungsskript* in German). While other instructional texts like textbooks have received quite a bit of attention by scholars interested in Languages for Special Purposes, lecture notes have gone widely unnoticed as a particular sub-group of instructional texts. I have started to collect *Vorlesungsskripte* for the purpose of a detailed corpus linguistic analysis from my Irish students of Chemistry with German on their return from their period of study abroad in German-speaking countries. In the process I noticed that it is not only the lecture notes themselves that are of some interest but also what students do with them.

2. Lecture notes and text-typology

Instructional texts in the form of textbooks are relatively well researched although there are considerable differences when it comes to naming and categorising the larger group of texts which are used in the process of turning laypeople into experts. The concept of instructional text (*Lehrbuch*) appears in many different shapes and forms in the relevant literature of the last two decades: Hahn's (1983) label is *Vermittlungstext* (mediating text), it appears as *didaktisiernd-instruierender* (didactic-instructional) text in Göpferich (1992), or *elementarisierend* (reverting to fundamentals) in Ickler (1997).[1]

The effort of categorising instructional texts results in their appearing as subject-internal texts (*fachintern*, Göpferich 1992), as well as subject-external texts (Gläser 1990) or their not explicitly being mentioned at all (Hoffmann 1987).

The subgroups of instructional texts included in these text typologies include textbooks (*Lehrbuch*), correspondence course lessons (*Lehrbrief*), technical and instructional manuals (*Handbuch, Gebrauchsanweisung*), as well as experimental reports (*Versuchsprotokoll*) and lectures. Ancillary text forms like black board notes, overhead transparencies, Power Point presentations and so on, are not included.

The training provided in the sciences makes a very pronounced distinction between the theoretical which is taught in lectures, sometimes accompanied by tutorials, and the practical, typically conducted in laboratories. Accordingly the *Skript* takes two main shapes, namely that of lecture notes and manual-type notes for the lab sessions. Both are very similar in appearance, character and function and are treated the same for the purposes of this study.

It is part of the position of the *Skript* in the German-speaking academic world that it is frequently seen as a precursor of a published textbook or laboratory manual. Looking at one of those (Fischer 1994) allows us to trace back the origins of his handbook to a *Skript*. In his introduction Fischer speaks of the "provisional and unsatisfactory raw form" of a previous edition. The editing process involves "improving text and graphics" and the "addition of a register and a list of references". In other words, the *Skript* is seen as an incomplete text on the level of content, structure, design and language.

A review of about 12 *Skripten* of chemistry in Germany produced a great variety of forms and styles of this text type, from fully

1 These examples, and those in the following paragraph, are taken from researchers in German-speaking countries because of the strong cultural difference between the German *Vorlesungsskript* and the English *lecture notes*.

handwritten varieties to quite sophisticated text designs (of the latter many can be found on the Internet). Some of the major characteristics they share are the following: *Skripten* are texts that emerge from the everyday work of academic teaching. They are meant to help students identify major points of the course content and to support their memory (the latter function applies partly to the lecturer, as well). Publication of the *Skripten* beyond the classroom is not necessarily intended although the conversion into a text form that is made accessible to a larger audience via a publisher's is not uncommon. *Skripten* often show signs of having been put together under the strains and stresses of everyday academic life, and therefore they contain typing errors, incomplete sentences, ungrammatical sentences and spelling errors. In terms of argumentation and structure, they are often characterised by logical jumps and starts and inconsistencies in content and layout for example in discontinuous page numbering, different font styles and seizes, unequal margins and so on. Figures are often inserted on an *ad hoc* basis as can be seen from missing, incomplete or wrong legends/keys; in a considerable number of cases, figures or tables are sketched in manually. In many cases, as in the one cited below, the situational rootedness of the text type *Skript* and lecture note is underlined by the fact that there is no mention of the authors or authors' name anywhere, and equally, references and index are usually not part of the *Skript*.[2]

All of these characteristics (incompleteness, jumps and start, missing logical links, errors) are shared with oral language usage, and as in the case of oral language they can only be measured against an idealised perfection and completeness of usage.

The rootedness of the *Skript* in everyday academic business is possibly the reason why it is, perhaps more than other academic text type, culturally quite different between the various countries and intellectual styles. This becomes quite obvious in a strongly condensed overview of research done on the *Skript* in Mechanical Engineering by Eßer/Little (2000). In reading the overview it should be kept in mind

2 This pertains in later published versions like Fischer (1994), who is named as the editor of the *Praktikum in Allgemeiner Chemie* without any mention of the other contributors to the two volumes of his work.

that above remarks about the provisionality were made about the German-language *Skript* which, in the following table (Table 1), appears to be more carefully crafted than the English-language lecture notes.

	Vorlesungsskript	*Lecture notes*
Function	Transcript of lecture	Supplementary information
Content	Structured, detailed, complex	Less structured; past exam and tutorial questions
Length	130 pages	56 pages
Structure (topic hierarchy)	Subordination of topics Third degree sub-points	Co-ordination of topics Listing of topics
Style	Writer presence: minimal Reader address: minimal	Writer presence: strong Reader address: present
	Formal, impersonal language (passive voice, reflexive constructions)	Mixture of formal and colloquial language

Table 1. German- *Skript vs. English lecture notes.*

The fact that the picture which emerges from Eßer and Little's lecture notes and *Skripten* in Mechanical Engineering is in some respects different from my observations on the *Skript* in Chemistry indicates that there might be a disciplinary culture (in our case between Mechanical Engineering and Chemistry) that overrides differences anchored in language (English vs. German) and/or intellectual style (Anglo-Saxon vs. Teutonic).

Following these few remarks on the text type of lecture notes or *Vorlesungsskript* the focus is now redirected towards the traces in the text which were left by a student in the form of annotations and short translations. These are a valuable indicator as to how the *Vorlesungsskript* is read and understood by a student of Chemistry for whom German is a second language. The annotations and translations in the *Skript* do not give a clear indication as to when and under what circumstances they were produced by the student. There are, however, indications that they were inserted at different stages, i.e. before, during or after the respective tutorials and laboratory sessions.

3. Case study

The *Skript* in question is entitled *Praktikum "Quantitative Instrmentelle Analytik". Grundlagen und Versuchsinhalte. 5. Semester Diplomstudiengang Chemie/Umweltchemie.*[3] It was used in the University of Leipzig in the Academic Year of 1999-2000. On its 64 pages it contains sections on administrative and safety issues, an introduction to the theory of the analysis of elements and four experimental parts (with subgroups) on Atom Spectroscopy (*Atomspektroskopie*), X-Ray Fluorescence Analysis (*Röngtenfluoriszenz-Analyse*), Differential Puls-Polarography, and Amperometric Enzyme Electrodes.

The section on X-Ray Fluorescence Analysis contains, under the subsection "Introduction to Theory" (*Theoretische Grundlagen*) in a further subsection entitled X-Rays and X-Ray Fluorescence Analysis, the following passage:

> Beim Beschuss /**bombardment**/ von Atomen mit energiereichen Photonen-(Röntgenstrahlen) oder Teilchenstrahlen /underlined but not annotated/ (Elektronen, Ionen) können Elektronen aus inneren Schalen /**shells**/ der Elektronenhülle /**X-Ray Fluorescence Analysis** / der Atome herausgeschlagen /**knock out**/ werden. Eine solche Vakanz /**vacancy**/ in einer inneren Schale wird jedoch sehr schnell durch Elektronen von energetisch höher liegenden Niveaus /**level**/ aufgefüllt /**fill up**/. Dabei wird ein Photon der Wellenlänge $\lambda = c/\nu$ emittiert, dessen Energie $h\nu$ gleich der Bindungsenergiedifferenz zwischen den beteiligten /**involved**/ Elektronenniveaus /**electron level**/ ist. Da eine Vakanz, etwa in der K-Schale, unter Beachtung der quantenmechanischen Auswahlregeln /**choice rules**/ von vielen darüberliegenden /**higher**/ Niveaus her aufgefüllt werden kann, kommt es zur Herausbildung / underlined but not annotated / von Serien /**series**/ solcher Röntgenemissionslinien (K-Serie, L-Serie usw.). Die Röntgenübergänge /**Xray; transition/crossing**/ werden im einfachsten Fall durch den Namen der Serie und einen nachfolgenden griechischen Buchstaben bezeichnet /**shown**/. Beispielsweise kennzeichnet /**identifies**/ α die Auffüllung /**filling up**/ einer Vakanz aus der folgenden /**following**/ Schale. Die Abbildung 1 gibt einen Überblick über erlaubte /**allowed**/ Röntgenübergänge /**Xray transition**/ und deren Bezeichnung /**Marking**/. Es gelten /**worth**/ Dipolauswahlregeln: $\Delta l = 1$, $\Delta j. = 0; 1$. Die auf die beschriebene Weise /**way**/ erzeugten /**produce**/ Linienspektren sind charakteristisch für die je-

3 Note the similarity in the title with Fischer (1994).

weiligen Elemente. Voraussetzung /**Condition**/ für die Anregung /**Excitation**/ dieser charakteristischen Röntgenstrahlung ist, dass die Anregungsenergie zum Entfernen der Elektronen aus den inneren Schalen der Elektronenhülle ausreicht /**be enough**/, d.h. dass sie energetisch über dem Wert der entsprechenden Absorptionskanten liegt.

The student's annotations are shown between forward slashes and in bold typeface. In the original *Skript* all annotations were written between the lines over the respective German words and expressions, and in two cases word were simply underlined but not annotated.

The passage is quite typical for this *Skript* and the annotations contained therein in terms of density and character of annotations. This passage comprises 180 words (the three equations have been excluded from the count). After the deduction of function words (including articles, prepositions, conjunctions, modal and auxiliary verbs, none of which was annotated), 100 content words are left as tokens, and 70 as types. Of the types 29 are annotated, two of these by underlining without the addition of an English equivalent. In other words, around 40% of all content words in this passage were annotated which indicates that the student submitted it to a thorough reading.

3.1. The position of verbs in the LSP of Chemistry

Of the annotated lexical items 17 are nouns (simple nouns: 5, compound nouns: 7; verb derivatives: 5) and 11 are verbs. Of the verbs 6 are in the predicate position, 5 are used as attributive participles (present participle: 2, past participle: 3). The following table shows the nouns and verbs concerned and the translated version as they appear in the student's annotations.

Word-type	*Word (line*)*	*Translation*
Noun		
Simple	Schale (2) Vakanz (3) Niveau (4) Serie (9) Weise (14)	shell vacancy level series way
Compound	Teilchenstrahlen (2) Elektronenhülle (3) Elektronenniveau (6) Auswahlregel (7) Herausbildung (8) Röntgenübergang (9) Röntgenübergang (12)	[no translation] shell electron level choice rule [no translation.] Xray transition/crossing Xray transition
Verb derivative [verb]	Beschuss (1) [beschießen] Auffüllung (11) [auffüllen] Bezeichnung (13) [bezeichnen] Voraussetzung (15) [vorausset-zen[] Anregung (15) [anregen]	bombardment filling up marking condition excitation
Verb		
in predicate position	herausschlagen (3) auffüllen (5) bezeichnen als (11) kennzeichnen (11) gelten (13)[3] ausreichen (17)	knock out fill up shown identifies worth be enough
attributive		
Present ParticipleI	darüberliegend (8) folgend (12)	higher following
Past Participle	beteiligt (6) erlaubt (12) erzeugt (14)	involved allowed produce
*the line-number refers to the original *Skript*		

Table 2. Nouns and verbs and their translated version in the student's annotations.

Counting the five verb derivates as verbs in terms of background knowledge required, since they cannot be comprehended without a sufficient knowledge and understanding of the verbs from which they derived, it is the verb which receives the majority of the student's attention. Compared with the tendency of LSPs – and the LSP of Chemistry is no exception – towards the use of nominalised forms, this seems to be a strong indication that the results of research into the structure and quantitative spread of parts of speech should not be transferred to the didactics of Specific Purpose Language directly. In other words: although the verb has a receding position in more specialised forms of discourse, the comprehension of texts by L2 learners (and probably also by readers in the first language) strongly hinges on the comprehension of the content and function of the verb or verbs in the text.

In the same way LSPs are much more than specific lexis and terminology, the reading of LSP texts by students are much more than just decoding individual words. This will be shown with two examples from the script in question and the work done on it by the student, namely with a view to interplay between content and form of the annotations in the passage from the *Skript* quoted above, and the translation of another short passage.

3.2. The connection between form and content

While our first look at the annotated passage focused on the lexical level of text comprehension, further interesting insights can be gained by looking at the relationship between the (grammatical) form of the annotations in relation to the original *Skript*, which can reflect insecurities and uncertainties in the reading process in the LSP of the foreign language. It is the verb form of the English-language annotations in comparison with the German originals that will be used as the measuring stick for the purposes of this case study. The verb forms can either take up the German forms directly (for example reflecting 3rd person, active, indicative, present tense in both languages) or indirectly (for example a present participle in German as an *–ing* form in adjective position in English), or they can be neutralised, usually by reflecting a conjugated verb form in German as the infinitive form (without *to*) in English.

Most verbs in the attributive position are rendered in the annotations as participles or in the *–ing* form, or they are translated as adjectives (for example, *darüberliegend* as '*higher*'), thus indicating correct comprehension of the original text. An exception is made with the verb *erzeugen* which occurs in an extended attributive phrase: *Die auf die beschriebene Weise* ['way'] *erzeugten* ['produce'] *Linienspektren*, where the German participle is annotated as an infinitive form in English. Similarly, in one of the two simple passive constructions the infinitive, again, is the translation of choice (*aufgefüllt – 'fill up*'), and this also pertains in the passive plus modal verb construction (*können [...] herausgeschlagen werden – 'knock out'*). In the same vein, finite verbs can duplicate the form (as in *kennzeichnet – 'identifies'*), but they can also appear in the annotations as nominalisations (*gelten – 'worth'*) or neutralised as an infinitive form (*ausreicht – 'be enough'*). All of these instances taken together point toward an uncertainty in the interpretation of the original verb phrases which is borne out when seen in the context of a particular form of annotation which is the translation of certain short text passages.

3.3. Translation and metaphor

In most cases the annotations confine themselves to the insertion of single lexical items. However, there are some short passages throughout the *Skript* which were translated by the student. The reasons for these are not known, it can only be surmised that these particular passages were perceived to be either particularly important or particularly difficult, or both, which would explain the change from the less exacting annotation to the more time-consuming translation.

One example for this can be found in the chapter on one form of Atom Spectroscopy (page 18). The following is the original text with the student's annotations followed by the translation.

> Atomspektroskopische Analysenverfahren können für die qualitative und quantitative Stoffanalyse eingesetzt / apply / werden. Es ist in jedem Falle erforderlich / necessary /, die Probe (Feststoff, Lösung, Gas) durch Energiezufuhr /Energy supply/ in den Plasmazustand (hocherhitztes, teilweise ionisier-

tes Gas) zu überführen / pass over /. Die Probe liegt / have arrived / in Form freier Atome vor, die selber elektromagnetische Strahlung aussenden / transmit / oder solche, die VIS und UV absorbieren können.

Translation (hand written)

Atomspectroscopy analysing methods can be applied for quantitative and qualitative analysing. It is necessary to pass the sample through the energy supply in the plasma state. The sample (arrives) in the form of free Atom, which can themselves transmit electromagnetic stream or such, the VIS and UV can absorb.

Some words remain untranslated, but these instances will not be discussed here. There is also the replacement of one plural in the German as a singular in English (*Atome – 'atoms'*), but this is interpreted as a simple writing error. It is, however, remarkable that the forms of only one or two of the verbs in this passage are translated without a change, thus underlining the point that was made above, namely that insecurity in the annotation of *forms* is a reliable indicator of difficulty with the comprehension of a text.

But there is a second source of misunderstanding which has to do with the metaphorical level in this LSP text. A pattern can be established which is based on the fact that misunderstandings are not isolated instances of false comprehension but they are tied into a semantic net around the concept of "movement from place A to place B" which give the author of the translation a wrong feeling of consistency, thus avoiding the impression of contradiction or lack of coherence which could lead to a re-assessment of a failed attempt at translating. In other words: the mistranslations support and amplify each other.

Most of the misunderstandings can be traced back to the annotations in the passage, but there is also an example for a non-annotated word getting caught up in the web of misapprehension.

The sentence

> Es ist in jedem Falle erforderlich / necessary /, die Probe (Feststoff, Lösung, Gas) durch Energiezufuhr / Energy supply / in den Plasmazustand (hocherhitztes, teilweise ionisiertes Gas) zu überführen /pass over/.

is translated as

> It is necessary to pass the sample through the energy supply in the plasma state.

The annotation to *überführen*, i.e. *pass over* which appears in the translation as the verb *pass* with the preposition *through* shows that the verb was not understood correctly in this context. The German original speaks of the transition from one state to another. We are, therefore, confronted with a metaphor in Johnson and Lakoff's (1980: 31-32) definition. In this case a physical state is conceptualised as a container. The metaphor is not recognised in this instance, a problem that had been recognised by Bhusan and Rosenfeld as a possible problem in the didactics of LSP in their interesting article on metaphorical models in chemistry (1995: 578):

> If one accepts that metaphors are pervasive in scientific thinking, what are the consequences of failing to recognize that a given scientific claim, or scientific model, is metaphorical rather than literal?

Our example is, in Andrew Goatly's (1997) terms, an asymmetrical metaphor, i.e. a metaphor which is not recognised by the recipient (or, *vice versa*, a non-metaphorical expression which is processed as a metaphor). The consequences of such an asymmetrical processing can be studied in this instance.

The misunderstanding deepens. The use of the local variety of the preposition *through* instead of the intended instrumental one is to be seen as a continuation error from the misapprehension of the verb, and the accumulation of these errors is carried through to in the next sentence.

> Die Probe liegt / have arrived / in Form freier Atome vor, die selber elektromagnetische Strahlung aussenden /transmit/ oder solche, die VIS und UV absorbieren können.

is translated as:

> The sample (arrives) in the form of free Atom, which can themselves transmit electromagnetic stream or such, the VIS and UV can absorb.

There are a number of problems and difficulties, which are partly perceived by the student herself.[4] The translation of *vorliegen* as '*have arrived'* is put into brackets in the translation which shows that there is an awareness of a problem. But the more important problems lie in the expressions *aussenden* and *Strahlung*, translated as '*transmit'* and '*stream'* respectively. '*Stream'* fits with the local interpretation of *überführen* as '*pass over / through'*, whereas '*transmit'* (instead of the correct translation '*emit'*) suits the semantic field of "movement from point A to point B" since '*transmit'* presupposes the presence of a sender as well as a receiver, while the intended meaning does not require a receiver position.

4. Conclusions

Student annotations are hardly accessible by other means than individual and manual analysis, but this is worth the effort. They provide a window on the language-learning process as it takes place not in a language-learning but in a subject-related context. Through this window much more can be seen about the L2 learning process than the few glimpses presented in this chapter. It is important to note that all the examples shown above are not isolated incidences but that they

4 It has to be said, in fairness to the student, that the problems may be partly due to the original text: the syntactic structure and cohesion of the sentence is somehow flawed as the case of *solche,* which refers to *freier Atome* (=genitive) should also be the genitive. This is one example for the lack of stylistic care, which is so typical for the *Vorlesungsskript.*

form part of a consistent pattern, at least for this particular set of lecture notes and this particular student which shows that the verb plays a pivotal part even in de-verbalised LSP texts, that lexis and syntax form parts of a unity, and that metaphors in the definition of Lakoff and Johnson are a vital part of the LSP of chemistry which lead to specific learning problems for students. But looking at students' annotations does not only provide an insight into the learning of an LSP from the point of view of an L2 learner, and, as a consequence, the chance to develop some novel ideas for the teaching of LSPs, it also provides an insight into the LSP itself and the way it functions in the process of imparting expert knowledge to future specialists.

References

Bhusan, N. / Rosenfeld, S. 1995. Metaphorical Models in Chemistry. *Journal of Chemical Education* 72/7, 578-582.

Eßer, R. / Little, R. 2000. German for academic purposes: A comparison of English and German lecture notes for students of mechanical engineering. In Ruane, M. / O'Baoill, D. (eds) *Integrating Theory and Practice in LSP and LAP. Papers from the ALC/IRAAL conference*. March 1998, Part 1 and 2, Dublin: IRAAL, 1-13.

Ehlich, K. 1994. Die Lehre der deutschen Wissenschaftssprache. In Kretzenbacher, H.-L. / Weinrich, H. (eds) *Linguistik der Wissenschaftssprache*. Berlin/New York: de Gruyter (Akademie der Wissenschaften zu Berlin, Forschungsberichte 10), 325-351.

Fischer, H. ^{2}1994. *Praktikum in Allgemeiner Chemie. Ein umweltschonendes Programm für Studienanfänger mit Versuchen zur Chemikalien-Rückgewinnung* 2 Bd. Basel: Verlag Helvetica Chimica Acta / Weinheim: VCH.

Fromherz, H. / King, A. ^{5}1968. *English – German Chemical Terminology. An Introduction to Chemistry in English and German. 5th rev. ed. Englische und deutsche chemische Fachausdrücke.*

Ein Leitfaden der Chemie in englischer und deutscher Sprache. Weinheim: Verlag Chemie.

Goatly, A. 1997. *The Language of Metaphor.* London/New York: Routledge.

Göpferich, S. 1992. Eine pragmatische Typologie von Textsorten der Naturwissenschaft und Technik. In Baumann, K.-D. / Kalverkämper, H. *Kontrastive Fachsprachenforschung.* Tübingen: Narr (Forum für Fachsprachen-Forschung 20), 190-210.

Hahn, W. von 1983. *Fachkommunikation. Entwicklung, linguistische Konzepte, betriebliche Beispiele.* Berlin/New York: Springer.

Hoffmann, L. ^{3}1987. *Kommunikationsmittel Fachsprache: eine Einführung.* Berlin: Akademie Verlag (Sammlung Akademie Verlag 44: Sprache).

Hund, E. 1998. naheliegend und weit hergeholt – unterrichtspraktische Überlegungen zu Raum und Körper in der Wissenschaftssprache. In Barkowski, H. / Wolff, A. (eds) *Alternative Vermittlungsmethoden auf dem Prüfstand. Beiträge der 26. Jahrestagung Deutsch als Fremdsprache vom 4. bis 6. Juni 1998, Regensburg: Fachverband Deutsch als Fremdsprache* (Materialien Deutsch als Fremdsprache 52) 290-320.

Ickler, Th. 1997. *Die Disziplinierung der Sprache. Fachsprachen in unserer Zeit.* Tübingen: Narr (Forum für Fachsprachen-Forschung 33).

Lakoff, G. / Johnson, M. 1980. *Metaphors we live by.* Chicago/London: Chicago University Press.

Lechleiter, H. 2002. *Die Fachsprache der Chemie in Theorie, Praxis und Didaktik.* PhD Dissertation, Dublin City University.

Part Five
Challenges in LSP translation

The layperson's view of LSP translation is often that of a word substitution exercise in which specialist dictionaries can fill the gaps in the translator's inadequate vocabulary. The translation of belletristic texts may, however, be judged more generously as a cultural intellectual challenge in contrast to "commercial" [*sic*] translation. Reasons for such judgements may include the more ephemeral nature of the subject matter in what the translation studies literature has called "pragmatic" texts (*Gebrauchstexte*) and the assumption of easier equivalences lacking in cultural nuance. The chapters in this fifth and final Part all deal with an aspect of specialist translation, and leave the reader in no doubt of some of the complex issues surrounding the translation of specialist texts, changing professional profiles and translation curricula in our information age. Today's specialist translators are continuing in a tradition stretching back millennia in which translators have played a key role in the transfer of knowledge between languages and cultures.

In a challenging opening chapter, Kirsten Malmkjær tackles head on the issue of equivalence in "specialised" and literary texts, posing the question whether there are two types of concept-term (or meaning-form) relation according to established but potentially contradictory views. On the one hand, invariant meanings are said to facilitate the equivalence of different forms across languages as in technical translation. On the other hand, in literary translation form and meaning are intimately linked, implying the impossibility of translation. By closely analysing the use of two adjectives in a short tale by Hans Christian Andersen, Malmkjær demonstrates that it can be important to preserve observed lexical patterns of distribution in a literary text so that consistency becomes as important as in technical translation. Ultimately, however, it becomes clear that concepts evolve, whether in a discipline over time or within a particular literary text, and it is this very "impermanence" which makes translation possible, according to Malmkjær.

The issue of metaphor in translation, or more specifically "grammatical metaphor", is addressed by Mall Stålhammar in the second chapter on four different language versions of the Treaty on European Union: English; French, German and Swedish. Grammatical metaphor is understood as a personification of inanimate nouns as in:

"This paper reports…". English and French are found to exhibit the closest parallels, with Swedish tending to follow similar patterns but German mostly choosing [*sic*] alternative structures such as passives. Interestingly, as Stålhammar points out, personifications are not universally considered acceptable – even in English – by some experienced scientific and technical writers; teachers of English for Specific Purposes may also welcome guidance on the semantic restrictions on grammatical metaphors such as acceptable noun-verb collocations. More data are needed, Stålhammar notes, for such restrictions to be adequately described.

The theme of the expanding professional sphere of translators is taken up again by Anastasia Parianou and Panayotis Kelandrias, who analyse the translation of instructions for use for a range of domestic appliances. They point to the difficulties of dealing with inconsistencies in the use of terms in the source text and of the problems posed by finding translation solutions in target languages where there is no tradition – or no recent tradition – in the relevant domain. The issue of lexical "gaps" in the target language is also explored by Anne Kari Bjørge in connection with Norwegian technical terms which have either no English dictionary equivalent or multiple possibilities without adequate contextualisation. Her main question is: how do student translators deal with such terms? Her proposed answer, based on a corpus of examination papers, suggests that the strategies employed in the translation of sociocultural texts are also appropriate here, thereby indicating that translational competence applies equally to technical subject fields where expectations of direct equivalence may be higher. Bjørge demonstrates the false optimism of this assumption. Whereas Bjørge looks at the strategies used by student translators under examination conditions without access to the World Wide Web, in the following chapter Marella Magris and Lorenza Rega compare the use of specialist dictionaries with the WWW as a lexical resource. They conclude that of the 51 translators who completed their questionnaire, only one never uses specialised dictionaries, most use them very often and a minority only rarely. Some respondents use specialised dictionaries more frequently than on-line resources, but more use them as or less frequently. The study demonstrates that paper resources have not yet been superseded by electronic resources and that translators show different preference patterns in their use of resource types.

On a didactic theme, Ioannis Saridakis and Georgia Kostopoulou outline the introduction of a corpus-based approach to the teaching of specialist translation in Greece. Their objective is to help students establish a pragmatic and semantic framework for later translation decisions by comparing at a discourse level in the first instance parallel corpora in the source and target languages which they themselves have compiled according to specified design criteria. They illustrate how such as analysis can aid decision-making at the lexical level.

This final Part of the volume presents a range of views about the possibility, practicability, methodology, teachability and necessity of specialist translation, raising issues related to the role of lexical resources, specialist knowledge and translation strategies. A common theme is the lack of determinacy in written verbal communication – including in technical and other specialist texts – a characteristic which is often only revealed by the specialist translator's attempts to understand the source text and to find appropriate solutions for the emerging target text.

KIRSTEN MALMKJÆR

Language and special translational purposes

1. Introduction

This article addresses three issues: (1) The relationship between literary translation and special-purpose translation; (2) the nature of specialised terms; and (3) the nature of meaning. I use, in section 5, a case study presented elsewhere (Malmkjær 2003), though in a different context to a different end, and I draw in section 7 on a discussion of equivalence which forms part of Malmkjær (2002).

2. Special-purpose translation

Special-purpose translation is usually thought to include, centrally, the translation of text types such as legal, medical, technical, scientific, public service, and possibly political texts just as LSP usually deals with texts written for use within reasonably clearly defined interest spheres or discourse communities (Swales 1990). Literary translation might logically be thought of as a special type of translation, but, perhaps because it is difficult to say what the purpose of literature is, it is rare to see literary translation classified as special-purpose translation.

I would like, nevertheless, to draw out some similarities between literary and special-purpose translation, without, I hope, losing sight of the differences between them, and in the hope that the comparison will highlight features that might help conceptualisation within both sub-disciplines.

3. Literary translation, special-purpose translation and specialisation

Both literary translation and special-purpose translation may be informed by genre studies. In the case of literary translation studies, the genres studied tend, naturally enough, to be literary and the approach taken to them tends to be informed by literary theory. Special-purpose translation studies, on the other hand, tend to look to the type of genre analysis exemplified by Swales (1990).

Both types of genre study offer the possibility of infinite genre refinement, as we might call it, through increasingly detailed definitions of the genres under attention. For example, we could identify within the genre, business communication, the subgenre, business letters; and within that, the subgenre, letters written from within company A; and within that, the subgenre, letters written within company A by employer B; and within that, the subgenre, letters written within company A by employer B to employer C; and so on. In literary stylistics, this kind of finely defined genre is very often the subject of individual studies. For example, there are a number of editions and studies of the letters of Dorothy Osborne to Sir William Temple (for example Hart 1968; Parker 1987; Parry 1914). Obviously, this feature of genre studies mirrors individuals' tendency to specialise, and this tendency is also to be found in translation studies. Translators' specialised areas can become very specialised indeed as they grow in their profession. For example, someone who set out translating or interpreting political discourse in general can end up as a personal translator, interpreter and speech writer for one politician; or someone who set out translating horticulture in general can end up specialising in one particular plant; or someone who set out translating for the automotive industry can end up translating only for, for example, Ford.

There are two main reasons for this. One arises from a clear overlap between LSP and special-purpose translation: an area of specialisation has its own highly detailed and often vast discourse consisting of sets of terms and phrases and text structures which only someone very familiar with the area will have a sure and steady grasp of.

Since a translator need this grasp for both languages, it often makes sense to specialise.

The other reason is linked to globalisation and increased competition in the market place, which combine to make speed of the essence in the translation profession (Eckersley 2003). For example, each time Ford or some other car manufacturer releases a new model, they will want the accompanying manual to be available simultaneously for the languages of all of the countries where the vehicle will go on sale. And they often think of this rather late in the day, once everything else is in place. Furthermore, they will want the manual to conform to the conventions governing all of Ford's manuals. Therefore, they tend to use a small number of large, specialised and highly technologialised translation companies who use translation memories as aids in the production of the manuals and other literature. This means that only minimal change is required in a new manual or other text type: The memory will recognise and automatically reproduce all those parts that are unchanged from previous manuals, so that the new work the translator has to do is minimal. But it also means that only those with the requisite software, trimmed and trained to Ford's house style, are able to produce Ford manuals fast and consistently enough. This tends to be large companies specialising mainly in translating for a few large clients whose translators, in turn, tend to end up specialising in the same.

The need to respond to market trends has also led to a conceptualisation of translation quality that closely mirrors the understanding of quality that predominates in the production industries. Quality, as a property of the kinds of translations that translation companies sell most of (not translations of literature), is defined in the fit-for-purpose sense: A quality translation is a translation that will fulfil the purpose the client wants and needs the translation to fulfil in the community it is to function in. And with the recognition that this is how translation quality needs to be defined in commercial terms have come new, so-called functional approaches to translation (Reiss 1971) such as *Skopos* theory (Vermeer 1978; Reiss/Vermeer 1984).

According to *Skopos* theory, the primary determinant of the characteristics of a translation should be the purpose the translation has to serve, rather than a quest for equivalence with the source text.

In the case of some texts, it is obvious that equivalence with the source text is not going to guarantee fitness for purpose of the translation. A famous example is the Coca-Cola advert slogan "Drink Coca-Cola" which, because of its imperative mood, would be insulting in some countries/cultures. Obviously, it is much more important not to insult one's potential customers, in such a case, than it is to reproduce as many features of the source text as possible in the translation, including its mood. But in clear cases like the Coca-Cola advert which may end up having nothing in common with the source text except possibly the trade mark term, perhaps we are not talking about translation at all, but about a quite different text, originally created, albeit falling within the same genre, advertisement, as the other text, and having the same purpose: To advertise Coca-Cola.

Other similar if less clear cases include for example company reports, business letters or newspaper articles, in the case of which structural and move conventions often differ in different languages. And in those cases it is less easy to declare the new text an original.

I won't delve further into that very difficult question, only into the underlying question of translational equivalence.

4. On translational equivalence

Until not so long ago, the quest for equivalence with the source text seemed the overriding criterion for translation success in all translation, and, of course, it is still the case that in many translations, the desired purpose is that they communicate as completely and clearly as possible whatever the source text communicates. This is particularly so in the case of, for example, legal texts, where it tends to be believed that the form of expression is very important in conveying the precise meaning of a piece of text. But it is also often still the case in literary translation that what translators claim to aim for and what some critics criticise them for not having achieved is faithfulness to the original in as many aspect as possible – which is to say, optimal equivalence.

But wherein can equivalence reside? It may seem that what you get from having a really good grasp of specialised terminology in two languages is some level of guarantee of equivalence, the guarantor being the extension (the set of things) that the specialised term stands for: You can have equivalence of signified and of sense in spite of formal variation in the signifier, as pointed out by for example Saussure (1916) and before him by Locke (1690: Book 3, Chapter 2).

Except, it has been said, where literary translation is concerned. In the translation of literary texts, equivalence across languages is often held to be quite impossible: The meaning of the source text is intimately tied in with its form, and as translating imposes a different form on the translation than that enjoyed by the source text, literary translation must, strictly speaking, give way to what Jakobson (1959: 238) called creative transposition (see for example Ingarden 1931/1973; 1937/1973).

Funnily enough, it is quite common for one and the same person (see for example Jakobson 1959) to hold to both of these views: (i) that specialised texts *can* be translated faithfully because of the invariant extensions for terms and expressions that differ in different languages; and (ii) that literary texts *cannot* be translated faithfully because of the impossibility of disassociating exactly these two phenomena: extension and expression or, as we might say, meaning and form.

So one and the same person can have in their heads two quite different ideas about how languages relate to concepts. One idea (for non-literary texts) might be pictured like this:

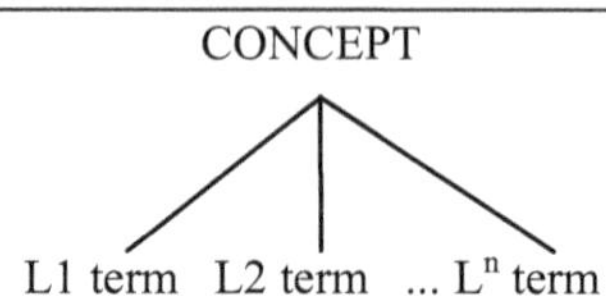

The other (for literary texts) might be pictured like this:

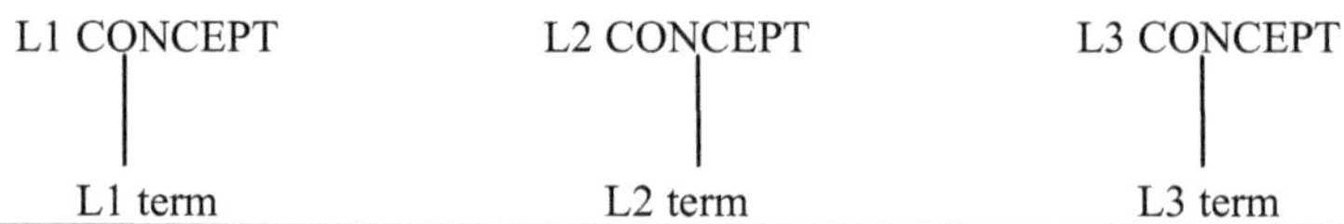

Figure 1. Different concept for one idea.

How can that be? Does language work differently in literature and in other text types normally known as special-purpose text? Is there only one way (though it may be a very complicated way, see Evans 1983) in which language relates to what it is about, or are there two ways (or more)? And is meaning actually just a question of this relationship between concepts and terms?

In the remainder of this article, I intend to work towards providing a set (among several possible sets, no doubt) of answers to these questions.

5. Specialised terms in literary translation

Let me begin by demonstrating how terms can be specialised in literary texts, and how they can be identified so that they can be properly represented in translations of literary texts.

Consider the following small story, in which I have left a few terms (underlined) untranslated:

(1) **The princess on the pea (1835 Hans Christian Andersen; my translation)**
There was once a prince; he wanted to have a princess, but she would have to be a *rigtig* princess. So he travelled all around the world to find one, but everywhere something was wrong, there were plenty of princesses, but whether they were *rigtige* princesses he could not quite figure out, there was always something which was not so rigtigt. So then he came home again and was very sad, for he wanted so much to have a virkelig princess.
Then one evening there was a dreadful storm; there was thunder and lightening, the rain poured down, it was quite frightful! Then someone knocked on the town gate, and the old king went to open it.
It was a princess who was standing outside. But God what a sight she was from the rain and the evil weather! Water was running down her hair and her clothes, and it was running in at the toes of her shoes and out at the heels, and yet she said that she was a virkelig princess.
"Well, we'll soon see about that!" thought the old queen, but she didn't say anything, went into the bedroom, took all the bedclothes off and laid a pea on the bottom of the bed, then she took twenty mattresses, laid them on top of the pea, and then another twenty eiderdown quilts on top of the mattresses.
That was where the princess was to lie that night.
In the morning they asked her how she had slept.
"Oh, frightfully badly!" said the princess, "I have hardly closed my eyes the whole night! God knows what there was in the bed? I have been lying on something hard, so that I am quite black and blue all over my body! It is quite frightful!"
Then they could see that she was a rigtig princess as she had been able to feel the pea through the twenty mattresses and the twenty eiderdown quilts. No one but a virkelig princess could be that tender skinned.
So the prince took her as his wife, for now he knew that he had a rigtig princess, and the pea was put in the Royal Collection, where it is still to be seen, if no one has taken it.
You see that was a rigtig story!

This a text of 383 word tokens of which 62 are nouns and 21 are adjectives:

Nouns
prince x 2; princess x 10; princesses x 2; world; something x 3; evening; storm; thunder; lightening; rain x 2; town; gate; king; God x 2; sight; weather; water; hair; clothes; toes; shoes; heels; queen; bedroom; bedclothes; pea x 4; bottom; bed x 2; mattresses x 3; eiderdown x 2; quilts x 2; night x 2; morning; eyes; body; wife; Collection; story

Adjectives
rigtig x 4; rigtige; rigtigt; sad; virkelig x 3; dreadful; frightful x 2; old x 2; evil; whole x 2; hard; tender skinned; royal

If we now look for combinations of the relatively few adjective tokens with the relatively more noun tokens, we find, unsurprisingly, that most noun tokens (44), are not modified by an adjective and that 5 adjective tokens are not attached to a noun, only to a dummy pronoun. We won't worry any further about those, because we are looking for patterns. This leaves the following combinations of adjective + noun:

Adjective-Noun combinations
rigtig princess x 3; virkelig princess x 3; rigtige princesses; something [something which was not so rigtigt]; dreadful storm; old king; evil weather; old queen; whole night; Royal Collection; rigtig story.

What we know so far, partly on the basis of this analysis and partly on the basis of background knowledge, is:

- The most frequent noun tokens are forms of the lexical item PRINCESS;
- The most frequent adjective tokens are forms of the lexical item RIGTIG
- The most frequent combination is of those lexical items
- PRINCESS is modified by one other adjective in this story, namely VIRKELIG
- This is the next most frequent adjective form in the story
- The two adjectives *rigtig* and *virkelig* fall within the same "semantic field": both indicate a quality of being a good example of a kind.
- The combination, PRINCESS + RIGTIG/VIRKELIG is also focal semantically because the story is about finding a princess who has the characteristic(s?) the adjectives stand for: The prince wants a princess who is rigtig/virkelig.
- One other noun, *story*, is premodified by one of these adjectives, *rigtig*.

This raises two questions which a translator might be interested in:

a) Do the two adjectives which are formally different but semantically similar differ subtly in meaning in this story?
b) What quality does the princess share with the story which allows both to be described as *rigtig*?

Looking in a dictionary will not help resolve these issues, because for both *rigtig* and *virkelig*, a dictionary will provide a selection of definitions (if it is monolingual) or translations (if it is bi-lingual) falling within the "good example if its kind"-field, most of which will work very well in each of the contexts in question. This is a reflection of the closeness in meaning of the two adjectives, of course, and it shifts the focus of inquiry sharply onto the prepositional phrase at end of our first question: Do the two adjectives differ in meaning *in this story*?

At this point, a translator might seek guidance in previous translations. Translations of Hans Christian Andersen's stories into English have appeared regularly since the mid-1800s, so there is quite a corpus available, relatively speaking, and I present here the solutions to the adjective-problem provided by translators within a sub-corpus consisting of copies that I have access to (see list in Appendix 1):

Anon: real princess x 6; real princesses; true story
Blegvad: *real* princess; real princesses; real princess x 5; a story
Corrin: *truly real* princess; *real* princesses; *real* princess x 2; real princess x 2; true princess; true story
Corrin and Corrin: *truly real* princess; *real* princesses; *real* princess x 2; real princess x 3; real story
De Chatelain: real princess; real ones; real princess x 5; real story
Dulcken: *real* princess; real one; *real* princesses; real princess x 4; true princess; true story
Hersholt: real one; real Princesses; real Princess x 3; a Princess; real Princess; true story
Haugaard: real one; real princesses; real princess x 4; real story
Kingsland: real princess x 6; real princesses; true story
Lewis: real princess x 5; the genuine article; fine story

Peachey: real Princess; real Princesses; real Princess x 5; "Was not this a lady of real delicacy"
Peulevé: genuine Princess; real Princesses; real Princess x 5; good story
Spink: *real* princess; real princesses; real princess 5; real story
Wehnert: real Princess; real Princesses; real Princess x 5; true story

It is not immediately obvious that this evidence is going to help us answer the questions we are concerned with (do *rigtig* and *virkelig* differ in meaning in this story and what property do the princess and the story share which makes both *rigtige*?): Two translators, Corrin and Dulcken, use two adjectives and use one of them for the story as well as for the princess; Lewis and Peulevé also use two adjectives for the princess, but have a third for the story; Anon, Blegvad, Hersholt, Kingsland and Wehnert distinguish in their adjective use between the princess and the story; Corrin and Corrin, De Chatelain, Haugaard, Peachey and Spink draw no distinction whatsoever.

It is difficult to determine whether this has the potential to matter, from just looking at this story alone. But one way to find out is to look at how Andersen uses the two adjectives in other stories.

The opus yields the following data (I report representative but select data, i.e. only data which do not raise additional questions to those currently in focus; I report the data in an English gloss type translation which, again, leaves the adjectives, underlined, in Danish):

From *The swineherd* (1842)
"Fie Papa!" she said, "it isn't artificial, it is *virkelig*!"

From *The nightingale* (1844)
1. it was a little piece of artistry lying in a box, an artificial nightingale that was supposed to look like the live one but which was covered all over with diamonds, rubies and sapphires; as soon as it was wound up, the artificial bird could sing one of the pieces the virkelige one sang,

2. the virkelige nightingale sang in its own way, and the artificial bird was clockwork;

3. Then the artificial bird must sing alone. – It was as popular as the virkelige one, and besides it was much prettier to look at: it glittered like bracelets and brooches.

4. that it [the artificial bird] was better than the virkelige nightingale,

5. in the case of the virkelige nightingale you can never predict what is going to happen, whereas in the case of the artificial bird, everything is arranged in advance!

6. But the poor fishermen who had heard the virkelige nightingale said: "it [the artificial bird] sounds beautiful all right, and it does resemble it, but something is missing, I don't know what!"

From *Holger Danske* (1845)
and here is a likeness of him!"
And it cast its shadow right up the wall, even a little way along the ceiling, it looked as if it was the virkelige Holger Danske himself

From *The shepherdess and the chimney-sweep* (1845)
Have you ever seen a rigtig old wooden cupboard, quite black with age and carved with intricate patterns of leaves?

From *The puck at the grocer's* (1853)
There was a rigtig student, he lived in the attic and owned nothing; there was a rigtig grocer, he lived on the ground floor and owned the whole house

In these data, *virkelig* is regularly opposed to terms indicating artificiality or artistry, and *rigtig* tends to indicate stereotypicality. This suggests to me that Andersen uses the adjectives *rigtig* and *virkelig* to distinguish between that which is genuinely and inherently what it purports to be, and that which either is a *stilleben* or (merely) conforms to socially held values, norms and expectations. Since this distinction is important thematically in much of Andersen's work, it is likely that the use of the adjectives is a deliberate way of supporting a theme lexically. In other words, the adjectives function for Andersen as specialised terms, which might be a reason for some translators to want to reproduce the kinds of patterns they enter into in the text.

I have suggested elsewhere (Malmkjær 2003) that one way of doing this might be to use 'real' for *rigtig* and 'genuine' for *virkelig*: According to the *COBUILD* dictionary, something 'real' (sense 2.1.) "has all the characteristics or qualities that such a thing typically has" whereas "something which is genuine is real and exactly what it appears to be, and is not fake or an imitation".

Obviously, in our focal story, this distinction is important: The prince is looking for the genuine article, as Naomi Lewis's translation has it, but is rather unsure about how to recognise it when he sees it. The princess who presents herself claims to be it, but fails to conform to expectations on the surface and has to be tested. The test reveals that she possesses the sensitivity inherent in princesses. It is not clear that the prince, whose point of view predominates in the story, is any clearer towards the end about the difference, since both adjectives are used for the princess in views attributed to him, and *rigtig* is the one he uses at the end ("he knew that he had a rigtig princess"); I take this to be a fine touch of irony. But it is significant that the princess herself claims to be *virkelig*, that it is this claim that the queen (who is the seat of wisdom in the story, who knows a test for princess-hood) sets out to test, and that it is this quality which is said to be possessed by the tender-skinned. And this is certainly a "real", stereotypical story with the expected, Proppian fairytale characters in it.

So it seems to me that the two terms, *rigtig* and *virkelig* function as specialised terms in this text just as much as *brake* and *accelerator* might in texts about cars, and that it may be just as important to retain them in translation, although the consequences of not retaining them are fuzzier than they might be in the case of the *brake* and *accelerator* – and this, in turn, may be why there is not such a concentration on specialist terminology in literary translation. In fact, one could even speak of a blindness to it among literary translators, which leads them to adopt the cavalier attitudes to literary terminology that we see exemplified in the translations above.

At the same time, though, it would plainly be absurd to suggest that all of the existing translations of this text are not translations of it. This point was made by Toury (1981), who suggests that a primarily Source Text-oriented theory of translation leads to the absurd position where none of the many translations that we find around us can be true translations. According to Source Text-oriented theories of translation, (a) only equivalence at all levels can qualify a text as a true literary translation, but (b) this equivalence can never be obtained. Ergo, nothing is a proper literary translation, so the theory has no empirical basis against which to test its claims or from which they may be derived. Instead, Toury advocates Target Text-oriented studies, which take existing literary translations to be what they are, namely actual empirical phenomena which function as literary translations and which can show us which terms actually constitute translational equivalents in certain text. Nowadays, of course, this is exactly what very many studies of corpora of original texts and their translations look for.

6. Some implication of the Andersen study

I argued in the previous section that many of the translational equivalents for *rigtig* and *virkelig* in the Andersen corpus are not the most helpful ones; but that this ought not lead one to suggest that all the existing translations of the story are bad, let alone that they are not translations.

What this suggests is the rather obvious idea that there is more to translation than specialised terminology, and I think this is certainly true in the case of special-purpose text translation too. Getting the special terminology right is not going to produce a good text if other features are inaccurate: A misplacement of a simple and very general word like *not*, for example, can be disastrous.

What I have called specialist terminology in the Andersen text is probably local to this one author: Not of course that he is the only one to use this terminology; but he may be alone is using it to reinforce exactly the story theme I have mentioned. This is less likely to happen in the case of texts that are usually thought of as special-purpose texts, the important notions of specialisation and special company house styles (see section 3) notwithstanding.

On the other hand, the fact that a writer can take a pair of existing terms and turn them to special use in the manner of Andersen points to the extraordinary variance there can be in the connection between concept and term; and this is good reason to prefer picture one from section 4 (Figure 1) to picture two, even for literary texts.

In the final section of this chapter, I would like to draw out some further implications of this for our understanding of meaning.

7. Meaning

When English A-level students got their results in August 2003, there was, as usual, much discussion about whether the increased percentage of passes at A-grade, now standing at 1 in 5, or 20%, indicates that the standard of the exam has fallen. The education minister, David Miliband, sought to dismiss this suggestion through an analogy with a possible argument that it must be becoming easier to run the London Marathon because Paula Radcliffe broke the record last time she ran, and because many people now run the Marathon faster than the winner ran it during its early years. Surely, Mr Miliband suggested, students are succeeding in greater numbers because they are taught better and work more efficiently year by year (the record has risen steadily over recent decades).

Whatever one's views of the question of A-level standards, I find it difficult to accept Mr Miliband's analogy, because it assumes that the distance covered by the route of the London Marathon is something similar to the knowledge and skills possessed by an A-level student, and that running the distance is similar to expressing part of the skills and knowledge base appropriately in an exam; but distance is a very different phenomenon than a knowledge and skills base is: Distance is invariant whereas knowledge and skills can develop and alter.

The traditional notion of translation equivalence, however, is based on a distance-type notion deriving from the first of Euclid's (ca

300 B. C.) 'common notion': "Things that are equal to the same thing are equal to one another". This implies that there has to exist a measure of equivalence: the same thing – $thing^1$ – which pre-exists the other things – $things^{2\text{-}n}$ – and which functions as a measure or guarantor of their equivalence.

This Euclidean picture of equivalence is an excellent account of how equivalence is established between things: If you go to buy ten meters of ribbon, the seller will measure a meter against a measuring stick ten times. Normally, they won't measure one meter of ribbon and then another against the first piece and so on. If I want to tune three guitars, I will tune each to a tuning fork rather than to another guitar – at least ideally, to prevent gradual distortion; if a constant is used to measure all new instances, minor inaccuracies in individual instances will not be replicated or increased for other individual instances.

But this picture cannot be transferred to language. Languages are subject to continuous, observable, gradual change; and language cannot be used to create identicals, be they meanings or states of mind. Instead, language promotes cognitive development: it gets you from one mental state to another, different mental state. It cannot get you from one mental state to another, identical mental state, whether your own or somebody else's. Finally, language items are inherently flexible and multifunctional in their semantics, as we saw in section 5.

In the discipline of terminology, which is fairly closely related to LSP, it is accepted that individual terms relate to concepts belonging to a particular domain such as law or medicine and that these domains are systems whose concepts, for which the terms stand, are defined within the theories to which they relate and that their meanings, therefore, are theory internal and theory specific. Within many specialised domains, concepts are perceived as dynamic, rather than static. Sager (1998/1999: 48), for example, points out that legal concepts develop on the basis of a combination of statute and case law.

In this, specialised terms begin to look rather like terms that Gallie (1955-1956) refers to as "essentially contested concepts" – concepts that develop along with the societies in which they are used, such as *liberty* and *democracy*. Though when we come to think about it, almost all so-called natural-kind terms develop along with their theories, and almost all manufactured-kind terms develop as manufacturing develops, just as Gallie's social-kind terms, as we might call them, develop along with their societies.

Every theory is in constant development: we will never know it all. So every term defined within a theory stands for a concept that is evolving. In LSP, the terms tend to remain stable while what they stand for evolves. In the case of literary texts, a concept is developed in a text and terms are adapted or refined to reinforce it. Yet both kinds of term are translated, which suggests that not only is there not, as Saussure and Locke pointed out so long ago (see section 4), any one-to-one correspondence between signifier and signified: there are no fixed correspondences whatsoever, because the signified is in flux and terms are multiply adaptable to new, more or less specialised uses. There are more or less impermanent relationships of meaning which are functions of the relationships between utterers, times, utterances, and background knowledge (Lewis 1974). But far from interfering with translation, this is what makes translation possible – we might even say that this is what translation *is*, essentially: the creation of one such relationship on the basis, partly, of some informed guesses about a previous relationship and who and what it was a relationship between. Sometimes, especially in the case of special-purpose texts the guessing process is helped along by an agreement among special interest groups to hold certain relationships between terms and concepts more stable than they are in most cases. But there is always far more involved in translation, whether specialised or not, than a simple reproduction of a set of relationships between linguistic forms and predetermined denotations.

References

Eckersley, H. 2003. Quality in the translation profession. Paper presented at Middlesex University, 2 February 2003.

Evans, G. 1983. *The Varieties of Reference*. Oxford: Oxford University Press.

Gallie, W. 1955-1956. Essentially contested concepts. *Proceedings of the Aristotelian Society* LVI, 167-198.

Hart, K. (ed.) 1968. *The Letters of Dorothy Osborne to Sir William Temple*. London: The Folio Society.

Ingarden, R. 1931 / 1973. T*he Literary Work of Art: An Investigation on the Borderlines of Ontology, Logic, and Theory of Literature. With an Appendix on the Functions of Language in the Theatre*. Translated, with an introduction by G. G. Grabowicz from the third edition of *Das literarische Kunstwerk* copyright 1935 by Max Niemeyer Verlag, Tübingen. Evanston: Northwestern University Press. First published in 1931 in German by Max Niemeyer.

Ingarden, R. 1937 / 1973. *The Cognition of the Literary Work of Art*. Translated by Crowley, R. A. / Olson, K. R. from *Vom Erkennen des literarischen Kunstwerks* copyright 1968 by Max Niemeyer Verlag, Tübingen. Evanston: Northwestern University Press. First published in 1937 in Polish as *O poznawaniu dziela literackiego* Lvov: Ossolineum.

Jakobson, R. 1959. On Linguistic Aspects of Translation. In Brower, R. A. (ed.) *On Translation*. Cambridge, MA: Harvard University Press / New York: Oxford University Press, 232-239.

Lewis, D. 1974. Radical Interpretation. *Synthese* 23, 331-344.

Locke, J. 1690. *An Essay Concerning Human Understanding.* (1977) Glasgow: Fount.

Malmkjær, K. 2002. Reversing a common notion: Translation and examples in contrastive linguistics. In Makri-Tsilipakou, M. (ed.) *Selected Papers on Theoretical and Applied Linguistics*. Department of Theoretical and Applied Linguistics, School of English, Aristotle University of Thessaloniki, 24-37.

Malmkjær, K. 2003. On a pseudo-subversive use of corpora in translator training. In Zanettin, F. / Bernardini, S. / Stewart, D. (eds) *Corpora in Translator Education*. Manchester: St. Jerome, 118-134.

Parker, K. (ed.) 1987. *Letters to Sir William Temple by Dorothy Osborne*. London: Penguin Books.

Parry, E. A. (ed.) 1914. *The Letters of Dorothy Osborne to Sir William Temple*. London: The Wayfarers Library.

Reiss, K. 1971. *Möglichkeiten und Grenzen der Übersetzungskritik. Kategorien und Kriterien für eine sachgerechte Beurteilung von Übersetzungen*. Munich: Max Huber.

Reiss, K. / Vermeer, H. 1984. *Grundlegung einer allgemeinen Translationstheorie*. Tübingen: Niemeyer.

Sager, J. 1998 / 1999. In Search of a Foundation Towards a Theory of the Term. *Terminology* 5/1, 41-57.

Saussure, F. de 1916. *Cours de linguistique générale*. Lausanne and Paris: Payot.

Swales, J. 1990. *Genre Analysis: English in Academic and research Settings*. Cambridge: Cambridge University Press.

Toury, G. 1981. Translated literature: System, norms, performance: Toward a TT oriented approach to literary translation. *Poetics Today* 2/4, 9-27.

Vermeer, H. 1978. Ein Rahmen für eine allgemeine Translationstheorie. *Lebende Sprachen* 23/3, 99-102.

Appendices

Appendix 1: Hans Christian Andersen translations referred to, in chronological order of publication date

Danish Fairy Legends and Tales. Caroline Peachey, London: William Pickering, 1846. Second, enlarged edition, 1852.

Tales and Fairy Stories. Madame de Chatelain, London: Routledge & Co, 1852.

Andersen's Tales for Children. Wehnert, Alfred, London: Bell & Daldy, 1861.

Stories and Tales. Henry William Dulcken, London: Routledge, 1864.

What the Moon Saw, and other tales. Henry William Dulcken, London: Routledge, 1865.

Hans Christian Andersen's Stories for the Household. H.W. Dulcken, London: Routledge, 1866. Re-issued as *The Complete Illustrated Works of Hans Christian Andersen*. London, Chancellor Press, 1983; 1994.

The Complete Andersen: All of the 168 Stories by Hans Christian Andersen. Jean Hersholt. New York: Limited Editions Club 1942-47. Available in electronic form on MAGNUS, from CD-Danmark A/S, Palægade 4, P.O. Box 9026, DK-1022 Copenhagen K, Denmark.

(Anon) *Hans Christian Andersen: Fairy Tales*. Translator not named. London: Hamlyn. 1959.

Eighty Fairy Tales. Translated by R.P. Keigwin. Odense: Skandinavisk Bogforlag. 1976. With an introduction by Elias Bredsdorff, New York: Pantheon Books, 1982 (This translation first published by Flensted (Denmark) in 1950).

Hans Christian Andersen. Fairy Tales and Stories. Translated, with an Introduction, by Reginald Spink. London, 1960. Republished in the series Everyman's Library Children's Classics, London 1992.

Tales from Hans Andersen. Translated by Stephen Corrin.1978. London: Guild Publishing. 1989.

Hans Christian Andersen. Stories and Fairy Tales selected, translated and illustrated by Erik Blegvad. London, 1993.

The Complete Fairy Tales and Stories. Translated from the Danish by Erik Christian Haugaard. Foreword by Naomi Lewis. London: Gollanz, 1974. Also published, with a foreword by Virginia Haviland, New York, Doubleday & Co. New Edition, Gollancz Children's Paperbacks, 1994.

MALL STÅLHAMMAR

Translation of grammatical metaphor

1. Introduction

Translating metaphors is an intricate part of any translation, even between closely related languages and cultures. Unfortunately it is also one of the least researched aspects of translation, or contrastive linguistics. What little there is, tends to suffer from the misconception that metaphor belongs primarily in literary language. But, as we all know, metaphor is an integral part of language and thus of all genres of text. LSP genres abound in metaphor, as shown in previous analyses of various areas (Stålhammar 1995, 1996, 1997, 2001). One genre that is often believed to be free from metaphor is legal language, or the language of administration, where neither the need to illuminate nor the wish to affect – often the main reasons for the use of metaphor – are supposed to motivate the writers of such texts. However, there may be other reasons for using metaphorical language, as well as there are different kinds of metaphor.

The particular variety of metaphor under discussion here is what Michael Halliday has termed “grammatical metaphor” (Halliday 1986/1994; Halliday/Martin 1993; Halliday 1998), roughly equivalent to what others before him have called ‘animisme’, i.e. personification (Vinay/Darbelnet 1960; Malblanc 1968). If an “ordinary” metaphor, being a lexical transformation, can be defined as the substitution of one word by another, a grammatical metaphor, being a grammatical transformation, is “a substitution of one grammatical class, or one grammatical structure, by another” (Halliday/Martin 1993: 79). For the present purpose it may be defined as the packaging of processes into nouns or nominalisations which in turn are provided with verbs that would “properly” be associated with the subject of the process packaged in the nominalisation. The result is experienced by the reader as if the inanimate noun itself, the package, were personified. (It could be argued that the "metaphor" properly speaking is a metonymy, since contiguity rather than similarity is the basis of the substitution). Of these two terms, the concept of grammatical metaphor serves the purposes of analysis better (revealing what is underlying the choice of verb), whereas the notion of personification may explain the reactions to the use of certain verbs (showing why certain verbs are more or less acceptable with certain subjects). There may also be overlap between lexical and grammatical metaphor (see Lassen 1997).

English and French, among other languages, readily use grammatical metaphor, especially when space is at a premium, and/or the subject "proper" (i.e. the congruent subject of the process) is anonymous, in reality or by convention. Both these qualities characterize certain genres in LSP, and often result in the alternative use of passive constructions (with or without adverbials). A typical opening could thus be phrased either "This paper reports..." or "In this paper (it) is reported..."

As Halliday points out, there are wider consequences following from the choice of grammatical metaphor:

> Ideationally, the nominalising grammar creates a universe of things, bounded, stable and determinate; and (in place of processes) of relations between things. Interpersonally, it sets itself apart as a discourse of the expert, readily becoming a language of power and technocratic control. In both aspects, it creates maximum distance between technical scientific knowledge and the experience of daily life. (Halliday 1998: 228).

Investigating the occurrence of grammatical metaphor is thus highly relevant to the study of LSP.

Comparing the use of similar examples in different languages shows, however, that the construction does not have a similar distribution. Germanic languages seem to prefer the passive, with/without adverbials, whereas the grammatical metaphor seems more acceptable in English and French. (Differences between French and German usage are touched upon in Malblanc 1968; the use in Danish is discussed in Hansen 1996, Korzen 1997). Some of the underlying reasons may be found in the history sketched by Halliday, where the usage is traced back to "the explosion of process nouns in scientific Greek from B.C. 550 [*sic*] onwards" (Halliday 1993: 116), later brought into English through Latin translations from Greek.

It should be pointed out that even highly experienced, native writers of scientific English still react to this widespread usage, perhaps experiencing it as personification without recognising the grammatical substitution. Reactions like the following occur, from a handbook in scientific writing, co-written by two scientists and an experienced writer / editor of scientific texts:

> [...] these lazy verbs should not be coupled with nonhuman subjects. For example, a scientist will write 'the results demonstrate', which results, being inanimate, cannot do. [...] This misuse is so widespread that most readers have come to accept it. (Matthews/Bowen/Matthews 2000: 155).

The (mis)use of a common case of animation in linguistics is also criticised by a linguist who cautiously analyses his own use:

> Languages are not entities and it can be seriously misleading to make them the subjects of active verbs [...] I have, for brevity's sake allowed myself to say that languages 'spread', meaning that the use of what may be called 'the same language' extends over a wider area than it did before. For brevity, again, I have allowed myself to say that a language 'has' roles or functions, meaning that its users use it for these purposes. If I say that a language 'changes', I mean that users of 'the same language' are using it differently in some particular detai [...]. (Dalby 2003: x).

Judging from other reactions (for example, Low 1999, a study involving acceptance of similar constructions among ESP teachers), there seem to be (semantically defined) restrictions as to which verbs may be used together with such grammatical metaphors. One of the aims of the present analysis is to attempt a definition of such restrictions, but more material is needed.

In order to compare the use of the construction in at least two languages, I chose to analyse texts translated by highly experienced professional translators, supported by legal advisors from the same nation/language: the Treaty on European Union, popularly known as the Maastricht Treaty. It may be argued that the texts of the European Union represent a particular language that is increasingly moving away from its respective native usage towards a medium for accommodation and compromises. At the same time, the language of these texts will have a pervasive influence on the languages of the Union by force of its status and distribution.

Although all EU texts are defined as "authentic" and no text or language should be identified as official Source Text (ST) or Source Language (SL), or Target Text (TT) or Target Language (TL), Swedish is clearly a TL in this case, Sweden having joined the Union at a later date than the creation of the Treaty.

2. Material and method

The texts used were the official versions, published in parallel columns by the Institute for European Law at Stockholm University in *Fördrag om Europeiska unionen – Treaty on European Union – Traité sur l'Union européenne – Vertrag über die Europäische Union*.

Examples of grammatical metaphor in English were collected and compared with Swedish, but also with French and German. For comparison, electronic searches were performed on certain subjects, using other EU texts and Swedish newspaper corpora.

3. Results and discussion

A total of 17 examples (some including more than one instance of grammatical metaphor, but registered and numbered as one occurrence) were found in the English version. The French version was parallel to the English version in all respects relevant to the present purpose. In the German version, the most frequent solution was adverbial and passive, sometimes verb (*be*) and predicate, or a static verb. Only one German example followed the English/French pattern.

In the Swedish version, nearly half of the examples were translated into Swedish following the English version, and the remaining examples were translated using other constructions. Most other alternatives involved the use of passive verb forms, or a verb (*make/be*) and a predicate, like the German version. The low figures are a result of the nature of the text, where almost all subjects are animate, consisting of the different groups of human beings in the Union: the Commission, the Council, the Parliament, Member States, and so on, i.e. subjects which are excluded for present purposes.

All examples are numbered in their order of appearance in the Treaty; each example has a reference to the Treaty. The notations provided for each example (static verb, predicate, and so on, are meant as brief indications of the differences between constructions, and no further attempt will be made to discuss such definitions.

The examples were divided according to type of translation into Swedish and comparisons with the other languages involved. First, cases of complete agreement or lack of agreement are described. Next, examples where the Swedish version is comparable to the German one, and finally an interesting group of examples where German and Swedish deviate for what seems to be semantic reasons.

3.1 *Comparisons: English and French versus German and Swedish*

Complete agreement (between all four languages) was found in only two cases:

(1) [...] measures which take account of [...]
[...] des mesures qui tiennent compte de [...]
[...] Massnahmen [...] die [...] Rechnung tragen.
[...] åtgärder som tar hänsyn till [...]
Article 136 Title XI (Social policy, education, vocational training and youth)

(2) Equal pay [...] means [...]
L'égalité de rémunération [...] implique [...]
Gleichheit des Arbeitsentgelts bedeutet [...]
Lika lön [...] innebär [...]
Article 141:2 Title XI (Social policy, education, vocational training and youth)

The converse, i.e. lack of agreement between English and the other three languages occurred only once, in a stipulative definition:

(3) 'Companies or firms' means [...]
Par sociétés, on entend [...] (adv+impers)
Als Gesellschaften gelten [...] (adv+static)
Med "bolag" förstås [...] (adv+pass)
Article 48 Title III (Free movement of persons, services and capital)

Here, English could have chosen an adverbial construction similar to that in the other languages [*by 'companies or firms' is meant...*]. This more economical construction of 'mean' (in the sense 'signify') overlaps with the use of 'mean' in the sense 'result in', as used in example (2), where the different senses are brought out in the other languages. Whereas the verb in (2) is static and collocates with both animate and inanimate subjects, the verb in (1) is more commonly used with animate subjects.

One category where Swedish translators seem prepared to use active verbs normally associated with human agents involves some kind of metonymic relationship (*politics* for *politicians*:)

(4) The common commercial policy shall take into account [...]
La politique commerciale commune tient compte de [...]
Bei der gemeinsamen Handelspolitik werden [...] berücksichtigt [...] (adv+pass)
Den gemensamma handelspolitiken skall ta hänsyn till [...]
Article 131 Title IX (Common commercial policy)

Alternatively, the subject is an explicitly named collective (*the Community*), i.e. another case of near-metonymy:

(5) Community action [...] shall fully respect [...]
L'action de la Communauté [...] respecte pleinement [...]
Bei der Tätigkeit der Gemeinschaft [...] wird [...] im vollem Umfang gewahrt [...] (adv+pass)
När gemenskapen handlar [...] skall den fullt ut respektera (nom=>clause)
Article 152:5 Title XIII (Public health)

In the example above, Swedish differs from the other languages in treating the Community itself as the subject of the sentence [*when the C acts, it shall respect*], i.e. unpacking the grammatical metaphor, where the other languages have Community action as the subject. It should, however, be mentioned that neither construction is frequent in Swedish newspaper corpora, where neither politics nor policies normally take active verbs. The translator has thus preferred to follow the source text(s) rather than contemporary Swedish usage.

3.2 Germanic similarities

In both German and Swedish there is the option of using an adverbial with a passive verb, as in examples (6) and (7) (*in [...] shall be indicated/defined*), a solution preferred by German in the majority of cases.

(6) [...] these guidelines shall identify projects of common interest[...]
[...] ces orientations identifient des projets d'interêt commun[...]
[...] in diesen Leitlinien werden Vorhaben von gemeinsamen Interesse ausgewiesen (adv+pass)
[...] i dessa riktlinjer skall projekt av gemensamt intresse preciseras [...] (adv+pass)
Article 155:1 Title XIII (Public health)

(7) Common strategies shall set out their objectives [...]
Les stratégies communes précisent leurs objectifs [...]
In den gemeinsamen Strategien sind [...] anzugeben. (adv+pass)
I de gemensamma strategierna skall anges [...] (adv+pass)
Article 13:2 Title V (Provisions on a common foreign and security policy)

There is also the option, in both German and Swedish, to use a verb with a predicate, as in examples (8) [*be binding*] and (9) [*be guiding/guidelines*], where the German version uses the same construction:

(8) Joint actions shall commit the Member States[...]
Les actions communes engagent les États membres [...]
Die gemeinsame Aktionen sind für die Mitgliedsstaaten bindend [...] (be+pred)

Gemensamma åtgärder skall vara förpliktande för medlemsstaterna[...] (be+pred)
Article 14:17 Title V (Provisions on a common foreign and security policy)

(9) [...] the conclusions [...] and the overall approach [...] will continue to guide the action ...
[...] les conclusions [...] et l'approche globale [...] continueront de guider l'action [...]
[...] die Schlussfolgerungen [...] und [...] das [...] Gesamtkonzept [...] weiterhin die Richtschnur [...] bilden werden (be+pred)
[...] slutsatserna [...] och den övergripande strategi [...] kommer att vara vägledande [...] (be+pred)
Protocol on the application of the principles of subsidiarity and proportionality C. Protocols annexed to the Treaty establishing the European Community Title VIII – Final provisions II. Protocols

Finally, agentless passive verbs (without adverbials) were used where the grammatical subject of the source text(s) was both (relatively) concrete and inanimate, as in example (10), rephrased as [*if duties have not been restored*] and example (11) [*this organisation shall be formed*]. It should be pointed out that in (11) Swedish could equally well have used a static verb like the German *bestehen* ['consist']. However, the Swedish translator seems to have followed the English, more process-oriented concept of creating different "forms":

(10) Products [...] if they have not benefited from a total or partial drawback ...
[...] les produits [...] qui n'ont pas bénéficié d'une ristourne totale ou partielle [...]
[...] Waren [...] für die [...] Zölle [...] rückvergütet worden sind (pass)
Varor [...] om [...] hel eller partiell restitution av [...] tullar [...] inte har lämnats (pass)
Article 24 Title I (Free movement of goods)

(11) This organisation shall take one of the following forms [...]
[...] cette organisation prend l'une des formes [...]
Diese [Organisation] besteht [...] aus einer der folgenden Organisationsformen (static)
[...] skall denna organisation utformas på något av följande sätt (pass)
Article 34:1 Title II (Agriculture)

3.3 *Differences between German and Swedish: legal concepts and verb choice*

Among examples where Swedish parallels English (and French), there is one category of subjects that by tradition collocates with certain animate verbs, namely concepts that may be associated with *law / lag*. This in turn has a long history of use with active verbs such as *say*, *decide*, *allow*, *protect*, and so on, in both English and the Scandinavian languages and may be traced back to early oral presentations of legal regulations, or influences from biblical language. There are few examples in this particular treaty (see above), although the pattern is frequently used in other EU documents. Among examples of similar concepts are *rule / regel*, *regulation / förordning*, *guideline / riktlinje*, in EU texts also *programme / program* and *common strategies / gemensamma strategier*. In the present material, *framework programme / ramprogram*, *common positions / gemensamma ståndpunkter*, and *joint actions / gemensamma åtgärder* are also used with verbs that collocate in Swedish with *lag / law*, and so on, which may indicate the legal status of these new concepts.

A search on similar subjects in other EU documents of comparable status confirmed the tendency for the Swedish versions to use active verbs with concepts such law, rules, regulations, and so on. This is the only category where the German versions differ consistently from the Swedish ones, which may be due to different traditions in German regarding verbs collocating with law, rules, regulations, and so on. Since this is a common construction in other Germanic languages such as Norwegian and Danish, this difference seems worth investigating.

In example (12), the Swedish version follows the English and French very closely, resulting in a less idiomatic translation where an adverbial with passives (see the German version) would have come closer to common usage. Assuming legal status for the framework programme, however, renders the Swedish translation logical.

(12) The framework programme shall: establish the [...] objectives; [..]. indicate the broad lines [...] ; fix the [...] amount [...] and the [...] rules [...]

Le programme-cadre: fixe les objectifs [...]; indique les grandes lignes [...]; fixe le montant [...] et les modalités [...]
In dem Rahmprogramm werden die [...] Ziele [...] festgelegt; die Grundzüge ... angegeben; der ... Betrag und die Einzelheiten ... festgelegt. (adv+pass)
Ramprogrammet skall fastställa de [...] mål [...], ange huvudlinjerna [...] , fastställa [...] beloppet och de närmare villkoren [...] establish [...] indicate [...] set]
Article 166:1Title XVIII (Research and technological development)

As seen from examples (13) and (14), a static verb (*avse* / *concern*) for *address* may act as a compromise in Swedish, although both examples also include other verbs indicating more animate activity (*ange* / *define*) for lay down and define, respectively.

(13) Joint actions shall address specific situations... They shall lay down their objectives [...]
[des actions communes.] Celles-ci concernent certaines situations [...] (static) Elles fixent leurs objectifs [...]
Gemeinsame Aktionen betreffen spezifische Situationen [...] (static) In den gemeinsamen Aktionen sind ihre Ziele [...] festgelegt. (adv+pass)
De gemensamma åtgärderna skall avse specifika situationer [...] (static) De skall ange mål [...] [concern [...] define]
Article 14:1 Title V (Provisions on a common foreign and security policy)

(14) The Council shall adopt common positions. Common positions shall define [...]
Le Conseil arrête des positions communes. Celles-ci définissent [...]
Der Rat nimmt gemeinsame Standpunkte an. In den gemeinsamen Standpunkten wird [...] bestimmt. (adv+pass)
Rådet skall anta gemensamma ståndpunkter. Dessa skall ange [...] [define]
Article 15 Title V (Provisions on a common foreign and security policy)

Static verbs (*make it possible to*) acting as compromise solutions also occur in examples (15) (*contain*), (16), (17):

(15) The regulations shall lay down detailed rules for [...]
Le règlement prévoit les modalités particulières [...]
Die Beteiligung [...] wird in der Haushaltsordnung im einzelnen geregelt. (adv+pass)
Budgetförordningen skall innehålla närmare bestämmelser [...] (static) [contain]

Article 274 Title XX (Development cooperation) Title II (Financial provisions) Part five – Institutions of the Community

(16) Subsidiarity is a dynamic concept [...] It allows Community action [...] to be expanded [...] (obj+inf.pass)
La subsidiarité est un concept dynamique [...] Il [sic] permet d'étendre l'action [...] (obj+inf)
Die Subsidiarität ist ein dynamisches Konzept [...] Nach dem Subsidiaritätsprinzip kann die Tätigkeit [...] erweitert werden [...] (adv+pass)
Subsidiariteten är ett dynamiskt begrepp [...] Den gör det möjligt att [...] utvidga räckvidden[...] (static+pred+inf) [makes it possible to[...].]
Protocol on the application of the principles of subsidiarity and proportionality: 3. C.Protocols annexed to the Treaty establishing the European Community Title VIII – Final provisionsII.Protocols

(17) [...] the Community's existing competition rules allow [...] to be taken into account in full.
[...] les règles de concurrence en vigueur dans la Communauté permettent [...] de prendre pleinement en compte.
[...] die bestehendenWettbewerbsregeln der Gemeinschaft es zulassen [...] zu berücksichtigen.
[...] gemenskapens befintliga konkurrensregler gör det möjligt att ta full hänsyn till [...] (static+pred+inf) [make it possible to[...]]
Declaration on public credit institutions in Germany

The use of a static verb, as a compromise between a verb associated with animate subjects and a totally different syntactic construction, is thus a solution frequently used. It enables the translator to follow the syntax of the source text (thus facilitating later amendments) while avoiding what might be seen as explicit personification, a less idiomatic, or less frequently used alternative.

4. Conclusion

Of the four languages involved, the English and French versions present the closest parallels. The Swedish version is noticeably close to the English and French versions, including a certain overuse of Swedish *skall*, corresponding to English *shall*, in such cases where Swedish legal language has the option to use the present indicative, like French and German. In spite of the Swedish option of using constructions corresponding to the German ones in almost every single case, the Swedish translators occasionally prefer less idiomatic solutions that are closer to the English and French versions. One possible reason may be found in the official Swedish recommendations to avoid the use of passives in legal and administrative language (see, for example, *Statsrådsberedningen* 1992: 99), another reason may simply be the economy of the construction (and the greater ease to insert later amendments).

Certain restrictions may be deduced from the choices made between different options, but more material is needed. Further studies will also have to take account of the process types involved.

It remains to be seen if these tentative results are part of a more widespread tendency to use the construction as a syntactic loan in the Swedish language in general, or perhaps in LSP texts, or if it remains associated with the particular text type of EU legislation.

References

Dalby, A. 2002 / 2003. *Language in Danger*. London: Penguin Books.

Halliday, M.A.K. 1986/1994. *An Introduction to Functional Grammar*. 2nd ed. London: Edward Arnold.

Halliday, M.A.K. 1998. Things and relations. In Martin, J.R. / Veel, Robert (eds) *Reading Science. Critical and functional perspectives on discourses of science*. London: Routledge, 185-235.

Halliday, M.A.K. / Martin, J.R. 1993. *Writing Science. Literacy and discursive power*. London: Falmer.

Hansen, E. 1996. Animismen – et falsk sprogrigtighedsproblem. In *Språket lever! Festskrift till Margareta Westman*. Stockholm: Svenska språknämnden, 17-35.

Korzen, H. 1997. Ser man det [...] Noget om at “se” på dansk og fransk. *Sprint, Sproginstitutternes tidsskrift* 1997/2. Copenhagen: Handelshøjskolen i København, 17-35.

Lassen, I. 1997. On the Cohabitation of Grammatical Metaphor and Conventional Figures of Speech. In Lassen, I. (ed.) *Interactional Perspectives on LSP . Language and Cultural Contact 22*. Aalborg: Aalborg University Press, 67-83.

Low, G. 1999. "This paper thinks [...]" Investigating the acceptability of the metaphor AN ESSAY IS A PERSON. In Cameron, L. / Low, G. (eds) *Researching and Applying Metaphor*. Cambridge: Cambridge University Press, 221-248.

Malblanc, A. 1968. *Stylistique comparée du français et de l'allemand*. Paris: Didier.

Matthews, J.R. / Bowen, J.M. / Matthews, R.W. [2]2000. *Successful scientific writing. A step-by-step guide for the biological and medical sciences*. Cambridge: Cambridge University Press.

Statsrådsberedningen 1993. *Kommittéhandboken. Särtryck om betänkandens utformning*. Ds 1992: 99. Stockholm: Regeringskansliet.

Stålhammar, M. 1995. The "market" – a changing word in a changing world. In Brekke, M. / Andersen, Ø. / Dahl, T. / Myking, J. (eds) *Applications and Implications of Current LSP Research*. Bergen: Fagbokforlaget, 789-796

Stålhammar, M. 1996. The use of metaphoric expressions in different types of medical texts. In Wilske, D. (ed.) *Fackspråk och översättningsteori. 16th VAKKI Symposium*. Vaasa: University of Vaasa, 235-246.

Stålhammar, M. 1997. *Metaforernas mönster i fackspråk och allmänspråk*. Stockholm: Carlsson.

Stålhammar, M. 2001. Through the computer screen. In Aijmer, K. (ed.) *A Wealth of Languages. Studies in Honour of Göran Kjellmer*. Gothenburg: Gothenburg Studies in English 81, 2001, 114-122.

Vinay, J.P. / Darbelnet, J. 1956. *Stylistique comparée du français et de l'anglais*. Paris: Didier.

i) Electronic sources

<http://europa.eu.int/eur-lex/en/index.html>

<http://spraakdata.gu.se/lb/konk>

ANASTASIA PARIANOU AND PANAYOTIS I KELANDRIAS

Instructions for use and their translation in a global age

1. Introduction

Localization plays an important role in software and product documentation. The actual translation process is only one step among several others which precede it. These other steps include "the use of multilingual terminology databases, controlled writing, disambiguity tagging, and the integration of MT" (Pym 2000: 1). Technical texts, such as instructions for use, must combine the appropriate technical terminology with the necessary amount of information for the prospective non-expert reader. Finding the appropriate technical terms, their usage and translation are facilitated with the aid of the above-mentioned tools. The question is whether non-expert readers will be able to understand the various functions of an appliance. When this goal is achieved, the communicative function of the text will have been accomplished.

2. Communicative function of LSP texts in instructions for use

Instructions for use are part of our everyday life. Yet, their producers[1] and receivers remain unknown to each other and rarely communicate

1 There are two different "producers" of a set of instructions for use, the text initiator (company) and the text author (person(s) or company) specialized in

with one another. The only thing they have in common is the content of the instructions and their mutual will for the proper use of the appliance described therein. Thus, the important thing for the producer is to write something that the recipient wants to read and will understand (Sager 1994). This is best accomplished when the technical writer and later the translator produce readable texts. In this case they must follow *les principes de la lisibilité* ('the principles of readability') (Gémar 1995: 60). These comprise the following three criteria:

- Clarity
- Simplicity
- Concision

Technical texts such as instructions for use serve functional communication. As such they must be understood immediately and without effort by a variety of people[2]. This implies the understanding of both the referential meaning of the technical terms and the general meaning of the text. In this way the criterion of *clarity* is served.

Simplicity in technical texts is assured when there are no vague or ambiguous terms and, at the same time all the necessary information is provided. In practice this implies the exclusion of polysemes, synonyms or what Thurmair calls *Doppelterminologie* 'double terminology') (Thurmair 1995) and the inclusion of controlled language techniques[3].

Concision implies a restricted amount of lexical features and avoiding superfluous stylistic features.

These three criteria contribute to the explanation of the function of an appliance. However, they are not always followed by the technical writer or the translator, resulting in problems for the user. The user

technical documentation and authorized by the text initiator to write the instruction for use (Zirngibl 2003).

2 Hensel (1987) and Hoffmann (1984) use the expression *generalisierte Mehrfachadressierung* .

3 In practice controlled language is not widely used as two companies, Bosch and Braun, informed us. (E-mail communication with the International Key Accounts Manager of Bosch, Fotios Katsardis and communication expert of Braun, Jochen Krämer.)

will be unable to use the appliance as described in the instructions. The major problems for the user of an instruction for use will be discussed below.

2.1 Technical details

A new product is always accompanied by documentation containing a large number of technical details and terminology. The object of new technological developments in household appliances should be to spare the reader from all these details. Thus, the technical writer's effort is to furnish the recipient with fewer technical details to avoid the confusion (Krämer 2003). Lehrndorfer (2003) has found that professionals dealing with technological details use simpler linguistic, visual and didactic means when technology becomes too complicated. Consequently, the technical writer must find exactly where to draw the line between technical information and functional communication.

2.2 Terminological vagueness in the target language (TL)

Things are more complicated when the TL does not generate its own terminology and is dependent on the translation from the source language (SL) to enrich its special language. This is mostly the case in countries with a so-called peripheral language and/or culture where terminological vagueness is unavoidable because:

- No important progress has taken place in the TL
- Product/term is not widely used in the TL country/region
- Product/term has just recently been introduced into the TL country/region
- No terminological data bank exists or is only just emerging

In our study of instructions for use we have noticed that precise terminology is used in the source text where strictly technical terms are concerned. Whenever terminological vagueness appears, it is the translator who has introduced it in the target text[4]. We shall examine examples employing terms that are not purely technical, i.e. terms with cultural, legal and administrative features. In the following examples (1, 2 and 3) two so-called central languages (English and German) and a peripheral language (Greek) are involved:

(1) *Example 1: CaféPresso Crematic Krups (Cappuccino and Filter* Coffee Machine)

- Disposal
- Entsorgung
- Απόσυρση

(2) *Example 2: Bosch BMS 2* (Vacuum Cleaner)

- Dispose of the packaging material correctly.
- Verpackungsmaterial ordnungsgemäß entsorgen.
- Επιβάλλεται κανονική οικολογική απαλλαγή των υλικών συσκευασίας.

(3) *Example 3: Neff Joker 150 D clou* (Electric Cooker)

- Dispose of packing material properly
- Verpackungsmaterial ordnungsgemäß entsorgen
- Η απόρριψη της συσκευασίας να εκτελείται σύμφωνα με τους κανόνες.

These three examples show us that while the two central languages use terms from the same word family (*disposal/dispose* in English and *Entsorgung/entsorgen* in German), the Greek language uses a different expression each time. This is part of the terminological vagueness and expresses on the one hand the almost complete absence of waste disposal policies in Greece in contrast to other countries and on the other hand the recent appearance of these terms in the Greek language.

The next five examples show the legal terminology involved in instructions for use and its translation into a peripheral language:

(4) *Example 4: Braun MP 80 Multipress automatic* (Automatic Juice Extractor)

- This product conforms to the EMC Requirements as laid down by the Council Directive 89/336/EEC and to the Low Voltage Regulation

4 We do not intend here to underline translation mistakes but rather to outline more general and comprehensive features connected with terminological vagueness.

(73/23 EEC).

- Dieses Gerät entspricht dem EMV-Gesetz (EG-Richtlinie 89/336/ EWG) sowie der Niederspannungsrichtlinie (73/23 EWG).
- Αυτό το προϊόν πληροί τις προδιαγραφές EMC, όπως αυτές έχουν οριστεί από την οδηγία του Συμβουλίου 89/336/EEC και τους Κανονισμούς Συσκευών Χαμηλής Τάσης (73/23 EEC).

(5) *Example 5: Braun K 3000 MultiSystem* (Kitchen Machine System)

- This product conforms to the EMC-Requirements as laid down by the Council Directive 89/336/EEC and to the Low Voltage Regulation (73/23 EEC).
- Dieses Gerät entspricht dem EMV-Gesetz (EG-Richtlinie 89/336/ EWG) sowie der Niederspannungsrichtlinie (73/23 EWG).
- Αυτό το προϊόν ανταποκρίνεται στις απαιτήσεις της Ευρωπαϊκής κοινότητας, όπως αυτές αναφέρονται στην οδηγία του Συμβουλίου 89/336/ΕΟΚ και με τις διατάξεις περί Χαμηλών Ηλεκτρικών Τάσεων (73/23 ΕΟΚ).

(6) *Example 6: Braun MX 2050 PowerBlend* (Blender)

- This product conforms to the EMC-Requirements as laid down by the Council Directive 89/336/EEC and to the Low Voltage Regulation (73/23 EEC).
- Dieses Gerät entspricht dem EMV-Gesetz (EG-Richtlinie 89/336/ EWG) sowie der Niederspannungsrichtlinie (73/23 EWG).
- Το προϊόν αυτό είναι σύμφωνο με τις προδιαγραφές της EMC όπως αυτές έχουν οριστεί από την υπ'αριθμό 89/336/ΕΟΚ Οδηγία του Συμβουλίου και από τον 73/23/ΕΟΚ Κανονισμό.

(7) *Example 7: Braun G 1300 K PowerPlus 1300* (Meat Grinder)

- This product conforms to the EMC-Requirements as laid down by the Council Directive 89/336/EEC and to the Low Voltage Regulation (73/23 EEC).
- Dieses Gerät entspricht dem EMV-Gesetz (EG-Richtlinie 89/336/ EWG) sowie der Niederspannungsrichtlinie (73/23 EWG).
- Το προϊόν είναι σύμφωνο με τις απαιτήσεις της ΕΜΟ όπως καθορίζονται από την Οδηγία 89/336/ΕΟΚ και τις διατάξεις περί Χαμηλών Ηλεκτρικών Τάσεων (73/23/ΕΟΚ).

(8) *Example 8: Braun MR 5500 BC, BC-HC, M BC-HC Multiquick/Minipimer professional* (Hand Blender)

- This product conforms to the EMC-Requirements as laid down by the Council Directive 89/336/EEC and to the Low Voltage Regulation (73/23 EEC).

- Dieses Gerät entspricht dem EMV-Gesetz (EG-Richtlinie 89/336/ EWG) sowie der Niederspannungsrichtlinie (73/23 EWG).
- Το προϊόν αυτό είναι σύμφωνο με τις προδιαγραφές της EMC όπως αυτές έχουν οριστεί από την υπ'αριθμό 89/336/EOK Οδηγία του Συμβουλίου και από τον 73/23/EOK Κανονισμό.

We can remark here that the central languages (English and German) use consistent terminology and phraseology in all five examples, while in the peripheral language we see four different translation proposals, i.e. only two examples out of five, 6 and 8, are identical.

It seems that in the near future terminological vagueness in the peripheral languages will be eliminated since more and more companies will use terminology data banks to achieve consistency in technical and other terms in these languages[5]. At the moment, it is either the translators of peripheral languages who have to refrain from using too many different terms and use existing terminology data banks[6] or the product manager in the peripheral country that is responsible for the "fine tuning"[7].

2.3 Corporate terminology

It is well known that each company has its own *corporate culture, corporate image* and *corporate identity* (Pogarell 1993)[8]. Corporate terminology is part of every company's identity and equally important to its products. Corporate terminology applied in instructions for use comprises product names, designations and terminology of technical

5 This assumption was confirmed by Braun's communication expert Jochen Krämer in an e-mail communication (31 July 2003).

6 Information given by Jochen Krämer from Braun (e-mail dated from 31 July 2003).

7 Information given by Fotios Katsardis, the International Key Accounts Manager of Bosch (e-mail dated 4 August 2003).

8 Apart from the product name, the corporate image comprises the logo, packaging, innovative product shapes, cartoon characters, website address names (domain names) and unique product characteristics. Even the look and feel of a business site on the Internet (web page) are increasingly becoming important means for a business to identify itself and its products in the marketplace (Elias 2003).

details. A corporate terminology may emerge either unintentionally or intentionally.

Bosch admitted that it is intentionally promoting its own corporate culture using its own terminology and rhetoric[9]. Braun, on the other hand, does not intentionally use a corporate terminology, with the exception of expressions such as *Food Processor* instead of *Kitchen Machine*[10]. In *Braun CombiMax K 650 Food Processor* we find *Food Processor* incorporated in the product name[11]. Other companies such as Bosch, Philips and Kenwood use both *Food Processor* and *Kitchen Machin* in their product names[12].

As far as technical details in descriptions are concerned, each company uses its own corporate terminology to describe the same technical parts. For example, in the description of a steam iron of different types (see Figure 1) Braun uses a corporate terminology of its own:

(9) *Example 9: Braun SI 4000, SI 8580, SI 6575, SI 6230, SI 6530, SI 6220, SI 6510, SI 6210* (Steam Iron)

- Water tank opening (English)
- Wassertanköffnung (German)
- Système d'ouverture et de fermeture du réservoir (French)
- Boca del depósito de agua (Spanish)
- Bocal do depósito de água (Portuguese)
- Οπή (του) δοχείου νερού (Greek)

Other companies have their own corporate terminology for the same technical items:

(10) *Example 10: Rowenta: ActiLine DM 110, 115, 120; PowerLine DM 130, 140* (Steam Iron)

- Water filling inlet (English)

9 See footnote 7.

10 See footnote 6.

11 Yet, in the description of *Braun K1000 5 in 1 Kitchen Machine Type 3210* we find the terms *food processor bowl*, *food processor cover* and and so on.

12 For example *MUM 4420 Compact Series Kitchen Machine* and *MCM 5000 Food Processor* (Bosch), *Philips HR7754 Essence Food Processor*, *Philips Combi 3000 Kitchen Machine HR 7805*, *Kenwood FP690 Food Processor*, *Kenwood KM600 Kitchen Machine*.

- Wassereinfüllöffnung (German)
- Ouverture de remplissage d'eau (French)
- Orificio para llenado de agua (Spanish)
- Orificio de enchimento do reservatório (Portuguese)
- Στόμιο πλήρωσης νερού (Greek)13

(11) Example 11: Philips HI 515/25/35/45 Azur Excel Plus (Steam Iron)14

- Turbo Steam Druckschalter (German)
- Bouton vapeur Turbo (French)
- Pulsante Turbo vapore (Italian)
- Turbo buhar düğmesi (Turkish)

It becomes clear that the variety of different corporate terminologies for the same function or technical part is likely to confuse the recipient. Only a careful reader of the text and the illustration will not be distressed by the different corporate terminologies of the technical details. On the other hand, the companies – even if they were willing to cooperate – are not obliged to use the same terms since this would lead to terminological, technical and legal problems (for example patent rights, trademark law).

2.4 Illustration and localization

A good illustration is very helpful and is almost always accompanied by a text. The illustration and its localized text are responsible for a

13 A very characteristic example of corporate terminology comes from the automobile industry. The German term for tinted glasses differs from company to company. The style sheets of Volkswagen/Audi and Toyota prescribe the terms *athermische Scheiben* and *Wärmeschutzverglasung*, Mercedes-Benz the term *wärmedämmendes Glas*, BMW the term *grünes Wärmeschutzglas*, Opel *wärmedämmende, getönte Rundumverglasung*, Nissan and Saab *getönte Scheiben'*and *Lancia Colorglas* (Stolze 1999).

14 No English version available. The expression *Turbo* seems to be used by different companies. Braun uses it in connection with *on/off switch for turbo speed* in English (example MR 5500 BC, MR 5500 BC-HC, MR 5550 M BC-HC), *Ein-/Ausschalter für Turbo-Geschwindigkeit* in German, *Interrupteur marche/arrêt pour utilisation avec la vitesse turbo* in French, *Interruptor de máxima potencia (turbo)* in Spanish, *διακόπτης (on/off) για ταχύτητα turbo* in Greek.

successful understanding of the instructions for use (Homberger 1972, cited in Nord 1988). However, a good illustration must avoid the following pitfalls:

- Pictures or illustrations that are too small.
- Unreadable text accompanying the illustration.
- Incorrect contrast between background and illustration.
- Disproportion between text and illustration.
- Explanatory text in the SL instead of the TL which leads to non-localized illustration-texts where the text is in a central language only, mostly in English.

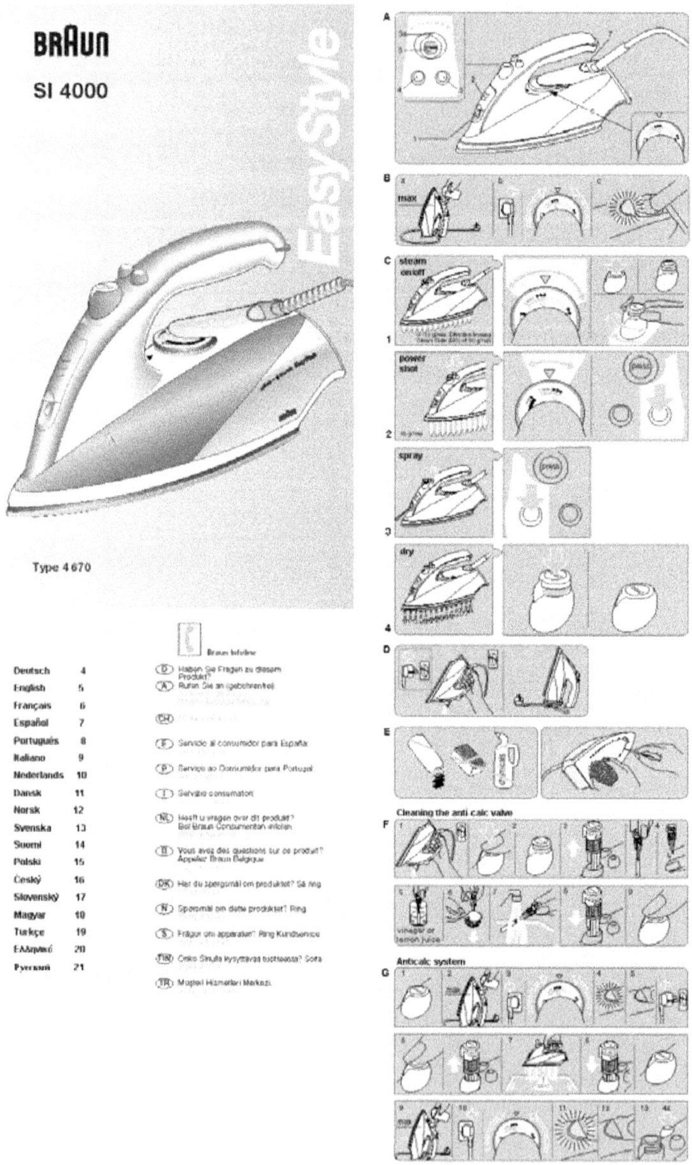

Figure 1. Braun steam iron: illustrations as part of instructions for use.

The instructions for use in Figure 1 have been translated into 18 languages. The illustrations depicting each step necessary for the proper use of the steam iron include the steps stated below:

(12) *Example 12: Braun SI 4000 Type 4670* (Steam Iron)

A. Description
B. Before starting off
C. Ironing
D. After ironing
E. Maintenance and cleaning
F. Cleaning the anti-calc valve
G. Anticalc system

However, the descriptions of the following illustrations are only given in English:

C.1. steam on/off
C.2. power shot
C.3. spray
C.4. dry
F. vinegar or lemon juice

Readers who are conversant English are therefore not particularly helped by the illustration.

In Example C.1. *steam on/off* is not very confusing since the words *on/off* are arguably easily understood even by non-English speakers. An attentive non-English speaking observer of the illustration may even understand the word *steam*[15].

In Example C.2., however, *power shot* is quite confusing to someone with inadequate knowledge of the English language. The reader who does not know the meaning of *power shot* will be puzzled when it occurs for the first time and without explanation. What is needed here is either a localized term or the English term with an explanation in the TL.

15 In the translation of the instructions, the English words *steam on/off* appear in three languages only, namely Greek, Russian and Portuguese, curiously enough not in C.1. but in different places (for example in D. and in F.).

The illustration as part of the instructions for use shows us that technical details and communicative function are equally important for a sound understanding of the instructions. For example, an illustration containing all the parts of an electrical appliance with their corresponding technical terms is as important as the translation where the text produced is written according to the "product or expectancy norms of the reader" (Chesterman 1997: 64). If the translator is aware of their responsibility "to ensure maximum communication between the parties"[16] (Munday 2002: 119), s/he should also be aware of the product or expectancy norms of the readers of a translation. To this end, a good illustration accompanied by relevant, and preferably localized text is necessary.

3. Conclusions

From the above examples and remarks we can extract the following three features that should be given particular attention by those (but not only those) involved in the localization process in a peripheral language.

3.1 Localization and internationalization

The degree to which text in instructions for use is localized manifests itself in two ways: first, as unlocalized text in illustrations which are accompanied by a mostly English text, which remains in English in all the other languages used in the instructions. This may hinder understanding (see Example 12). Secondly, as far as the rest of the non-illustrated text is concerned, it manifests itself in a lack of localization in favour of internationalization. If we follow the evolution of instruc-

16 For Chesterman the "communication norm" belongs to the "professional norms" and is "subordinate to and determined by expectancy norms" (1997: 67).

tions for use over the years, we find that in the beginning instructions were unlocalized and reminded us of the language and the cultural patterns of the country where they were first written. In instructions produced more recently, culturally- and country-specific expressions are deleted because internationalization is replacing localization. Almost all texts nowadays are internationalized[17] so the product can be sold in different countries without the need for redesign (Pym 2001). This lack of cultural patterns deprives the reader of a certain degree of acquaintance and intimacy with the text.

3.2 Inappropriate use of special language

Undoubtedly, the use of special language is necessary for both the technical writer and the translator. Yet, there are two different situations where the use of special language has entirely different consequences. The first situation has to do with reference to technical details, such as the different parts of the appliance mentioned in the descriptions that are always depicted in the illustration sheet. Here, understanding is facilitated by the illustration even if the terminology is very unfamiliar to the reader. The producer of an appliance needs technical terminology to name the product and its parts and functioning. The second situation is entirely different and has to do with understanding the text itself regardless of the quantity of the terminology used. Where certain actions are described and certain objects (non-technical parts) are used that are neither mentioned nor depicted, they should be expressed in a communicative and functional way that is easily understood by everyone. Two of the most common problems are:

- The excessive use of special language hinders understanding and readability.
- Not placing the explanations of the technical details and their descriptions in the layout of the manual diminishes readability (see Example 12).

17 For an American product this involves taking the product and deleting all elements that were in some way specific to the American market (Pym 2000).

A last remark concerning inappropriate use of special language relates to the non-technical terms (legally or culturally-bound terms) which, when translated, are not given the same attention as purely technical terms.

3.3 End-user's expectation and knowledge

On the one hand, following the principles of readability the language of instructions for use should contain the particular features of *clarity, simplicity* and *concision*, as we have seen. On the other hand, LSP uses "specialized vocabulary, collocations, [and] stylistic features" (Bowker/Pearson 2002: 27). Yet, the recipients of the instructions for use are mostly non-experts, these are "people who, for one reason or another, find themselves in a situation where they must use an LSP with which they are not familiar" (Bowker/Pearson 2002: 27). How can a communication situation succeed when non-experts come into contact with features such as specialized vocabulary, collocations and stylistic features? Here again, we must think about the end-user, a non-expert and his communication with the expert who is writing the technical text. If the expert wants to be understood he must unavoidably limit the specialized language, sometimes use LGP words instead of LSP terms and produce good illustrations. The non-expert recipient does not want to become an expert on the linguistic or conceptual knowledge of the text. What s/he wants is to learn quickly, how to use an appliance and have it function efficiently. Function is the basic reason why instructions for use are produced. Special knowledge and time are what the majority of the recipients do not possess. Hence, we argue that instructions should be presented in a clear, simple and concise way.

References

Bowker, L. / Pearson, J. 2002. *Working with Specialized Language*. London/New York: Routledge.

Chesterman, A. 1997. *Memes of Translation*. Amsterdam/Philadelphia: John Benjamins.

Elias, S.R. 2003. *Trademark: Legal Care for Your Business and Product Name*. Berkeley, CA: Nolo.

Gémar, J.-C. 1995. *Traduire ou l'art d'interpréter. Langue, droit et société: Éléments de jurilinguistique. Applications* 2. Québec: Presses de l'Université du Québec.

Hensel, C. 1987. *Produktbegleitende Texte – der Versuch einer Analyse unter illokutionärem Aspekt*. Leipzig [Diss.].

Hoffmann, L. 1984. Mehrfachadressierung und Verständlichkeit. *LiLi* 55, 71-85.

Krämer, J. 2003. Gebrauchsanleitungen – Ideal und Alltag. *technische kommunikation. Fachzeitschrift für Technische Dokumentation und Informationsmanagement* 3, 18-21.

Lehrndorfer, A. 2003. Handlungen à la carte. *technische kommunikation. Fachzeitschrift für Technische Dokumentation und Informationsmanagement* 3, 22-27.

Munday, J. 2002. *Introducing Translation Studies: Theories and Applications*. London/New York: Routledge.

Nord, C. 1988. *Textanalyse und Übersetzen*. Heidelberg: Groos.

Pogarell, R. 1993. Corporate Identity in der Sprache technischer Dokumente. *tekom-Nachrichten* 2, 18-21.

Pym, A. 2000. Localization and the Changing Role of Linguistics. Available: <http://www.fut.es/~apym/on-line/locling/locling.html> [accessed August 2, 2003].

Pym, A. 2001. Localization and Linguistics. Available: <http://www.fut.es/~apym/on-line/loclinguistics.pdf> [accessed August 2, 2003].

Sager, J.C. 1994. *Language Engineering and Translation. Consequences of automation*. Amsterdam/Philadelphia: John Benjamins.

Stolze, R. 1999. *Die Fachübersetzung. Eine Einführung.* Tübingen: Narr.

Thurmair, M. 1995. Doppelterminologie im Text oder: hydrophob ist wasserscheu. In Kretzenbacher, H.L. / Weinrich, H. (eds) *Linguistik der Wissenschaftssprache*. Berlin/New York: de Gruyter, 247-280.

Zirngibl, M. 2003. *Die fachliche Textsorte Bedienungsanleitung.* Frankfurt a.M., Berlin/Bern/Bruxelles/New York/Oxford/Wien: Lang.

ANNE KARI BJØRGE

"The person in thc middle": Strategies in translating LSP texts

1. Introduction

In this chapter I am going to discuss some observations with respect to translating LSP texts. The language pair is Norwegian and English, and the text material is translations written by candidates sitting for the Norwegian translator accreditation examination. Candidates passing the examination receive the prestigious qualification of accredited translator. They translate four texts, one dealing with a general topic, and three which would be described as LSP texts, dealing with technical, economics and legal subject matter respectively.

Three issues are basic in this context: First, there is the selection of LSP texts, which should have an appropriate level of complexity, and be representative of the three topics selected for testing. LSP is not interpreted in the sense of referring to communication among specialists only (as in Sager/Dungworth/McDonald 1980: 69), but rather to communicate information of a specialist nature at any level (as in Picht/Draskau 1985: 3). The second issue concerns the fact that the translations have been carried out under examination conditions, which raises the issue of strategies to cope with limitations of time and access to information. The third is the issue of evaluation, or which criteria to use when deciding whether a candidate is to pass the examination and receive accreditation.

Whether a text is perceived as difficult to translate or not may depend on a number of factors, for example syntactic complexity and lack of corresponding concepts in the target language. One approach is to look at the number of variant translations of the same text as an indication of translational difficulty. This is the approach I shall adopt in the following, using the choice network analysis (CNA) as set out in Campbell 2000, and Hale/Campbell 2002. This analysis compares a number of translations of the same translation item. A large number of alternatives will be taken as an indication of translational difficulty. The kind of alternative chosen by the candidates – Campbell's "person in the middle" (2000: 30) – will be linked to translation strategies set up by Chesterman (1998, 2000: 15-16), namely syntactic, semantic or pragmatic strategies.

On this basis, I shall address the following research questions:

1. Can the number of variant translations of the same translation item be an indication of how difficult it is to translate?

2. What strategies have been used by candidates when bilingual dictionaries do not have an equivalent term?

3. What criteria are relevant when comparing the quality of the different variants?

2. Data

The material used for this chapter is an LSP text in Norwegian, set as part of the translator accreditation examination in 2002. Candidates were asked whether they would permit the use of their translations for research purposes, and 19 candidates gave their assent, which resulted in a corpus of 19 different translations of the same text into English. The length of the Norwegian text is 266 words. The texts were translated under examination conditions, and candidates had approximately 2.5 hours to translate the text. Dictionaries were allowed, but not access to the Internet, which means that candidates' ability to do an Internet search for relevant terminology and collocations was not tested.

Candidates sitting for the examination have a minimum of three years' university education, but there are no requirements for English to be included as part of their university course. Many of them work as translators, but lack the accreditation given by the exam. I therefore feel justified in referring to this corpus as a *parallel* or *bilingual corpus*, consisting of "original, source language-texts in language A and their translated versions in language B" (Baker 1995: 230, quoted in Shuttleworth/Cowie 1997: 120), or, in the words of Johansson/Oksefjell (1998: 4), as a *translation corpus*, defined as a corpus consisting of an original text and its translations.

The text to be discussed deals with a technical topic, more specifically with the insulation of external walls in wooden houses. Unlike texts dealing with economics and legal topics, technical texts are generally regarded as being non-cultural. However, technical descriptions may also refer to objects and processes that are specific to one culture. A case in point is the construction of houses, which will vary according to climate and local conditions. Thus, in Norway, private houses are generally wood constructions and, being built for a cold climate, are very well insulated.

The text was accompanied by an illustration showing the construction in question.

3. Methodology

To address the question of translational difficulty I shall discuss whether a large number of variant translations of the same item is an indication of difficulty, using the choice network analysis as set out in Campbell 2000 and Hale/Campbell 2002. Choice network analysis regards the target text to be "a tangible source of evidence of mental processing in translation" (Campbell 2000: 32). The variant translations of one source text thus reflect the behaviours of the subjects translating the text, and represent choosing an alternative from a set of potential options.[1]

The alternatives chosen by the candidates will be linked to the translation strategies set up by Chesterman (1998, 2000: 15-16), namely whether the strategy chosen is primarily of a syntactic, semantic or pragmatic nature.

Translation accuracy is notoriously difficult to pin down. However, I shall try to assess what criteria are relevant when assessing the accuracy of the alternatives chosen by the candidates. Decisions on relative accuracy will be made on the basis of how the terminology in question appears – if at all – in relevant textual material appearing on the Internet, using GOOGLE as a search engine.

Invariably, some of these alternatives will be regarded as being "preferable to" or "more accurate than" other less successful variants. In evaluating a candidate's performance, one will necessarily also have an opinion on degree of accuracy or acceptability (Hale/Campbell 2002). When it comes to translating terminology with respect to the language pair English/Norwegian, the alternatives presented by the candidates may be evaluated by a comparison with documentation available on the Internet.

Assessing the text as a whole would be beyond the scope of the present study. I shall thus focus on three examples: the variant translations of one brief sentence, one technical term which is specific to Norwegian culture, and one technical term realised by a complex noun phrase,

1 In Hale/Campbell (2002: 18) a distinction is drawn between *options*, i.e. "the set of possibilities available to a subject when faced with the translation of a specific item". This is an empirical notion, based on the number of translations of an item in a sample. The term *alternative* is used about the actual choice made by the translator. *Choice* is used "as the overarching term, covering the whole process of selecting alternatives from options" (2008: 18).

4. Results

4.1 Analysis of one brief sentence including general vocabulary

English and Norwegian share many features of syntax. In some cases, translating from Norwegian into English can be a question of translating word by word. Thus, a CNA analysis of the sentence *Eldre hus er ikke så godt utstyrt* yielded the following results:[2]

Eldre	hus	er	ikke	så	godt	utstyrt.	No. of cand.
Older	houses	are	not	so	well	equipped.	10
				that			7
				*as			1
				*equivalently			1

Figure 1. Alternative translations of *Eldre hus er ikke så godt utstyrt.*

It will be clear that the similarity between the two languages here allows the candidates to translate word by word, and that the majority of them have chosen the acceptable alternatives *so* and *that.*

A word-for-word strategy is thus successful in this case.

4.2 CNA analysis of murtvang

In this case, we have a term which has no corresponding concept in the target language. The Norwegian word *murtvang*, (word-for-word translation **brickwork compulsion*), refers to outdated building regulations prohibiting the building of wooden houses in Norwegian towns to prevent fires from spreading. As a minimum requirement, a brick front could be added to the wall facing the street. Since the concept is unknown in the target culture, Norwegian-English dictionaries do not give a translation of the term.

A word-for-word "translation" could look like this:

2 An asterisk indicates unacceptable/unidiomatic translation.

mur	tvang
*brickwork	*compulsion

Figure 2. Word-for-word translation of *murtvang.*

So how did our candidates cope with this situation? The 19 candidates came up with 17 different variants for the concept.

Three of them opted for a syntactic strategy involving a word-for-word translation, choosing one lexeme for *mur* (*brick wall*, *masonry*, *wall*) and one to express the mandatory aspect (*compulsion*, *obligatory*).

The other 16 candidates, however, opted for the pragmatic strategy of explicitation, either by means of a noun phrase, for example *an obligation to build in brick or stone,* or by means of a finite clause, for example *brick walls were made compulsory.*

In this case, it is my opinion that a pragmatic strategy of explicitation is preferable, since the concept is culture-specific.

4.3 Analysis of technical term realised as a complex noun phrase

When it comes to terminology, one would expect the situation to be fairly straightforward, and most terms to be available in technical dictionaries. However, finding lexical equivalents of technical terms may present major problems. The term in question may not be found in the dictionary, or the dictionary may provide a number of alternative translations without guidelines for which alternative is the most appropriate one.

A number of the terms in the text yielded eight or more alternative translations. They included terms requiring explicitation due to cultural factors, for example *murtvang,* which we have just looked at, and terms realised by noun phrases with an underlying argument structure, for example a subject-verb or object-verb relationship. Head-modifier relationships also gave rise to a number of alternatives.

For closer analysis, I have chosen the term *diffusjonsåpen vindsperre.* This refers to a membrane or layer of material inserted in the insulation to allow damp air from inside the house to escape, while keeping out draughts.

The term – or its component parts – looks deceptively easy to translate, but is not found in the relevant dictionaries.

One might, however, easily come up with the following word-for-word translation:

	PREMODIFIER	HEAD		
Norwegian term	diffusjonsåpen	vindsperre		
Word-for-word translation	diffusion	open	wind	barrier

Figure 3. Norwegian term *diffusjonsåpen vindsperre* and word-for-word translation.

Norwegian-English dictionaries give neither the premodifier nor the head, but do include *diffusion* for *diffusjon*. The term *diffusjonsåpen*, however, is a common one in Norwegian, giving 225 GOOGLE hits, the first 10 of which all refer to relevant contexts, namely to membranes / barriers / coatings of various types that allow diffusion, i.e. that allow the migration of damp air.

In the following CNA chart, I have tried to relate the 19 candidates' alternatives to the translation strategies set out in Chesterman (2000: 15-16), concentrating on the translation of the modifier *diffusjonsåpen*:

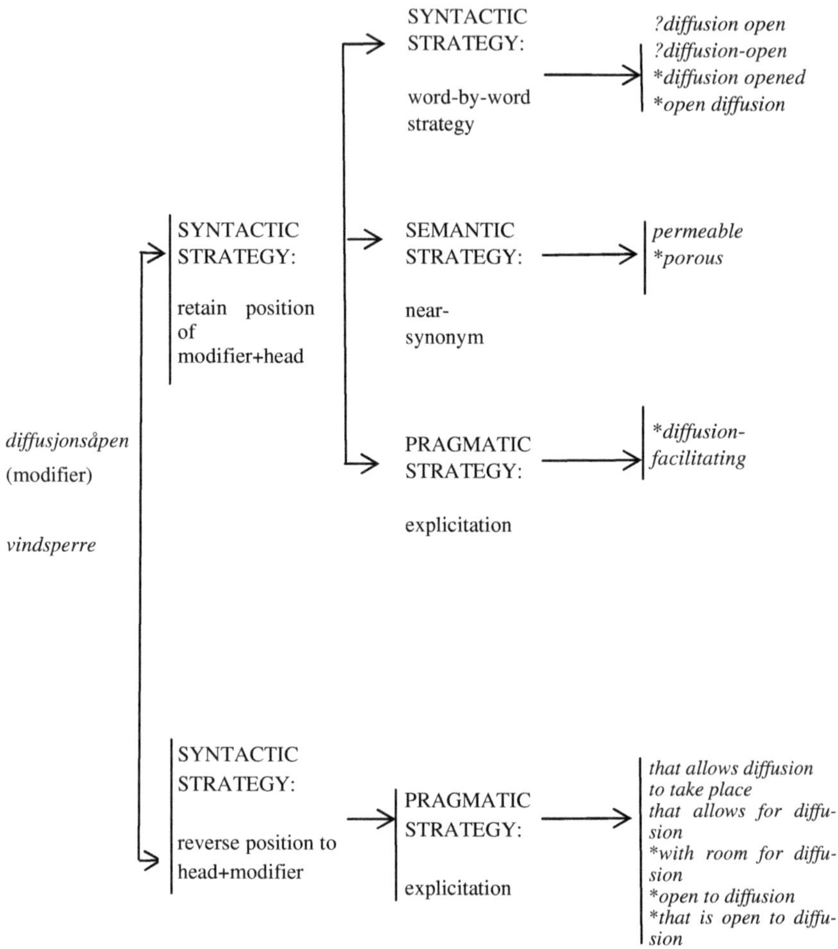

Figure 4. CNA chart illustrating alternative strategies used to translate *diffusjonsåpen*.

The initial choice made by the candidates is whether the modifier is to be translated as a premodifier or a postmodifier. For the ones who chose the premodification solution, the strategies varied from a word-for-word translation, via the use of near-synonym to explicitation. The postmodification solutions, however, are probably best described in terms of explicitation, reflecting a choice where the candidates did not trust the closest version – *diffusion open* – but preferred to explain the process involved.

The British National Corpus had no citations for *diffusion open*, while a GOOGLE search yielded 246 results. A check of the first 50 yielded 13 relevant contexts (the others mainly referred to computer contexts, including its use as a loan-word in French). However, none of these 13 contexts originated in an English-speaking country. The relevant websites – in English – were German (4) 'insulate and feel well', Danish (3), Austrian (2), Norwegian (1), Swedish (1), Slovenian (1) and Czech (1). These results should make the translator suspect that *diffusion open* may not be the preferred term, and instead follow Newmark's advice (1988: 154) in preferring a descriptive term.

Another strategy is to hypothesise on the basis the concept of *diffusjonsåpen* and approach it through near-synonymous concepts like *permeable* and *porous* in combination with *vapour*. Thus, a GOOGLE search for *vapour permeable* gave 2,320 results. A check of the first 10 revealed relevant contexts.

In the Norwegian text, *diffusjonsåpen* modifies *vindsperre* (literally *wind barrier*). The similarity of *vind* and *wind* is probably the reason why all 19 candidates included *wind* as one of the components. (However, *wind* entered into 12 different combinations, for example, *wind barrier* and *wind-proof sheeting*).

A GOOGLE check of the first 20 occurrences of *vapour permeable air barrier* vs *vapour permeable wind barrier* (*air barrier* vs *wind barrier*) gave the impression that *air barrier* was probably to be preferred, since there were in fact websites entitled "vapour permeable air barriers", defined as "a material which resists the passage of air and bulk water but allows the passage of moisture vapour through diffusion under a difference in pressure" (<www.bakor.com/USA/Tech Talks>).

The candidates, however, did not have access to the Internet. How, then, to assess the merit of the alternatives chosen by the candidates in the examination situation? In my opinion, in this case the candidate coming up with the best alternative would be the one who did not opt for a word-for-word solution. I would thus agree with Newmark (1988: 154) that it is safer to opt for a descriptive term. Hence, the best candidates in my opinion would be the ones who were discriminating enough to go for explicitation, preferably by postmodification:

	PREMODIFIER	HEAD
Norwegian term	diffusjonsåpen	vindsperre

Figure 5. Norwegian term *diffusjonsåpen vindsperre.*

Syntactic strategy Word for-word translation	diffusion	open	wind	barrier

Figure 6. Alternative using a word-for-word translation.

Semantic strategy Using a near-synonym	vapour	permeable	air/ wind	barrier

Figure 7. Alternative using a near-synonym.

Pragmatic strategy: explicitation	wind	barrier	that allows diffusion to take place

Figure 8. Alternative using explicitation.

Had the candidates had access to the Internet, however, I would have expected them to come up with *vapour permeable air / wind barrier*, through a process similar to the one I have one outlined above.

For the other terms referred to, various solutions were adopted. Thus, explicitation was the preferred alternative for terms having an underlying argument structure (subject-verb / object-verb). Some candidates, however, gambled on a word-for-word solution being acceptable. In all these cases, the choice of strategy would have to be evaluated on the basis of the acceptability of the alternative chosen by the candidate.

This preference for explicitation may be one of the factors behind the 19 translations of the 266-word long Norwegian text being, on average, more than 20 per cent longer than the source text.

5. Conclusion

Technical translation is generally regarded as being non-cultural, presenting different problems of terminology from translations where cultural factors are basic when choosing appropriate terminology. However, when the dictionaries fail to give the term, when dictionaries give a number of alternatives without guidelines for choice, or when the process involved is not clear to the translator, he or she will have to fall back on the same translation strategies as those used for other types of text.

In this chapter I have used a Choice network analysis (CNA) to analyse the variant translations of a number of technical terms, illustrated in more detail by two examples. I found this a useful way to approach the problem of evaluating the level of difficulty of the text in question. When the examination situation makes it impossible for the candidates to carry out a quality check on their chosen alternative, evaluation may be based on how successful he or she is in choosing an appropriate translation strategy.

References

Baker, M. 1995. Corpora in translation studies: An overview and some suggestions for future research . *Target* 7/2, 223-243.

Campbell, S. 2000. Choice network analysis in translation research. In Olohan, M. *Intercultural faultlines*. Manchester: St. Jerome, 29-42.

Chesterman, A. 1998. Communication strategies, learning strategies & translation strategies. In Malmkjær, K. (ed.) *Translation and language teaching*. Manchester: St. Jerome, 135-144.

Chesterman, A. 2000. Memetics and translation studies. *Synaps* 5, 1-17.

Hale, S. / Campbell, S. 2002. The interaction between text difficulty and translation accuracy . *Babel*, 48/1, 14-33.

Newmark, P. 1988. *A textbook of translation*. New York: Prentice Hall.

Picht, H. / Draskau, J. 1985. *Terminology : an introduction*. Department of Linguistic and International Studies monographs 2. Guildford: University of Surrey, Department of Linguistic and International Studies.

Sager, J. C. / Dungworth, D. / McDonald, P. F. 1980. *English special languages : principles and practice in science and technology*. Wiesbaden: Brandstetter.

Shuttleworth, M. / Cowie, M. 1997. *Dictionary of translation studies*. Manchester, UK: St. Jerome.

MARELLA MAGRIS AND LORENZA REGA

Riflessioni sull'uso dei dizionari specialistici italiano-tedesco-italiano nell'era di internet

Internet è diventato uno degli strumenti di informazione più importanti ad ogni livello di ricerca, tanto più nell'ambito della traduzione specializzata, che è particolarmente dipendente da una informazione rapida che tenga conto degli ultimi sviluppi in qualsiasi settore della società. A fronte di questa considerazione ci si è chiesti se il dizionario specialistico cartaceo abbia ancora una sua validità per i traduttori oppure se ormai il reperimento degli equivalenti avvenga soltanto mediante il ricorso all'informazione in Internet, sia che essa sia rappresentata da banche terminografiche mono- o plurilingui oppure da testi veri e propri accessibili grazie ai motori di ricerca.

In una precedente ricerca (Magris/Musacchio 2001) si era accertato che i traduttori semi-professionisti (in questo caso neo-laureati con qualche esperienza lavorativa) non disdegnano affatto di abbinare alle ricerche in rete il ricorso ai dizionari cartacei e che anzi, in alcuni casi, risultano dare la priorità a questi ultimi. Si è quindi rivolta l'attenzione ai traduttori professionisti, inviando loro un questionario che tenesse conto dei seguenti fattori: tipo di attività, fascia di età, titolo di studio, uso/non uso del dizionario specialistico, valutazione del grado di utilità del dizionario in generale e rispetto alle risorse di Internet, carenze riscontrate, interesse per la pubblicazione di altri dizionari.

Ovviamente si è consapevoli dei limiti del questionario quale metodo di indagine e della sua minore informatività rispetto ad un altro possibile strumento, ovvero il protocollo (per un confronto tra i due metodi si veda ad esempio Nielsen 1994: 13-33)[1]. Il metodo del

1 Questo secondo metodo applicato allo studio dell'uso dei dizionari prevede di assegnare ad un gruppo di soggetti un compito (ad esempio una traduzione)

protocollo consente di ottenere dati non solo molto più dettagliati, ma anche non influenzati dalla formulazione delle domande da parte del ricercatore. Pur tuttavia, in questa sede si è scelto di ricorrere al questionario come prima indagine conoscitiva, anche considerando che la realizzazione dei protocolli è un procedimento che richiede molto tempo e che difficilmente avrebbe incontrato ampia adesione da parte del gruppo studiato, composto, come si diceva, non da studenti ma da professionisti. Significativo sembra essere il fatto che alla richiesta di specificare autonomamente "altre carenze" presenti nei dizionari, pochi abbiano risposto a questo punto del questionario.

Al questionario hanno risposto 51 persone. Più della metà sono traduttori ad alto livello che operano all'interno di grandi organizzazioni internazionali. I traduttori liberi professionisti, pari a un 1/5, sono in larga misura anche docenti di traduzione. Si rileva dunque un certo squilibrio del nostro campione verso la figura del traduttore dipendente altamente specializzato: come si vedrà in seguito, si può ragionevolmente ipotizzare che ciò abbia rilevanza per quanto riguarda nello specifico il rapporto tra dizionari cartacei e Internet.

Per quanto riguarda l'età, il gruppo più numeroso in assoluto è costituito dalle persone che rientrano nella fascia dai 40 ai 50 anni (17); seguono poi quelli delle fasce comprese tra 30 e 40 anni (15) e tra 50 e 60 anni (10), mentre sono meno rappresentate le fasce comprese tra 20 e 30 anni (8) e tra 60 e 70 (1). Si tratta dunque di traduttori, oltre che di alto livello, anche di grande esperienza.

Quanto ai titoli di studio, più della metà ha una laurea in traduzione o interpretazione, più di 1/3 una laurea in lingue e letterature straniere (laddove va evidenziato che 4 persone hanno sia la laurea in lingue, sia in traduzione o interpretazione).

I dizionari specialistici continuano ad essere usati da tutti (ad eccezione di una sola persona che ha dichiarato di non utilizzarli affatto). 33 li usano spesso, 17 raramente. Rispetto alle risorse on-line, tuttavia, 12 li usano più frequentemente e 14 li usano con la stessa

chiedendo loro di annotare su appositi moduli tutti i problemi incontrati e le strategie usate per risolverli, relativamente alla consultazione del materiale lessicografico (un'indagine simile applicata proprio all'uso dei dizionari specializzati è stata condotta ad esempio da Duvå e Laursen [1994]).

frequenza: ben 24 persone hanno dichiarato di usarli meno frequentemente, un intervistato (funzionario del quadro linguistico UE) non li adopera mai e un altro (traduttore free-lance giovane e qualificato) adopera soltanto materiale cartaceo.

Qui va ricordato che più della metà dei traduttori operano in grandi organizzazioni internazionali dotate di una struttura informatica che consente loro di tenere i terminali sempre accesi senza aggravio di spesa per se stessi, di grandi risorse terminologiche in casa (ad esempio un servizio di terminologia), di banche testuali multilingui e di biblioteche cartacee ampiamente fornite. Si tratta inoltre di traduttori specializzati in settori ben determinati, per cui il ricorso ai dizionari, anche specialistici, può essere considerato quasi superfluo. Dei 12 che hanno dichiarato di usare più frequentemente i dizionari cartacei, la maggior parte sono traduttori liberi professionisti che, solitamente, non dispongono di risorse terminografiche e testuali altrettanto complete. Inoltre essi debbono essere più "generalisti" dei traduttori dipendenti, devono muoversi in una gamma di tipologie testuali e di argomenti più diversificata, e ciò riduce la possibilità di disporre di pre-conoscenze specialistiche sempre adeguate al compito da svolgere. In questo caso si ipotizza che il dizionario cartaceo costituisca il punto di partenza classico, se non per individuare l'equivalente definitivo di un termine, almeno per reperire delle prime ipotesi di traducente da verificare in rete o su testi paralleli[2]. E questo è anche il percorso che viene indicato da tutti gli intervistati che, oltre al questionario, hanno voluto fornire anche delle precisazioni supplementari.

Per quanto riguarda l'utilità attribuita ai dizionari cartacei, va rilevato che soltanto tre persone li ritengono poco utili, mentre la grande maggioranza li ritiene mediamente utili (31), ben 16 intervistati li ritengono molto utili.

Ne emerge un'immagine dell'uso dei dizionari che si discosta per esempio da quella descritta da Galisson (1983, citato in Campoy Cubillo 2002: 207), i cui intervistati consideravano i dizionari una fonte di informazione prestigiosa e inesauribile, anche nei casi in cui

2 Cfr. anche Bretthauer (2000: 123): "Je weniger Fachwissen vorhanden ist, desto stärker ist die Tendenz, Zuflucht beim mehrsprachigen Wörterbuch zu suchen."

la singola consultazione non produceva alcun frutto. Confrontata con questa immagine, la "media utilità" attribuita da molti dei nostri soggetti potrebbe apparire ben poca cosa: bisogna però considerare che, mentre i soggetti di Galisson erano studenti di lingue, nel nostro caso si tratta di utenti particolarmente raffinati e attenti, che hanno del dizionario un'immagine che si è delineata spesso in decenni di "frequentazione". E l'indicazione di "media utilità" va confrontata d'altra parte anche con la volontà di Bretthauer (2001: 168) di sensibilizzare i traduttori in quanto utenti professionisti affinché essi diffidino sostanzialmente dei dizionari bilingui, anche di quelli considerati più validi. Ma il traduttore professionista è a priori consapevole di tale fatto, e i traduttori semiprofessionisti vengono addestrati ad esserlo.

Un dato piuttosto positivo è che, paragonati alle risorse on-line, quasi la metà degli intervistati li ritiene ugualmente utili (23). 8 li ritengono meno utili per ragioni di tempo, 4 per l'attendibilità e ben 14 per la minore probabilità di trovare il termine cercato. Mentre quest'ultimo aspetto trova un ampio consenso da parte di tutti, per quanto riguarda il fattore tempo e l'attendibilità vi sono anche pareri contrari, con rispettivamente 5 e 6 persone che considerano i dizionari più utili proprio per questi due motivi.

Le critiche più rilevanti rivolte ai dizionari riguardano le carenze nella specificazione dei settori e sottosettori (23) e le indicazioni relative ai tecnicismi collaterali (26) e, in assoluto, le indicazioni relative agli equivalenti nella lingua di arrivo (32)[3]. Come detto, pochi, soltanto un terzo, hanno risposto alla richiesta di precisare "altre" carenze: la critica principale riguarda comunque il mancato aggiornamento oltre alla carenza di contesti e di spiegazioni. Pochi auspicano categorie diverse da quelle tutto sommato già esistenti, che però, per l'appunto, sono sottoposte a critiche.

Anche in letteratura si nota in generale che la pubblicazione di un nuovo dizionario specialistico bi- o plurilingue è accompagnata da recensioni che ne mettono in luce le carenze pur riconoscendone nel contempo i meriti. Del resto, i dizionari di questo tipo non sembrano

3 Sul problema dell'equivalenza nei dizionari specialistici bi- o plurilingui cfr. Werner (1998).

trovare difficoltà di mercato, come è dimostrato anche dal numero[4] di dizionari specialistici pubblicati negli ultimi tempi presso grandi case editrici.

Significativa riguardo al problema delle critiche ai dizionari plurilingui è comunque la discussione sviluppatasi sulla scorta dell'analisi di due dizionari giuridici tedesco-francese-tedesco (cfr. Bretthauer 2000 e 2001, Fleck 2000). Al di là delle questioni concrete affrontate da Bretthauer e Fleck, il merito di questi tre contributi va individuato nell'avere posto in modo chiaro l'accento su quello che è il dilemma per eccellenza dei dizionari specializzati, ovvero l'equilibrio tra la volontà di fornire quante più precisazioni possibili e i vincoli oggettivi di varia natura (economica, di numero di pagine ecc.) imposti a un volume stampato.

Si deve tuttavia sottolineare che alla base di tale problema v'è già il fatto che i dizionari specialistici sono tali in realtà fino a un certo punto. Conte-Boss, che è peraltro un assai buon dizionario, si intitola *Dizionario giuridico ed economico*, Troike Strambaci-Mariani sceglie *Vocabolario del diritto e dell'econom*ia, il recente dizionario del Gabler Verlag curato da Hartung-Thönes/Pierallini restringe il campo e sceglie il titolo *Wirtschaftswörterbuch Deutsch-Italienisch* e allo stesso modo si comporta anche Köbler *Rechtsitalienisch – Deutsch-italienisches und italienisch-deutsches Rechtswörterbuch für jedermann.* Per coprire tutti i sottosettori degli ambiti menzionati (con relative collocazioni e eventuali esempi) il numero dei termini dovrebbe essere assai rilevante. E' evidente che il criterio di scelta dei termini da inserire deve necessariamente essere all'insegna del risparmio: per es. del numero di termini e delle indicazioni di varia natura che sarebbe opportuno accompagnassero il termine. E' ovvio che sarà inutile andare a cercare in questo tipo di dizionari un termine quale *Mutterschaftsurlaub – Astensione facoltativa dal lavoro* o *Schutzfrist vor der Entbindung – Astensione obbligatoria prima del parto*: si tratta infatti di termini sì giuridici, ma talmente specifici del settore della tutela della donna nel diritto del lavoro, che il compilatore di un

4 Per es. Conte-Boss (2001-2003), Hartung-Thönes/Pierallini (2002), Hoepli (2000), Marolli/Guarnieri (1999/2002), Taino (c.d.s.). Si tratta di un numero alto se si considera l'impegno necessario per questo tipo di pubblicazione.

dizionario giuridico non può permettersi di rilevarli, anche se si tratta effettivamente di entrate che potrebbero essere interessanti e utili[5]. Il traduttore esperto sa già in realtà che in questi casi deve ricorrere direttamente ai testi paralleli oppure a Internet nella speranza di trovare quanto cerca in qualche banca dati terminografica plurilingue oppure in documenti a disposizione in rete. Ed è anche ovvio non tentare di trovare in un dizionario cartaceo delle glosse così ampie come quelle per esempio proposte da Schneider (2000a/b). Del resto la possibilità di avere questo tipo di glosse, oppure dei contesti definitori, che aiutano l'utente a vedere come il termine è effettivamente impiegato, o, ancora, come detto, di avere dei termini assai specifici era stata ed è alla base del progetto TERMit[6], come pure – riteniamo – di altre banche dati terminografiche. Il problema di fondo è invece che talvolta si ha l'impressione che il compilatore del dizionario specialistico plurilingue – che generalmente non è un lessicografo, ma un esperto del settore – non abbia sempre chiarezza sui criteri sottostanti alla redazione di un tale dizionario, per es. riguardo alla scelta del corpus e delle entrate nonché all'inserimento delle informazioni di minima necessarie. In realtà sono proprio queste ultime a essere le più richieste in particolare dai traduttori, ma anche dagli esperti, anche se questi ultimi in generale si possono anche accontentare di capire "più o meno" a quale referente una denominazione rimanda.

Non va infatti dimenticato che destinatari dei dizionari specialistici non sono soltanto traduttori di testi specialistici[7], ma possono essere anche altri utenti. Anzi, si è rilevato che in realtà il destinatario principale non è probabilmente il traduttore[8]. Quindi anche i dizionari

5 I termini sono stati rilevati da Silvia Reggio sulla scorta della sua tesi di laurea *La tutela della donna nel diritto del lavoro*. Università di Trieste, a.a. 1999-2000, e quindi inseriti in TERMit, la banca dati terminografica della SSLMIT dell'Università di Trieste (v. <http://www.sslmit.units.it/termit>).

6 V. nota precedente.

7 Secondo Duvå/Laursen (1994: 248), "The basis of bilingual LSP lexicographic research must be a knowledge of the problems and (the) needs of the LSP translator".

8 Cfr. per es. Rossenbeck (1994: 138): „Als Benutzer zweisprachiger Fachwörterbücher wurden erstens fortgeschrittene Studenten eines bestimmten Faches und zweitens Fachleute, die beide hin und wieder fremdsprachige Fachtexte verstehen oder auch produzieren müssen, sowie drittens professionelle Über-

specialistici, come quelli generali, si trovano a servire due padroni (cfr. Marello 1996: 130), col rischio di servirli entrambi male.

Le indicazioni semantiche, indubbiamente di minima, sono comunque l'aspetto più rilevante nella voce di un dizionario specialistico, in quanto soltanto esse possono contribuire a dare chiarezza al traduttore sul referente e, quindi, ad aiutarlo nelle sue scelte. Per indicazioni di minima si intende anche semplicemente ricordare se un termine appartiene per es. in un dizionario giuridico al diritto civile o penale, oppure se esso trovi un equivalente relativamente analogo[9] nella LA, o ancora se si tratti di una proposta di traduzione per un termine senza referente nella LA. Assai meno rilevanti sono invece indicazioni di tipo grammaticale[10] oppure etimologico, in quanto – per avere questo tipo di informazioni – si può generalmente ricorrere a un dizionario generale e, comunque, in un'ottica di scelta dei criteri, la priorità non dovrebbe essere data a questo tipo di informazioni.

Nei dizionari specialistici più antichi, per esempio ottocenteschi, la tendenza era quella di fornire un unico traducente per ogni termine: tale fatto era tipico di uno stadio ancora iniziale della specializzazione del sapere e, quindi, di lingue speciali ancora in formazione: tuttavia esso rendeva in realtà più semplice il compito all'utente del dizionario che non doveva decidere sulla folla di traducenti che oggi gli vengono offerti da un dizionario specialistico. Soltanto in alcuni sporadici casi si trovano tutt'al più due proposte: nella *Strenna linguistica-commerciale pel 1875. Prontuario di 1000 voci mercantili ordinate alfabeticamente ad uso del corrispondente in italiano-*

setzer, die in ihrer Praxis mit Fachtexten konfrontiert werden, ins Auge gefaßt."

9 Si parla di "relativamente" in quanto per es. già in un termine che si supporrebbe equivalente nelle due lingue, come *Frühgeburt* e "parto prematuro", si deve constatare una differenza a livello giuridico: nel determinare il parto prematuro vengono presi in considerazione in Germania sia il fattore peso (feto al di sotto dei 2500 grammi) sia quello temporale (fine prematura della gravidanza). In Italia, invece si tiene conto unicamente di quest'ultimo fattore (espulsione del feto dopo il 180° giorno e fino al 266° giorno di gestazione). Cfr. la tesi di laurea di Silvia Reggio, *La tutela della donna nel diritto del lavoro*, Università di Trieste, a.a. 1999-2000.

10 A meno che, ovviamente, il genere e il numero non svolgano un ruolo di discriminazione del significato che ne imponga l'indicazione.

tedesco-francese-inglese (Trieste 1874, a cura di Giacomo Pincherle), per "importo" si trova *Betrag* e *Belauf*; per "incassare" *Eincassiren* e *Einziehen*, ma in generale la corrispondenza è sempre biunivoca. Interessante notare come in questo dizionarietto-prontuario vengano inseriti anche numerose collocazioni fisse ("Estinguere una cambiale"- *Einen Wechsel ausloeschen*), tecnicismi collaterali ("Essere a giorno" – *A' jour sein, orientirt sein, genau unterrichtet*) e parole ad alta frequenza nel diritto e nella prassi commerciale ("Favore a" – *Zu Gunsten*). All'epoca, inoltre, il dizionario specialistico che aveva fini eminentemente pratici (ma la situazione non è mutata neppure oggi) era forse non tanto rivolto ai traduttori, quanto piuttosto a degli esperti veri e propri ai quali bastava una corrispondenza per capire, come già si diceva, "più o meno" di cosa si trattava. Analizzando la bibliografia dei dizionari specializzati italiani del XIX secolo (Zolli 1973), in cui rientrano anche alcuni dizionari bi- e plurilingui, si nota che, per quanto riguarda la coppia tedesco-italiano, esistevano un discreto numero di dizionari tecnici (dall'infermieristica alla nautica), e alcuni nel settore giuridico-commerciale destinati agli addetti ai lavori che nella maggior parte dei casi vivevano in una realtà plurietnica, plurilingue, ma monogiuridica[11]. Ancora oggi, nonostante i mutamenti socio-economici verificatisi, che hanno modificato la tipologia degli utenti e le loro esigenze, alcuni dizionari continuano a fornire semplici equivalenze biunivoche (p. es. Köbler 1996), e Rossenbeck (1994: 155) nota che un dizionario di questo tipo può costituire tutt'al più un ausilio a chi già possiede conoscenze specialistiche. Si pensi per esempio al termine *Überhangmandat*, per il quale vengono forniti come traducenti "mandato in eccedenza" (Troike Strambaci-Mariani) o "mandato eccedente" (Conte-Boss), proposte poco trasparenti per chi non conosca già il sistema elettorale tedesco.

Oggi il dizionario specialistico deve tenere conto di una realtà specialistica sempre più complessa e ormai da tempo presenta per un termine più traducenti. Tale fatto non si è però accompagnato a una maggiore consapevolezza terminografica, per cui il dizionario specialistico plurilingue ha cominciato in qualche caso a creare difficoltà al

11 Non è forse casuale che quali luoghi di edizione di tre dei quattro dizionari pubblicati prima del 1918 compaiano Trieste, Vienna e Zara.

suo utente presentandogli sì tutta una serie di proposte, magari valide, ma in realtà tali da ingenerare confusione quando sono prive di alcune specificazioni che, sole, possono aiutare l'utente a muoversi in una realtà che non conosce come la realtà di ogni giorno mediata dai dizionari generali.

In tale contesto si è provato a testare anche per l'italiano i termini oggetto del dibattito Bretthauer-Fleck, e più precisamente *Angeklagter*, *Angeschuldigter* e *Beschuldigter* nei due dizionari di diritto più accreditati, ovvero Troike Strambaci-Mariani e Conte-Boss, prendendo in esame peraltro anche Köbler, che però già a priori rinuncia a qualsiasi tipo di informazione supplementare, limitandosi a fornire soltanto dei traducenti di cui specifica tutt'al più il genere.

Troike Strambaci-Mariani:
Angeklagter accusato; imputato; **Haupt~** principale imputato; **Mit~** coaccusato; coimputato; ~ in Abwesenheit imputato contumace; ~ auf freiem Fuß imputato a piede libero
Angeschuldigter accusato, incolpato
Beschuldigter accusato, imputato, incolpato
Conte-Boss:
Angeklagter m imputato, accusato (S); **abwesender** imputato contumace; **flüchtiger** ~ imputato latitante; ~ **in Abwesenheit** imputato contumace; **den ~ freisprechen** prosciogliere l'imputato; **den ~ verurteilen** condannare l'imputato; **den ~ vernehmen** interrogare l'imputato
Angeschuldigter *m* imputato
Beschuldigter m indiziato (di reato), imputato
Köbler
Angeklagter (M.) imputato (M.), accusato (M.)
Angeschuldigter (M.) imputato (M.)
Beschuldigter (M.) imputato (M.), indiziato (M.) di reato

Quando un traduttore si trova davanti a una situazione di questo genere, ovvero a una mancanza di chiarezza nella decisione che deve necessariamente prendere, la prima cosa che tende a fare, dopo avere ovviamente analizzato il contesto, è quella di cercare un riscontro nella direzione opposta (nel caso specifico, dall'italiano al tedesco), la seconda di frugare nella sua memoria e, quindi, di ricorrere a testi paralleli se non li ha già sottomano.

Troike Strambaci-Mariani
accusato Angeklagter; Angeschuldigter; Beklagter; Beschuldigter.
imputato Angeklagter; Begklagter; Beschuldigter; **banco degli ~i** Anklagebank; **principale ~** Hauptangeklagter; **~ a piede libero** Angeklagter auf freiem Fuß; **~ contumace** Angeklagter in Abwesenheit.
incolpato Angeklagter; Angeschuldigter; Beschuldigter.
Conte-Boss
imputato m Angeklagter m; **principale** Hauptangeklagter; **contumace** Angeklagter in Abwesenheit
indiziato m Verdächtiger m.
Köbler:
imputato (M.) Angeklagter (M.), Angeschuldigter (M.), Beschuldigter (M.)
accusato (M.) Angeklagter (M.)
indiziato (M.) di reato Beschuldigter (M.)

E' evidente che a questo punto l'utente specialista ha più o meno capito di cosa si tratta, il traduttore invece, che deve decidere per un termine, comincia nuovamente a interrogare la sua memoria, oppure a cercare in dizionari enciclopedici monolingui le definizioni dei termini cercati. Se sa che *Angeklagter* (il termine in realtà meno complesso in quanto si tratta di un referente che esiste praticamente senza distinzioni in entrambe le realtà italiana e tedesca) è senza ombra di dubbio l'imputato, comincerà a ricercare in questo campo semantico e penserà per es. a "indagato" per operare dei distinguo tra i vari termini offertigli.

Troike Strambaci-Mariani
indagato Beschuldigter im Ermittlungsverfahren; **registro degli ~i** Register der Beschuldigten, gegen die ein Ermittlungsverfahren eingeleitet wird.
Conte-Boss
indagato *m (persona sottoposta alle indagini preliminari)* Beschuldigter *m*.

persona sottoposta alle indagini (proc. pen.) Beschuldigter *m*.
Köbler
non riporta i due termini qui proposti.

A questo punto il problema rimane *Angeschuldigter* che non si vuole qui discutere: ci si limita a accennare al fatto che *Angeschuldigter* dovrebbe essere in realtà colui che è iscritto al registro delle notizie di reato e *Beschuldigter* colui che ancora non lo è, laddove entrambi sono persona sottoposta alle indagini preliminari.

Insomma, ciò che sembra mancare, non è tanto l'informazione, ma la coerenza nel fornirla. E questo dovrebbe essere un parametro imprescindibile per un dizionario specialistico.

Nel momento in cui gli intervistati dicono che vi sono carenze nelle indicazioni relative agli equivalenti nella lingua di arrivo, si pensa però anche ad altri tipi di termini. Si pensi ad es. a *Verfolgter*, parola che non è forse termine a tutti gli effetti, ma che è altamente occorrente in qualsiasi testo riguardante una procedura di estradizione, e che quindi il traduttore tende a riconoscere come termine vero e proprio. Ma comunque, anche se di termine vero e proprio non si tratta, esso è certamente un tecnicismo collaterale ad altissima frequenza che un dizionario specialistico dovrebbe contenere.

Troike Strambaci-Mariani
Verfolgter perseguitato.
Conte-Boss
Verfolgter *m* perseguitato; **politischer** perseguitato politico.
Köbler
non riporta il termine.

Il problema è dato dal fatto che la parola *Verfolgter* nel senso di "perseguitato politico" rientra piuttosto nel lessico comune, tanto che lo si trova anche nei dizionari generali. Il traduttore sa benissimo che non può adoperare "il perseguitato" in un testo in cui con tale parola ci si riferisce a un criminale già riconosciuto in quanto tale. Cerca allora nella sua memoria e giunge a "il perseguito" oppure "il ricercato" che, però, probabilmente non lo convincono. Deve allora cominciare a consultare dizionari enciclopedici: va detto che il dizionario Creifelds

(Weber 1999) riporta la parola soltanto nell'accezione di perseguitato politico, più correttamente Köbler – pur non riportando *Verfolgter* – rimanda il verbo *verfolgen* a *Ermittlungsverfahren.* A questo punto il traduttore avrà quanto meno la certezza che non si tratta di un termine autentico, ma di uno pseudotermine. Se consulterà Internet, troverà *die Auslieferung des Verfolgten* con occorrenza assai alta, ma comunque gli sarà difficile avere la corrispondenza italiana. Ricorrerà ai testi paralleli e comincerà a capire che l'italiano non ha neppure tale tecnicismo collaterale, ma che parla di "estradando", oppure ripete il nome e cognome o, ancora, usa forme di tipo anaforico, del tipo "il summenzionato", "la persona in questione". Nella Convenzione europea di estradizione[12] scoprirà che *Verfolgter* è in italiano "la persona richiesta, reclamata" oppure "l'estradato". Anche se l'esempio proposto non è particolarmente complesso, esso evidenzia che, come ricorda tra gli altri Bretthauer (2001: 168), la soluzione ad un problema terminologico va spesso ricercata a livello frastico o testuale. In questi casi il dizionario può fornire solo un primo aiuto verso la soluzione: è infatti impensabile inserire stringhe di testo che costituiscano una sorta di grammatica della traduzione, anche se sarebbe auspicabile che venissero riportati esempi sulla scorta di quanto fa la lessicografia generale.

Nel caso specifico sarebbe già utile se il tecnicismo venissse specificato anche nell'accezione assunta nell'espressione *die Auslieferung des Verfolgten (estradizione della persona richiesta)* che è in realtà quella più comune nella lingua del diritto penale, ma meno nota al traduttore che invece certamente conosce la parola nel significato di perseguitato politico. Al traduttore resterebbe poi la scelta tra la traduzione proposta ed altre soluzioni per es. di tipo anaforico.

Altro problema ancora è quello di distinguere se l'equivalente fornito è un traducente a tutti gli effetti o meno. In alcuni casi si può trattare di una *nonce word* creata dal lessicografo (Nielsen 1994: 174), come può essere il caso del termine tedesco *Delibation* fornito come traducente di "delibazione" e in realtà non usato nel diritto tedesco.

12 Consultabile al sito <www.giustizia.it/pol_internaz/atti/penale/non_ufficiali/conv_eu_estr.htm>.

Troike Strambaci-Mariani
delibazione Delibation (Beschluß über die Vollstreckung eines ausländischen Urteils); **giudizio di ~** Gültigkeitserklärung; **procedimento di ~** Delibationsverfahren; **sentenza di ~** (*di una decisione straniera*) Vollstreckungsurteil; **~ di decisioni straniere** Anerkennung ausländischer Entscheidungen; **~ di sentenze straniere** Anerkennung ausländischer Entscheidungen
Delibation delibazione
Gültigkeitserklärung **convalida; convalidamento; convalidazione; delibazione; giudizio di delibazione; legalizzazione; legittimazione; sanatoria;**
Anerkennung ausländischer Entscheidungen **delibazione di decisioni straniere; delibazione di sentenze straniere;**
Anerkennung eines ausländischen Urteils **delibazione di (una) sentenza**
Conte-Boss
delibazione f. Prüfung eines ausländischen Urteils, dessen Anerkennung beantragt wird.
Anerkennung f. **eines ausländischen Urteils** riconoscimento di sentenza straniera, delibazione di sentenza straniera.
Köbler
non riporta il termine

Un ulteriore, rilevante problema è che la mancanza di informazioni semantiche rende difficile al profano verificare la validità dei traducenti forniti. Si consideri *Aufsichtsrat*:

Troike Strambaci-Mariani
Aufsichtsrat (ARat): consigliere di sorveglianza; consigliere di vigilanza; consiglio di sorveglianza; consiglio di vigilanza;
Abberufung des ~s revoca del consiglio di sorveglianza; **Arbeitnehmervertreter im ~** rappresentante delle maestranze nel consiglio di sorveglianza; **Besetzung des ~s** composizione del consiglio di sorveglianza; **Betriebsvertreter des ~s** rappresentante del personale nel consiglio di vigilanza; **Entlastung des ~s** approvazione dell'operato del consiglio di controllo (di sorveglianza/di vigilanza)
Consiglio di sorveglianza Aufsichtsrat

Conte-Boss
Aufsichtsrat m. (1) (*als Gremium)* collegio sindacale; (2) (*als Einzelperson*) sindaco
Collegio sindacale, dei sindaci (*società*) Aufsichtsrat m., Kontrollstelle f. (S), Revisionskommission f. (S), Revisorenkommission f. (S)
Organo di controllo Kontrollorgan, Aufsichtsorgan
Köbler
Aufsichtsrat (M.) (einer Gesellschaft) collegio (M.) sindacale
Collegio sindacale (M.) Aufsichtsrat (M.)
Hartung-Thönes/Pierallini
Aufsichtsrat m. consiglio m. di vigilanza, consiglio di amministrazione

Ciola, Coluccia, Maganzi, Mayer

Collegio sindacale n.m.	**Aufsichtsrat** n.m.	**IT, AT, DE**
DEFINIZIONE	(Südtirol genormt)	
CONTESTO	KONTEXT IT	
	DEFINITION AT	
	KONTEXT AT	
	DEFINITION DE	
	Prüferkollegium n.n.	**IT**
	AR n.m.	**DE**
	KONTEXT DE	
	Revisionsstelle n.f.	**CH**
	(*bei Aktiengesellschaften*)	
	KONTEXT CH	
	Aufsichtsstelle n.f.	**CH**
	(*Kommanditaktiengesellschaften*)	
	KONTEXT CH	
	Kontrollstelle n.f.	**CH**
	(*bei Genossenschaften*)	
	KONTEXT CH	

Taino[13]
Aufsichtsrat m. (abbr. AR) [comm., dir.] consiglio di sorveglianza, comitato di sorveglianza, commissione interna, consigliere di sor-

13 Il dizionario è attualmente in fase di revisione prima della stampa, per cui sono possibili ancora delle modifiche.

veglianza. Aufsichtsrat eines Unternehmens [comm., dir.] consiglio di sorveglianza dell'impresa. Im Aufsichtsrat sitzen [comm., dir.] sedere nel consiglio di sorveglianza, far parte della commissione interna. **Consiglio di sorveglianza** m. [comm., ec. az, dir.] Aufsichtsrat m. (abbr. AR); [pubbl. amm.] Verwaltungsrat m. (negli enti di diritto pubblico, corrispondente allo "Aufsichtsrat" delle società per azioni); **consiglio di sorveglianza dell'impresa** (comm., dir.) Aufsichtsrat eines Unternehmens

Tale termine è particolarmente complesso in quanto la sua composizione e le sue funzioni coincidono solo parzialmente con il collegio dei sindaci nella realtà italiana: appare evidentemente forte la tentazione di indicare quest'ultimo come corrispondente funzionale, ed è quanto fanno in toto Conte-Boss e Köbler. Altra è la posizione di Ciola et al. che partono da una realtà italiana e che forniscono però ulteriori traducenti per la realtà tedesca, austriaca e svizzera: in effetti *Aufsichtsrat* si trova per coerenza editoriale nell'elenco dei termini tedeschi, ma l'intero dizionario deve fare i conti con la terminologia in lingua tedesca attestata in Alto Adige già da molti decenni. Troike Strambaci-Mariani forniscono dei traducenti assolutamente accettabili, anche se ci chiede la necessità di variare tra sorveglianza e vigilanza. Hartung-Thönes/Pierallini forniscono come secondo termine "consiglio di amministrazione", che può ingenerare notevole confusione. In entrambi i casi ("collegio dei sindaci" e "consiglio di amministrazione") sarebbe stato per lo meno opportuno inserire un'avvertenza sul grado (non assoluto) di equivalenza, come è stato rilevato per esempio nel caso del termine *Grundbuch* in Troike Strambaci-Mariani[14].

Nei dizionari pubblicati fino a oggi, queste indicazioni vengono fornite tuttavia, come si è visto, soltanto in rari casi, in particolare nei dizionari di Ciola et al. e di Taino. Utili al traduttore e a qualsiasi altro utente sono per l'appunto la struttura e i contenuti delle entrate presentate da questi autori: in particolare, sebbene sia stato rilevato più volte che i dizionari cartacei non possono riportare spiegazioni approfon-

14 **Grundbuch** (*in etwa zu vergleichen mit*): catasto, libro delle ipoteche, libro fondiario, registro delle ipoteche, registro fondiario, registro immobiliare. Tale indicazione rimane però praticamente un'eccezione.

dite, negli esempi forniti si evidenzia come anche una glossa breve possa fornire indicazioni preziose e concretamente utili. Non a caso tutti questi autori sono linguisti e, o si sono occupati del settore, oppure operano a stretto contatto con specialisti.

Conclusioni

La "metalessicografia" si è occupata tutto sommato poco dei dizionari specialistici; in molti casi ci si limita a constatarne la qualità carente, senza passare a critiche più costruttive, come nota per esempio Bergenholtz (1994: 43).

Secondo Pilegaard (1994: 211) questa considerazione riguarda soprattutto la lessicografia specializzata bilingue, mentre per l'ambito monolingue una maggior attenzione da parte dei lessicografi avrebbe portato anche ad un miglioramento nella redazione dei dizionari. Duvå/Laursen (1994: 266) hanno sottolineato come i problemi connessi all'equivalenza siano entità complesse che possono essere suddivise in: incertezze relative all'argomento, al contenuto semantico delle parole, alla collocazione delle parole nell'"universo", all'uso delle parole, alle loro possibilità combinatorie. Il dizionario ideale dovrebbe contribuire ad eliminare tali incertezze fornendo ad esempio il settore o sottosettore, una definizione, discriminazioni di significato ecc.

In realtà, negli anni'90 vi è stato un cambiamento di tendenza, segnato ad esempio dal manuale di lessicografia specializzata di Bergenholtz/Tarp (1995) o dal testo di Nielsen (1994), in cui si tracciano i principi su cui basarsi per creare dizionari specializzati più utili ed affidabili. Anche la pratica segna notevoli passi in avanti, come dimostrato dal dizionario terminologico di Ciola et al. e da Taino.

Purtroppo però rimangono ancora frequenti i casi in cui non sembra che le scelte lessicografiche siano guidate da alcun insieme coerente di principi: spesso non vi è coerenza nella scelta dei lemmi (ad esempio vengono inclusi termini estranei alla disciplina trattata, o vengono incluse come voci a sé stanti forme flesse di uno stesso lemma), non viene prestata sufficiente attenzione ai problemi legati alla polisemia e alla sinonimia e non si trova traccia del percorso seguito dal lessicografo per arrivare a stabilire l'equivalenza interlinguistica. In particolare, un'importanza fondamentale riveste la scelta del corpus da cui estrarre i termini.

Riassumendo, i dizionari cartacei sembrano avere comunque ancora un futuro, e questo per quanto riguarda sia quelli più generici (dizionario del diritto, dell'economia e via dicendo) sia quelli altamente specialistici (sull'esempio del Dizionario terminologico del diritto societario italiano/tedesco). E' necessario che i primi si ispirino ai secondi nella concezione di fondo e, in particolare, tengano presenti i seguenti punti:

1. scelta del corpus;
2. coerenza nella scelta dei termini;
3. coerenza nell'attribuzione ai singoli settori e sottosettori;
4. indicazione se si tratta di equivalenze autentiche, oppure di proposte del lessicografo.

Soltanto se si terranno presenti questi fattori il dizionario specialistico plurilingue potrà continuare ad avere e ad aumentare la propria importanza nei confronti della ricerca in Internet. Cloaca massima e Biblioteca di Alessandria al tempo stesso, secondo la definizione che ne dà Jean Starobinski (Corriere della Sera, 23 luglio 2003, p. 29), Internet rimane, almeno per il momento, come dimostrato dalle risposte degli intervistati, uno degli ausili per il reperimento della terminologia accanto al dizionario specialistico cartaceo al quale ben pochi traduttori sono in realtà disposti a rinunciare.

Riferimenti bibliografici

Bergenholtz, H. 1994. Zehn Thesen zur Fachlexikographie. In Schaeder, B. / Bergenholtz, H. (Hrsg.) *Fachlexikographie: Fachwissen und seine Repräsentation in Wörterbüchern*. Tübingen: Narr, 43-56.

Bergenholtz, H. / Tarp, S. (eds) 1995. *Manual of Specialised Lexicography. The Presentation of Specialised Dictionaries* / Philadelphia: John Benjamins.

Bretthauer, P. 2000. Das zweisprachige Fachwörterbuch: die Krücke des Übersetzers . *Lebende Sprachen* 3, 121-123.

Bretthauer, P. 2001. Nochmals zur Krücke des Übersetzers. Eine Replik auf Klaus E.W. Fleck: „Beschuldigte Fachwörterbücher auf der Anklagebank" in LES 4/2000, S. 171-2 , *Lebende Sprachen* 4, 168-170.

Campoy Cubillo, M.C. 2002. Dictionary use and dictionary needs of ESP students: an experimental approach. *International Journal of Lexicography* 15/3, 206-228.

Ciola, B. / Coluccia, S. / Mayer, F. / Maganzi, F. 2000. *Terminologisches Wörterbuch zum Gesellschaftsrecht italienisch/deutsch*. München/Bolzano-Bozen/Wien/Bern: C.H. Beck'sche Verlagsbuchhandlung/Athesia/Linde/Stämpfli.

Conte, G. / Boss, H. 2001-2003. *Wörterbuch der Rechts-und Wirtschaftssprache*. München/Basel/Milano: Beck/Helbing & Lichtenhahn/Giuffrè.

Duvå, G. / Laursen, A.-L. 1994. Translation and LSP lexicography: a user survey. In Schaeder, B. / Bergenholtz, H. (Hrsg.) *Fachlexikographie: Fachwissen und seine Repräsentation in Wörterbüchern*. Tübingen: Narr, 247-267.

Fleck, K.E.W. 2000. Beschuldigte Fachwörterbücher auf der Anklagebank. Zu: Dieter Bretthauer: „Das zweisprachige Fachwörterbuch: die Krücke des Übersetzers" in LES 3/2000, S. 121-123 , *Lebende Sprachen*, 4, 171-2.

Hartung-Thönes, S. / Pierallini, P. 2002. *Gabler Wirtschaftswörterbuch – Deutsch-Italienisch*. Wiesbaden: Gabler Verlag.

Hoepli 2000. *Grande dizionario tecnico/Das große Wörterbuch der Technik*. Milano/Wiesbaden: Hoepli/Brandstetter.

Köbler, G. 1996. *Rechtsitalienisch – Deutsch-italienisches und italienisch-deutsches Wörterbuch*. München: Verlag Vahlen.

Magris, M. / Musacchio, M.T. 2001. La ricerca terminologica nella traduzione specializzata: un esperimento con approcci diversi . In Mayer, F. (ed.) *Language for Special Purposes: Perspectives for the New Millennium*. Tübingen: Narr, 311-319.

Marello, C. 1996. *Le parole dell'italiano. Lessico e dizionari*. Bologna: Zanichelli.

Marolli, G. / Guarnieri, O. 1999/2002. *Grande Dizionario di Tedesco Tecnico*. Milano: Garzanti.

Nielsen, S. 1994. *The Bilingual LSP Dictionary. Principles and Practice for Legal Language*. Tübingen: Narr.

Pilegaard, M. 1994. Bilingual LSP dictionaries. User benefit correlates with elaborateness of 'explanation' . In Schaeder, B. / Bergenholtz, H. (Hrsg.) *Fachlexikographie: Fachwissen und seine Repräsentation in Wörterbüchern*. Tübingen: Narr, 221-228.

Rossenbeck, K. 1994. Enzyklopädische Information im zweisprachigen Fachwörterbuch. In Schaeder, B. / Bergenholtz, H. (Hrsg.) *Fachlexikographie: Fachwissen und seine Repräsentation in Wörterbüchern*. Tübingen: Narr, 133-159.

Schneider, F. 2000a. Die Glosse im zweisprachigen Wirtschaftswörterbuch. Ein Instrument zur Erreichung von interkultureller Verstehenssouveränität und zum flexiblen Gebrauch von Äquivalenten . *Lebende Sprachen* 1, 22-25.

Schneider, F. 2000b. Die Glosse im zweisprachigen Wirtschaftswörterbuch (2. Teil). Ein Instrument zur Erreichung von interkultureller Verstehenssouveränität und zum flexiblen Gebrauch von Äquivalenten . *Lebende Sprachen* 2, 68-72.

Troike Strambaci, H. / Helffrich Mariani, E. 1997-1999. *Wörterbuch für Recht und Wirtschaft – Deutsch-Italienisch, Vocabolario del diritto e dell'economia – Tedesco-Italiano*. München/Milano: C.H. Beck'sche Verlagsbuchhandlung / Giuffrè.

Weber, K. (Hrsg.) 1999. *Creifelds Rechtswörterbuch*. München: C.H. Beck'sche Verlagsbuchhandlung.

Werner, R. 1998. Das Problem der Äquivalenz im zwei- und im mehrsprachigen Fachwörterbuch . In Hoffmann, L., Kalverkämper, H. / Wiegand, H.E. (Hrsg.) *Fachsprachen*. Berlin/New York: De Gruyter. Band 2, 1853-1884.

Zolli, P. 1974. *Bibliografia dei dizionari specializzati italiani del XIX secolo*. Firenze: Olschki.

IOANNIS E. SARIDAKIS AND GEORGIA KOSTOPOULOU

Modern trends in the pedagogy of specialised translation: LSP, text typology and the use of IT tools

1. Introduction

This chapter addresses different aspects of the pedagogy of specialised translation, such as LSP and terminology, text typology and style, all with regard to the use of monolingual and bilingual corpora in translator training curricula and processes. Moreover, it presents the first pedagogical findings stemming from the experimental inclusion of the corpus-based approach in a Greek translator-training curriculum.

2. LSP and translation

It is widely accepted that in order to adequately train future translators at a university level – both in terms of scientific methodology and professional orientation and attitudes – specialised translation pedagogy must take into account the essential matters of text typology, register and style. These can be readily addressed with the aid and exploitation of text corpora. This recent approach to the pedagogy of specialised translation adds to traditional methods dealing with the translation process itself and the various translation difficulties between languages in contact that are addressed in terms of LSP.[1]

1 As Sara Laviosa (2002: 18) states, the idea of complementing traditional translation studies with a corpus linguistics component was first put forward

Baker's general definition of "translation universals"[2] is consistent with the empirical finding that translation trainees tend to consider the difficulty in specialised translation mostly in terms of the source-text (ST) terminology. Indeed, students usually focus their attention on searching in specialised dictionaries and text-specific documentation material, as well as on Internet resources which they deem relevant to their task. The students' prevalent approach is, in this sense, the resolution of terminological and textual ambiguities pertaining to the co-text, and very rarely to the context.[3] In terms of lexico-semantic choices, consulting traditional and online terminological databases and customised personal term collections is, however, a technique which is not only inadequate, but can also be truly misleading in many respects.

in 1993 by Mona Baker, who predicted that the availability of large corpora of original and translated texts would enable translation scholars to "uncover the nature of translated text as a mediated communicative event".

2 "Explicitation, in the form of shifts in cohesion, insertion of additional information in the target language text and at syntactic level in the form of higher redundancy; disambiguation and simplification; textual conventionality in written translations; avoidance of repetitions that are present in the ST; tendency to over-represent features of the target language; and specific distribution of lexical items in translated texts vis-à-vis source texts and original texts in the target language" (Laviosa 2002: 18-19).

3 Using Hatim/Mason's definition, a *context* is the "extra-textual environment which exerts a determining influence on the language used. The subject-matter of a given text is part of the register and can thus determine, say the way the texts presents who is doing what to whom" (Hatim/Mason 1997: 215). In the case of translation teaching, the *context* essentially refers to the set of communicative, pragmatic and semiotic determinants that are inherent in the textual utterance of a given thematic domain and are reflected in the authors' "choices of discourse" at all language levels: morphosyntactic, pragmatic, lexico-semantic and stylistic. In a corpus-based methodology, the context is derived, both descriptively and quantitatively, from other co-texts, i.e. other textual utterances.

3. LSP, text typology and text corpora

It is not our intention to go into definitions of LSP; Sager, Schmidt, Rondeau, Rey, Hoffmann provide such definitions, to name only a few scholars. It is, however, worth mentioning that especially in English, there are three terms describing the concept of LSP, i.e. *special language, specialised language,* and *language for specific purposes* (*LSP*). For some, like Kocourek (1982) and Rondeau (1984), these terms are synonyms, while Sager/Dungworth/McDonald (1980) stress that the term *language for specific purposes* (*LSP*) derives from language teaching not from linguistics, and must therefore be limited to this area of study; so in lieu of *LSP*, they prefer using the term *special languages*, and in particular *special subject languages*.

It is often observed that translation trainees usually neglect the “universality” or “international character” of LSPs (*sensu* Beaugrande 1987) and thus tend to consider terminology as the major source of problems when translating. A practical outcome of this tendency is that students depend mainly on “ready-made” choices available to them in bilingual dictionaries and databases. However, bilingual specialised term collections, especially in culturally non-balanced language pairs such as those with a Greek component (for example EN-EL), are usually compiled on an intuitive and *ad hoc* basis, lacking contextual relevance and reference.

It has also been observed that, on the other hand, trainees consider the general language of a specialised text to be almost unimportant and easy to translate, thus neglecting essential aspects of the translation process, like style and register appropriateness and naturalness in the target language (TL) (Kostopoulou 1999).

The “international” character of LSP, as pointed out by Beaugrande, and the fact that English has become a *lingua franca* for specialised communication, seem to disorientate trainees and to have a two-fold function:

- positive, i.e. when students exploit LSP features by trying to decode the semantic field of a term within a particular text; and

- negative, i.e. when students rely solely on the recognisability and even "popularity" of an English term. The negative aspect of the students' perception of LSP terminology often results in mistranslations or raw translations, i.e. target texts (TTs) with terminology that is often incomprehensible for the target audience and is sometimes accompanied by the SL term, or even term borrowing, a method only randomly appropriate in terms of language style and register.

This is exactly where the notion of text typology and style can be of great help to the teaching of specialised translation. Specialised translation, or simply technical translation, in the view of many scholars, not only requires an in-depth understanding of the subject field and sufficient transfer of the technical concepts and terms into the target language – as pertains to content and information – but also, and sometimes even more importantly, the preservation and/or adjustment of the draft translation to the style and register that are appropriate for a particular text type and genre and a particular language community (Wright/Wright 1993).

According to Kussmaul (1997: 72), the English term *text type* is ambiguous, since it:

(a) refers to the so-called *Texttyp* in German, i.e. a general notion based on Reiss's distinction between informative, expressive and appellative text types; and
(b) it may serve as an equivalent for German *Textsorte* (for which the prevalent English equivalent is 'genre'), i.e. categories of texts such as manuals, instruction leaflets, weather reports, contracts, newspaper articles, academic discourse, and so on.

Many translation scholars have discussed the need to develop text types or text categories with a view to assisting translators in their decision-making process. For example, a well-known classification of texts is *expressive* (for example, literary), *informative* (for example, technical and legal documents) and *vocative* (for example, advertisements). In this sense, text typology is based on the perceived function of texts. However, as Hatim/Mason (1990) point out, such a distinction of text types can sometimes be misleading, since most texts present features from various genres, and are therefore multifunctional. Once more, the solution for the translator is to be found in the context. Of course, we have to bear in mind there are always some dominances, some traditionally defined types according to the function of texts, namely their contribution to human communication (see Beaugrande/Dressler 1981).

In terms of typology, texts created within the framework of scientific and technical communication, are mainly informative and descriptive, with their main function being referential and, to a lesser extent, metalinguistic and expressive (Cabré 1999). As pertains to LSP and text typology, the trainee translator must be aware of the content and possible boundaries of a particular LSP, and he/she must also be capable of correlating the special language – that is, the phraseology and terminology – of a particular domain with the type and genre of a given ST, in order to decide on the strategies and ways to approach the translation at its micro- and macro-structure level. Also, we should not forget that there are cases where a particular distinctive genre of one language may not exist in another, as in, for example, the case of academic novels.

4. LSP and English-Greek (en-el) translation corpora

One of the main reasons why trainees must be aware of the abovementioned LSP issues, is the fact that bilingual dictionaries and databases, on which students mainly depend, are less than sufficient as documentation tools, and "totally inadequate as a source of real world data for the purposes of translation studies" (Peters/Picchi 1998: 91). This is due to the fact that bilingual dictionaries, even those that are subject-area specific, are mainly mono-semantic and tend to present entries dogmatically and outside their naturally occurring co-text and pragmatic reference (context). Another limitation of context-free terminological entries in bilingual (for example, en-el) specialised dictionaries is to be found in the "equivalent" presentation of several translation equivalents for a concept within a specific thematic field (case of synonymy). Considering the fact that all such equivalents are context-free, the trainee translator is almost helpless in his/her attempt to select the appropriate term in the TL.[4]

This problem can be addressed with applied research aimed at implementing the methods and findings of corpus linguistics in modern lexicography and in the use of large text corpora for translation-teaching purposes. Bilingual text corpora, both parallel and comparable, can provide the trainee translator with documented, naturally-occurring linguistic data that pinpoint to "*how utterances or samples of text in one language can be rendered in another*" (Peters/Picchi 1998: 92). By exploiting bilingual parallel corpora, i.e. original texts with their translations in the target language (preferably multiple translations for comparison reasons; see Malmkjær 1998), trainees have the opportunity to examine LSPs and the terminology of STs always *en situation*, that is within the particular communicative environment of terms, phrases and general language constructs. As Laviosa (2002: 104) points out:

> translators often find that their intuition as native speakers of the target language and the information contained in descriptive and pedagogic grammars or dictionaries are not always adequate for suggesting the most appropriate equivalent. This is largely due to the fact that the meaning of words is generally provided without giving sufficient linguistic context or a sufficient number of authentic examples. Parallel corpora are invaluable resources of information for discovering typical and well established translation equivalents of given terms and expressions, while comparable corpora are particularly useful for discovering the typical co-text of assumed equivalent terms and expressions in the source and target language.

A major part of our pedagogical approach to technical translation in the English-Greek language pair is dedicated to the pragmatic analysis

4 The inadequacy of bilingual dictionaries as tools for translators and as soures of real world data within the context of translation studies is, inter alia, stressed by Hartmann (1994: 292): "the semantic abstraction that is built into the lexical inventory of the dictionary has deprived each of these words of their natural context, and the translator must compensate for the lack of contextual information from his/her own bilingual discourse competence, particularly in that most intractable area of 'culture-specific' vocabulary".

of the ST. Our effort lies in guiding students to tackle the pragmatic framework of the ST and the semantic breadth of its specialised terms, often by contrasting the pragmatics and semantics of the ST to other texts of related subject fields and their communication- and utterance-specific notions and terms. Utilising such a pragmatic and semantic approach, students are presented with a sound ST interpretation method aimed at clarifying the extralinguistic patterns and the linguistic means by which the scientific and technical knowledge of the ST is organised, materialised and conveyed. The extra- and intra-linguistic perception of the communicative environment and function of the ST gained in this way is an indispensable tool for the students' subsequent micro-textual approach, in which we include their efforts to identify appropriate equivalents for terms, to adopt ready-made solutions for translating particular terms and phrases, or even to suggest new lexical renderings or neologisms for concepts previously not identified by the translational and terminographical processes undertaken.

However, our experience shows that mastering the pragmatic and semantic – in other words, communicative – background of a ST requires significantly more effort than is common in descriptive approaches to translation studies and, of course, goes well beyond the instructions on how to utilise bilingual terminological documentation material. It is in this sense that the academic translation community has reached a consensus on the need to compile bilingual comparable corpora of naturally-occurring textual evidence.

As a first stage, the translation tutor provides students with the methodological tools that are indispensable for attempting such a corpus-based approach in technical translation. Text selection and corpus compilation criteria, which all aim to safeguard the appropriateness of the textual material gathered, have been detailed in previous publications. These are: text representativeness, specific intentionality of the author, terminological intensity of texts, text origin (only ST in English and Greek), date of publication and typical degree of textual specialisation (Saridakis 2001). Illustrations of how a corpus of this kind can be compiled must accompany the description of such a method. A matrix of the corpus design – based on the chosen design criteria – can help to orientate students in their terminological searches

At a subsequent stage, students are required to compile their personal- and team-work collections of documentation corpora and to utilise them for substantiating their translation choices, mainly in terms of pragmatic and semantic validity. At a more advanced level, students utilise corpus linguistic tools in order to further facilitate their corpus-based research work.

The first objective of this approach, always within the framework of our technical translation course, is to carefully study these comparable resources, not for identifying equivalents at a lexical level, but for examining issues pertinent to text type and genre. In other words, the students' efforts focus primarily on the identification of general patterns, on the observation of differences at the discourse level between English and Greek and on the systematic elicitation of variations in terms of register within a given thematic field.

Such variations and differences can, for example, be observed in tenor between a technical manual addressed to the end user of a vehicle and a technical manual addressed to automotive workshop personnel. In this way, when trainees are faced with the dilemma of the choice of the proper lexical equivalent for a given ST, they are already aware that, among the synonyms given in a dictionary entry, they would have to pick the entry most suited to the tenor and general style of the target text and audience, thus avoiding the randomness of their linguistic instinct and personal preference.

A typical example is the case of the English term *interface*, a lexeme widely used in modern English texts in the field of computer science. Based on the pragmatics of the text, the target audience and to some extent the level of formality, there is a whole set of Greek equivalents to choose from: (a) *διασύνδεση* (= [i] term related to the interconnection of electronic components, [ii] term extending also elliptically to the notion of man-machine-interface in texts of a high technical register); (b) *διεπαφή* (= [i] semantic overlap with (aii) in lower-register -but not jargon or common-language- texts); (c) *περιβάλλον επικοινωνίας* (= two-word equivalent referring generally [i] to the notion of electronic device or computer (man-machine communication) interfaces and, more specifically, [ii] to computer operating systems); (d) *περιβάλλον χρήσης* (= [i] hyponym of (ci) overlapping with (cii) and signifying the operating software of any electronic device, for example mobile phones, but not of personal computers); (e) *πρότυπο δικτύου* (= [i] a network communication protocol, semantically unrelated to notions (a) through (d)). This example is characteristic of a linguistic sign originally transferred from a donor language (English) to a host language (Greek) and translated initially using a single-word term (*διασύνδεση*), with the aim to cover all its potential – and future – semantic fields. However, usage has in the course of time differentiated the signifier of all the above lexemes (a-e), depending on the context, the pragmatics, and the "objective" register of a given text. The linking of signs (and notions) with time that is exemplified in the *usage* of this term is less observed in the donor language, where variation is attributable to the authors' personal choices of tenor. By contrast, the interchangeability in the usage of the terms is significantly less frequent in Greek texts. In terms of the host language (Greek), this remark illustrates:

(a) the normalisation-standardisation of the signifier according to the actual usage of the notion, i.e. the term's pragmatic reference and communicative situation;
(b) in the same sense, the variation of the term usage even within a single text; and
(c) the need to substantiate the lexical choice when translating this term or any other term with similar variation and adaptation characteristics of usage, on the actual frequency of use, as derived from the analysis of authentic pieces of language.

Consistent with scholarly remarks (see Baker 1993; Toury 1980; Vanderauwera 1985), translation trainees intuitively tend to over-represent features of the target language, to present shifts in cohesion and to insert unnecessary additional information in the TT. Based on our observations, such a systematic corpus-based documentation approach reduces unnecessary occurrences of over-simplification (i.e. redundancy) or over-complication of the TL register, and guides students towards a more sound and therefore acceptable technical discourse in the TL.

The above-mentioned "generic" corpus-based pedagogical approach to LSP is complemented by a more systematic corpus analysis in the context of another course on IT Applications in Translation (at the postgraduate level). As part of this analytical approach, which in this case relies on extensive bilingual parallel corpora, students are required to systematically observe and document the choices made by their fellow undergraduate students, at all language levels, for specific STs. With the use of WordSmith Tools software, students build word lists and concordances and examine variations at a lexico-semantic level with regard to specific term tokens, and to the use of general language components (for example, of common verbs and function words). Comparing the findings of such an analysis with the findings of a similar study based on professional bilingual translation corpora, the tutor is provided with an essential tool to intervene and to systematically address the students' misinterpretations and misrepresentations of LSP concepts. Even more importantly, it is obvious that this evidence-based approach is open to criticism by the translation trainees and as such, enables students to systematise their work in terms of translation revision, i.e. at a stage which is of major importance in the context of teamwork.

5. Conclusions

While still in an experimental stage, the systematic approach of the corpus-based documentation of the training of translators in the Greek-English language pair has proven to be encouraging for the tutor, in that it provides substantial evidence of actual language use and thus provides a way to focus the trainees' attention on the methodology of translation choices. Furthermore, this method, while complementing the traditional pedagogical approach, provides the basis for the compilation of extensive parallel and comparable corpora, text-linguistically characterised in terms of function and susceptible to easy annotation to facilitate further linguistic research. Last but not least, the method provides a coherent basis for the compilation of multilingual terminological databases, that is both practicable and linguistically sound, in an academic translator-training environment.

References

Baker, M. 1993. *Corpus linguistics and translation studies – implications and applications*. In Baker M. / Francis G. / Tognini-Bonelli E. (eds) *Text and Technology. In Honour of John Sinclair*. Amsterdam/Philadelphia: John Benjamins, 233-250.

Beaugrande, R. de 1987. Special Purpose Language and Linguistic Theory. *ALSED-LSP Newsletter* 10/2 (25), 2-10.

Beaugrande, R. de / Dressler, W. 1981. *Introduction to Text Linguistics*. London: Longman.

Cabré, M.T. 1999. *Terminology. Theory, methods and applications*. Amsterdam/Philadelphia: John Benjamins (Edited by Juan C. Sager and translated into English by Janet Ann DeCesaris).

Hartmann, R.R.K. 1994. The Use of Parallel Text Corpora in the Generation of Translation Equivalents for Bilingual Lexicography. In Martin, W. / Meijs, W. / Moerland, M. / ten Pas, E. / van Sterkenburg, P. / Vossen, P. (eds) *Euralex 1994 Proceedings*. Amsterdam, 291-297.

Hatim, B. / Mason, I. 1990. *Discourse and the Translator*. London: Longman.

Hatim, B. / Mason, I. 1997. *The Translator as Communicator*. London: Routledge.

Kocourek, R. 1982. *La langue française de la technique et de la science*. Wiesbaden: Brandstetter.

Kostopoulou, G. 1999. *Didactics of Specialised Translation. MA Thesis submitted in the Postgraduate Studies Programme*. Corfu: DFLTI, Ionian University.

Kussmaul, P. 1997. Text-Type Conventions and Translating: Some Methodological Issues. In Trosborg, A. (ed.) *Text Typology and Translation*. Amsterdam/Philadelphia: John Benjamins, 67-83.

Laviosa, S. 2002. *Corpus-based Translation Studies. Theory, Findings, Applications*. Amsterdam: Rodopi.

Malmkjær, K. 1998. Love thy neighbour: Will parallel corpora endear linguistics to translators? In Laviosa, S. (ed.) *L'approche basée sur le corpus / The Corpus-Based Approach*, Special Issue of *Meta* 43/4, 534-41.

Peters, C. / Picchi, E. 1998. Bilingual Reference Corpora for Translators and Translation Studies. In Bowker. L. / Cronin, M. / Kenny, D. / Pearson, J. (eds) *Unity in Diversity? Current Trends in Translation Studies*. Manchester: St. Jerome, 91-100.

Rondeau, G. 1984. *Introduction à la terminologie*. Québec: Gaëtan Morin.

Sager, J. / Dungworth, D. / McDonald, P.F. 1980. *English Special Languages: Principles and practice in Science and Technology*. Wiesbaden: Brandstetter Verlag.

Sager, J.C. 1997. Text Types and Translation. In Trosborg, A. (ed.) *Text Typology and Translation*. Amsterdam/Philadelphia: John Benjamins, 25-42.

Saridakis, I. 2001. Terminology and Terminography in the Modern Translation Environment: A Case Study on Terminology Extraction and Documentation. In Chabas, J. et al. (eds) *Proceedings of the 1st International Conference on Specialized Translation*. Barcelona: Universitat Pompeu Fabra, 186-189.

Toury, G. 1980. *In Search of a Theory of Translation*. Tel Aviv: The Porter Institute for Poetics and Semiotics,Tel Aviv University.

Vanderauwera, R. 1985. *Dutch Novels Translated into English: The Transformation of a "Minority" Literature*. Amsterdam: Rodopi.

Wright, S.E. / Wright, L.D. (eds) 1993. *Scientific and Technical Translation*. American Translators Association, Scholarly Monograph Series VI. Amsterdam/Philadelphia: John Benjamins.

Linguistic Insights

Studies in Language and Communication

This series aims to promote specialist language studies in the fields of linguistic theory and applied linguistics, by publishing volumes that focus on specific aspects of language use in one or several languages and provide valuable insights into language and communication research. A cross-disciplinary approach is favoured and most European languages are accepted.

The series includes two types of books:

- **Monographs** – featuring in-depth studies on special aspects of language theory, language analysis or language teaching.
- **Collected papers** – assembling papers from workshops, conferences or symposia.

Vol. 1 Maurizio Gotti & Marina Dossena (eds)
Modality in Specialized Texts. Selected Papers of the 1st CERLIS Conference. 421 pp. 2001.
ISBN 3-906767-10-8. US-ISBN 0-8204-5340-4

Vol. 2 Giuseppina Cortese & Philip Riley (eds)
Domain-specific English. Textual Practices across Communities and Classrooms.
420 pp. 2002.
ISBN 3-906768-98-8. US-ISBN 0-8204-5884-8

Vol. 3 Maurizio Gotti, Dorothee Heller & Marina Dossena (eds)
Conflict and Negotiation in Specialized Texts. Selected Papers of the 2nd CERLIS Conference. 470 pp. 2002.
ISBN 3-906769-12-7. US-ISBN 0-8204-5887-2

Editorial address:

Prof. Maurizio Gotti Università di Bergamo, Facoltà di Lingue e Letterature Straniere,
Via Salvecchio 19, 24129 Bergamo, Italy
Fax: 0039 035 2052789, E-Mail: m.gotti@unibg.it

Vol. 4 Maurizio Gotti, Marina Dossena, Richard Dury, Roberta Facchinetti & Maria Lima
Variation in Central Modals. A Repertoire of Forms and Types of Usage in Middle English and Early Modern English.
364 pp. 2002.
ISBN 3-906769-84-4. US-ISBN 0-8204-5898-8

Vol. 5 Stefania Nuccorini (ed.)
Phrases and Phraseology. Data and Descriptions.
187 pp. 2002.
ISBN 3-906770-08-7. US-ISBN 0-8204-5933-X

Vol. 6 Vijay Bhatia, Christopher N. Candlin & Maurizio Gotti (eds)
Legal Discourse in Multilingual and Multicultural Contexts. Arbitration Texts in Europe.
385 pp. 2003.
ISBN 3-906770-85-0. US-ISBN 0-8204-6254-3

Vol. 7 Marina Dossena & Charles Jones (eds)
Insights into Late Modern English.
2nd edition. 378 pp. 2003, 2007.
ISBN 978-3-03911-257-9. US-ISBN 978-0-8204-8927-8

Vol. 8 Maurizio Gotti
Specialized Discourse. Linguistic Features and Changing Conventions.
351 pp. 2003, 2005.
ISBN 3-03910-606-6. US-ISBN 0-8204-7000-7

Vol. 9 Alan Partington, John Morley & Louann Haarman (eds)
Corpora and Discourse.
420 pp. 2004.
ISBN 3-03910-026-2. US-ISBN 0-8204-6262-4

Vol. 10 Martina Möllering
The Acquisition of German Modal Particles. A Corpus-Based Approach.
290 pp. 2004.
ISBN 3-03910-043-2. US-ISBN 0-8204-6273-X

Vol. 11 David Hart (ed.)
English Modality in Context. Diachronic Perspectives.
261 pp. 2003.
ISBN 3-03910-046-7. US-ISBN 0-8204-6852-5

Vol. 12 Wendy Swanson
Modes of Co-reference as an Indicator of Genre.
430 pp. 2003.
ISBN 3-03910-052-1. US-ISBN 0-8204-6855-X

Vol. 13 Gina Poncini
Discursive Strategies in Multicultural Business Meetings.
338 pp. 2004, 2007.
ISBN 978-3-03911-296-8. US-ISBN 978-0-8204-8937-7

Vol. 14 Christopher N. Candlin & Maurizio Gotti (eds)
Intercultural Aspects of Specialized Communication.
2nd edition. 369 pp. 2004, 2007.
ISBN 978-3-03911-258-6. US-ISBN 978-0-8204-8926-1

Vol. 15 Gabriella Del Lungo Camiciotti & Elena Tognini Bonelli (eds)
Academic Discourse. New Insights into Evaluation.
234 pp. 2004.
ISBN 3-03910-353-9. US-ISBN 0-8204-7016-3

Vol. 16 Marina Dossena & Roger Lass (eds)
Methods and Data in English Historical Dialectology.
405 pp. 2004.
ISBN 3-03910-362-8. US-ISBN 0-8204-7018-X

Vol. 17 Judy Noguchi
The Science Review Article. An Opportune Genre in the Construction of Science.
274 pp. 2006.
ISBN 3-03910-426-8. US-ISBN 0-8204-7034-1

Vol. 18 Giuseppina Cortese & Anna Duszak (eds)
Identity, Community, Discourse.
English in Intercultural Settings.
495 pp. 2005.
ISBN 3-03910-632-5. US-ISBN 0-8204-7163-1

Vol. 19 Anna Trosborg & Poul Erik Flyvholm Jørgensen (eds)
Business Discourse. Texts and Contexts.
250 pp. 2005.
ISBN 3-03910-606-6. US-ISBN 0-8204-7000-7

Vol. 20 Christopher Williams
Tradition and Change in Legal English. Verbal Constructions in Prescriptive Texts.
216 pp. 2005.
ISBN 3-03910-644-9. US-ISBN 0-8204-7166-6

Vol. 21 Katarzyna Dziubalska-Kołaczyk & Joanna Przedlacka (eds)
English Pronunciation Models: A Changing Scene.
476 pp. 2005.
ISBN 3-03910-662-7. US-ISBN 0-8204-7173-9

Vol. 22 Christián Abello-Contesse, Rubén Chacón-Beltrán, M. Dolores López-Jiménez & M. Mar Torreblanca-López (eds)
Age in L2 Acquisition and Teaching.
214 pp. 2006.
ISBN 3-03910-668-6. US-ISBN 0-8204-7174-7

Vol. 23 Vijay K. Bhatia, Maurizio Gotti, Jan Engberg & Dorothee Heller (eds)
Vagueness in Normative Texts.
474 pp. 2005.
ISBN 3-03910-653-8. US-ISBN 0-8204-7169-0

Vol. 24 Paul Gillaerts & Maurizio Gotti (eds)
Genre Variation in Business Letters.
407 pp. 2005.
ISBN 3-03910-674-0. US-ISBN 0-8204-7552-1

Vol. 25 Ana María Hornero, María José Luzón & Silvia Murillo (eds)
Corpus Linguistics. Applications for the Study of English.
526 pp. 2006.
ISBN 3-03910-675-9 / US-ISBN 0-8204-7554-8

Vol. 26 J. Lachlan Mackenzie & María de los Ángeles Gómez-González (eds)
Studies in Functional Discourse Grammar.
259 pp. 2005.
ISBN 3-03910-696-1 / US-ISBN 0-8204-7558-0

Vol. 27 Debbie G.E. Ho
Classroom Talk. Exploring the Sociocultural Structure of Formal ESL Learning.
254 pages. 2006, 2007.
ISBN 978-3-03911-434-4

Vol. 28 Forthcoming.

Vol. 29 Francesca Bargiela-Chiappini & Maurizio Gotti (eds)
Asian Business Discourse(s).
350 pp. 2005.
ISBN 3-03910-804-2 / US-ISBN 0-8204-7574-2

Vol. 30 Nicholas Brownlees (ed.)
News Discourse in Early Modern Britain. Selected Papers of CHINED 2004.
300 pp. 2006.
ISBN 3-03910-805-0 / US-ISBN 0-8204-8025-8

Vol. 31 Roberta Facchinetti & Matti Rissanen (eds)
Corpus-based Studies of Diachronic English.
300 pp. 2006.
ISBN 3-03910-851-4 / US-ISBN 0-8204-8040-1

Vol. 32 Marina Dossena & Susan M. Fitzmaurice (eds)
Business and Official Correspondence: Historical Investigations.
209 pp. 2006.
ISBN 3-03910-880-8 / US-ISBN 0-8204-8352-4

Vol. 33 Forthcoming.

Vol. 34 Forthcoming.

Vol. 35 Vijay K. Bhatia & Maurizio Gotti (eds)
Explorations in Specialized Genres.
316 pp. 2006.
ISBN 3-03910-995-2 / US-ISBN 0-8204-8372-9

Vol. 36 Heribert Picht (ed.)
Modern Approaches to Terminological Theories and Applications.
432 pages. 2006.
ISBN 3-03911-156-6 / US-ISBN 0-8204-8380-X

Vol. 37 Anne Wagner & Sophie Cacciaguidi-Fahy (eds)
Legal Language and the Search for Clarity / Le langage juridique et la quête de clarté. Practice and Tools / Pratiques et instruments.
487 pages. 2006.
ISBN 3-03911-169-8 / US-ISBN 0-8388-5

Vol. 38 Juan Carlos Palmer-Silveira, Miguel F. Ruiz-Garrido & Inmaculada Fortanet-Gómez (eds)
Intercultural and International Business Communication: Theory, Research and Teaching.
343 pages. 2006.
ISBN 3-03910-954-5 / US-ISBN 0-8204-8356-7

Vol. 39 Christiane Dalton-Puffer, Dieter Kastovsky, Nikolaus Ritt & Herbert Schendl (eds)
Syntax, Style and Grammatical Norms: English from 1500–2000.
250 pages. 2006.
ISBN 3-03911-181-7 / US-ISBN 0-8204-8394-X

Vol. 40 Marina Dossena & Irma Taavitsainen (eds)
Diachronic Perspectives on Domain-Specific English.
280 pages. 2006.
ISBN 3-03910-176-0 / US-ISBN 0-8204-8391-5

Vol. 41 John Flowerdew & Maurizio Gotti (eds)
Studies in Specialized Discourse.
293 pages. 2006.
ISBN 3-03911-178-7 / US-ISBN 0-8204-8393-1

Vol. 42 Ken Hyland & Marina Bondi (eds)
Academic Discourse Across Disciplines.
320 pages. 2006.
ISBN 3-03911-183-3 / US-ISBN 0-8204-8396-6

Vol. 43 Paul Gillaerts & Philip Shaw (eds)
The Map and the Landscape: Norms and Practices in Genre.
256 pages. 2006.
ISBN 3-03911-182-5 / US-ISBN 0-8204-8395-4

Vol. 44 Maurizio Gotti & Davide Giannoni (eds)
New Trends in Specialized Discourse Analysis.
301 pages. 2006.
ISBN 3-03911-184-1 / US-ISBN 0-8204-8381-8

Vol. 45 Maurizio Gotti & Françoise Salager-Meyer (eds)
Advances in Medical Discourse Analysis:
Oral and Written Contexts.
492 pages. 2006.
ISBN 3-03911-185-X / US-ISBN 0-8204-8382-6

Vol. 46 Maurizio Gotti & Susan Šarčević (eds)
Insights into Specialized Translation.
396 pages. 2006.
ISBN 3-03911-186-8 / US-ISBN 0-8204-8383-4

Vol. 47 Khurshid Ahmad & Margaret Rogers (eds)
Evidence-based LSP: Translation, Text and Terminology.
584 pages. 2007.
ISBN 978-3-03911-187-9

Vol. 48 Forthcoming.

Vol. 49 Cristina Suárez-Gómez
Relativization in Early English (950-1250):
the Position of Relative Clauses.
149 pages. 2006.
ISBN 3-03911-203-1 / US-ISBN 0-8204-8904-2

Vol. 50 Maria Vittoria Calvi & Luisa Chierichetti (eds)
Nuevas tendencias en el discurso de especialidad.
319 pages. 2006.
ISBN 978-3-03911-261-6

Vol. 51 Forthcoming.

Vol. 52 Konrad Ehlich & Dorothee Heller (Hrsg.)
Die Wissenschaft und ihre Sprachen.
323 pages. 2006.
ISBN 978-3-03911-272-2

Vol. 53 Forthcoming.

Vol. 54 Norman Fairclough, Giuseppina Cortese & Patrizia Ardizzone (eds)
Discourse and Contemporary Social Change.
555 pages. 2007.
ISBN 978-3-03911-276-0

Vol. 55 Jan Engberg, Marianne Grove Ditlevsen, Peter Kastberg & Martin Stegu (eds)
New Directions in LSP Teaching.
331 pages. 2007.
ISBN 978-3-03911-433-7

Vol. 56 Dorothee Heller & Konrad Ehlich (Hrsg.)
Studien zur Rechtskommunikation.
322 pages. 2007.
ISBN 978-3-03911-436-8

Giuseppina Cortese / Anna Duszak (eds)

Identity, Community, Discourse

English in Intercultural Settings

Bern, Berlin, Bruxelles, Frankfurt am Main, New York, Oxford, Wien, 2005.
495 pp., num. fig. and tables
Linguistic Insights. Studies in Language and Communication. Vol. 18
Edited by Maurizio Gotti
ISBN 978-3-03910-632-5 / US-ISBN 978-0-8204-7163-1 pb.
sFr. 106.– / € 72.80 / €** 74.80 / € 68.– / £ 47.60 / US-$ 81.95*

* includes VAT – valid for Germany ** includes VAT – valid for Austria

Languages are inseparable from their contexts of use. They are not only congruent with, but also involved in the configuration of the worldviews and value systems manifested in cultures and embodied in texts. The spread of English worldwide foregrounds the issue of textual dynamics in intercultural settings. The production/reception of texts in English facilitates international contacts and exchanges, yet it also triggers hegemonic practices. The volume aims to investigate the representations and negotiations of sociocognitive identities in intercultural settings relevant for 'good practice'. Contributions explore 'languaging' strategies (verbal, visual, multimodal; English monolingual, bilingual, multilingual) through a range of methodological perspectives wherein the respect for sociocultural differences is a constitutive value.

With contributions by: Giuseppina Cortese – Anna Duszak – Ron Scollon – Suzie Wong Scollon – Suresh Canagarajah – Christer Laurén – John Douthwaite – Maurizio Gotti – Philip Riley – Maria Grazia Guido – Paola Evangelisti Allori – Edith Esch – Anna Mauranen – Elizabeth Rowley-Jolivet – Shirley Carter-Thomas – Małgorzata Sokół – Kristina Svartholm – Gigliola Sacerdoti Mariani – Giuditta Caliendo – Gabriella Di Martino – Marco Venuti – Rosa Maria Bollettieri Bosinelli – Elena Di Giovanni – Ira Torresi – Nicoletta Vasta.

The Editors: Giuseppina Cortese is Professor of English Linguistics at the University of Turin, Italy.

Anna Duszak is Professor of Linguistics at Warsaw University and Warsaw School of Social Psychology, Poland.

PETER LANG
Bern · Berlin · Bruxelles · Frankfurt am Main · New York · Oxford · Wien

Heribert Picht (ed.)

Modern Approaches to Terminological Theories and Applications

Bern, Berlin, Bruxelles, Frankfurt am Main, New York, Oxford, Wien, 2006.
434 pp.
Linguistic Insights. Studies in Language and Communication. Vol. 36
Edited by Maurizio Gotti
ISBN 978-3-03911-156-5 / US-ISBN 978-0-8204-8380-1 pb.
sFr. 97.– / € 66.90 / €** 68.80 / € 62.50 / £ 43.80 / US-$ 74.95*

* includes VAT – valid for Germany   ** includes VAT – valid for Austria

This volume comprises contributions originally presented at the 15th European Symposium on Languages for Special Purposes held at the University of Bergamo on 29 August - 2 September 2005. The volume is divided into four parts: Approaches to Terminological Theories; Terms in Discourse; Knowledge Elicitation, Ordering and Management; Term extraction and terminographical work.

The research presented in the various contributions to this volume clearly indicates that terminology as an inter- and transdisciplinary field of knowledge is firmly developing its theoretical foundations and practical applications in accordance with and within the framework of its overall goal: to ensure and to augment the quality of communication with professional content.

With contributions by: Heribert Picht – Serguey D. Shelov – Vladimir M. Leitchik – Larissa Alexeeva – Valentina Novodranova – Nina Pilke – Birthe Toft – Marie-Claude L'Homme – Rute Costa – Gerhard Budin – Margaret Rogers – Sue Ellen Wright – Bassey E. Antia – Richard Kamai – Elizabeth Schlomann Lowe – Christer Laurén – Maria Giovanna Nigro – Jan Roald – Bettina Mottura – Walther v. Hahn – Elizabeth Marshman – Niina Nissilä – Ana María Monterde Rey – Cristina Valentini – Magnar Brekke – Patrick Drouin – Natascia Ralli – Isabella Ties.

The Editor: Heribert Picht was until 2005 Professor of Terminology, LSP and Knowledge Representation at Copenhagen Business School and the Norwegian School of Economics in Bergen. His research work and publications are related to terminology theory, applied terminology, knowledge representation, semiotics related to terminology and terminology didactics. His most recent publications are *La representación de objetos y conceptos* (2002), *The Concept in Terminology. A Unit of Thought, Knowledge or Cognition?* (2003), *Überlegungen zum Gegenstand und zum Begriff in der Terminologie* (2004).

PETER LANG
Bern · Berlin · Bruxelles · Frankfurt am Main · New York · Oxford · Wien

www.ingramcontent.com/pod-product-compliance
Ingram Content Group UK Ltd.
Pitfield, Milton Keynes, MK11 3LW, UK
UKHW020202290926
15471UKWH00005B/1016

9 783039 111879